ADVANCE PRAISE FOR Visions in Global Education

"A cutting-edge effort on the part of its editor and authors. Any social studies educator, or any advanced graduate student, owes [it] to themselves to read this book and reflect on it for an informed perspective on twenty-first century education. Bravo!"

—*Anna S. Ochoa-Becker, Professor Emeritá, School of Education, Indiana University-Bloomington; Past President, National Council for the Social Studies*

"This book is a comprehensive treatment of the state of the art of global education and will serve as an excellent starting point for teachers, teacher educators, and researchers working in the field today. Past and current leaders in global education present case studies, syntheses of scholarship, and their visions for needed practice, research, and theory in the future."

—*Carole L. Hahn, Charles Howard Candler Professor of Educational Studies, Emory University*

"This collection makes a major and most welcome contribution to the theory and practice of global education. It comes at an especially fertile moment when 'global education' is all the rage but much that is done under its name betrays the very idea. Kirkwood-Tucker has given us an enormously thoughtful book."

—*Walter Parker, Professor of Education, University of Washington*

"Distinguished global educators have contributed their visions to this book. Chapters on the history of the movement and global education to build peace are the bookends, and in between the reader will find both general chapters on topics such as research and practice in teacher education and characteristics of a globally minded teacher, and specific case studies of schools in Miami-Dade County, Florida, and Russian education reform."

—*Angene Wilson, Professor Emeritá of Social Studies Education, University of Kentucky*

"This is an important and timely contribution to the urgent debate on appropriate education for present and future global citizens. The potential of global education for the creation of more just, peaceful, and sustainable societies is well illustrated, as are the complexities and challenges of the task ahead. Examples of successful initiatives in the past, alongside a comprehensive history of the global education movement, provide a substantive platform on which contemporary global educators can build and shape their demands for public education that is relevant and responsive to the world in which we live."

—*Graham Pike, Professor and Dean of International Education, Vancouver Island University, Canada*

"Kirkwood-Tucker's book provides a useful overview of recent research and time-honored projects in global education. The book is a unique compilation of conceptual, empirical, and case studies about the development of the field and many will find value in this book."

—*William Gaudelli, Associate Professor of Social Studies and Education, Teachers College, Columbia University*

Visions in Global Education

omplicated

A Book Series of Curriculum Studies

William F. Pinar
General Editor

Vol. 29

PETER LANG
New York • Washington, D.C./Baltimore • Bern
Frankfurt am Main • Berlin • Brussels • Vienna • Oxford

Visions in Global Education

The Globalization of Curriculum and Pedagogy
in Teacher Education and Schools

Perspectives from Canada, Russia,
and the United States

Edited by
Toni Fuss Kirkwood-Tucker

PETER LANG
New York • Washington, D.C./Baltimore • Bern
Frankfurt am Main • Berlin • Brussels • Vienna • Oxford

Library of Congress Cataloging-in-Publication Data

Visions in global education: the globalization of curriculum and pedagogy
in teacher education and schools: perspectives from Canada, Russia,
and the United States / [edited by] Toni Fuss Kirkwood-Tucker.
p. cm. — (Complicated conversation: a book series of curriculum studies; v. 29)
Includes bibliographical references and index.
1. International education—Curricula—Canada.
2. International education—Curricula—Russia (Federation).
3. International education—Curricula—United States. 4. Teachers—
Training of—Canada. 5. Teachers—Training of—Russia (Federation).
6. Teachers—Training of—United States. I. Kirkwood-Tucker, Toni Fuss.
LC1090.V56   370.116—dc22   2008053502
ISBN 978-1-4331-0309-4
ISSN 1534-2816

Bibliographic information published by **Die Deutsche Bibliothek**.
Die Deutsche Bibliothek lists this publication in the "Deutsche
Nationalbibliografie"; detailed bibliographic data is available
on the Internet at http://dnb.ddb.de/.

Cover design by Joshua Hanson

The paper in this book meets the guidelines for permanence and durability
of the Committee on Production Guidelines for Book Longevity
of the Council of Library Resources.

© 2009 Peter Lang Publishing, Inc., New York
29 Broadway, 18th floor, New York, NY 10006
www.peterlang.com

Printed in the United States of America

To
Jan L. Tucker
My beloved husband and mentor
and to
My beloved children, Andrée and David
who give meaning to my life

Contents

III. Pedagogy and Possibilities in the Postmodern World

Foreword

International global education, like the world it seeks to understand and explain, is constantly changing. Its aims and purpose, like the educational institutions in which such studies are embedded, are shaped by the larger culture in which they exist. This volume provides a wide-ranging collection of current thinking, historical foundations, extant research, and examples of large scale efforts to implement programs of global studies on two continents.

Among the special features of the book are (1) an insider's report of an award-winning large-scale Global Awareness Program in one of this nation's largest and most culturally diverse school districts; (2) a detailed analysis on global education in Russia—teacher education and educational reform; (3) a comprehensive history of global education as well as a discussion of the conceptual development of the field as revealed in the early documents that provided the foundations for the movement; (4) a research-derived list of the characteristics of global-minded teachers; and (5) a vision of needed changes in global education to encompass shifting parameters of power and influence and more effective use of new technology. This timely, wide-ranging, and insightful collection of essays provides a basis for reviewing the status of the movement and offers some rich resources for updating, revising, and developing new approaches. The global education movement needs to be reviewed not only in the context of the educational institutions in which it is embedded but also in the changing nature of the larger world it seeks to understand and explain.

Globalization is the dominant term used to describe many of the major changes in the larger culture in the last 100 years. Historians often cite globalization as one of the greatest achievements of humankind, lifting hundreds of millions of people out of poverty. They divide the current 100-year phase of an age-old phenomenon into three stages.

Globalization Stage I began in the 1890s and came to a halt with World War I. Major concentrations of power and influence centered in Europe with Great Britain playing a key role until 1945. Stage II began when the victors of World War II fashioned a number of new institutions to revive worldwide trade and cooperation. They reflected a new distribution of power and influence. The United States has played a key role in this stage. The Cold War (the Soviet Union versus the United States) created a bipolar world. Once the Berlin Wall came down, the United States dominated the finances, trade, and technology for a decade of booming global prosperity. Stage II seems to be coming to an end as we near the end of the first decade of the new century. The United States and the West no longer dominate world finance and investment. China's and India's demonstrated capability in manufacturing, development of nuclear power, and success in software offer evidence of major shifts in the global balance of technological skill and economic power. The fact that the West accounts for barely 15 percent of the world's population (Walker, 2007) suggests our share of the market will shrink even further. This is a new age in which people, money, jobs, and goods move worldwide as never before. The free flow of information, technology, capital goods, services, and people has spread opportunity and influence far and wide. No single nation or group has the status or the resources to deal with the biggest challenges shaping the future: that is, the forces, plus and minus, of globalization, climate change, terrorism, failed states, competition for resources or weapons of mass destruction—issues that increasingly require global, not just regional or national, solutions.

The decades-old view of the world as divided between rich and powerful and the developing others is no longer accurate or useful. The unipolar position of the United States is being replaced by what scholars are calling a multipolar or nonpolar world with dozens of actors exercising different kinds of power and influence. Hundreds of organizations now regulate the global dimensions of trade, civil aviation, health, telecommunications, and the environment. Examples are multinational corporations and a variety of other kinds of nongovernmental organizations as well as official government efforts. The fast-changing world is challenging many of the international institutions that helped stabilize the world after the massive devastation of World War II. A new and more balanced map of influence and responsibility is needed. Education, as yet, has not adequately responded to the new maps of power and influence that are emerging. New maps of the "flat world" signal a need to take to heart the lessons learned in the more than 40 years since the global education movement began (see chapter 1). The identities, loyalties, rights, and responsibilities developed in the old international system may no longer be adequate.

Thomas L. Friedman's widely cited book *The World Is Flat* (2005) is one description of the new worldwide opportunities and well-being. The flat world puts different peoples, societies, and cultures in greater contact with one another. It fosters people-to-people contact in ways for which they have little preparation. The education and training needed for cross-cultural cooperation is sorely lacking. Educational efforts to cope with the flat world seem to focus largely on technical skills, job training, or the preparation of scientists and engineers—all of which are necessary, but not sufficient to meet the challenges of a world where more people have increased cross-cultural interactions. Markets have expanded and tied people together; environmental, social, political, and military interdependence have increased demonstrably. However, the emphasis on competing in the global marketplace may keep us from dealing effectively with the more important needed changes in the distribution of power. Markets have unequal effects, and the inequality that results often has powerful political consequences (Nye, 2001). Democratic governance requires that people be informed participants if their needs are to be met. Our diplomatic, human relationships and efforts to globalize "civic education" need at least as much attention and support as our economic, technical, and military preparations.

Citizenship education with a global perspective is a key ingredient in preparing students to participate not only in the global marketplace but in playing a positive role in improving the political system—governance at the global level—in order to deal with problems that plague the planet as well as the nation. This book offers several different versions of how to improve and expand the current global education movement. Each of these approaches seeks to sharpen and clarify the focus of the current movement. Included are (1) efforts to build on the historic approaches provided by F. L. Anderson, Becker, Hanvey and others but using human rights as the main pillar of a new approach; (2) a proposed merger (an integrated approach) of multicultural and global education emphasizing citizenship education; and (3) global education to build peace. Such approaches may be interesting and attractive because they include a moral dimension. However, to make major changes, extensive dialogue among the advocates of the three proposals cited above is needed.

Given the different perspectives, history and the objectives of these approaches, a "coalition of the willing," would be a big and important step toward developing new and improved ways of studying our constantly changing world. Whatever choices and directions are considered, this volume offers some historical perspectives and research-based evidence rich in experience to guide those seeking to make needed changes in global education.

James M. Becker
Professor Emeritus Indiana University

Acknowledgments

I am indebted to many individuals who have made this book a reality. First, I wish to thank my friend and colleague Bárbara C. Cruz who encouraged me to undertake the project. Second, and of equal importance, my appreciation is extended to my colleagues who had the trust and confidence in me to write in this book.

I extend my sincere gratitude to Mr. Chris Myers, Managing Director, Peter Lang Publishing, who accepted our proposal for this book. I deeply thank Professor William Pinar, Series Editor, for his critical comments in polishing our book. I wish to thank all staff members of Peter Lang Publishing who lent their expertise in shaping this book. A special hug goes to Ms. Sophie Appel, Production Supervisor, who never tired of my thousand questions.

I owe deep gratitude to the hundreds of teachers, media specialists, principals, and administrators in the Miami-Dade County Public Schools who welcomed me into their classrooms and offices to participate in our new venture of school reform in global education. And I extend a very special thank you to Frank de Varona, *mi Hermano Cubano*, former Area Director, Area Superintendent, and Associate Superintendent of the Miami Public Schools, both for giving me entrée into the schools and classrooms and for his critical input to my chapters.

I am forever grateful to my friend and technical editor, Mia Shargel, who was also a consistent and unending source of psychological support in times of self-doubt and discouragement. Very special thanks to my reliable graduate research assistant Naheel Baker. My friends Gittl and Christel: many hugs to you for your interest in my work and steadfast support.

My deepest gratitude is extended to my deceased parents Leonhard and Franziska Fuss and my sister and best friend Rita, who from the very beginning of my border crossing have supported and encouraged me to pursue my dreams.

Acknowledgments

[illegible faded text]

Personal Profile

Toni Fuss Kirkwood-Tucker

Our philosophy of life begins to take root in early childhood memories and continues to be formed, altered, and reshaped as the journey of life heaps experience after experience across our path. Inspired by the lived experiences of my colleague and friend Bill Gaudelli expounded in his book, *World Class: Teaching and Learning in Global Times* (2003) and the work by Merryfield, Van Manen, and Wilson (Merryfield, 2000a, b; Van Manen, 1990; Wilson, 1984; 1993a, b; 1998), I draw on the theory and research of the experiences of teachers that have shaped their worldview in their work and in their commitment to multicultural and global education. I have deconstructed some of my own vivid memories to provide the reader some insight into the processes that have carved my philosophy of education: growing up during the war in the Nazi era, international study, and my border crossing experiences.

My childhood years during the Nazi era were filled with stark images of a population scarred by war and yearning for peace. Too many death notices from the two fronts had decimated the male population in my farming village of 1,500 residents in the foothills of the Alps. Husbands, sons, brothers, uncles, and cousins were missing in action, either detained as prisoners of war or killed. The image of my mother fainting when the notice of the death of her oldest brother, a scout in Siberia, arrived is still fresh in my mind. I remember hundreds of refugees, from as far as the Sudetenland to as near as Munich, 100 kilometers away, seeking shelter in the village; the first group migrating from Polish lands conquered by the Nazis; the city-dwellers hungry and homeless from the bombing. Memories of my grandmother's primeval scream when the death notice of my father's youngest brother, who had fallen in France at the age of 17, have haunted me for years. I remember fearing that we would be bombed to death. I could feel a blanket of despair hovering over my village nestled along the Ammer River until it was liberated in April 1945 by U.S. tanks.

This was Catholic Bavaria. The mayor, priest, and teachers were the prominent individuals in the village. I clearly remember the scene when our village priest entered our classroom one morning, climbed on a chair, removed the hand-carved crucifix from the wall behind the teacher's desk, and replaced it with a framed picture of Hitler he pulled out from under his black frock. He stepped down from the chair and told the class, "From now on, when your teacher comes into the room, you will no longer pray. Instead, you stand up, salute Hitler, and shout 'Sieg Heil' three times. Only then are you allowed to sit down. Second, when you greet people in the street you no longer greet them with 'Gruess Gott, Frau 'such and such' but you raise your arm and say, 'Sieg Heil, Frau such and such.'" As a first grader I thought Jesus coming down from the wall was cool. I always felt sorry for him having to hang from a cross. When I informed my father of this exciting event, he grabbed me by my arms and spoke in no uncertain terms: "I forbid you to salute Hitler in the classroom or in the streets, do you understand? Do not let me catch you." From the next day on, I had to remain one hour longer in school every day cleaning blackboards, floors, and windows until the Americans came. From then on, Herr Pfarrer disliked my family.

Another vivid memory is the daily clicking of a young woman's passing footsteps—heading daily for the train station expecting her fiancé to arrive home from the war on the 10:30 night train. It must have been a year before the feet stopped clicking by. He never arrived; he had died in one of history's bloodiest battles in Stalingrad at the age of 23.

When my little brother was born in our house in 1944, I asked my mother why Dr. Kohlmeier did not deliver him just as he had delivered my sister and me; she responded that he was not around any more. My father, just arriving from Munich where he worked in the Messerschmitt factory after being injured in the war, yelled at my mother, "Tell her the truth. Dr. Kohlmeier is a Jew, and he was taken away. Who knows in which concentration camp he and his family were killed." My mother started moaning, and I begged my father to tell me about the camps. He ranted for hours as he spoke to his seven-year old first-born of the horrors happening in concentration camps, especially Dachau.

The images of war and genocide of my early childhood (there are more) have shaped me into a questioning individual distrusting governments and authority, and hating war. For most of my life, I felt ashamed to be German, wondering how so much darkness could emanate from such hardworking, cultured, and gifted people and tried to make sense of the nightmare. The shame eventually turned into pain and, for nearly all of my life, I carried it silently as I did not have the courage to discuss the horror in my high school or university classes in South Florida, an area with a large Jewish population.

My beliefs about the larger world have been shaped by memorable experiences of travel-study trips to England, Vietnam, Cambodia, Europe, and Japan; to international conferences in Russia and Siberia, Korea, South Africa, Zimbabwe, the Caribbean, Canada, Peru, and Mexico; and two Fulbright Fellowships, to China and Russia. These experiences have taught me that the world is filled with kind, caring, talented people many of whom have been victims of corrupt governments, colonialism, and greed. Their deprivation did not prevent them from moving forward selflessly to improve the lives of others. I am forever touched by their commitment, resourcefulness, gentleness, and hope to improve education. I discovered how much we teachers of the world are philosophically and culturally interconnected.

The traumatizing experiences of my border crossing as a transplant from Southern Germany to the Deep South of America in the early 1960s are deeply embedded in the affective domain. The immigrant existence is best articulated by W. E. B. Du Bois' (1903) notion of double consciousness; he clearly understands the dilemma of the ever-present veil that separates you permanently from your new country. My cultural and linguistic background and ability to speak Goethe's German and the Bavarian vernacular has resulted in an accent, linguistic errors, persistent struggle with the pronunciation of "th," and the ever-present enunciation of the American "v" for the German "w." The immigrant experience teaches you to perform your responsibilities with 200 percent efficiency to prove your worth. I believe that one will always remain marginal to a degree as duality steeped in two cultures is engrained.

The unanticipated consequences of my border crossing introduced me to different victims of discrimination and the notion of slow and early deaths. I was traumatized not only by shotgun houses, rocking chairs on front porches, and humidity in 100 degree weather, but also by the segregation of African Americans confined to the back of the bus and other things such as my mother-in-law's maid Yvonne refusing to eat at the same table with me and asking me to drop her off at the corner of the housing-project when she finally consented to let me drive her home. I experienced cities burning, demonstrators beaten and killed by the police, and unnerving race riots. At the height of integration in Miami's schools, I learned that my bussed-in middle-schoolers from the poverty-stricken inner city had never seen the Atlantic Ocean nor knew swimming. My German education did not prepare me for this. This was difficult for a young girl from the Bavarian countryside until I could put the pieces together and came to understand this as another form of genocide in slow motion in a country to which most of the world's people want to emigrate. The positive side of this existence is that I identify with minorities, relate to their struggle for acceptance and equality, and feel empathy. I had, in effect, developed the cultural sensitivity that Schuerholz-Lehr (2007) believes contributes to world-mindedness and effectiveness in cross-cultural competence.

Why do I possess a proclivity and commitment to multicultural and global education? Guichun Zong (2008), a friend and colleague, provides one answer. As a Chinese American she has reconciled her duality and her marginality in our country and uses them as assets to advance teaching from a global perspective; our immigrant experimental cultural and linguistic backgrounds result in a unique potential to make significant contributions shaping colleges and universities to global institutions.

My childhood memories of war and genocide shaped my view of the world and my determination to prevent them. The experiential learning of my adult years in foreign countries has sensitized my cross-cultural awareness and increased my knowledge base and the poverty and despair I have witnessed in developing nations has scarred me. The border crossing at the age of 22 into unknown territories and cultures of the unfamiliar affected my perspectives. I have experienced the social and racial injustices of interrelationships across identity, power, and experience that lead to a consciousness of other perspectives and a recognition of multiple realities grounded in international sensitivity, intercultural competence and world-mindedness (Merryfield, 2000a, b).

My life in the United States evolved as a hard journey of golden opportunities. I chose the road less taken. While I was a high school teacher, global facilitator, social studies coordinator, and eventually coordinator of the International Global Education Program of the Miami-Dade County Public Schools, I earned my doctorate at Florida International University under the mentorship of Jan L. Tucker. I was selected as Assistant Professor of Social Studies Education at Florida Atlantic University (FAU) where I was tenured and promoted to Associate Professor. My primary research focused on the integration of global perspectives in teacher education and schools, minority and global issues, and global citizenship education. One of my golden opportunities was to work with the Russian Ministry of Education and Russian colleagues in its education reform after the fall of the Berlin Wall in globalizing curriculum and instruction in teacher education and schools.

After 30 years in Florida's schools and universities, I retired to Tallahassee, Florida, to be near my adult children David and Andrée. Missing the Academy, I served as Adjunct at Florida Agricultural and Mechanical University (FAMU) and Florida State University (FSU) when Dr. Pamela "Sissi" Carroll, Chair of the School of Teacher Education, recently promoted to Associate Academic Dean, invited me to serve as Visiting Associate Professor at FSU. Her strong support led to the globalization of the traditional social science education program integrating new courses in global and multicultural education.

At last, after almost 50 years living in this good country, I am now psychologically able to discuss the horrors of the holocaust (with other genocides) from multiple perspectives. I have presented at the National Council for the Social Studies, and I am an invited speaker at the Annual Holocaust Institute at Florida State University on "Do German Schools Teach about the Holocaust?" The answer is a resounding yes.

Dreams fulfilled.

I. Historical and Theoretical Foundations

Chapter 1

A History of the Global
Education Movement in the United States

Kenneth A. Tye

Nationalism is an infantile disease ...it is the measles of mankind.
—Albert Einstein

Prelude to Global Education

The education profession in the United States is known for its preoccupation with domestic affairs (Butts, 1969). Such a preoccupation is rooted in the view that our systems of government and economics, along with our commitment to individual freedoms, are somehow superior to those of other peoples of the world. In short, the curriculum in our schools is nationalistic. The fact is that the curricula of all schools of the world are nationalistic (Schleicher, 1993; Tye, 1999). But history urges us toward the antidote of a global education, which

> involves learning about those problems and issues that cut across national boundaries, and about the interconnectedness of system—ecological, cultural, economic, political, and technological. Global education involves perspective taking—seeing things through the eyes and minds of others—and it means the realization that while individuals and groups may view life differently, they also have common needs and wants (Tye, 1991, p. 5).

Thus, when one examines the development of the global education movement in the United States or anywhere else, it is important to relate that development to the broader historical national and international context. Schools operate within a deep *societal structure* that dictates what is taught to their students (Tye, 2000). Before World War I, the major role of the schools in the United States was to assimilate waves of immigrants, mainly European, into the "American Way of Life." This explains why American history, civics, and economics were taught throughout the K-12 years of schooling. It does not, however, explain why they are still taught in a specific sequential order in U.S. classrooms today.

The post–World War I era was characterized in large part by the Wilsonian passion for peace and the fear of rising totalitarianism throughout the world. This led many educators of the time to argue for the inclusion of a more international perspective in curriculum and instruction in U.S. schools. This perspective was not an anti-American movement, but did advocate a change in our foreign policy, which at the time reflected a reluctance to participate in international affairs (Lamy, 1989). Although the existing foreign policy did make an effort to stress open-mindedness and international goodwill, the 1937 *National Society for the Study of Education (NSSE) Yearbook* made clear that it was deemed wise to avoid all controversial issues such as pacifism, disarmament, the World Court, and politics in general. In short, the curriculum at that time was isolationist and skirting controversial issues. As Shane (1969) stated rather tersely in the 1969 *NSSE Yearbook* after examining the elementary and secondary social studies curricula of the nation, "One would infer that, except for a few well-intentioned statements from scholars and authorities and occasional pioneering by rare and temerarious classroom teachers, meaningful education for world understanding in any modern sense of the term was neglected before 1940" (p. 275).

During the brief period of World War II, quite understandably the schools of the nation emphasized a curriculum focused on nationalism and patriotism. It was the post–World War II era that began to bring global and international emphasis to the curricula of the schools of the United States, albeit with only marginal success and not without conflict.

Beginning immediately after the end of World War II, there was an emergent focus on the workings of the United Nations (UN) as well as efforts on the part of the U.S. government to encourage various aspects of international education. The *1959 NSSE Yearbook* characterized the former as an effort to aid the people of the newly independent underdeveloped nations to improve themselves by educational means, formal and informal (Henry, 1959). The United Nations Educational, Scientific and Cultural Organization (UNESCO) emphasized the need for world peace and a belief in international organizations as a bulwark against narrow chauvinistic nationalism (www.icomos.org). One major UNESCO (2008) educational initiative has been the Associated Schools Project Network (ASPnet). Founded in 1953, it is a global network of some 8000 educational institutions in 177 countries, ranging from pre-school to teacher training institutions that work in support of quality education. Its focus has been on education about human rights, democracy, tolerance, intercultural learning, international cooperation, the role of the UN system and the millennium goals of the United Nations. The network sponsors a variety of projects that include collaboration among schools around the world. The most familiar education effort about the United Nations in

U.S. schools is the Model United Nations (MUN, 2008). This is a simulation of the United Nations in which high school or university students take on roles as diplomats, investigate international issues, deliberate, and develop solutions to world problems. Currently, more than 90,000 students take part in MUN Conferences in the United States. Though the MUN begun in the 1950s it is interesting to note that as early as the 1920s students in the United States were participating in collegiate simulations of the League of Nations (2008).

At the same time, the U.S. government also gave impetus to some interest in international education. Just after the end of World War II in 1946, the United States joined UNESCO, and Congress passed the Fulbright Act, which supported educational exchanges with countries around the world. The support for such exchanges was increased through a number of additional congressional acts over the years, and, in addition, many private for-profit and nonprofit organizations developed programs of international travel for secondary and tertiary students and teachers.

Unfortunately, however, almost immediately after the end of World War II much of the optimism about world peace and international cooperation came to an abrupt halt with the advent of the *Cold War*, which dominated foreign policy for more than four decades. Likewise, the rise of McCarthyism in the 1950s dominated much of educational policy in the nation. Punitive loyalty oaths and attacks on the schools for promoting "internationalism" and being "soft on communism" caused teachers to shy away from teaching about other countries, particularly communist nations. Yet paradoxically, it was the Cold War that gave rise to a decade of investment in international education. In October 1957, the Soviet Union launched *Sputnik*, the first man-made space satellite. The U.S. Congress responded in 1958 by passing the National Defense Education Act that, through its Title VI Program, required funding for foreign language and area studies centers located at universities across the country. The area studies centers were charged particularly to focus on lesser-known areas of the world. Included in the mandate for study centers was the idea of outreach for teacher-training and materials development for the pre-collegiate system.

The 1960s: Global Education Has Its Beginnings

The Report of the Study Commission on Global Education (1987) sponsored by Global Perspectives in Education noted that the widespread interest in the United States in international affairs generated by World

War II abated under "pressures for domestic change in the 1960s, and that the decline was exacerbated by disillusionment with overseas involvement during and following the Vietnam War" (p. 23). Even so, advances were made. At the federal level, adding to Title VI, the U.S. Congress passed the *Mutual Educational and Cultural Exchange Act of 1961* and the *International Education Act of 1966*. Although the latter act was ultimately not funded, both acts increased the flow of Americans to other countries and brought many more people from the rest of the world to the United States. By the 1967–1968 academic year, for example, there were 110,000 foreign students studying in the United States (Butts, 1969). These governmental acts also underlined the importance of increased knowledge of foreign languages. Tucker (1996) pointed out that a new worldview began to evolve in the 1960s and early 1970s. According to him, that global view was shaped by the works of numerous scholars:

> Rachel Carson (1962) described the harmful consequences of the use of pesticides. Pierre Teilhard de Chardin (1964) wrote of the convergence of human aspirations and history which included a progressive unification of humankind and intensification of our collective consciousness. Marshall McLuhan (1964) described the global village with its people linked through communications technology. Paul Ehrlich (1968) called attention to the stunning exponential growth rate of world population and impending ecological catastrophe. Alvin Toffler (1970) warned of impending future shock. R. Buckminster Fuller (1970) conceived of the metaphor of spaceship earth. Barbara Ward and René Dubos (1972) coined the notion of "thinking globally, acting locally." The Club of Rome ignited a global controversy regarding the rapid depletion of our non-renewable resources (Meadows, et al., 1972), and biologist Lewis Thomas (1974) portrayed Earth as a single living cell. (pp. 45–46).

This worldview was reflected, at least in part, in the developments in the social studies field. For example, *Man: A Course of Study*, influenced heavily by the work of Bruner, was initially designed and used widely in elementary schools in the United States and United Kingdom in the 1970s. Although *Man: A Course of Study* could not specifically be called global education, it did stress a cross-cultural, cross-disciplinary analyses of human behavior and emphasized the fact that an individual life can be viewed as an integral part of the larger flow of human existence (Bruner, 1965). The curriculum was much criticized in the United States by right-wing groups because of its emphasis on questioning such aspects of life as belief and morality.

There were other developments in social studies education that set the stage for global education. For example, Taba (1962), who participated with Tyler in the Eight-Year Study as an evaluation expert focusing on alternatives to standardized testing, was an influential progressive educator in the development of the elementary school social studies. The Social Studies Development Center at the University of Indiana (now the Center for Social Studies and International Education), founded in 1968, made its primary mission outreach to social studies teachers through in-service education and the development of instructional materials with a particular emphasis on international education (University of Indiana, 2008). According to Tucker (1996), "In 1968, the idea of global education emerged from a landmark report by the Foreign Policy Association, funded by the U.S. Office of Education, titled *An Examination of Objectives and Priorities in International Education in U.S. Secondary and Elementary Schools*" (p. 47). This report resulted in the publication of a special issue of Social Education titled *International Education for the Twenty-first Century*, edited by Anderson and Becker that, according to Tucker (1996), boasted "a veritable who's who of international educators" (p. 47). This publication rejected the idea of international education as a study of a collection of nations. Instead, it proposed a focus on problems and issues that cut across national boundaries. As Tucker acknowledged, "Global Education was born."

The 1970s: Global Education Moves Forward

Throughout the 1970s and until the end of the century, Becker and Anderson provided critical leadership to the global education movement. Becker's work at the Mid-America Program for Global Perspectives at the University of Indiana created a model for global education projects in individual states to link their products to the rest of the world and to demonstrate their interdependence to people and nations around the world. These endeavors resulted in projects such as Mid-America Trades with the World; Interdependence: Indiana and the World; Kansas in the World; and The World in Kentucky (Kirkwood-Tucker & Goldstein, 2007a). The idea of identifying cultural, economic and political links with one's home region, state, or city came from the work of Alger (1974) at the Mershon Center at the Ohio State University in the early 1970s, and resulted in *Your Community in the World/The World in Your Community*. Alger and his political science graduate students conducted exhaustive inventories of the ways various sectors in Columbus, Ohio, were linked to the global system. Sectors investigated included banking, medicine, religion, labor, real estate, research, education, agriculture, sports, media, and business.

Becker was a prolific and captivating writer and speaker. Using his Lincolnian way of presenting, he eschewed the role of scholar and worked to make connections between the theories and frameworks promoting global education and the needs of teachers working in the classrooms of our nation. Becker's many publications have been critical to the movement. The publication *Father of Global Education: Jim Becker* describes many of them quite well (Kirkwood-Tucker & Goldstein, 2007b). Three of Becker's publications call for special mention. The first, *Global Dimension in U.S. Education: The Secondary School* (1972) co-authored with East, set out an overview of secondary education programs and curriculum development programs and included an appendix identifying objectives for a global approach in secondary schools. The second publication, *The Wingspread Workbook for Educational Change Agents* (1976), co-authored with Hahn, described a variety of ways of introducing and using new global education practices and programs in schools. Becker's third edited publication was *Schooling for a Global Age* (1979). This book involved many of the global education leaders of the time. However, it was his chapter, "The World and the School: A Case for World-Centered Education," that earned him the title, *father of global education*.

If James Becker is known as the father of global education, Lee Anderson could certainly have been called the scholar of the field. In addition to editing with Becker the 1968 landmark foreign policy report described earlier, Anderson gave leadership to the field through numerous salient articles and spoken presentations. He was a political science professor at Northwestern University with a joint appointment to the University's School of Education, where his initial interests in civic education soon expanded to the international arena. His involvement in global education was evidenced in serving as the general editor for the Houghton Mifflin K-6 Social Studies Series, and his first published work, *Windows on Our World* (Anderson, 1976) represented a position on global education for which he was recommended by Howard Mehlinger, who was advisor to Houghton Mifflin and long-time director of the Social Studies Development Center at the University of Indiana as well as a major contributor to global and international education in his own right.

By the end of the 1970s, Anderson had added a number of important publications to the global education literature. His book, *Schooling and Citizenship in a Global Age: An Exploration of the Meaning and Significance of Global Education* (1979) was called *a must* by Tucker (1988) who at that time put together an annotated bibliography of global education writings. Merryfield, Jarchow, & Pickert (1997) referred to the book as one of the best rationales for global education ever written. In his book Anderson introduced the concept of the *J Curve* to explain the exponential increase in a variety of global phenomena: population growth, increases in carbon dioxide in the atmosphere, life expectancy, energy consumption, deaths attributed to war, and so on. In collaboration with his wife and lifelong professional colleague, Charlotte C. Anderson, he wrote "A Visit to Middleston's World-Centered Schools: A Scenario," which was the first chapter in *Schooling for a Global Age* (1979) described earlier. The chapter was a fictional (but possible) account of how the imaginary Terra and Futura Elementary schools, World Middle School, and 21st Century High School in Middleston designed and carried out programs in world-centered education. Lee Anderson (1982) also wrote the article, "Why Should American Education Be Globalized? It's a Nonsensical Question," a compelling argument for bringing a global perspective to the curriculum of our schools. Anderson reprised this argument and added additional evidence for the need for globalization of the curriculum in U.S. schools in "A Rationale for Global Education," the first chapter of the 1991 Association for Supervision and Curriculum (ASCD) Yearbook, *Global Education: From Thought to Action.*

A brief but important document titled *An Attainable Global Perspective* written by Hanvey (1976) and produced by the Center for Teaching International Relations (CTIR) at the University of Denver promoted and elaborated on five interdisciplinary dimensions in how to teach from a global perspective:

- *Perspective consciousness*: Awareness of and appreciation for different perspectives of the world.
- *State of the planet awareness:* An in-depth understanding of global issues and events and their cause-and-effect relationships.
- *Cross-cultural awareness:* Awareness of the diversity of ideas and practices in human societies around the world, and how they compare.
- *Knowledge of global dynamics*: Comprehension of traits and mechanisms of the world system, with an emphasis on theories and concepts that increase consciousness of global change.
- *Awareness of human choices*: Awareness of the problems of choices confronting individuals, nations, and the human species as consciousness and knowledge of the global system expands.

Though Hanvey never had the personal presence in the global education movement that Becker and Anderson did, this singular paper has been and still is extremely influential for those interested in global education. Kniep (1987), writing for the American Forum for Global Education, commented that "since its first publication, the work has been widely used, has been reprinted a number of times, remains timely, in demand, and valid. In many ways it is a classic in the literature of global education" (p. 82).

One leading organization in promoting global education has been the American Forum for Global Education. Founded in 1970 as Global Perspectives in Education, the American Forum has produced many curriculum materials, sponsored a variety of projects and conferences, and has been in the forefront of the global education movement. Of particular note are three publications all of which still have relevance today. The first, *Education for a World in Change* (King, Branson, & Condon, 1976) contains lesson plans and a special section on "goals of education with a global perspective." More than a decade later, this organization produced *The United States Prepares for its Future: Global Perspectives in Education*, a report of the Study Commission on Global Education (1987), a commission made up of a number of leading intellectual and political figures of the time brought together by the American Forum. The report pointed to the growing globalization of the world and outlined the implications of this change for the schools of the nation. It made concrete recommendations for improvements in schooling at all levels of the system, and contained appendices with helpful information for global educators. Finally, and also in 1987, Kniep wrote and edited *Next Steps in Global Education: A Handbook for Curriculum Development*, a highly practical document that sets forth concrete steps for the development of curricula at all levels of schooling, infused with a global perspective

The 1980s and 1990s: *The Golden Years*

Global education programs became fairly common during the 1980s and on into the 1990s. Along with the provision of instructional materials, inservice training of teachers, and travel-study courses provided by the Title VI Area Studies Centers at universities around the country, a number of foundations gave significant support to schools and various consortia willing to develop and pilot test global education programs. A select few of the major projects of the time are described here.

The Global Awareness Program

The Global Awareness Program (GAP), led by Jan Tucker and located in Miami at Florida International University (FIU), began in 1979 as a collaboration under Tucker's direction between FIU, the Miami-Dade County Public Schools, and the Florida State Department of Education. With funding from the Danforth Foundation, the U.S. Department of Education, local sources, and other foundations, and using the Hanvey framework described earlier, the program initially focused on the infusion of global education into the curricula and instruction of selected Miami-Dade County high schools, middle schools, and elementary schools, organized in feeder systems. Ultimately nearly two-thirds of Dade County schools were involved with GAP.

Over the years, the project set out to train global education master teachers who in their turn provided school-based leadership. The development of instructional materials and travel-study courses was also part of the program. Throughout the 1980s and 1990s, GAP provided national leadership through the dissemination of information about its Miami-Dade County initiatives. Travel-study programs to England, China, and Japan offered Miami's teachers opportunities to learn about the world. The FIU-Japan Program took 60 teachers and administrators from Miami's global schools to Japan, teachers who then implemented Japan studies in their respective schools. The program exists, but has been significantly modified over the years as funding has declined. Currently the focus is on the teacher education program at FIU (Florida International University, 2008).

The Bay Area Global Education Program

The Bay Area Global Education Program (BAGEP) began in 1979 when Global Educators (the West Coast Office of Global Perspectives in Education), the World Affairs Council of Northern California, and the Stanford Program on International and Cross-cultural Education (SPICE) joined forces to promote global education in K-12 schools in the San Francisco Bay Area. Each of the three partner organizations continued its own global education outreach activities—indeed, SPICE has been one of the major providers of high quality global education instructional materials—but their combined resources channeled through BAGEP brought global education to large numbers of schools in the region and served as a model program for other regions of the country. Early funding came from local and national foundations, federal government agencies, and California-based corporations. The strategy included training teachers who would in their turn teach teachers in their own schools, developing and providing instructional materials, and sponsoring of numerous study tours (Freeman, 1986).

In the mid-1980s BAGEP was merged into the California International Studies Project (CISP) based at Stanford University, led by Ron Herring and supported by a combination of state and local funding. BAGEP served as a model for what ultimately became a network of a dozen or so consortia located throughout California. CISP moved from Stanford to the University of the Pacific in 2003, and, under pressure to conform to statewide standards in order to receive funding from the state of California, became one of the California Subject Matter Projects (California International Studies Project, 2008).

Project Enrichment

Project Enrichment was begun by the Stanley Foundation in 1974 with a focus on assisting local Muscatine, Iowa, high schools and the community with a variety of global education activities. According to Jan Drum (1986), the original coordinator of the project, 50 such activities were completed in 1975; by the mid-1980s there were more than 200 projects per year. Activities included support for Model United Nations, sending international university students into high school classrooms to expose students to people from other nations, creation of a values institute, and provision of teacher travel expenses (Freeman, 1986). Paralleling these initiatives, the State Department of Education in Iowa in the 1980s became one of the early state education departments to support the implementation of global education programs in K-12 schools. At that point in time, this was one of the exemplary global education programs in the nation. Muscatine initiatives were replicated fairly widely in Iowa and elsewhere.

By the 1990s, however, with the advent of strict curriculum standards focused mainly on the so-called basics across the country and attacks by the right wing, interest in global education began to wane. By 2000, the Stanley Foundation still maintained a small education program (Stanley Foundation Programs, 2008) and the Global Community College program (Stanley Foundation, Community College Program, 2008). Currently the main program of the foundation is the production of position papers prepared by scholarly panels on such topics as the U.S. and global security, the United Nations and global institutions, and arms control. Unfortunately this movement away from supporting education in K-12 schools, including global education, and toward the production of position papers on broad national and international issues has become a common practice of American foundations. As easy and interesting as such a course might be for those who inhabit the halls of foundations, it does bring into question the value of allowing them tax-free status in the public interest.

Global Learning, Inc.

Global Learning, Inc. was originally conceived in 1973 as a three-year peace education project headed by Jeffrey Brown, who was struggling with questions about U.S. involvement in Vietnam. With a small grant from a close friend and joined by Paula Gotsch, who had a community organizing background, he became involved in the emerging field of global education. To the two primary values of peace and social justice, Global Learning added the values of economic well-being, ecological balance, and political participation to the concepts of the field. Hanvey's *An Attainable Global Perspective* (1976), along with works by movement leaders such as Alger, Anderson, and Becker, influenced the work of the organization. Programmatically, Global Learning began by organizing topical programs on global themes to raise teachers' awareness and to provide classroom resources. The first workshop was on the theme of human rights, with a keynote speaker from the United Nations. Over the years, grants were obtained from a wide variety of sources, and programs usually focused on specific topics such as world hunger and third-world development, conflict resolution, the more traditional international education, sustainable development, and more recently on energy. Procedures generally involved creating a volunteer project team of teachers, academics, and content specialists to provide content and classroom expertise. Though Global Learning's focus has been mostly in its home state of New Jersey, resulting publications have been disseminated in teacher workshops across the country, and the organization has participated with the American Library Association on two national projects. At this point, Global Learning finds itself mostly engaged with locally based energy conservation efforts sponsored by school-based Green Schools Teams (Brown, 2008).

The World Affairs Council of Philadelphia

The World Affairs Council of Philadelphia (WACP) has been in operation since 1949 and has sponsored a world affairs program for students and teachers in the region. From an initial effort limited to extracurricular programs for high school students, the council's program has grown to include a wide variety of classroom projects for elementary and secondary students and the co-sponsorship of the public Bodine High School for International Affairs. Currently, under the auspices of the Center for Teacher Excellence, a number of programs are also offered for teachers of the greater Philadelphia area. These programs include opportunities to interact with scholars, to share the best practices of the profession, to access a wide range of curriculum materials, and to train in the use of technology that enhances classroom learning. Other World Affairs Councils around the country offer programs for students and teachers; their services can be found on the Internet. The Philadelphia WAC Program, however, is still one of the most comprehensive and well known in the country (Lonzetta, 1986).

The International Education Consortium

The International Education Consortium (IEC) was founded in St. Louis in 1984 by a group of academics and citizens who represented the United Nations Association and the World Affairs Council. With support from the Danforth, Rockefeller, and James S. McDonnell Foundations, the IEC began its programming with teams of teachers who attended summer institutes and workshops that provided new information and pedagogical skills to teach about foreign cultures and the relationship of the United States with regions of the world. Owing to the influence of the Rockefeller Foundation, the IEC created a humanities framework for its programming, giving it a unique identity among international global education programs. In 1994, the IEC gave up its not-for-profit status and joined a local service agency, the Cooperating School Districts (CSD), which serves more than 50 school districts and one-third of Missouri's students. In the past 15 years, IEC has conducted summer institutes in world history and geography and has been the recipient of three grants from the U.S. Department of Education to improve the teaching of U.S. history. The IEC remains a leader in social studies education for the state of Missouri, offering networking for social studies coordinators and world history teachers (Lubeck, 2008).

The Center for Human Interdependence

The Center for Human Interdependence (CHI) was established in 1985 at what was then Chapman College (now Chapman University) in Orange County, California, with a grant from the Helen DeVitt Jones Foundation. CHI created a network of 11 collaborating schools (three high schools, four middle schools, and four elementary schools) organized in feeder systems. CHI used the principles learned from previous work at the Institute for the Development of Educational Activities (I/D/E/A) at UCLA under the leadership of John Goodlad, who was examining the educational change process. The CHI program focused its action on the single school, not on individual teachers or school districts. The CHI supported a variety of activities in the participating schools, most of them initiated by the schools. Workshops were organized around interests expressed by teachers. The Orange County and the World Project and the Middle School World Games Day were initiated and supported by CHI.

Following five years of support from the Jones Foundation, CHI received other small grants and carried on limited activities. The project was completed in 1991. One significant contribution of the project was that all its activities throughout its duration were carefully documented using a framework and methodology derived from *Symbolic Interaction Theory* (Blumer, 1969). Results of the study were reported in several publications (Tye & Tye, 1992).

Education for Global Involvement

Education for Global Involvement (EGI) was established in 1988 by a group of educators and community leaders concerned about the quality of international and multicultural education in schools; Charlotte Anderson served as its president throughout its life. Though EGI consulted with schools across the United States and internationally, its major focus was in Illinois, especially the Chicago schools. EGI conducted summer institutes for teachers at local universities in Chicago and neighboring districts and conducted several joint projects with major national and international organizations, including the ASCD, the Foreign Policy Association, the American Forum for Global Education, and the Matsuyama International Education Center, Japan. The Japan Studies project, funded by the United States-Japan Foundation, engaged teachers in 24 Chicago public schools in intensive seminars and study tours of Japan. Thirty Japanese teachers were hosted in Illinois Schools each year for three years. Other projects, focused on Japan and Latin America, involved seminars and travel abroad. EGI maintained a resource library for area teachers. After several years of raising considerable financial support from local and outside sources for its work, the project ended in 2000 (Anderson, 2008). A significant contribution of this project to the global education movement has been the development and testing of several frameworks and models useful to those who wish to carry out their own programs (see, e.g., *Global Understandings: A Framework for Teaching and Learning* (Anderson, Niklas, & Crawford, 1994).

The Center for Teaching International Relations

The Center for Teaching International Relations (CTIR) is the outreach arm of Denver Graduate School of International Studies. Founded in 1968 by Maurice East with a grant from the U.S. Office of Education, CTIR has gone through significant changes over time. Initially it established the Prospective Teachers Fellowship Program, which trained students to teach international relations at the secondary school level. Beginning in 1970, CTIR began to focus more on in-service training of teachers of the fifth through the eleventh grades. By 1975, it was working closely with schools in the region and, in collaboration with Global Perspectives in Education, began to develop curriculum materials for teachers across the country. At this point, thanks to federal funding, support from the university, local schools, teachers, and a creative staff, CTIR established itself as one of the largest teacher-training programs in international and intercultural studies in the nation (Schukar, 1986). In the 1980s, CTIR and global education in general came under attack from a variety of ultraconservative organizations (which is described more fully later in this chapter). Current programs include the International Studies School Association (ISSA, 2008), a network of well over 80 schools at all levels and all across the country that have a variety of global and international programs and whose faculty members meet every summer. In addition, CTIR offers online and on-campus courses as well as advanced placement (AP) summer institutes for secondary school teachers and other education professionals. A variety of publications and instructional materials are available to teachers at all levels of schooling, and a new program, World Affairs Challenge, has been developed for use by middle and high school students.

Continuing the Golden Years

Many other programs were also developed during this time. Among them were the Arkansas International Center at the University of Arkansas (2008), led by Walter Nunn; the REACH PROGRAM (2008) in Arlington, WA, led by Gary Howard; the Massachusetts Global Education Center, led by Paul Mulloy, and now part of the Massachusetts Geographic Alliance (2008); and the Global Education in Minnesota (GEM) program, led by Bob Erickson (1986). Many more programs existed during these golden years, many of which no longer exist at the time of this writing. Others have changed their foci for a variety of reasons but largely because of the need to find continued funding. For example, The Arkansas International Center, opened in 1988, worked in its early years with school programs such as the Gibbs Elementary Global Education Magnet School as well as in collaboration with the nearby Heifer Project. The Center continues operation with some education programs, but its major focus today is on various community exchange programs.

Numerous individuals in the country were also important to the global education movement during this time. Judith Torney-Purta, who has a psychology background and is based at the University of Maryland, has been an important researcher, writer, and consultant in the field. She has provided particular expertise in evaluation work (see, e.g., Torney-Purta, 1982a). Later in her career, she became associated with the International Education Association (IEA) for International Studies of Civic Education (Torney-Purta, Lehmann, Oswald, & Schulz, 2001). H. Thomas Collins, based at the Elliott School of International Affairs, Georgetown University, has been a consultant to many projects and state departments of education. He collaborated as a writer with Fred Czarra, director of International Relations at the Council of Chief State School Officers and with Andrew Smith, president of the American Forum for Global Education, on a number of important publications in the field (Collins, Czarra, & Smith, 1998). Working with Chadwick Alger at the Mershon Center at Ohio State were Richard Remy, Robert Woyach, and Eugene Gilliom. These scholars were involved in the *Your Community and the World* project. George Otero began Las Palomas de Taos at the Mabel Dodge Luhan House in Taos, New Mexico, in 1977, where countless global education conferences were held. Otero has been a consultant to many global education projects over the years in the United States and other countries and has developed a number of global education curriculum materials. John Cogan, at the University of Minnesota, a scholar in field with more than 100 publications relating to global education to his credit, has also been a consultant to many global education programs (Parker, Ninomiya, & Cogan, 1999). He worked extensively on global education issues in the Asia-Pacific region, particularly Japan. Angene Wilson began at the University of Kentucky in 1975 as a secondary school social studies professor. Her Peace Corps time in Africa led her to focus on how people with international experience can make an impact in teaching high school students about the world (Wilson 1986; 1993a; 1993b). She retired from the University in 2005, but is still active as a scholar and consultant. There are many other dedicated and talented people who made contributions to the cause of global education during its golden years; some continue their work to the present time.

More recently, to the names of Anne Baker, director of the National Peace Corps Association, Bill Gaudelli, Teachers College at Columbia, Elizabeth Heilman at Michigan State University, Toni Fuss Kirkwood-Tucker at Florida State University, and Guichun Zong at Kennesaw State University, one must add the name of Merry M. Merryfield at the Ohio State University as one of the current leaders in the field. She has many salient publications that clarify and move the field forward and has developed an outstanding website that can be used for the in-service training of teachers (Merryfield, 2008a).

Right-Wing Attacks on Global Education

Global education came under attack in the 1980s and early 1990s. Thomas Tancredo, a former Colorado legislator and once Republican candidate for President, was appointed by U.S. Secretary of Education William Bennett as Director of Region VIII of the U.S. Department of Education based in Denver. Tancredo expressed concern about the values implicit in programs in global education and hired a consultant, Gregg Cunningham, to write a report about the CTIR. The report also examined a number of other global education programs, including BAGEP. In the report, "Blowing the Whistle on Global Education," Cunningham (1986) charged CTIR with having a liberal bias that fostered "capitulationist" attitudes, moral relativism, and a "hard left" agenda. Tancredo took it upon himself to promote this attack throughout Region VIII, and according to Caporaso and Mittelman (1988) he was successful in causing "a wave of hysteria" to sweep through the Colorado schools. Conservatives in some communities accused teachers of "promoting communism, atheism, and anti-American ideas" (p. 37). As an example of how damaging such attacks could be, at the April 15, 1986, Pro-Family Conference in Colorado, Tancredo noted William Coors's remark, "If they do not disenfranchise the Center for Teaching International Relations, I'm resigning as a member of the Board of Trustees, and I'm withdrawing all financial support from the University of Denver" (Caporaso & Mittelman, 1988, p. 43).

The report was quickly picked up by conservative organizations nationwide as a call for action against global education programs (Schukar, 1993). The next major attack on global education was in Minnesota where a conservative policy think-tank group issued a report called "The Radicalization of Minnesota's Public Schools" (Kersten, 1988). It was an attack on the Minnesota Global Education Coalition that included the Minnesota Department of Education, the Global Education Center at the University of Minnesota, and the Global Studies Resource Center located in the Twin Cities Metropolitan School District. The charges focused on an alliance by the Coalition with the Central American Resource Center and the materials produced for use by teachers (Schukar, 1993).

A third attack occurred in Iowa in 1991. In the late 1980s, the Iowa Department of Education had received a mandate from the Iowa legislature to develop a global education component in all subjects for K-12. The result of the mandate was a resource and activity book prepared by an appointed task force of educators that consisted of more than 1,500 lessons, resources, and suggestions for implementing global education. Objections came from fundamentalist Christian groups, parents, and members of agricultural communities and organizations. Most of the criticism was directed toward the wording of a few activities and the failure of some of the activities to present contending perspectives (Schukar, 1993).

There were similar attacks across the country, particularly in California and in the state of Washington. It became apparent that these attacks were a clearly, carefully, and well-articulated political agenda driven by the conservative political right and fundamentalist Christian groups. For example, syndicated columnist Phyllis Schlafly (1986), head of the conservative Eagle Forum, in an article titled "What Is Wrong with Global Education?" criticized global education for eliminating patriotism, promoting moral equivalence, imposing particular worldviews, brainwashing, charging teachers that their curricular infusion techniques amounted to "indoctrination-by-deception" (p. 23). When the Northwest Regional Educational Laboratory published a report on global education in 1983, it was lambasted for suggesting that a "massive re-education of teachers" was needed in order to teach global education effectively. Schlafly (1986) alleged that global education was founded on "the myth of [country/cultural] equivalence" and objected to the curricular movement's advancement of world government, the alarming teaching of the world's depletion of resources, and called the movement a "cult" (p. 23).

As these attacks on global education were being made, Jan Tucker, director of the GAP in Miami described earlier, was serving as president of the National Council for the Social Studies (January 1987–June 1988). His presidential address focused on the urgent need for global education. He too came under attack. This time the affront came from conservative thinker Chester Finn, the same Chester Finn who was Assistant Secretary for Research and Improvement in the U.S. Department of Education and who two years earlier had written the article "Globaloney" with Gary Bauer, a virulent attack on both the United Nations and global content in American textbooks (Finn & Bauer, 1986). Finn also attacked Tucker's discussion of the rise of the trading state (Rosecrance, 1986) and his warning against the "nationalization of knowledge" (Finn, 1988). Harsh criticism also came from Diane Ravitch, Andre Ryerson, William Bennett, and the Thomas B. Fordham Foundation.

These attacks on global education represent the views of so-called *movement conservatives*. Most movement conservatives, according to Lamy (1991), "have a passion for international relations and seek to carry their conservative social reform movement to foreign lands" (p. 52). They reject the notion that there is any kind of equivalence in the world; the United States is superior in all ways.

The cumulative result of these attacks caused state departments of education, school administrators, teachers, and teacher educators to be much more cautious about offering programs under the name of global education. Foundation support of global education programs declined markedly. Even Global Perspectives in Education changed its name to the American Forum for Global Education. As we have seen, some programs closed. Others were modified to offer more U.S. history, environmental studies, multicultural education, education for sustainability, international education, and so on as means of obtaining funding support. As Barbara Tye (2000) has noted, education is embedded within a deep structure of pervasive social expectations. By the end of the mid-1990s, because of the politics of the time, the golden age of global education was on the wane.

The Contemporary Scene

At the turn of the twentieth century, the "Politics of the Right" continues to impede global education. The *No Child Left Behind* legislation with its orientation toward high-stakes testing coupled with the national standards movement has had very little success in reaching the goal of overall school improvement in the United States, yet has caused a significant reduction in the time spent on such subjects as the arts, social studies, even science. This turn of events has left little room for global education content.

Yet there are signs that global education is once again being recognized as important to the future of our children and youth as well as to the nation as a whole. One can see that there are new movements in the country toward the inclusion of a global perspective in teacher education and schools.

The website www.globaledyellowpages.org, which I developed in 2005–2006, is a description of more than 1,000 sources that provide global education materials, training programs to teachers, and includes links to many other sources (Tye, 2006). Using the definition of global education at the opening of this chapter and looking at the website, one can see that a variety of programs in the country can be said to have global content. For example, the website lists 50 Title VI Asian Studies Centers and 61 additional organizations that provide resources and training for teachers interested in teaching about Asia. The latter category includes the Asia Society, with a large array of instructional materials and the Goldman Sachs award for excellence in international education and many other Area Studies Centers and organizations that focus on additional regions of the world.

Under the entry *global education,* the website describes 94 organizations, including links to many other organizations that focus specifically on global education. Among these are the National Peace Corps Association, led by Anne Baker, with a wide array of programs for global education teachers; the Foreign Policy Association with its *Great Decisions Curriculum;* Global Classrooms with United Nations resources; the Global Studies Foundation, Facing the Future; the Global SchoolNet Foundation and i*EARN, which uses the Internet to create networks for more than 20,000 schools in over 100 countries that enable students to collaborate on service learning projects. Finally, the Longview Foundation for Education World Affairs & International Understanding is the one foundation in the country that uses all of its resources to support global education.

Other related topics on the website, most with additional links, are environment; foreign language; geography; human rights; multicultural education; peace and conflict resolution (58 sources, including Educators for Social Responsibility); sustainability education; and world history. Other topics include the arts, business, civics, teaching materials, technology, travel and exchange, and world affairs councils around the nation. The website also contains a section on those few state Departments of Education that support global education.

The final section of the yellow pages website lists actual schools that are working on global education per se. Though it does not include all schools working on related topics, the number is still impressive. In addition to a number of individual schools in the database, there are several networks of schools, including the Asia Society's International Studies School Network; The Global Classroom Initiative of the Canadian International Development Agency; InterConnections21 that includes schools affiliated with the Associated Schools Project of UNESCO (2008); The International Studies Association, with many schools, and sponsored by the Center for Teaching International Relations; The National Association of Independent Schools, and the National Association of Multicultural Schools. There are many other schools that are carrying out global education programs despite the emphasis on the so-called basics and high-stakes testing. Unfortunately, there is an imbalance. Many schools whose constituency is largely low-income families are being deprived of learning about the world.

A Look into the Future

There is no doubt that the right-wing attacks have had a negative impact on global education in our country. However, using a broad definition of the field, there still is a great deal of activity in the movement, including providing instructional materials and in-service training for teachers, harnessing technology for teaching and learning about the world, travel-study abroad, and exchange programs for students and teachers. Most important, there are a number of programs that are thriving in U.S. K-12 schools.

The rationale for the development of global education used in the 1980s and early 1990s to promote global education is still compelling. In the 1980s and 1990s, most people argued for global education because we had moved into a world that was undergoing rapid globalization. Global trade and multinational corporate structures, the Internet and other forms of communication, worldwide media, rapid transportation, and massive human migration all made the need for global education perfectly obvious. Such conditions continue to exist and, in addition to environmental degradation, a growth in hunger and poverty, and expansion of conflicts around the world, makes the need for global education even more important today.

Unfortunately many political and business leaders have fallen into the trap of justifying global education on nationalistic grounds. They claim, based on international assessments, that our schools are failing and that our students cannot compete in the new world economy. However, the question needs to be asked, "Is this appeal to national and personal self-interest causing us to miss the opportunity to connect with people's hopes and values?" We are reminded by Priscilla Lewis of the

Rockefeller Brothers Foundation that even parents who want their children to succeed and to grow up in a secure world and, for the majority of the public that means not just militarily secure but also secure in other ways, comes from cooperating and living together according to fundamental norms of decency and fairness (2000).

We must teach our young people about the new world in which we live. This form of pedagogy is what can be called the *descriptive* side of global education: teaching about how the systems of the world work, and how humans interact within those systems. Such descriptive teaching is important because we know that a majority of individuals in the United States lack knowledge about the rest of the world. More important, however, is what I call *normative* teaching: teaching students to analyze issues and problems that involve value positions so that they can plan appropriate courses of action. If you wonder what issues and problems to focus upon, a good list comes from a 1999 survey of global education practices around the world (K. Tye, 1999). In order of importance they were the environment; sustainable development; intercultural relations; peace and conflict resolution; the role of technology; human rights; and social justice (including racism and sexism). Because of attacks from the right, some global educators adhere only to descriptive teaching and tend to shy away from normative teaching. However, as Schukar (1993) reminds us, "responsible citizenship demands that controversial issues be set aside out of fear or discomfort. To deny the role of controversial issues in education is to deny students a quality and essential education" (p. 57). There is some evidence that the deep structure of schooling, that is the political and economic system within which it resides, is changing, and that the time is coming when global education will be embraced more fully. If that is true, then we need to be prepared to respond to that change. In order to respond, there are some things we need to do. The list is not very long:

- As a society, we need to realize that knowing how the systems of the world work is as basic as knowing how to read, write, and work with numbers.
- We need to recruit more individuals who are knowledgeable about the world in which they live and who demonstrate analytical and critical thinking abilities into teaching.
- We need to improve teacher education so that potential teachers learn about the systems of the world, the skills, abilities of analysis, and critical thinking.

- We need to review materials of instruction so that we identify those that teach particular value positions, and we need to be able to teach students how to recognize and analyze such materials.

Global education has experienced difficult times in the recent past. Despite setbacks, the fact remains that the movement is currently strong and growing. It is now time to be optimistic about the future. It is also the time to increase our efforts to move the field forward for the benefit of our students, our nation, and our world.

Chapter 2

Terrains of Global and Multicultural Education: What Is Distinctive, Contested, and Shared?

Elizabeth E. Heilman

> The test of courage comes when we are in the minority. The test of tolerance comes when we are in the majority.
>
> --Ralph W. Sockman, 1969

Clearly there are links between the concepts and pedagogy necessary to multicultural and global education: both focus on cultural and cross-cultural understanding, for example. In this regard, global education appears to be a close cousin to multicultural education. However, as this chapter details, there are important differences and tensions and one approach does not easily substitute for the other. First, I describe the ways in which the fields are distinctive. They have very different origins and some distinctive aims; they developed with different origins; different justifications; different beneficiaries, proponents, and opponents; they have different policy profiles and different scopes. Next, I describe the ways the fields are similar and explore how each field includes similarly different "types" with different political and theoretical assumptions. In conclusion, I will identify elements that are definitive, important, and central to both. I discuss how democratic perspectives on diversity, difference, and power are increasingly important in the world, both philosophically and experientially and in terms of social and educational policy, and I offer a new way to think about them through cosmopolitanism, poststructuralism, and neopragmatism and a call for a new political-personal citizenship education. This chapter primarily addresses the ways in which these fields have been theorized and practiced, with many examples from the United States. However, I also deliberately make a few references to the ways in which these fields and their debates have taken shape in other nations.

What is distinctive between global education and multicultural education? To begin with, there are important ways in which multicultural education is distinct from global education.

Table 2.1. What Is Distinctive between Global Education
and Multicultural Education?

Distinctions	Multicultural Education	Global Education
Origin	Develops as an aspect of national minority struggles in the context of national political issues	Develops in response to international and national politics and global issues
Justification	Derives justification from and constitutional principles of democracies and is supported by law. Pragmatic justification focuses on interpersonal and community relations	Derives legitimacy from principles of national and global citizenship and human rights but has no legal authority Pragmatic justification focuses on participating in global economics and politics
Beneficiary	Perceived to benefit national minorities mostly and every citizen to some degree	Perceived to people outside of the nation and every citizen to some degree
Proponents & Opponents	Led mostly by minority and native people and scholars. Opposed by nationalists.	Led mostly by first world whites and scholars. National minorities are sometimes against it. Opposed by nationalists
Policy Profile	Subject to high-profile public debate. Explicit education policy is typical	Usually low profile unless national interests are evoked. Explicit education policy less frequent than in multicultural education
Scope	Multicultural education includes issues of curriculum, instruction, learner's culture and learning style and many aspects of school policy from hiring to funding	Global education focuses primarily on curriculum

Origins and Contexts of Global Education and Multicultural Education

Global Education

Global education and multicultural education have very different origins. Although some aspects of what might be called global education have been in the U.S. curriculum at least since the progressive era, global education began to emerge as a coherent educational field in the 1960s owing to four interrelated contexts: (1) an American domestic sphere increasingly dominated by foreign policy issues; (2) the emergence of global jurisprudence and global economic systems exemplified by the United Nations and the Bretton Woods financial institutions in the wake of World War II; (3) the emerging ecology and environmental education movement; and (4) the influence of a global focus in disciplinary academic study in areas ranging from anthropology to geography, world literature to history, and political science, among others.

Multicultural Education

The fields' respective attempts to understand across difference—by focusing inward on the needs of minorities and by focusing outward on those whom we affect and who affect us—correspond to the distinct historical origins of the fields. Efforts of minority groups to gain rights, notably African Americans, Native Americans, and Hispanics in the 1950s and 1960s provided the context for the development of multicultural education; however as with global education, there were precedents. James Banks (1993), one of the major architects of the field, documents emerging interest in culture and writings by and about ethnic groups such as African Americans in the early progressive era; the intergroup education movement of the 1950s; and, finally, the ethnic studies movement in the 1960s and 1970s. Although not directly generating multicultural education, these were important precedents to the current multicultural education movement. In addition, four scholars are mentioned as "specialists in other groups" and as having played early and significant roles in the evolution of multicultural education: "C. E. Cortes on Mexican-Americans; J. Forbes on American Indians; S. Nieto on Puerto Ricans; and D. Sue on Asian-Americans" (Banks, 1993, p. 12).

> Multiculturalism did not emerge from scholarship alone however as the political and legal national context was central to the development of multicultural education. Pushed by a growing civil rights movement and by the

legal challenge of the National Association of the Advancement of Colored People (NAACP), the Supreme Court declared racial segregation in education to be unconstitutional in *Brown v. Board of Education* (1954), an important triumph that set the stage for a major new development in American education: the desegregation of Southern schools. Such desegregation was slow and deeply resisted but, sustained work over a decade backed by the expanding resources of the federal government, brought an eventual end to legally sanctioned Jim Crow laws in education even if, 10 years after the Supreme Court decision, fewer than one percent of all black children in the South went to desegregated schools.

By the 1980s, equity was increasingly interpreted not just as having access to equally funded and openly available schooling but much more deeply as having equitable access to curriculum and instruction. James Banks (1981; 1989), for example, argued that in order to maintain a "multicultural school environment" all aspects of the school had to be examined and transformed including policies, teachers' attitudes, instructional materials, assessment methods, counseling, and teaching styles and how the field has moved through different stages. For Banks, it has gone from its ethnic studies phase to its multiethnic education phase designed to bring about structural and systemic changes in schools, into the third phase that introduced other minority groups, especially women, into the conceptualization and, finally, into the fourth and current phase that keeps at the forefront the development of theory, research, and practice that focus on the interplay of race, gender, and class.

Different Legal and Philosophical Justifications

In this section I describe the different legal and philosophical justifications for multicultural and global education. Multicultural education is most distinctive from global education because it has deep philosophical roots in democratic theory and because it can be mandated by law. Multicultural education is justified as necessary to assure justice, liberty, and freedom of expression, which are foundational to democracies and central to individual lives and micro-politics. Because democracy requires the just distribution of public goods and opportunities and equal treatment under the law, multiculturalism and diversity are perennial issues in our debates about our largest national policy concerns. Even issues such as the economy, healthcare, and education that are not explicitly about diversity often entail deep debates about how policies in these arenas are or should be enacted with justice with diverse people in mind. Though global issues are increasingly important in the economy, healthcare, and education, the debate is not about justice for global people but typically about *protecting* us from global problems—a stark difference.

Mediating minority rights and justice for diverse citizens is a necessary part of democratic policy-making, but rights for those outside of one's nation have no constitutional authority. One of the most important differences between multicultural education and global education is the fact that multicultural education policies are often mandated by law, and they have a judicial constitutional protection. In spite of differences across all democracies, Dahl (2003) says there are 22 basic principles and processes of democracy that are remarkably similar and include the need to balance the rights of the few against the rights of the many and to provide equality of protection under the law. This helps explain the fact that all democracies have some kind of multicultural education policy. Yet there are also differences in democracies and in their corresponding multicultural policies. Democratic societies, which range from the United States to France to Sweden to Singapore to India, conceive of certain aspects of democratic principles somewhat differently, and thus adjudicate them somewhat differently in law and in education. For example, the U.S. Constitution has the "right to bear arms" as one of the central rights and does not mention education or housing, whereas the Swedish constitution states that "public authority should especially safeguard the right to work, housing, and education and should promote social welfare, security, and a good environment for a good life." Swedes focus more heavily on positive freedoms and material equality while Americans focus more on negative freedoms and the right to protest or be free from government interference. Nations with large specific minority populations such as Singapore and Canada tend to include deeper rights to autonomous minority cultural expression, language, and education.

Multicultural education has roots in law and constitutional principles and is typically championed by constituent national minorities and by social progressives. Multicultural education emerges as part of a wider social movement for minority rights, which include not only the right to capital goods such as fair wages, housing, and equal spending on education, but more broadly, the right to include cultural values and curriculum in nation-states that previously had a de facto national identity. When the French Canadians in Canada or the Malay in Singapore gain explicit rights, these are multicultural societies. Nations are not considered multicultural by virtue of diversity alone. Many nation-states in Africa, Asia, and the Americas are culturally diverse and have long been "multicultural" in the sense that people from different cultures live there, but they are *not* multicultural if diverse people do not have equal rights to participate in society and to have their cultures recognized as worthy.

Global education lacks the constitutional legal-ethical grounding of multiculturalism, and it is a field that needs to argue for its ethical foundation rather than claim it within a defined legal-ethical system. A common move in global education is to justify it as a necessity for the practice of citizenship. This takes two forms: one has to do with the knowledge needed for active citizenship; the other with the philosophical perspectives needed for democratic thinking. One is formal and policy oriented; the other is more oriented to culture and philosophy. From the knowledge perspective it can be argued that global education is a practical necessity for citizens who vote about matters affecting the world. The argument is that American power and policies shape a great deal globally and that by the nature of these relations, American citizens are morally and civically implicated in how such policies and practices shape the lives of others. As the responsibilities of citizenship extend far beyond national boundaries, so must our education. From this perspective, many of the pressing issues of our time, from terrorism to global warming, are world problems that, if they are to be solved, require an understanding of the world and commitment to both a global civic culture and the skills of global citizenship.

From a philosophical perspective it can be argued that Americans need to recognize the human rights of everyone on the planet. The philosophical argument is that American democratic citizenship is based on a philosophical belief and on related constitutional provisions for human equality, human reason, and human rights together with a faith in democratic dialogue and decision-making. These are not qualities of Americans or Westerners alone but are thought to encompass all individuals. To believe in democracy is thus to believe in the rights of everyone inhabiting the planet. In theory, the rationale for a national democratic citizenship of human equality, human reason, and faith in democratic dialogue and decision-making does not allow for exclusion of people residing outside one's democracy. Even more broadly, philosophical arguments for global citizenship sometimes assert responsibility for all species and for the environment as well.

But global education has no legal or procedural basis in the way that multicultural education has. Although there is not yet any formal global citizenship, there are increasing venues for global rights and global cooperation—the United Nations and its Commission on Human Rights (UNCHR), the Organization for Economic Cooperation and Development (OECD), the Universal Postal Union (UPU), and the World Trade Organization (WTO) among many others. Philosophical recognition of global human rights has actually led to an increasing number of institutions for and examples of practical and legally negotiated tolerance. The Universal Declaration of Human Rights (UDHR) is widely endorsed: there are international standards for the rights of individuals and the treatment of prisoners of war and international agreements about biological diversity, endangered species, and sustainability. There is also increasing agreement about global standards in trade, communication, transportation, and environmental safety, and about global moral standards in such areas as child soldiers, child brides, international prostitution, torture, and child pornography. Although agreements are unevenly negotiated and enforced, they are enforced nonetheless, and global principles as norms are important. Agreement among diverse nations is a real global accomplishment considering that no such agreements existed at all 100 years ago.

Different Beneficiaries, Proponents, Opponents, and Scope

These different legal and philosophical positions have engaged somewhat different types of people and issues in the two approaches; the champions of multicultural and global education and their constituencies are different.

Often the leaders of multicultural education are minority and native people and scholars. The leaders of global education (called "international education" in an earlier phase) have tended to be educated white elites who have had a significant international or global experience. James Becker, for example, was influenced by his military experience outside of the United States, Merry Merryfield by her Peace Corps work in Africa, and Toni Fuss Kirkwood-Tucker by her immigrant border crossing.

Both movements tend to attract support from social progressives and liberal scholars and both are generally opposed by conservatives and nationalists. But given the legal-ethical context of multicultural education, its curricula are often the products of contentious public debates and ultimately formal resolutions, however uneasy. Global education does not share this high profile. Multicultural education as a movement is not only focused on curricula but also concerned with instructional techniques for specific real children and explicit school policies. In the field of global education, instruction and school policy are comparatively marginal aspects. In democracies there is a trail of what could be called multicultural education case law related to who gets to attend school; what forms of cultural and religious expression they may bring into the public school (such as head scarves); how children are taught; what is studied about various cultures and about prejudice and tolerance; and what teachers learn about how to teach diverse children and even about the diversity of teachers.

Global education tends to engage in issues in nations that are external to a student's country of residence; thus, it lacks a public focus on understanding and problematizing cultural diversity and national minority groups or students (see Gay, 2000; Ladson-Billings, 1994; Nieto, 1992, for example). It also lacks the political base and constituencies of multiculturalism, though several states have introduced requirements that global education be taught in schools; for example, between 1984 and 1994 almost three-fourths of the Miami-Dade County Public Schools integrated global programs in curriculum and instruction (see chapter 6). The precepts of global education are rarely an important aspect of curriculum debate by local or national advocates (or antagonists) working to make policy and a workable curriculum. Global education remains comparatively marginal both in policy discourse and in curriculum deliberation and development. When global education is highlighted (as for example in *A Nation at Risk)* it is most commonly justified from a neoliberal or ethnocentric perspective. For example, U.S. Secretary of Education Spellings (2006) observed that efforts to increase international student enrollment, encourage study abroad and emphasize language proficiency will help produce graduates adequately prepared to engage and lead in the new global economy. Ohio has mandated global education, but the rationale is to benefit Americans—specifically economic growth; for example, in a plan developed through the Council of Chief State School Officers (2006b) the aim is to create a system of international student and teacher exchanges and study abroad programs to offer teacher and student cultural immersion experiences and to stimulate economic development.

It is important that movements for multicultural education are generally led by minorities and benefit minorities and their children, and there are community-based grassroots calls for it. This rarely happens with global education; when it does, it is because citizens are concerned with their children acquiring knowledge to compete in a globalized society. The justification is often self-interest and not concern for the "other" or oriented to human rights. In further contrast, global education is sometimes perceived as being championed by white liberal elites, to

benefit elites, even potentially to take attention away from national minorities and national multiculturalism. In its more nationalist forms,
global education provides knowledge about other nations and people
that benefits the mainstream power holders.

The actual diversity of a nation is always less than the diversity of the
world, so national multiculturalists seem to face less diversity, although
perhaps more is at stake. Nations, for all their internal diversities, are
bound together by legal and political rights and a shared history, however contested that experience may be. Within a nation there also needs
to be a resolution. Therefore in national multiculturalism the process of
negotiating the boundaries of common and distinctive cultures and considering the need for tolerance of fewer functional and even practical
concepts is different from the process required in global education,
which entails all the diverse and contested politics, histories, and cultures
of the globe in the absence of a policy. The hard edges of identity politics
and its imaginaries of culture are simply less central.

Global education tends not to delve into the toughest issues of national culture and diversity. One form of cosmopolitan global education
endorses a form of post-identity and post-national (global) citizenship
and seeks to shift authority from the local and national community to a
world community that is a loose network of international organizations
and subnational political actors not bound within any clear democratic
constitutional framework. Multicultural education is a lively discourse
and contested practice in liberal democratic nations. Critiques of liberalism on the one hand, and of "identity politics" on the other hand, have
had a real influence in how culture is understood in education policy,
alternatively justifying common schools, the study of traditional American history, English-only policies, and, alternatively, public funding for
private schools, Afrocentric schools, and home schooling. The richness
and complexity of this philosophical engagement with the nature of culture, equity, and identity is mostly absent from the global education discourse, curriculum, and policy.

Similarities between Multicultural and Global Education

I now identify how each field includes similarly different "types"—each
with different political and theoretical assumptions. As this review suggests, multicultural education addresses cultural diversity, individual
and human rights, prejudice reduction, and social justice within the particular legal, political, and social context of the nation in which the student resides. It is about "us," while global education is about "us and the

Other." These distinctions, however, are becoming less and less clear, especially with increased immigration, deepening global communications, and the proliferation of transnational identities. Further, as mentioned earlier, the controversy between respecting other cultures and protecting one's own, and in finding the boundary between tolerance and critical judgment, remains a hot issue in both global and multicultural education. Understanding difference and redressing inequalities in power are important and central elements to both. These core themes of "difference" and "power" have been approached in *similarly different ways* in both fields as both emerged in response to monoculturalism and ethnocentric hegemonic presentations of difference, culture, and power (Duarte & Smith, 2000; Gaudelli & Heilman, 2009; Sleeter & Grant, 2003).

Making distinctions among different related approaches is much more common in multicultural education than in global education. Global education theorists often seek to locate commonalities across theories rather than differences. For example, Case (1993) argued, "We should not automatically assume that greater clarity about the goals of global education is necessary. Loosely defined coalitions...often permit otherwise disparate factions to ally in pursuit of common or, at least, compatible goals" (p. 319). Tye (1999) researched global education in more than 50 countries and identified "common issues" that (in order of frequency) were ecology and environment, development, intercultural relations, peace, economics, technology, and human rights. Identifying general common themes in global education theory, however, obscures the very real differences in approaches, as I detail below. Differences in approaches to global education are political and are also related to differences in their origins in the distinct fields of social studies education, science education, environmental education, multicultural education, critical theory, peace education, education for human rights, and development education, all of which include theorists who call for globally focused curriculum (Anderson, 1994; Calder, 2000; Calder & Smith, 1996; Case, 1993; Cogan, Grossman, & Liu, 2000; Giroux, 1997; Gur-Ze'ev, 2001; Kirkwood, 2001a; Lister, 1987; McLaren, 2006; Tye & Kniep, 1991; Willinsky, 1998). These theorists come from a wide range of philosophical and curricular positions and thus present a range of curricular approaches and theoretical understandings of the political, educational, moral, and economic issues at stake.

Shared Discourse in Global and Multicultural Education

Distinctive approaches to global and multicultural education and to the general issue of diversity include monoculturalism, particularism, pluralism, liberalism, and criticality. While this list is certainly an overview and is not exhaustive, it allows us to see quickly how each instantiates the relationship between diversity and power and differences in how diversity is understood.

Table 2.2. Shared Discourse in Global and Multicultural Education

Type	Examples and related movements	Curricular Rationale and Goal	View of Diversity
Monoculturalism	English-only Traditional National History	Solidifies national identity, unity and power. Enhance feeling for the nation	Defend against diversity
Particularism	Ethnic Studies Indigenous Studies Afro-centric Education. Public funding for religious schools	Minority groups need and deserve autonomy to maintain their culture. Cultural autonomy is a right. Fosters the cultural, linguistic and religious autonomy of minority groups	Defend and enhance diversity
Pluralism	Human Relations Pluralism Neoliberalism	Cross-cultural understanding as a means to improve life for everyone or maintain and enhance power/capital	Explore and use diversity as a resource to maximize benefit
Liberalism	Critical Thinking Human Rights Education. Liberal theory	Reconciliation and deliberation amongst groups and balancing the rights of the individual against group rights	Negotiate diversity and balancing the rights of individuals and groups through deliberative process
Criticality	Critical Theory Critical Race Theory Postcolonial Studies Anti-imperial Education	Explore, critique experiences of oppression or uneven power relations and develop resistance and transformative potential.	Critique the ways diversity intersects with oppression.

Monocultural Approaches: Defending Against Diversity

Monoculturalism is both an old approach to diversity and a very current one as the need for nation-making in new emerging democracies is inevitable (as it was in the eighteenth- and nineteenth-century democracies). Monoculturalism is also a common reactionary approach to diversity in many contemporary societies. The leaders of new democracies in nations with a great deal of regional, political, and cultural diversity, such as France, the United States, and India, felt a need at the time of nation formation to promote national and nationalist identities from heterogeneous and divisive societies. Education has always been a useful tool in such efforts. In 1776, most Americans rooted their identity in their towns or in their distinctive colonial regions (as Bostonians or Virginians), while others were culturally rooted in such European identities as British, Dutch, or French. My Dutch ancestors, for example, had been in New York since 1720 and fought in the American Revolution; yet they considered themselves in many ways Dutch, sharing language, regions, and customs with the European Dutch. (My ancestors are also German Jews, Irish Catholics, Scotts, and a British debtor who was sent to the colonies for indentured labor.) At any rate, schooling became newly important with the establishment of the new nation in 1776, which required civic propaganda to create a sense of nationhood without a shared past, customs, language, or religion, only a shared future. Examples of this civic propaganda were evident when the American flag was invented and quickly fetishized and mythologized; when Noah Webster wrote the standardized American dictionary, based on mostly arbitrary distinctions; and when many untrue stories about national heroes, like that of George Washington chopping down the cherry tree, were taught to nurture national identity and pride. Such efforts are hardly unique to the past or to the United States. Taiwan has had to create and maintain a national identity distinct from Chinese identity; multiethnic Malaysia had to create a national unity to transcend stark differences. Right now, Tajikistan is separating from its Russian identity and trying to bring coherence and to develop unity among various ethnic identities. I argue that an element of monoculturalism is inevitable at the founding of a democracy, and it also emerges to challenge both multicultural education and global education whenever national unity seems to be threatened. Since fear is often involved, it is difficult for policy in these contexts to maintain both pluralistic and nationalistic approaches to identity and culture. For those of us interested in resisting monoculturalism, it is important to understand its dynamics and its inevitability. Every democracy, even the more culturally homogeneous, must engage in a process of myth-making to create a new national identity.

Monoculturalism, however, is not just a phenomenon of new nations. It often emerges in response to immigration and globalization and is sometimes a direct reversal of earlier multicultural and global policies. For example, the U.S. Congress mandated teaching "traditional American history" after years of more multicultural curriculum. Burack (2003), in *Where Did Social Studies Go Wrong?*, argues that students should study an American history that emphasizes "true heroes of the American story" and be free of exposure to the darker side of American history. Teachers should sidestep irrelevant emphases on multicultural differences and above all should be freed from the alleged globalist influence in social studies curricula, which, in its emphases on multicultural celebration, cultural relativism, and "transnational progressivism," aims at substituting another set of loyalties for those of American patriotic pride. Similarly Arthur Schlesinger, Jr. (1991) argues that multicultural education will contribute to increased racial and cultural division and tension. When the state of California revised its curriculum to be more culturally inclusive, many argued that there was too much emphasis on diversity (Kirp, 1991). The United Kingdom, France, and Germany have had similar critics and official campaigns to promote national unity and individual identification with the nation. The French prohibitions on Islamic dress in schools and the promotion of official national history with exhibitions about national heroes in the Netherlands have sparked international debate. These policies are often responses both to immigrations and to extreme particularistic multiculturalism and global education.

Particularistic Approaches: Defending Diversity

Particularistic multiculturalism fosters the cultural, linguistic, and religious autonomy of major minority groups and helps to reify their cultural attributes. These kinds of policies often emerge in response to explicit ethnocentrism and exclusion, for example, the Irish versus the nineteenth-century Protestant American school wars that led to the American Catholic school system; the American Indian struggle to gain control of their schools; and the struggle of French Canadians against assimilationist-oriented Anglos that led to constitutional protection for French Canadian culture. Sometimes particularism is perceived to be too divisive or is thought to foster too much autonomy, and public pressure is exerted in opposition. This includes school multicultural curriculum, special schools for minority groups, ethnic studies, area studies, and various forms of "centrism," such as Afrocentrism.

Critics point out that these policies always anoint some marginal cultures and in doing so more deeply marginalize other marginal cultures that are not formally recognized in law or in school policy. For example, in the United States, African Americans, Hispanics, Native Americans, and Asians are typically recognized; black Americans from Africa, the Caribbean, Europe, Australia, and other places, and Hispanics who are not Mexican are generally not recognized. In Canada, French and English speakers have constitutional language rights but Spanish speakers do not. Asians are rarely the beneficiaries of affirmative action and the incredible breadth of Asian diversities is rarely considered. White ethnicity is rarely addressed. Particularistic multiculturalism *affirms* recognized alternative identities and the "politics of difference" and often critiques the Marxist perspective that economic factors are at the base of injustice and existence. Instead, culture is central. In this approach, markers of identity such as race, religion, and gender are central in explaining and redressing oppression. The dominant policy perspective is respect for difference. Schools aiming to reinforce the identity and expression of marginalized groups include schools for girls only, Afrocentric curriculum and schools (e.g., Asante, 1992; 1998) and publicly funded religious schools in parts of Europe. Another problem, as implied earlier, is the difficulty in defining culture. In criticism of particularistic approaches, Michaels (1995) comments from the Canadian context:

> Without some way of explaining how and what people used to do but no longer do constitutes their real identity while what they actually do does not, it cannot be said that what the former French speakers, current English speakers have lost is their identity....My point then is not that nothing of value is ever lost but that identity is never lost (pp. 181–182).

Particularistic approaches are often critiqued for reinforcing difference and promoting tolerance for cultures above tolerance for the content of any given culture.

Pluralistic Approaches: Resourcing Diversity

Pluralists do not deny or defend against culture differences; instead they see diversity as inevitable and as something to understand, use, and learn from, as a resource that can enhance the individual, the dominant culture, and the economy. Pluralistic approaches are common to both global and multicultural education. Triandis (1976), for example, argues that the majority culture can be enriched by considering the viewpoints of several minority cultures that exist in America rather than trying to force these minorities to adopt a "monocultural, impoverished, provincial viewpoint which may in the long run reduce creativity and effective adjustment in a fast-changing world" (p. 181). Historian Ronald Takaki (cited in Shea, 1993) optimistically believes, "We can all get along and function as a community if we take the opportunity to learn about each other." Christine Sleeter and Carl Grant (2003) describe this type of curriculum as "human relations multiculturalism" that seeks to teach similarity out of difference and ignores how difficult it can be to get along especially given institutional racism, sexism, and discrimination. Students are to appreciate the beliefs, traditions, and values of different cultural groups and for schools and other institutions to create policies and events to celebrate diversity. Such an education situates learning about people as a form of commodity, not in its economic sense but as a tool, such that learning about others is principally based on enhancing oneself. James Becker (1982) offers this self-directed pluralistic rationale for global education: "In an interrelated world...our survival and well-being is intimately related to our capacity to understand and deal responsibly and effectively with other peoples and nations" (p. 230). Typically global educators focus on cultural universals more than cultural differences and on an optimistic cross-cultural understanding, open-mindedness, and the ability to have knowledge and appreciation for other peoples' points of view (Case, 1993; Hanvey, 1976; Kniep, 1986).

Within global education, there is often a neoliberal twist to this pluralism. There is a type of global education that is directed at private interests and is primarily concerned with preparing entrepreneurs and consumers through learning about the world or with preparing corporate citizens who are able to move easily from place to place in a global world. The University of Central Florida Business School (2005) explains, "One out of every four new jobs created in the U.S. is tied to international business....Rewarding career opportunities await those students who acquire a solid business education with a global perspective." Even without travel the neoliberal global consumer can enjoy the food, music, art, textiles, and consumer goods of many places. This education tends to be problem based, and the problem is how to maximize economic advantage. People are both commodities and technologies, and students are encouraged to know the Other in a potentially exploitative way that situates the Other as a technology or tool that can serve as means to personal ends, those being building capital wealth. Michigan State University, for example, offers this as one potential goal in internationalizing the student experience so that graduates will have the cultural competence to engage with people, ideas, and activities from other cultures as a means of personal and professional development (Renn & Lucas, 2007).

Liberal Approaches: Negotiating Diversity

In the liberal view, cultures are not to be consumed as a resource, accepted at face value, or "tolerated" but something very different. Diversity is to be encountered critically and negotiated. Advocating a pluralistic appreciation for multiple perspectives denies or underestimates the discomfort of real difference. For example, how can a person simultaneously value something like equality for women and appreciate a nation that legislates that women are intrinsically inferior? Should we educate that this sort of national diversity is an asset? What would it mean to tolerate this? By embracing the other, many theories of global education highlight and consider difference, especially third-world difference, yet avoid the politics of non-Western marginalization and the discomfort connected with encountering intractable difference by discovering and celebrating Otherness relatively uncritically. In liberal theory, diversity brings inevitable difficult issues of difference that can best be understood and even mediated through public discussion and politics with critical analysis and rationalist, legalistic discourse. All forms of difference are to be explored, debated, and negotiated. In John Stuart Mill's (1869) famous letter, "On Liberty of Thought and Discussion," he details the reasoning behind liberal toleration for diverse views that have resulted in the constitutional protection of the freedom of speech in democracies. Mill explains the value of protecting freedom of speech on differences, even differences that are clearly troubling and antithetical to the core values of most Americans. Mill provides distinct grounds for the freedom of opinion and freedom of the expression of opinion. He argues:

> First, if any opinion is compelled to silence that opinion may, for all we can certainly know, be true. To deny this is to assume our own infallibility. Secondly, though the silenced opinion be an error it may, and very commonly is, contains a portion of truth; and since the general or prevailing opinion on any subject is rarely or never the whole truth, it is only by the collision of adverse opinions that the remainder of the truth has any chance of being.

And then Mill warns,

> Thirdly, even if the received opinion be not only true but the whole truth unless it is suffered to be and actually is vigorously and earnestly contested,

it will by most of those who receive it, be held in the manner of a prejudice, with little comprehension or feeling of its rational grounds.

The purpose of classical liberalism is not to maintain any view or affirm any culture. Mill would like for any potential cultural value or option to be explored in a public setting and to allow anyone to defend and potentially modify their beliefs, including cultural beliefs and practices. In order to have meaningful conversations in which diverse views are explored, contested, and treated with the sort of seriousness and respect that allows each person to be willing to learn something, a certain measure of tolerance is required. Yet this is a very active and demanding idea of tolerance, and requires something Nussbaum (1997) calls "world citizenship." Nussbaum cites Marcus Aurelius in describing how the world citizen should become "a sensitive and empathetic interpreter" but explains that "world citizenship" does not and should not require that we suspend criticism toward other individuals and cultures:

> The world citizen may be very critical of unjust actions or policies and of the character of people who promote them. But, at the same time, Marcus [Aurelius] refuses to think of the opponents as simply alien, as members of a different and inferior species. He refuses to criticize until he respects and understands. He carefully chooses images that reflect his desire to see them as close to him and similarly human (p. 65).

As Nussbaum suggests, liberal multiculturalism, with its notions of world citizenship, does not advocate an uncritical "celebration of cultural difference." Furthermore, this active tolerance requires educated processes and emotional sophistication. The liberal approach to debate also relies on faith in the process of rational argument that transcends identity. In education and cultural life in the democratic public sphere, differences in belief, including metaphysical beliefs, are to be explored and aired.

Critical Approaches: Intersecting Diversity with Oppression

Critical thinkers on diversity question the neutrality of any exploration of diversity including what Mill envisioned and draw attention to the socially constructed nature of race and difference and the power-laden nature of the public sphere. Critical theories are all concerned with the intersections of power, knowledge, and identity and are motivated by an ethos of justice. Yet the ways that oppression, emancipation, agency, subjectivity, knowledge, and power are thought about and described vary across critical educators. Though Hanvey (1976), Case (1993), and

Kniep (1986) propose a global education that involves an awareness of a variety of perspectives, they do not address the uneven balance of power and influence among nations, regions and cultures; thus these are not critical approaches but are pluralist.

The best exemplar of a critical orientation to global education is offered in Bigelow and Peterson's (2002) *Rethinking Globalization*. Through a wide range of narratives, cases, and illustrations, they provide a rich compendium that urges students and teachers to act with knowledge about and for those who are oppressed. They explain:

> We hoped that students would consider that whether one works in a "sweatshop" or not, our lives here are directly affected by the global "race to the bottom" that pits workers around the world against one another. People here do have a moral imperative to help people everywhere. But we also have a personal stake in challenging the poor conditions around the globe that exert a downward pull on conditions here (p. 5).

Critical global education seeks to illustrate the intricate ways in which people are related to each other around the world and how these relationships are set against a historical legacy of hegemony. Critical multiculturalism analyzes inequality of power and privilege and explores how cultural differences have been politicized. Critical perspective considers the nature of national and global knowledge and identities, yet at the same time explores by what social and economic processes space and place are constructed and how these constructions can be explored within discourses and practices tied to various positions of power. Such a curriculum has the potential to focus on human perception and personal experience, and it captures the complexity of lived experience, identities, and cultural visions that are produced and troubled through global education.

Yet critical global education and multicultural education are also not without problems. Critical analyses are not always related to personal meaning and are often massive, directed at an amorphous disembodied thing called *global society* or *transnational capitalism* to which it is difficult to respond. Students tend to read about *global heroes* and the *global oppressed* from nowhere, and their study often goes in the same direction— that is, nowhere. Personal connections are not easily made. Critical work is most often described as conducted by heroes, the likes of Ché and Gandhi, not the work of teachers or of pedestrian citizens (Heilman, 2005). This critical pedagogy focuses on *making sense* and does not always move toward the *making of self*. Critical global education theory and pedagogy is often rationalistic, positivistic, masculine, and rooted in a utopian, revolutionary meta-narrative. As critics have suggested, the relationship to the Other is as one to liberate, which is condescending.

The language of much critical theory is more dualistic than multiple, originating from the dialectical approach created by Hegel, and adapted by Marx, which focuses on the contradiction of opposites and their continual resolution. In a dialectical model, all human, anthropological, and epistemological processes are moving toward an end state that is more desirable. For Plato, this was true knowledge; for Hegel, absolute self-consciousness; and for Marx, the collapse of society. Most elements of global education and multicultural education are not dialectical in the traditional sense because the theoretical focus is on the process of seeing in multiple ways, not on the outcome. Of course, we can argue that the outcome of seeing in multiple ways would be the attainment of true knowledge or the collapse of an inequitable society. The distinction, however, is an important one for education in a democracy. Critical theorists and pedagogues want social justice.

Joining the Fields through Poststructuralist Pragmatist Citizenship Education

What does each of these approaches show and hide? Each approach to global education and multicultural education has it limits and dangers, and each has worth. A better understanding of their distinctive origins and beneficiaries and also of their shared opponents can bring the fields together. I argue for a poststructuralist pragmatist approach to citizenship education that can include a *creative synthesis of multicultural and global education*. The four most definitive, important, and central elements to both are (1) an ethical dimension based in the recognition of human rights; (2) a technical dimension in which knowledge about cultures, history, politics, and global dynamics matters; (3) an imaginative dimension related to the need to understand across difference; and (4) a civic dimension recognizing and requiring action to redress injustice and inequalities in power. Of course settling on these four points leaves out monoculturalism, particularism, and pluralism, which are arguably not defensible within a global education rooted in recognition of global human rights or even, as some argue, liberal democratic theory. To understand what the more democratic approaches to multicultural education and global education have in common, and what poststructuralism and pragmatism have to offer, it may be more useful to focus on the segment *multi* than on the segment *cultural*. The essence of multicultural and global education may be in approaching key dimensions of education with a multiplicity of perspectives. In place of the familiar monocultural unequivocal curriculum, in place of ethnocentric and hegemonic ideas of power, and in place of static rigid conceptions of the learner are multiplicities of ways to see, think, learn, and act.

A key aspect of the change from *mono* to *multi* is a change from the hierarchical valuing of knowledge and relationships to a more equitable valuing of knowledge and relationships in which the hand of power is seen from a critical perspective. The potential of multicultural and global education is not in creating new theories, subject matter, or institutions but, inspired by poststructuralist methods, in literally reordering and restructuring the ones that exist. Among the many elements that are restructured or unstructured with a poststructural approach to multicultural and global education could be perspectives on the self, perspectives on the self in relation to the Other, perspectives on time, perspectives on cultures, perspectives on nonstatic processes and elements that create and recreate culture, and perspectives on power in groups, institutions, and states.

In recent decades the focus of both global and multicultural education has been mostly on macro-political issues, next on interactions, and least focused on identity, personal meaning making, and response. To a large degree, both multiculturalism and global education have been structural practices. While structuralism has meant different things in different disciplines, it is a particularly modernist way of thinking characterized by a reliance on logic and often binary rational choices to determine the structures of the world, both natural and social, including linguistic, psychological, political, and cultural structure.

A Call for a New Political-Personal Citizenship

I am calling for a fundamentally different approach to global education and multicultural education and, more broadly, to citizenship education. Citizenship education has typically been focused on politics. Instead I think we need to focus more on the political-personal. A citizenship education for politics focuses on the public sphere and prepares you to participate in a current social order. This approach focuses on what the student knows, how you make claims, and what you do. From this perspective, healthy institutions and legitimate processes help to create good lives and a good society. This citizenship education for politics relies on insights from political science and from liberal democratic deliberative theory; students learn about the qualities of different cultures, the reasons for government and its branches and functions, current social issues, and the sort of actions a citizen can take both alone and with others within the system, or ways to improve the system. Our citizens have to live up to what our democracies have become.

A citizenship education for the political-personal is different. It relies on insights from radical democracy and poststructuralism and, much more broadly, on the arts, popular culture, psychoanalysis, and social science—indeed the whole social cloth. It is self-reflexive education that begins with an interrogation of the concept of difference itself. It blurs the boundaries between the seemingly separate disciplines and spheres of the public, the economic, the private, and the personal, and it even aims to undo the seemingly separate boundaries within the self. I have come to believe that one of the most import educative techniques for both multicultural and global education is to be able to critically deconstruct social meanings. As we make ordinary choices as citizens in any particular circumstance or as we live and imagine a life plan, we make reference to the available discourses, socially valued characters, ideals, archetypes, objects, and images. We use the kinds of plots, genres, narrative conventions, and the verbs, adjectives, sentences available to us. These often seem neutral but they are not.

From this perspective, the democratic polity relies on the quality of *our* political-personal imaginations and the quality of relationships, communities, and polities that our imaginations lead us to enact. It focuses on who you are, how you imagine, how you have become, why you act, and in what ways you might quest for another imaginary, another self, and a better and more just, free, and peaceful world, reflective of our imaginaries. Our democracies have to live up to who we have become.

One of the less discussed aspects of democracies is that any given government is not intended to be treated as a final authoritative arrival on how best to do things. There is no fixed authority or inherently good government in a democracy. Democracy replaced the immutable social order, the truth of aristocracy and religious orthodoxy, and the judgment of queens and priests with a mutable social order and mutable theories to be discussed and tested among human equals. In fact, democracy gives us nothing but a process and some loose principles to replace previously fixed beliefs. Democracy is a method of governance that is legitimated not by its *content* but by its *process,* and the process is intended to change the content. Multicultural education and global education, then, is best understood not simply as introducing new cultures but rather as deconstructing and revaluing them.

The pragmatic stance also allows for incompatibility and seeks *a reasoned eclectic approach*. Each approach described above reveals both problems and possibilities, particularly when viewed in light of their ideas about power and culture. I suggest humbly that teachers, teacher educators, and curriculum designers first need to be clear about the nature of various approaches and then reflectively to make choices about how, when, and why to teach from a particular paradigm. Globalization, which increases the moral reach of human concern, has the potential to increase the critical, imaginative, and ethical dimensions of our education and our capacities and dispositions to respond to our world. We face a seeming battle of theoretical camps and paradigms about the intentions and forms of education that requires us to reconcile the national and global, the ethical and the technical, and to deny neither. We can be critical in our approaches to national histories and yet embrace the commitments to rights and justice at the core of the nation; we can be cosmopolitan in orientation to humans elsewhere in the world and yet be practical in terms of participation in national politics and policy. The possibility for a more just world rests on the educated imagination.

Chapter 3

Toward a Philosophy of Global Education

Hilary Landorf

> Even while cherishing our diversity, we need certain shared values if we are
> to work together for our common good—perhaps our survival as a species.
> —Kofi Annan, 1999

Human rights play an integral part in today's process of globalization. They have become the language of global political dialogue and the basis of a moral imperative for a global world order. In education the increasing pace of globalization has resulted in increasing demands to bring global perspectives into the K-20 curriculum. Global education is at the forefront of this movement to international human rights.

It is my belief that global educators need to clearly and publicly articulate the central concepts and philosophy upon which our field is based. Upon examination of its content, it is evident that global education is philosophically based on human rights, and especially on the core human rights concept of moral universalism. However, this phenomenon is rarely acknowledged or discussed. I believe that such an articulation would allow those working in global education to have a voice in framing the conversation and policies regarding its scope, methods, curriculum, and direction.

In this chapter, I show how the fundamental concepts of human rights are embedded in global education by examining global education documents and policies revealing the similarities of global education and human rights in terms of goals and content, the somewhat parallel expansion in the development of global education and human rights, and their conceptual convergence. In order to fully appreciate and understand the dynamic between human rights and global education, we must first examine human rights—what they mean, what they are today, their origins, and the values they bring to the philosophical underpinnings of global education.

Meaning, Historical Development, and Application
of Human Rights

Human rights usually refers to a body of rights based on public moral behavioral norms and attitudes held by all people in all countries that are respected and protected by nations throughout the world. Today, in most discussions of human rights it is accepted that we are referring to those rights codified in the articles of the UDHR (1948) and the subsequent expansion of those rights in various international documents, covenants, and treaties.

The field of human rights is large and complex with origins and modern-day relevance to the fields of philosophy, jurisprudence, religion, economics, democracy, government, and legal systems. Although it is often claimed that the concept of human rights originated in Western philosophy, the values and justifications for human rights are found in a combination of worldwide religious practices, cultural traditions, philosophical constructions of universal, natural moral rights, and demands for certain standards of behavior from civil society. Many of the issues and controversies in today's discussion of human rights have their genesis in the diverse historical and topical perspectives and documents that have contributed to our contemporary understanding of human rights. To understand these issues in their relationship to global education, it is helpful to examine the definition and the development of human rights.

Any discussion of human rights is premised on the philosophical definition of rights. Rights determine our abilities and freedom to take a place in the world; rights form the basis of the rules and norms of interaction of people in civil society. To have a right to something means that one has an entitlement to exercise, enjoy, or claim it. A right belongs to an individual, but it can involve others if they have the ability to prevent or influence the exercise of that right. As such, rights can also impose restraints on other individuals or groups. For example if one has a right to vote, then the people administering the voting system have a duty not to interfere with the voter.

While all rights are "human rights," legally and philosophically human rights are defined as a special class of rights. First, human rights are essentially moral rights; they relate to how we should behave in civil society. However, they do not present themselves as a fully comprehensive moral doctrine such as a religion or a code of ethics. Rather they represent a limited set of specific, public high-priority moral norms of behavior without which civil society would fall apart. Second, belief and respect for human rights are inherent in all human beings. It is this characteristic that makes human rights universal, as they transcend all individual communities, cultures, ethnicities, governments, and nations (Donnelly, 2003). Third, human rights are not inalienable although they are often referred to as such. A rightholder can always lose a right in a particular situation (consider defamation versus free speech). By the same token, human rights require very little trade-off in most situations, for example, torture is considered indefensible (Nickel, 2006). Today it is a commonly held view that the protection of human rights transcends national interests and provides the fundamental moral imperative for regulating the contemporary political world order and justifying international intervention in cases of human rights abuse.

Historical Background of Human Rights

The underlying concept of human rights comes from the notion of a moral world order, one that can be found in most religions in Western philosophy going back to the Greeks. Many Western philosophers have long maintained that there is a rationally identifiable moral world order, one that applies to all human beings everywhere and the legitimacy of which precedes any social or political organization. Usually described as moral universalism, this concept claims that there exist certain identifiable trans-cultural and trans-historical moral truths. This perspective is strongly tied to the origins of human rights and is still important to the defense and justification of much of human rights doctrines today. The origins of this moral universalism are usually attributed to Aristotle and the Stoics, who asserted the existence of a natural and rational moral order as distinguished from man-made legal systems. This concept was adopted by the Roman Stoics and many Christian theologians. In a parallel development, several charters codifying freedoms and rights that embodied a concept of rights were drawn up in Europe. These included the Magna Carta (1215), the Union of Utrecht (1579), and the English Bill of Rights (1689) among others. These documents specified rights and freedoms in relation to a ruler that could be claimed in specific circumstances by virtue of rank, although they did not embrace a philosophical concept of universal human liberty.

The development of human rights concepts based on one's status as a human being came in the eighteenth century, European Age of Enlightenment. Philosophers such as Locke, Kant, and Rousseau developed the concept of natural rights, rights that belonged to a human being regardless of status, memberships, or citizenship. These rights included life, liberty, and property. Throughout the eighteenth and nineteenth centuries, human rights served as an ideology for effecting political change and produced documents such as the United States Declaration of Independence (1776), the United States Bill of Rights (1789), and the French Rights of Man and the Citizen (1789) (*Declaration des Droits de l'Homme et du Citoyen*). These documents reflect the emerging international theory of universal rights and the particular enumeration of specific rights. These concepts of universality and particularity are important characteristics of human rights and are considered essential for the transformation of a cause or issue into a protected human right today.

The development of rights continued throughout the nineteenth and twentieth centuries in different forms. The classic rights of the individual and the freedom of equality in the French and American declarations were incorporated in almost all subsequent national constitutions. Claiming rights became a force for effecting political and social change and was used as the philosophical basis for political activity tied with ethnic, religious, or political struggles to end or protest oppressive or colonial regimes. Other specific civil rights movements centered on issues such as slavery, suffrage, and workers' rights

It was only after World War II that it became clear that human rights were not a domestic or local issue and that state sovereignty could not be absolute. The defeat of the Axis powers caused international alliances to be galvanized by the idea of fundamental and universal freedom for all humans. The prominence of human rights as a moral imperative in the war is clearly evident in President Franklin D. Roosevelt's 1941 "Four Freedoms" speech.[1] The subsequent revelations of the violations of human rights during World War II pointed to a need for the protection of individuals from without as well as from within. Thus, there emerged a consensus that human rights were a universal concern for all individuals, that there was a compelling need for the international protection and promotion of these rights, and that this should be a fundamental goal of the new international body, the United Nations.

The United Nations

The United Nations Organization Charter of 1945 committed the United Nations to promoting and protecting human rights and fundamental freedoms. Subsequently the Universal Declaration of Human Rights (UDHR) was adopted by the United Nations Assembly in December 1948. This document is based on the recognition of the inherent dignity and equal and inalienable rights of all members of the human family that are the foundations of freedom, justice, and peace in the world. The document consists of a Preamble and 30 articles that identify specific human rights. These rights are divided into two classes: (1) civil and political rights articulated in Articles 3–21, and (2) cultural, social, and economic rights articulated in Articles 22–27. The last three articles of the declaration, Articles 28–30, place the enumerated rights in the context of limits, duties, and the social and political order in which they are to be realized.

The UDHR was followed by a large number of international conventions and treaties particularly designed to protect the rights stated in the document. The most important of these are the United Nations International Covenant on Civil and Political Rights (United Nations, 1966a) and the United Nations International Covenant on Economic, Social and Cultural Rights (United Nations, 1966b). The UDHR and these two covenants are also referred to as the International Bill of Human Rights. Other important conventions cover such areas as racial discrimination, genocide, and women's rights. Especially relevant for global education is the Convention on the Rights of the Child (1989). All these conventions and treaties have been ratified by most countries of the United Nations and incorporated in national constitutions of most countries of the world grounded in specific laws.

The importance of the UDHR cannot be overstated. It represents the first time in human history that an international body has presented a standard of basic civil, political, economic, social and cultural rights to which all human beings are entitled, together with the intent to promote and protect those rights for individuals. The UDHR is more than a declaration. Its writers and signatories assert a belief in a universal moral world order, one where all humans are equally entitled to human rights. Although there is still philosophical discussion of rights without specific reference to the UDHR, our knowledge and discussion of human rights today are largely based on the list of rights contained in the UDHR. What began as a declaration of human equality and dignity and the intent to provide rights for all people by imposing specific moral standards on national governments has become the foundation of a human rights movement, the basis of international law, and a cornerstone of world political dialogue.

The Three Generations of Human Rights

The evolution of human rights since the creation of the UDHR is often couched in terms of three accumulating generations of rights as initially proposed by the Czech jurist Karel Vasak (1977) and corresponding to the themes of the French Revolution: *liberté, egalité,* and *fraternité.*

Civil and Political Rights. First generation rights (*liberté*) consist of the first rights in the UDHR, the group of civil and political rights that promote classical freedoms and ensure security, property, and political participation. The constant theme in these rights is the liberty of the individual and the protection of that individual against the abuse of authority by government. They also include the fundamental freedoms associated with democracy: freedom of expression, association, assembly, opinion, belief and religion, and movement. After World War II these were the rights that dominated the discussion and activity in human rights up until the 1970s. Many new countries were born during this time and much of the political struggle to gain self-determination involved the claiming and protection of these classical freedoms. As such these first generation rights are associated with this postcolonial era of national liberation culminating in the triumph of the antiapartheid movement in South Africa. Many of the constitutions of the world today incorporate these rights, yet there are still many that do not respect or protect these rights.

Social, Economic, and Cultural Rights. Second generation rights (*egalité*) are essentially claims to social equality: social, economic, and cultural rights. They began to be recognized in the early part of the twentieth century and are associated with the UDHR (Articles 23–29) and the International Covenant on Economic, Social and Cultural Rights (1966). These rights ensure such things as a right to work, education, housing, health care, and social security. In contrast to the first generation rights that focus on individual entitlements, these rights are often referred to as group rights or collective rights, in that they refer to the well-being of whole societies and are rights that are held and exercised by all the people collectively or by specific subsets of people. In contrast to first generation rights, second generation rights require affirmative government action for their realization.

There is still considerable debate as to whether these rights should be recognized as human rights because courts are generally unable to enforce affirmative duties on states and such rights can be considered only as statements of aspiration. Similarly, few states have the economic resources for the realization of affirmative obligations such as education, health, and an adequate standard of living (Wellman, 1998). Despite considerable discussion on how these rights should be quantified and implemented, they are still considered underdeveloped.

Solidarity Rights. Third generation rights (*fraternité*) are still evolving and comprise a broad spectrum of rights known as "solidarity rights." They took hold in the 1990s and assumed particular importance in human rights discussions today. Solidarity refers to the mutual support and cohesiveness within a group, especially among individuals with strong common interests, sympathies, or goals. These rights include the right to self-determination, the right to peace, the right to a clean environment, the right to participate in and benefit from the Earth, and the right to development. Third generation rights are quite complex and interdependent on other rights, which makes recognition, justification, or enforcement very difficult (Weston, 2006, p. 22). These rights have been recognized in various documents such as the 1972 United Nations Stockholm Declaration on the Human Environment, the Declaration on the Right to Development (1986), and the 1992 Rio Declaration on Environment and Development.

Other Rights. Three of these rights reflect the rising expectations of developing countries in terms of global redistribution of power, wealth, and other important values or capabilities. These are self-determination, development, and the right to participate in and benefit from the Earth. These rights are associated with different approaches to thinking about human rights such as the human capability approach of Amartya Sen (1999) and philosopher Martha Nussbaum (2000). Some writers have suggested a fourth generation of human rights that should include women's rights, rights for future generations, rights of access to information, and rights to communication.

However, as useful as it is to see the progress of contemporary human rights in terms of these generations of rights, it should be emphasized that while Vasak's model suggests a linear process in which one generation of rights evolves or gives way to the next generation, this is not the case. Rather, in this model all rights are still viewed holistically; certain rights do not have priority over others; and all rights exist together at the same time. This was affirmed in the Vienna Declaration and Programme of Action of the World Conference on Human Rights (1993) which states, "All human rights are universal, indivisible and interdependent and interrelated" (para. 5).

Today the idea of human rights has widespread international acceptance. The human rights doctrine forms the basis of a robust and important international human rights movement outside national governments. Increasingly, most social, economic, and political issues are framed as human rights issues, be it the issue of Tibetan monks protesting a Chinese regime, poor fishermen in Thailand protesting multinational corporations, women raped in the Congo, starvation in Darfur, or Mexicans trying to cross the border into the United States. The drive for social justice and an ideal world is usually described in human rights terms and any group who wants a say in the future global world order seeks to gain recognition of their cause in terms of formal human rights with the attached protection and enforcement of national and international bodies.

Evolution of a Philosophical Framework for Global Education

Some global educators have stated that there is a moral imperative underlying global education (Darling-Farr, 1994; Heilman, 2007; Kirkwood, 2001a; Tucker, 1982b). It is my contention that the source of this moral imperative lies in the concepts of human rights. When one examines the various definitions of global education, key global education documents, the parallel development of global education and human rights, and the issues most frequently discussed in both human rights and global education, it is clear that global education is based on a human rights philosophy.

The Meaning of Global Education

Since the inception of global education, scholars and practitioners have defined global education in a variety of ways. Global education has been referred to as a field of study (Gaudelli, 2003; Heilman, 2007; Merryfield, 1996), a movement (Tye, 1991), a curriculum (Gaudelli, 2003; Kniep, 1986; Lamy, 1991), an approach to learning (Werner and Case, 1997), and, for many, as components and objectives (Becker, 1979; Case, 1993; Hanvey, 1976; Heater, 1984; Merryfield 1997b; 2006). Kirkwood (2001a) in her analysis of principal definitions of global education concluded that the commonalities among the various definitions far outweigh their differences. No matter how global education is defined, the key elements of the endeavor clearly relate to four of Hanvey's five dimensions of a global awareness: multiple perspectives, state of the planet awareness including global issues, comprehension and appreciation of other cultures, the world as an interrelated system, and the significance of human choices. These dimensions of developing a global perspective are a critical component of the contemporary philosophy of human rights.

Although Hanvey's (1976) dimensions of global education avoid an overt discussion of any overarching moral imperative in global education comparable to the philosophy of moral universalism in human rights, human rights have played a key role in global education since its inception. Early global educators such as Tucker (1982b) and Torney-Purta (1982b) argued that human rights *should form* the framework of global education. Tucker (1982a, b), for example, writes that the International Bill of Rights can provide a normative framework for the content of global education. He cites UNESCO's 1974 Recommendation Concerning Education for International Understanding to illustrate that human rights should be a part of this framework. Subsequently, global educators have claimed, as I do, that human rights and global education *are* grounded in the concept that all people are created equal and are entitled to certain unalienable rights (Kirkwood, 2001a; Kirkwood-Tucker, 2003; Reardon, 1995). For example, in *Our Global Age Requires Global Education: Clarifying Definitional Ambiguities*, Kirkwood (2001a) writes that, among the four assumptions that constitute the philosophical underpinnings of global education, is the notion that "human beings are created equal regardless of age, ability, class, ethnicity, gender, nationality, sexual orientation, socioeconomic status, or race" (p. 10).

Global Education in a Human Rights Context

The premise of this chapter is that human rights concepts form a moral imperative that is the basis of global education as evidenced by global education policy, documents, and curricula. Before reviewing global education, it is useful to examine the development and convergence of contemporary human rights and global education (Figure 3.1). Here we can see that the three generations of human rights are clearly tied to the three stages of global education. Just as the first generation of human rights deals with individual freedom and participation in political and civil life, the first stage of global education focuses on the individual's place in an interconnected world system. Second generation human rights are related to social and cultural equality, similar to the second stage of global education, in which the emphasis is on respect for other cultures. Third generation global education terms like *cosmopolitanism* and *global responsibility* are indistinguishable from the right-based approach to development and global human rights with an emphasis on individual responsibility combined with a collective consciousness.

Figure 3.1. Global Education and Human Rights Development

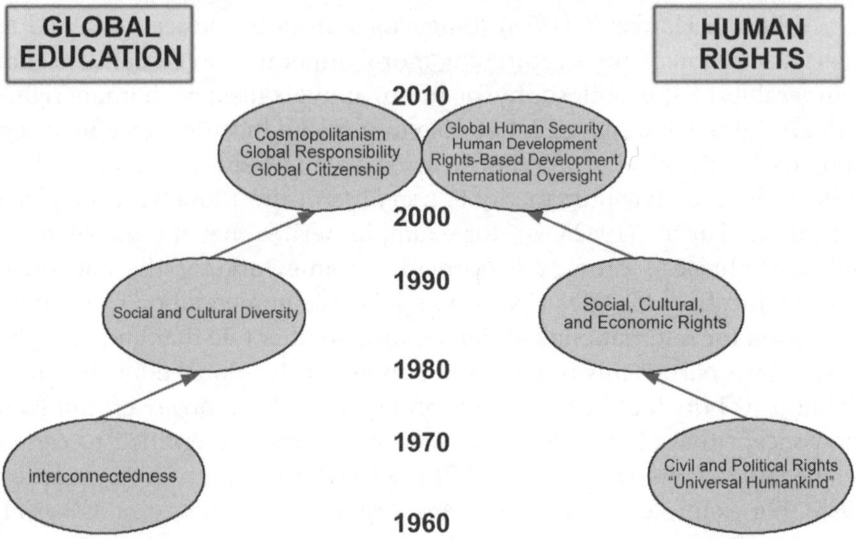

The developments of global education and human rights are also contemporaneous with developments and priorities in human rights subsequently reflected in global education. In addition, the developments of both global education and human rights are expansive. In the first stage, the focus is on the individual; the second stage encompasses the community; in the current stage rights and responsibilities span the globe. By examining the documents and policies in each of these three stages of global education and considering them in the context of the equivalent generation in human rights, the human rights basis of global education clearly emerges.

First Stage Global Education:
Equality, Interconnectedness, and Common Values

The first stage of global education emphasizes equality, interconnectedness, and common values. This was also the apex of the time of first generation human rights, those fundamental civil and political rights that include, among other things, freedom of speech, the right to a fair trial, freedom of religion, and voting rights. The birth of many new countries based on claiming these rights to self-determination and these freedoms along with a changing international world order coincided with the birth of the concept of international education.

According to Tucker (1996) one of two documents that marked the beginning of global education in the 1960s is a "landmark report by the Foreign Policy Association, funded by the U.S. Office of Education, titled *An Examination of Needs, Objectives and Priorities in International Education in U.S. Secondary and Elementary Schools*" (p. 47). At the beginning of this report, authors Lee Anderson and James Becker (1968) state that in their search for prevailing conceptions of international education they found that no one claimed a philosophy of the field, "This does not mean that school curricula are not grounded in, or conditioned by, operating, albeit unarticulated, conceptions of what world affairs education is all about" (p. 17). Belief in the civil rights for all humans to be treated as equals was the unstated framework for the call for curriculum, research, and training in international education at this time, though it would take until almost the 1980s, during the "golden years" of global education, that human rights would be voiced and accepted as such.

Beside the landmark global education document published by the Foreign Policy Association (FPA) mentioned earlier, the importance of global education was also highlighted by U.S. government policy documents of the time. The two most significant were the Mutual Educational and Cultural Exchange Act in 1961 followed by the International Education Act in 1966. Although the latter act was not funded, both acts signaled recognition on the part of U.S. government policy-makers that in order for the United States to grow and prosper as a country, it was essential that U.S. students learn to understand and respect people from other economic, political, social, and cultural contexts.

Man: A Course of Study, known as MACOS, directed by Jerome Bruner (1965), was one of the first elementary social studies curriculum projects in which exploration of the human being's place in the world entailed a cross-cultural analysis of human behavior (see chapter 1). Bruner wrote, "The content of the course is man: his nature as a species, the forces that shape and continues to shape his humanity" (p. 4). Similar to the framework of the 1968 FPA document, in which the rights of human being in the world were the unstated focus, the MACOS curriculum is designed for students to examine an individual's relationship to the world. In both the FPA document and the MACOS curriculum, the role

of a human being is as an individual faced with an increasingly globalized world.

Along with the political and civil human rights concepts inherent in
the founding documents and curricula associated with global education,
global educators in the 1970s understood that humans were living within
a world system and asked each individual to gain knowledge and respect
for himself or herself and others within this system. In *Schooling for a
Global Age*, James Becker (1979) explicitly situates global education in a
human rights framework, one that focuses on both the rights and the responsibilities of the individual. Becker gives examples of ways in which
human rights and human responsibilities are tied to each goal, while
providing curricular content that includes human rights documents such
as the UDHR and the Convention of the Child. Noteworthy in this chapter is that while Becker concurred with his colleagues in placing the
rights and needs of the individual as primary in the face of a growing
recognition of the world as a system, he also foresaw the convergence of
global education and human rights by emphasizing the essential role of
global responsibilities.

Second Stage of Global Education: Communities and Cultures

Whereas the first stage of global educators emphasized the world as a
system with the goal that the individual would learn to take care of his or
her world, the second stage in the 1980s and 1990s focused on communities and cultures, with an emphasis on respect for all (Case, 1993; Heater,
1984; Kniep, 1986; Merryfield, 1993; Wilson, 1982). Around this time the
world of human rights was expanding with an increasing emphasis on
the second generation rights; the social, economic, and cultural rights
that seek to ensure that all citizens of all states receive equal treatment
and equal economic conditions no matter what their culture, ethnicity, or
status. This second stage mirrors these developments in human rights
with an increasing emphasis on the collective, holistic approach to a
global perspective. Second generation global educators also advocated
for a more active approach to the individual's role in the world with the
notion that students should seek knowledge and understanding so they
can participate in the power dynamics of our interdependent cultures,
societies, and economies. This social justice approach is also integral to
the promotion of second generation human rights. Examples in teacher
education show that the sphere of global education moved from highlighting the individual's stewardship of the world system to the need of

both the individual and the group for knowledge of and respect for cultural diversity based on a value system.

In an article titled "Reflective Practice in Global Education: Strategies for Teacher Educators" (1993), Merryfield highlights the social and cultural competencies in global education. In this article, she gives three examples of how she uses reflection with her graduate students to increase their learning of global education. In the first example, she has her students sketch a "tree of life" to symbolize their own lives and to reflect on the values and beliefs that shaped them as people. As Merryfield describes the goal of this exercise, it is for students to "identify and reflect upon what values, beliefs, experiences, and knowledge have shaped their multicultural and global perspectives" (p. 28). In other words, the point of this exercise is for students to reflect on and share with others the ways in which they learn cultural norms.

Another example is found in "Education for a Global Perspective: A Plan for New York State, 1982–2000" (1981) for infusing global education into the curriculum. Its purpose was to provide K-16 students with opportunities to learn about the past and the future interdependence of nations, political and social change including learning to understand and live with peoples who are different from oneself while preserving one's own cultural traditions. In both its purpose and its content, there were two foci to the New York State plan: learning to understand the world as a system and gaining multicultural competence.

Postcolonial and anti-imperialism studies were a part of this second stage of global education (McCarthy, 1998; Said, 1993; Willinsky, 1998). By facilitating the learning of the history, form, and content of hegemonic relationships between the core and the periphery states, global educators sought to raise student awareness of issues of power between nations and social and cultural groups. Global educators also tried to give students the tools with which to fight against power and gain acceptance and respect, both as individuals and as members of their natural and their self-selected groups.

With this emphasis on acknowledgment of and respect for other cultures, human rights continued to be the grounding of second stage global education; this acknowledgment and respect for other cultural and social structures is encoded in the UDHR as well as in the International Covenant on Economic, Social and Cultural Rights. The fact that human rights was in the forefront of global educators' vision of the field is also evident in documents in which human rights is the subject, such as: Reardon's (2005) book *Educating for Human Dignity:*

Learning about Rights and Responsibilities; Boulding's (1988) *Building a Global Civic Culture: Education for an Independent World*; and Torney-Purta's (1982b) co-edited NCSS Bulletin on *International Human Rights, Society, and the Schools.*

In the 1980s and 1990s, human rights education also became a subject of study in itself. Tibbitts (1996), who called for human rights education in an article that appeared in *Social Education*, later became the director of Human Rights Education Associates (HREA), a center for human rights education activity and a repository for human rights education resources. Other educators who have come to be associated with human rights education through their publications and advocacy include Nancy Flowers, George Andreopoulos, David Shiman, Paul Spector, and Garth Meintjes, just to name a few.

In a chapter in *Human Rights, Education, and Global Responsibilities*, Tarrow (1992) discusses different types and levels of human rights programs and curricula. After addressing the content, process, and conceptualization of human rights education in different settings, Tarrow points to the distinctions others such as Shafer (1987) have made between human rights education, moral education, global education, and civics and social education. She then describes how she herself views human rights as the link between these various programs of education for global citizenship: "Human rights can serve as the unifying factor which cuts across current efforts to produce informed and active citizens of their communities, their nations and an interdependent world" (p. 30).

Third Stage of Global Education:
Global Citizenship vis-à-vis Solidarity Rights

Global responsibility, cosmopolitanism, and global citizenship—these are some of the terms associated with the third and current stage of global educators. These terms, which emphasize the role of the individual, have also been used with reference to the third generation human rights. They include such rights as the right to peace, development, and a clean environment. These "solidarity" rights are based on an understanding that their realization is predicated not only on the actions of states, but also on the social behavior of each individual within a communal context. None of these objectives is possible without the concept of global responsibility and the actions and support of like-minded global citizens. It is at this intersection of individual responsibility where we see that global education today is firmly grounded in human rights philosophy and practice.

As global education has come into the post–9/11 age, its researchers have become more numerous, its advocates come from a wider political and social spectrum, and its needs are more important than ever. Much as the 1960s, when President Lyndon Johnson passed the International Education Act, and the Foreign Policy Association defined international education in broad terms, the terrain for global education has opened widely again. While there has been a movement to co-opt global education in the name of global security, accountability, and international academic competition, there have also been exciting positive developments in global education. Theorists such as Martha Nussbaum (2000) and Amy Gutmann (2003) have written of the critical need for an ethical and moral citizenship education that facilitates respect for the other, the world, and the planet. Educational psychologist Gardner (2006) has classified respect for differences among human beings and fulfillment of responsibility toward others among the five cognitive abilities needed to live successfully in the twenty-first century. Naming these abilities "the respectful mind" and "the ethical mind," Gardner pinpoints the nexus of the current generation of global education concepts, global recognition of human rights, and human responsibilities as essential capacities for the future. In linking human rights with education in our increasingly globalized world, these researchers go a long way toward validating the infusion of human rights based global education into the curriculum.

Cosmopolitanism

In the field of global education, several researchers have recently turned to cosmopolitanism as a promising concept for articulating, teaching, and enacting responsible global citizenship (Banks, 2004; Gaudelli & Heilman, 2009; Merryfield, 2006). Just as the third generation of human rights is focused on the rights and responsibilities of individuals as members of a world community, cosmopolitanism also embodies the notion that human beings are citizens of the world and as such are entitled to certain rights and responsible in certain ways to and for one another. Cosmopolitans are "people whose allegiance is to the worldwide community of human beings" (Nussbaum, 2002, p. 4). As such, one tenet that cosmopolitans hold is that every human being has obligations to every other human being (Appiah, 2006). Third generation human rights, such as the right to development, the right to natural resources, and the right to a healthy environment, also require that human beings act responsibly. For example, in order to guarantee that an individual in New York has access to safe drinking water, individuals in Vancouver have a responsibility not to pollute their own waters. According to Banks (2004), individuals who exemplify cosmopolitanism are at the highest stage of development of global citizenship, possessing the "knowledge, skills, and attitudes needed to function effectively within their own cultural communities, within other cultures within their nation-state, in the civic culture of their nation, and in the global community" (p. 297).

Global Responsibility

In addition to advocating cosmopolitanism, some global educators have focused on global responsibility as a way to promote a move from the insistence on rights alone to recognition of the obligations inherent in human rights (Kirkwood-Tucker, 2003). When referring to global responsibility, they articulate the idea that all humans are equally charged with obligations toward humankind to participate in creating a more just and peaceful world (Bickmore, 2002; Carter, 2002).

The Universal Declaration of Human Responsibilities, proposed by the United Nations Interaction Council under the leadership of former West German Chancellor Helmut Schmidt (1997) and expounded by German philosopher Hans Küng (1991), encapsulates this balance between freedom and responsibility. Formulated by 24 former heads of state, this document is meant to serve as an explicit complement to the UDHR. It consists of 19 Articles that are divided into five sections: (1) Fundamental Principles for Humanity; (2) Non-Violence and Respect for Life; (3) Justice and Solidarity; (4) Truthfulness and Tolerance; and (5) Mutual Respect and Partnership. Each article proclaims a responsibility that is tied to a human right as expressed in the UDHR. Thus, for example, under Non-Violence and Respect for Life, Article 5 begins with the statement, "Every person has a responsibility to respect life," and goes on to proclaim that no one has the right to torture, injure, or kill another person. This is a complement to Article 5 of the UDHR, which proclaims the right of an individual not to be "subjected to torture or to cruel, inhuman or degrading treatment or punishment" (United Nations, 1948). While the UDHR Article 5 is a negative right, in the sense that it states what the government cannot do to an individual, the Universal Declaration of Human Responsibilities' corresponding Article 5 clearly couches the right of one in terms of the responsibilities of others. It begins with the individual's obligation and goes on to state that an individual is forbidden to torture and to injure another. By spelling out the responsibilities that go along with human rights, the Universal Declaration of Human Responsibilities can serve as an important document in global education pedagogy and practice. It can give students the support to move actively from a freedom of indifference to a freedom of involvement.

Global Citizenship Education

A third key discussion in current global education is global citizenship education (Gaudelli & Heilman, 2009). Often interchangeable with cosmopolitan education (Marshall & Arnot, 2008), global citizenship education attempts to bridge the love of country, highlighted by traditional citizenship education, with respect for the other, the purview of global education. The goal of global citizenship education is to "enable young people to learn about their rights and responsibilities and equip them with skills for democratic participation, at all levels, from local to global" (Ibrahim, 2005, p. 27).

Gaudelli and Heilman envision a global citizenship education curriculum that combines human rights, which they see as part of cosmopolitan education, environmental education, and education for social justice (Gaudelli & Heilman, 2009). However, human rights are not only part of cosmopolitan education. They are also the basis of environmental education, as in the right to a healthy, clean environment, and education for social justice. Human rights are at the root of all current iterations of global education. The conceptual basis and values advocated in global citizenship education, cosmopolitan education, and global responsibility are the same as the conceptual basis for the third generation of human rights—a fundamental respect for all people that balances individual rights and ethical responsibility to the global and local community that one calls home.

Important Issues in Global Education and Human Rights

The view that human rights concepts form the grounding of a philosophy for global education is further supported by the convergence of issues and challenges in human rights and global education today that can be seen in two key areas of discussion: cultural relativism and globalization.

Cultural Relativism

One of the long-standing arguments against the UDHR and, indeed, the concept of human rights is that they impose obligations on countries without regard to the cultural and social mores of that country. For example what would be considered a right in one country is forbidden in another, such as child betrothal versus the freedom to marry whom one chooses. This debate between the universalists and the relativists is long-standing and is in the forefront of discussion, implementation, and enforcement of human rights today. Despite the globalization process, or perhaps because of it, we are assailed with many examples of rights being invoked to protest the behavior of one side, who then invokes the cultural difference argument to justify that behavior. From a legal standpoint, however, there is general international consensus that *cultural difference should not be allowed to obscure the universality of fundamental human rights*, which do not depend on the culture or status of the individual. There is also general consensus through international covenants and treaties that cultural relativism should not be used as a strategy to place limitations on speech, subjugation of women, torture, imprisonment, and other violations of human rights.

Likewise one of the main criticisms of global education is that it is culturally relativistic, that it espouses the notion that because each culture is unique, there are no universal standards by which to judge actions within a culture. The Fordham Foundation's report, "Where did Social Studies go Wrong?" (Burack, 2003), suggests that "by discouraging students who might wish to criticize negative aspects of other cultures, teachers seek to suppress what is likely an irrepressible natural human tendency to make moral judgments. Such pressure and hectoring probably fosters cynicism and indifference in students, not a true spirit of tolerance" (p. 48).

It would seem as if global education and human rights are at odds on the issue of cultural relativism. A human rights based approach claims that human rights exist without regard to social and cultural mores. For example you can't use cultural differences to justify torture. Using the cultural relativism argument, global education curriculum would be criticized for sanctioning torture because it is culturally appropriate in certain circumstances. However, by clarifying that the basis of global education is human rights, the cultural relativism criticism is no longer relevant. There is general international consensus that cultural difference should *not* be allowed to obscure the generally accepted universality of human rights that do not depend on the culture or status of the individual.

Globalization

In light of the intensity of the present globalization process, global education is crucial to help students understand and navigate the complexity of issues and the various domains of global activity. It is especially important that in today's world even seemingly small decisions taken by individuals can have considerable global impact. Global education has responded to the globalization process by focusing on notions like cosmopolitanism, global citizenship, and global responsibility.

How is globalization affecting human rights? Although globalization has been characterized as a locomotive for productivity, opportunity, technological progress, and uniting the world, the integration of markets, free trade, and increased economic and political migration, along with the growth of multinational companies, also creates an environment ripe for increased impoverishment, social disparities, and violations of human rights. In addition, globalization has created a situation where the rights of an individual now depend on a wide range of global forces and institutions, many of which are outside sovereign state governments with whom the individual has no connection, let alone is able to influence. Thus the World Bank, multinational corporations, NGOs, and international peacekeepers increasingly affect and control the lives of millions of people throughout the world.

On a positive note for human rights, globalization has resulted in the growth and communication of international prescriptive norms and institutions for the protection of human rights. Global civil society provides opportunities for appeal and support for those citizens who are oppressed by their own states. An international regime for human rights, new forms of advocacy and communication, humanitarian intervention, and global monitoring by watch dogs such as Amnesty International have led to increased awareness of human rights entitlement and protection from abuse (Donnelly, 2003).

Globalization has created new opportunities to challenge the state from above, through international bodies, state governments, and INGOs, and from below, through grassroots international movements aided by NGOs like Amnesty International and Human Rights Watch (Brysk, 2002). Global education can enable students to understand that many decisions affecting their own lives are made outside traditional national, state, and local governments.

Conclusion

As global educators, we have a responsibility to promote the idea that processes of globalization should be subject to moral considerations, including the ethical and legal principles entailed by human rights. The former UN High Commissioner for Human Rights, Mary Robinson (2002) asks whether, in the upward or downward shifting of power, human rights scrutiny should not also follow in both directions—in a world where markets, ideas, and peoples impact one another as never before, the time has come to reconsider how we think about human rights and develop a shared sense of responsibility for their realization.

On the eve of the tenth anniversary of the signing of the UDHR, Eleanor Roosevelt (1958) declared that "the destiny of human rights is in the hands of all our citizens in all our communities" and urged people everywhere to improve human rights conditions "in small places, close to home" (para. 2) as the first step toward global progress.

In countless incidents and events, the international community is charged with the promotion and protection of human rights. Today human rights is the language of international dialogue in almost all global issues, be they social, political, cultural, or economic, or disputes between sovereign states. It is the task of global educators to facilitate students acquiring the knowledge, skills, and attitudes that will allow them to understand these challenges so that they will actively participate in support of community efforts and promote actions. Realization of this task starts with understanding that students need to be able to bring a human rights perspective to issues, that all peoples should enjoy the protection and implementation of human rights not just in their local communities but in their global community as well, a perspective based on a philosophy of unequivocal moral universalism.

Global educators need to embrace human rights as a philosophy and work to make global education replete with a moral imperative for global citizenship based on human rights. To those who question the case for human rights in global education, I ask the reader to imagine a world without human rights.

Note

1. In his annual address to Congress on January 6, 1941, Franklin D. Roosevelt presented his reasons for continued American involvement in World War II, which at that stage consisted of continued aid to Great Britain and greater production of war industries at home. President Roosevelt stated that the United States was fighting for the universal freedoms that all people possessed: the freedom of speech, the freedom

of worship, the freedom from want, and the freedom from fear. Once America entered the war, these "Four Freedoms" became the moral basis of America's aim in fighting the war (Franklin D. Roosevelt Presidential Library and Museum, n.d.).

II. From Theory to Practice

Chapter 4

Global Perspectives in Teacher Education Research and Practice

Guichun Zong

The new global reality intensifies the difficulties that we face in educating our young. It clearly calls for a global education that permeates the curriculum and provides a far more extensive and sounder education than schools have previously provided about the nature of the human species, the planet that we call home, and the ways we organize ourselves on the face of the Earth.

—Anderson, Niklas, & Crawford, 1994

Teacher educators today are faced with an urgent responsibility to transform curriculum and pedagogy to better prepare teachers in educating the young generation about the increasing global interdependence and their role in the emerging global society. Scholars in education and professional organizations in education such as the American Association of Colleges for Teacher Education (AACTE), the National Council for Accreditation of Teacher Education (NCATE), and the National Council for the Social Studies (NCSS) have long called for global education in both K-12 classrooms and preservice teacher education programs. In its newly published *Professional Standards for the Accreditation of Teacher Preparation Institutions*, NCATE requires teacher education programs undergoing accreditation reviews to show evidence of how the curriculum and field experiences address such perspectives. Standard 4 on Diversity states, "Regardless of whether they live in areas with great diversity, candidates must develop knowledge of diversity in the United States and the world, dispositions that respect and value differences, and skills for working in diverse settings" (NCATE, 2008, p. 36). It continues, "One of the goals of the diversity standard is the development of educators who can help all students learn and who can teach from multicultural and global perspectives that draw on the histories, experiences, and representations of students from diverse cultural backgrounds" (p. 36). The organization defines global perspective as "an understanding of the interdependency of nations and peoples and the political, economic, ecological, and social concepts and values that affect lives within and across national boundaries; it allows for the exploration of multiple perspectives on events and issues" (p. 87).

Over the past two decades, colleges and universities have attempted to respond to these calls by increasingly adding a global dimension to their teacher education programs. They have done so through a variety of initiatives, including encouraging the study of foreign languages, creating internationally focused courses, organizing cross-cultural fieldwork experiences, offering extracurricular activities that are internationally oriented, and other policies and practices to help prospective and practicing teachers gain knowledge, skills, and dispositions to teach from a global viewpoint (Cushner & Brennan, 2007; Merryfield, Jarchow, & Pickert, 1997; Quezada & Cordeiro, 2007). What is known about the impact of these policies and practices? What is the research base that demonstrates the effects and complexities of these initiatives? Under what conditions and in what contexts are these efforts successful? What are the challenges facing teacher educators while they engage in global practices?

In the latest edition of the *Handbook of Research on Teacher Education: Enduring Questions in Changing Contexts* by Cochran-Smith, Feiman-Nemser, McIntyre, and Demers (2008) there is no mention of global education or globalization. A thorough search of the entire index will reveal the fact that neither the word *global* nor the word *international* is mentioned. Similarly, in the much publicized AACTE-award-winning book on teacher education research, *Studying Teacher Education: Report of the AERA Panel on Research and Teacher Education* (Cochran-Smith & Zeichner, 2005), neither *global education* nor *globalization* is included. Though the word *international* is mentioned twice, we find that they appear in the context of international datasets and the International Council on Exceptional Children.

This chapter aims to fill this gap by reviewing and analyzing the growing body of literature on teacher education in global perspectives with a primary focus on teacher preparation. I seek to synthesize research in the field to determine what might be learned about practices in globalizing teacher education and the impact of these practices. The chapter is organized around three major ideas, each of which is presented in the following three sections: (1) a brief overview of the history and evolution of teacher education for global perspectives; (2) a review of the existing literature to examine the impact of current practices in global education on preservice teachers' development; and (3) discussion of the implications of the findings for future global perspectives in teacher education and practice.

Historical Tracing and Conceptual Framework

Global education became a mainstream concern during the late 1960s and early 1970s when "visionary thinkers, best-selling books, and unexpected events changed the American public to the implications of global interdependence" (Tucker & Cistone, 1991, p. 3). As world events such as American astronauts and Soviet cosmonauts returning with radiant images of the Earth and the landmark United Nations Conference on the Human Environment coining the now familiar phrase "think globally, act locally" gradually changed public awareness, global education for teachers began to take shape through books and articles that spoke to the necessity of embedding global perspectives within the knowledge, skills, and dispositions of teacher education programs, as well as the scholarship and actions of teacher educators (Becker, 1973; Hanvey, 1976; Reischauer, 1973; Taylor, 1970). In *The World as Teacher*, Taylor (1970) argues that teacher education institutions in the United States could become genuine educational laboratories serving as places of international dialogue for educators from around the world, and that international education should be the integrating focus of study and activity in schools and colleges of teacher education.

The first teacher education program for global perspectives began at the Center for Teaching International Relations (CTIR) at the University of Denver in 1969. In the early 1970s, global teacher education programs were also initiated at the Mershon Center of the Ohio State University (1971), the University of South Dakota (1972), and the Stanford Program on International and Cross-Cultural Education (SPICE, 1973). More programs were initiated in the 1980s (Merryfield, 1991), an era in global education development that Tye in chapter 1 refers to as "the golden years of global education." However, progress in the infusion of global perspectives into teacher education programs was hampered by emerging attacks on global education beginning in the mid-1980s (Merryfield, 1991; Schukar, 1993; Tucker & Cistone, 1991; also see chapter 1). Merryfield's (1991) study, however, found that "most teachers in the United States learn to teach global perspectives through brief in-service education programs and professional conferences (p. 1).

Rapid global changes since the 1990s, such as the accelerating growth of global interdependence in the economy, technology, politics, and culture, have brought global perspectives to the forefront of teacher education again. The recognition that the United States is part of an interdependent and interconnected global system is becoming increasingly apparent (Anderson, 1991; Tucker & Cistone, 1991). Professional organizations such as AACTE, NCATE, NCSS, the Association of Teacher Educators (ATE), and the Association for Supervision and Curriculum Development (ASCD) joined scholars in supporting global education through publications, position statements, and various other measures. In 1996, AACTE established the global and international teacher education Best Practice Award to recognize exemplary practice or programs in the intercultural, global, cross-cultural, and international arenas.

What does it mean to teach from a global perspective? What are the core elements in teacher education programs that are globally oriented? What are the evolving scope, focus, and direction of these fields? Although different teacher educators and scholars emphasize different aspects of interdependence, they all share the idea that a global perspective course is more than courses on world geography and world history and requires a holistic approach that gives students an understanding of themselves and their relationship to the world community (Avery, 2004; Kirkwood-Tucker, 2003; 2004; Merryfield, 1993; 1997b; Quezada & Alfaro, 2007a; Tucker & Cistone, 1991). A global perspective also seeks to develop an outlook that helps us to see the world in which we live as a "sociopolitical, planetary biosphere" (Gutek, 1993, p. 19). Global education should prepare teachers to build bridges across cultural boundaries and citizens to be able to communicate and collaborate with those whose attitudes, values, knowledge, and ways of doing things differ significantly from their own (Cushner & Brennan, 2007).

Merryfield's (1991) in-depth study of 30 exemplary secondary social studies teacher education programs in the United States indicated a common understanding among teacher educators on the core content of global teacher education: knowledge and appreciation of cultural differences and similarities in the United States and around the world; multiple perspectives on cultures, events, and issues and tolerance toward diversity; understanding of the world as a system among nations and peoples; and need for teachers to be prepared to address contemporary global issues. In a later publication, Merryfield, Jarchow, & Pickert (1997) laid out a comprehensive framework to guide teacher education programs in incorporating global perspectives that included the following essential elements: conceptualizing the field, infusing global content, promoting cross-cultural experiential learning, and practicing global pedagogy. In this chapter, I have adopted Merryfield's framework in identifying, selecting, and reviewing research on teacher education for global perspectives.

Selection and Evaluation Procedures

To examine what teacher educators are doing in scholarship and practice to bring a global dimension to teacher education and the preparation of teacher candidates, I reviewed articles published since 1990. It is commonly acknowledged that this is the period in which the process of globalization has significantly accelerated (Friedman, 2000; 2005). The focus of this review is on scholarship that has dealt directly with the preparation of candidates for global perspectives in the context of teacher education programs, although some reference is made to studies on the professional development of teachers in general. In identifying articles for review, I initially combined the descriptors of teacher education, preservice, and global perspectives to search three databases that included ERIC, EBSCO, and ProQuest. I also conducted a hand search of the past 10 years for Action in Teacher Education, Teachers College Record, Teaching and Teacher Education, Teacher Education Quarterly, Journal of Teacher Education, and Theory and Research in Social Education and examined the bibliographies of recent studies to identify publications that might have been overlooked. I searched particularly for empirical research studying the preparation and learning of preservice teachers, although some conceptual and theoretical literature is also included. The articles reviewed comprise those published in refereed journals and as chapters in books. Overall, the articles included here are by no means exhaustive but they are representative of what exists in the field to date. As Grant and Agosto (2008) stated, the importance of review lies in the fact that scholars keep up with the development of their field by reading the literature in their area.

Research on Global Perspectives for Teacher Education

Over the past two decades, teacher educators have increasingly focused on preparing preservice teachers with knowledge, skills, and attitudes to be effective intercultural teachers in a global age. As a result, a growing body of literature has developed that documents and analyzes a number of key issues in this area. Several books have been published to report scholarship on bringing global dimension to teacher education. Among them are *Developing the Global Teacher: Theory and Practice in Initial Teacher*

Education (Steiner, 1996); *Preparing Teachers to Teach Global Perspectives: A Handbook for Teacher Education* (Merryfield, Jarchow, & Pickert, 1997); and *Intercultural Student Teaching: A Bridge to Global Competence* (Cushner & Brennan, 2007). An increasing number of articles have also appeared in major educational journals. For instance, the Journal of Teacher Education, Theory into Practice, and Teacher Education Quarterly devoted separate issues to global education in 1991, 1993, and 2007 respectively.

Written by teacher education scholars from various academic backgrounds, these publications on global education in the teacher education context have addressed a range of topics, such as historical origins and intellectual foundations of global education, content, pedagogy, faculty development, school-university collaboration, cross-cultural experiences in teacher education courses, international field experiences, and student teaching overseas. Some of them are theoretical and conceptual in nature, some are empirical reports based on research studies in teacher education settings. Others deal with program planning and best practices in implementing global initiatives. There are also a number of studies focusing on particular components of teacher education programs.

Much of this research examines effects of international field experiences, particular overseas student teaching, on the global awareness of teacher candidates. A number of studies report the effects of various pedagogical approaches designed to facilitate global understanding among preservice teachers. The review also found a few studies that examine teacher education students and faculty members about their preparedness for teaching globally. I organize the review results around Merryfield's (1997b) framework and five major themes emerging from the existing literature: (1) international field experiences; (2) global content; (3) technology; (4) teacher education students' prior knowledge and global-mindedness; and (5) teacher education faculty.

International Field Experiences

Field experiences have long been identified by both teacher educators and prospective and experienced teachers as a major part of preservice teacher preparation. It is broadly assumed that field experiences are the key components of preparation where teacher candidates learn to bridge theory and practice and develop pedagogical and curricular strategies for meaningful learning. Designing international field experiences is one of the major ways teacher education programs have attempted to improve the preparation of teachers with global perspectives. These internationally based field experiences are organized in various ways, and range in duration from two weeks to daily full-time student teaching for a semester. Proponents argue that carefully structured international field placements provide a unique experiential learning approach and open opportunities for practicing and prospective teachers to learn about other views of the world and thus become more global in their thoughts and actions. A good number of research studies has been conducted to examine the impact of these international experiences on the development of global perspectives among preservice teachers.

Short-Term Experiences

Pence and Macgillivray (2008) reported their study of 15 teacher education students from James Madison University who completed a four-week international practicum working with teachers and students at a private school in Italy. Using multiple data sources, which included preservice teachers' reflections and comments collected from their personal journals, focus groups with supervisors, observation notes, a final reflection paper, course evaluations, and a questionnaire completed one year after the experience, the authors concluded that while there were a few negative experiences, the results indicated overall benefits that included both personal change and professional growth, such as a better appreciation of and respect for differences of others and other cultures.

Similarly, Kambutu and Nganga's (2008) inquiry explored the effectiveness of two to three weeks of cultural immersion experiences in Kenya in improving the global understanding of 12 preservice and in-service American rural teachers. The pre-visit data indicated that the participants were apprehensive about the planned trip, doubtful of formal educational opportunities in Kenya, and associated Kenya with poverty. Post-visit reflections showed evidence of cultural change and appreciation among the most participants even though there were indications of ethnocentrism. The trip also helped teachers develop a new understanding of the multifaceted nature of the factors involved in poverty and the complexity connected with globalization.

Spalding, Savage, and Garcia's (2007) study presented the impact of another initiative taken by teacher educators to promote teachers' global understanding through short-term international programs. Twelve participants, including five preservice teachers and seven graduate students in counseling psychology and school psychology, participated in a field-based program in Poland focusing on the effect of the Holocaust and the March of Remembrance and Hope on teachers. All participants took a semester-long seminar before the actual international trip. A post-trip seminar was organized for the participants to share what they had learned. Based on various data sources collected from an in-depth case study of three participants a year after the completion of the trip, the authors concluded that although the academic preparation was critical to participants' understanding of the Holocaust, it was the authentic learning from the international field experience that had the greatest impact on these teachers' thinking about human diversity and their willingness to take action against social injustice.

Long-Term Experiences

A growing number of studies also explore the impact of such long-term international and intercultural immersion experiences as overseas student teaching on the global knowledge and global-mindedness of teacher candidates. Kenneth Cushner and Sharon Brennan's (2007) edited book, published in partnership with the Association of Teacher Educators, is a collection of research and reflection on three long-standing initiatives in this field: the Consortium for Overseas Student Teaching, the International Teacher Education Program in the California State University System, and the cultural immersion projects at Indiana University. The results of a number of research studies on international student teaching have also been published in peer-reviewed journals. Drawing on data sources such as teacher candidates' reflective journal entries, program evaluations, anecdotal notes, feedback from host country educators, and results from questionnaires or surveys, many studies have highlighted the positive impact of international student teaching experiences on pre-service teachers' professional and personal development, a shift in consciousness and perspective, an empathetic understanding of the world and its people, an appreciation for other cultures and perspectives, and an awareness of both global and domestic diversity (Clement & Outlaw, 2002; Kuechle, O'Brien, & Ferguson, 1995; Mahan & Stachowski, 1990; Mahon & Cushner, 2002; Quezada & Alfaro, 2007b; Roberts, 2004; Stachowski & Chlebo, 1998; Vall & Tennison, 1991). This line of research also reveals essential factors to ensure successful completion of student teaching programs: structuring and monitoring systems, attention to orientation and preparation prior to departure, close supervision during the placement period, and structured debriefing sessions upon return (Cushner & Brennan, 2007; Quezada & Alfaro, 2007b).

Global Content

Leading scholars in the field have long argued that global content should be an essential part of efforts in globalizing teacher education to help prospective and practicing teachers acquire the knowledge of the world and its people (Merryfield, Jarchow, & Pickert, 1997; Tucker & Cistone, 1991). A fair amount of literature describes and documents various measures teacher education programs have taken in providing current scholarly knowledge the teachers need to teach from a global perspective. Mayer (1997) provides a case study of a globally oriented science education program, Earth Systems Education. He explains that the earth systems education evolves a concept of science literacy that is more attentive to the post–Cold War global intellectual climate that places Earth at the center of the science teaching and learning. He detailed how this new paradigm of science education has influenced the curriculum development and teachers' learning.

Wilson (1997) documents how University of Kentucky social studies teacher education students learn global content, along with cross-cultural experiential learning, global pedagogy in the methods class, and practice in the field. Teacher candidates were encouraged to look at their entire program and take courses that will both prepare them to teach about the various regions of the world and give them a global perspective on topics such as population or politics. Wilson conducted several research studies on the impact of her program-wide infusion approach on the development of global perspectives among social studies teacher candidates. For example, in 2001 she investigated the growth toward a global perspective of her 15 social studies preservice teachers who participated in a year-long initial certification graduate program. Beginning with their application essays on previous cross-cultural experiences and then through classroom observations, taped interviews, and documents such as lesson plans and teaching philosophies, Wilson found that as preservice teachers talked about influences on their teaching from a global perspective they emphasized learning specific content about the world both in earlier schooling and in social studies methods classes.

In another teacher educator's self-study, Kirkwood-Tucker (2004) examined the impact of integrating global content and pedagogy into a global education elective course with a group of 53 practicing elementary teachers and preservice secondary teachers, using a United Nations General Assembly simulation. She required students to study *A Global Agenda: Issues Before the General Assembly of the United Nations* (Ayton-Shenker & Tessitore, 2002) and *What Citizens Need to Know about World*

Affairs (Goldstein, 2000) and to ground their simulated debate in the framework of the Universal Declaration of Human Rights (1948) and the Convention of the Rights of the Child (1989). The findings indicated that through the simulation of General Assembly deliberations, students developed an open-mindedness toward those who are ethnically and culturally different, concerns for human rights and global stability, and in recognizing the importance of peace-building competence. The participants' lesson plans reflected a global education framework grounded in themes of persistent problems and interconnectedness of issues.

Technology

The promotion of technology in teacher education over the past decade has shifted emphasis from technology taught as a separate course to technology integrated into academic courses. As more teacher educators begin to integrate technology into teaching and learning, researchers have begun to focus more and more on the effectiveness of various technology-based initiatives in the development of prospective teachers' global understanding and commitment to teach from a global perspective. As Adler (2008) noted, "the biggest change in research on social studies teacher education is the large increase in the number of studies of technology and teacher preparation" (p. 338). Teacher education scholars have been particularly interested in exploring the potential of Internet-based technology, such as computer-mediated communication (CMC), in building cross-cultural understanding and promoting global awareness among preservice teachers.

Merryfield (2000b) analyzed the strengths and weaknesses of integrating online discussions into her graduate courses in social studies and global education over a period of several years. She compared the content and patterns of interaction on online discussions with face-to-face discussions. Based on content analysis of online messages and other data, which included formative and summative course evaluations, she found that class discussions online progressed quite differently than face to face. This was especially the case in discussion of sensitive and controversial topics like prejudice, privilege, inequity, injustice, and imperialism. Overall, the asynchronous nature of most online pedagogy increased both depth of content and equity in participation. She further cited four ways that online pedagogy made a difference in maximizing cross-cultural learning: diffusing triggers of difference; increasing the depth of study and the meaningfulness of academic content; facilitating immediate and detailed feedback and extended discussion of ideas and resources; and creating communities of diverse learners and connections to a larger world.

Gaudelli (2006) studied the experiences of two beginning social studies teachers with a nine-week web-based distance learning course designed to enhance pedagogy for global and multicultural education. Using a phenomenological approach, he collected and analyzed data from participant interviews, observations of teachers' participation in the course, e-mail correspondence throughout the school year, and periodic observations of the two teachers' classroom instruction in urban settings to explore their interpretations of the online learning experience before, during, and after the web-based distance course. Gaudelli's research revealed that even though the web-based learning had an impact on the beginning teachers' motivation and their pedagogical skills in teaching from global and multicultural perspectives, their decisions to implement a technology-based approach to facilitate global learning were severely tempered by factors such as the demanding teaching schedule in urban schools and the digital divide "between high-tech post-secondary environments to lower-tech middle school and high school situations" (p. 112).

Zong (2002) examined how the participation of two preservice social studies teachers in a technology-enhanced global education course influenced their understanding of global education. The preservice teachers participated in International Communication and Negotiation Simulations (ICONS), a worldwide simulation network that uses both synchronous and asynchronous communication characteristics of the Internet to teach international negotiation and intercultural communication to university and high school students. She followed the two teacher candidates through their student teaching, noting the ways in which they attempted to infuse a global perspective into student teaching. Both teacher candidates reported that the ICONS simulation project shaped their understanding of the importance of teaching global perspectives and believed the potential of Internet-based technology lies in two equally important features: the advantage of instant access to updated worldwide information from various sources and a tool for communication across time, space, and culture.

More recently, Zong (2007) reported the results of a three-year study exploring the impact of participation in a semester-long web-based multinational discussion project coordinated by International Education and Resource Network (iEARN) on the development of preservice elementary and middle school teachers' understanding of cultural diversity and global awareness. Drawing on social constructivist learning theory, the study examined whether, and if so how, participation in this online project in which students and teachers from more than 20 countries discussed issues related to cultural diversity and global challenges could have an impact on future teachers' conceptual understanding of global education. Overall findings suggested that the computer-mediated communication projects provide an authentic context in which to learn about other countries and cultures, global issues such as child labor in Asia, hunger and poverty in Africa, and multiple perspectives on world events, particularly on the U.S.-led wars in Afghanistan and Iraq. The project also had limited impact on preservice teachers' critical understanding of globalization.

As the literature on CMC develops, the initial optimism regarding the potential of this new communication technology in facilitating interaction and communication across cultural, geographical, institutional, and linguistic lines has been tempered by the more recent research studies in the field. Both Merryfield's (2000a) and Zong's (2007) studies have demonstrated the inconclusive and sometimes contradictory impact of electronic technologies on the global understanding of preservice and practicing teachers. Other studies have also demonstrated that CMC projects do not automatically increase cross-cultural understanding and may have little impact on people's misinformation and misperceptions (Belz & Muller-Hartmann, 2003; Kern, 2000; Kramsch & Thorne, 2002; Roberts, 2003; 2004). For example, Ware and Kramsch (2005) described an extended episode of misunderstanding between a German female college student and an American male college student discussing their versions of recent German history during a classroom-based asynchronous tele-collaborative project between learners of German in the United States and learners of English in Germany. Similarly, in their review of literature on telecommunication projects in education, Fabos and Young (1999) noted that many of the expected benefits of telecommunication exchanges were "inconclusive, overly optimistic and even contradictory" (p. 249). A more critical approach to analyze the impacts of telecommunication projects on teaching and learning is clearly needed.

Teacher Education Students' Prior Knowledge and Global-Mindedness

Another line of research is to investigate student teachers' prior knowledge of and dispositions toward global education. In a survey study of 856 preservice teachers combined with in-depth interviews, Holden and

Hicks (2007) found that the teacher candidates reported knowing most about the reasons for war and famine and least about the reasons for economic problems in less economically developed nations and human rights abuse. Teacher candidates' perceived levels of knowledge varied according to the grade level they planned to teach and their own education level (graduate or undergraduate). Male participants were three times as likely to say they knew a lot about the reasons for wars and twice likely to claim knowing about the reasons for environmental issues. The study also revealed that while the majority of preservice teachers expressed strong motivation to learn more about global issues and to feel that they can make a difference in their future students' awareness and understanding of the critical issues, some expressed the concern that global issues are "sensitive, controversial and complex" (p. 22).

Osunde, Tlou, and Brown (1996) focused more specifically on examining the knowledge and perceptions of preservice social studies teachers about a single region, Africa. Their study involved the administration of a questionnaire to 100 randomly selected preservice social studies teachers from two universities in the United States. The questionnaire listed various concepts that might be applied to Africa from which the respondents were to choose those that they considered relevant to the country. The results indicated that the concepts most often associated with Africa are *wild animals, malnutrition, disease, huts, tribes, elephants, jungles, poor, deserts, villages, tigers, natives,* and *superstition.* Other stereotypical concepts ascribed to Africa by the preservice teachers included *spears, underdeveloped, illiterate, naked, witch doctors, primitive, violence, racial problems, pygmies, savages,* and *backward.* The authors conclude,

> Even though preservice teachers are exposed to an increasing amount of information on Africa through their college courses and seminars and even though the media now presents news on Africa with more frequency, the results of our data analysis showed that a majority of the preservice social studies teachers had the same misconceptions about Africa that their grandparents and parents had several decades ago. (p. 120)

Duckworth, Levy, and Levy (2005) investigated the global-mindedness of 93 preservice and in-service teachers by administrating a 55-item questionnaire that included a section taken from the Global Mindedness Scale (GMS) developed by Jane Hett (1993). Two-thirds of the participants were born in the United States; the rest came from Canada, the Middle East, Europe, Africa, Asia, South America, and Australia (p. 289). About 82 percent of the participants were female and the same percentage reported that they had lived outside of the United States for at least six months. This demographic information might help to explain the intriguing findings of their study: most participants demonstrated a high-level global-mindedness as measured by Hett's scale, and there were no significant correlations between scores on the GMS and such factors as gender, age, ethnicity, or experiences outside of the United States. The authors argued that more research needs to be conducted in this area.

In a much larger scale survey study, Kirkwood-Tucker and Morris (in review) provided further insight into the readiness of U.S. preservice teachers to embrace teaching from a global perspective. Their study examined the global-mindedness of 644 teacher candidates enrolled in the requisite social studies methods course at five of Florida's largest public universities. Participating teacher candidates were juniors and seniors with various ethnic backgrounds pursuing their undergraduate degrees in either elementary education or secondary social science education. The instrument used was a two-part Worldmindedness Survey composed of 24 demographic questions and 30-item statements based on Hett's (1993) GMS. The results revealed that the teacher candidates' high world-mindedness scores were related to the following variables: attending classes with global content, foreign language proficiency, high grade-point average, birthplace, political orientation, and gender. The study also demonstrated that teacher candidates' age, international experiences, and membership in professional organizations were all significantly correlated to their world-mindedness scores.

Teacher Education Faculty Development

Many scholars in education have argued that to successfully globalize teacher education there is a critical need to foster teacher education faculty commitment to, understanding of, and support for the movement. Ochoa (1986) laid out three practical strategies used in engaging faculty involvement at Indiana University: recruitment, seminar participation and module development, and rewards and recognition. Gilliom (1993) suggested the following to mobilize teacher education faculty to participate in global teaching: effective leadership from administrators, collaboration among colleagues, visibility, a reward system, and a sense of community among faculty members. Case and Werner (1997) examined the impact of a faculty professional development project to globalize teacher education in four universities in Canada. They found that the underlying factors that contribute to the success of the project are perceived need, disciplinary relevance, strong advocacy, meaningful incentives, and institutional resources and structures; the lack of conceptual clarity was the most significant impediment.

Another emerging area of research on faculty development is exploration of the influence of the personal and professional backgrounds and life experiences of teacher educators on their conceptualizations of and commitment to global education. Merryfield's (2000b) study identified 80 teacher educators recognized by their peers for their success in preparing teachers in both multicultural and global education. These exemplary teacher educators reflected upon their experiences in areas such as childhood and family, education, traveling, and their own teaching and identified "encounters with people different from themselves, experiences with discrimination, injustice or outside status, and their felt contradictions in dealing with multiple realities" as the most influential factors. Merryfield's study also revealed that "most people of color acquired an experiential understanding of discrimination and outsider status by the nature of growing up in a society characterized by white privilege and racism" while "many of the middle-class white teacher educators had their most profound experiences while living outside their own country" (p. 429). She further explained that experiences alone do not make a person a global educator. Rather "it is the interrelationships across identity, power, and experience that lead to a consciousness of other perspectives and a recognition of multiple realities" (p. 440).

In a collaborative self-study among three teacher educators in an international context (Rios, Montecinos, & van Olphen, 2007), a teacher education faculty from the United States examined overseas teaching experiences through dialogues with colleagues from Latin America to better understand how to build authentic international teacher education activities. The guiding research question was to explore "what visions, questions, and challenges (visiones, preguntas, y desafios) arise in the context of carrying out teacher education in a Latin American country that might help us rethink teacher education in the U.S." (p. 64). The primary data came from the U.S. teacher educator's reflective journal kept while he was teaching a multicultural education course at a Chilean university on a Fulbright Fellowship. The authors concluded for international experiences to be meaningful, teacher education programs need to emphasize the following key aspects: (1) reflective practice as we reconsider our assumptions and clarify our expectations, (2) flexibility and creativity in acknowledging our always-evolving identities from an open-minded perspective, (3) understanding teaching as a political activity, and (4) seeking and strengthening "authenticity" without trivializing these experiences (p. 73).

Zong (2005) reflected on her own journey from growing up during the Mao Ze Dong era of China to a faculty member teaching in two research universities in the United States. Drawing on theory and research related to understanding lived experiences, the influence of teachers' stories and narratives, and the contribution of cross-cultural experiences to the development of multicultural and global educators, she examined the impact of her border crossing experiences on her identity and pedagogy. In particular, Zong discussed how she had used her experiences as assets to advance teaching from a global perspective. She argues that, given their cultural and linguistic background, knowledge of their nations of origin and diverse cultural perspectives, immigrant professors have a unique potential to become a bridge between cultures and to make significant contributions to making colleges and universities institutions of global learning.

The research by both Merryfield and Zong seems to be consistent with the results of Schuerholz-Lehr's (2007) review of empirical studies on how higher education faculty's experiences, background, and disciplinary affiliation affect their international sensitivity, intercultural competence, and world-mindedness. Although not specifically directed at teacher education faculty, Schuerholz-Lehr's review also indicates that few studies have been carried out to explore whether the level of intercultural competence and world-mindedness of individual faculty enhances his or her cultural sensitivity and the appropriateness of his or her teaching for global literacy. Clearly, more studies, particularly those based on classroom observations, are needed.

Discussion and Conclusion

Since there is no current comprehensive review of literature concerning the intersection of global education and teacher education, this chapter has presented in broad brushstrokes several key aspects related to the field. Fifteen years ago, Johnston and Ochoa (1993) commented that there was a surprising and unacceptable paucity of empirical research on global perspectives in teacher education despite years of advocacy and rich experiences of program development. Judging from the publications reviewed in this chapter, it seems that progress has been made over these years. Teacher education researchers have explored a range of topics related to the preparation of teachers for an increasingly interdependent world. The practice and research reviewed in this chapter consist of short-term and long-term international field experiences including student teaching abroad, the integration of technology in teacher education, faculty development for teaching global perspectives, and teacher education students' knowledge of and attitudes toward global education. Methodologically, the author has featured various qualitative and descriptive approaches to data collection and analysis that provide readers with an opportunity to replicate similar studies. This review also points to some gaps in the existing research that limit both our understanding of the dynamics of teaching and learning from a global perspective and the potential impact of current research on future teacher education policy and practice.

The most important theme that emerged from this review is that the research on teacher preparation for global perspectives reflects the state of teacher education in more general terms. This is to say, the majority of the studies have been conducted by teacher educators engaging in self-study by taking their own professional programs and projects as sites for inquiry, especially in professional education courses and field experiences (Adler, 2008; Grossman, 2005; Sleeter, 2008). There are also many small studies conducted in individual courses or programs because global issues are generally not well integrated into teacher preparation as a whole. These studies provide insights into specific cases and tend to be either descriptive or qualitative in nature. This approach to research has engaged teacher educators both in systematic reflection on their work and in contributing to the body of literature in the field. On the other hand, there is little to date that links these individual studies and leads to a strong empirical base that would allow readers of the research to consider broader generalizations. Merryfield's (1991) study was an exception. Studies of similar design and situated in broader teacher education contexts are needed.

Moreover, there exist very few longitudinal studies in the literature to date. Although several studies report short-term positive gains, there is little evidence about whether these gains are sustained over time. Researchers suggest that the experiences of a teacher education program or project can make a difference in the expressed attitudes of prospective teachers. Much less is known, however, about whether—and if so, how—these expressed attitudes of prospective teachers translate into practice to influence candidates' actions and effectiveness in the K-12 classroom. Most studies conducted by teacher educators ended at the conclusion of a particular course or with the conclusion of student teaching. Future research might be directed as follow-up studies into teachers' beginning years in the classroom to examine the long-term impact of preservice teacher education initiatives in global education and to address the extent to which teacher candidates could apply what had been learned to produce a positive (or negative) impact on learning for K-12 students.

The studies in the category of international field experiences were conducted in various countries and under a variety of conditions, in both English-speaking and non-English-speaking countries. Some studies were conducted in economically more developed nations such as Australia and Italy; some were in developing countries such as Kenya and Mexico. However, relatively little is known about these settings, particularly the role of mentors and supervisors or cooperative teachers who work in the field. Future studies might focus on comparing the impact of different fieldwork settings to better inform teacher education programs that are about to set up similar initiatives. Given the reality that the majority of teacher candidates cannot participate in international field experiences because of financial and other constraints, teacher educators are encouraged to explore the international resources in their community to plan similar cultural immersion experiences. Wilson's (1993a; 1993b) work has significantly contributed to the examination of the impact of such cross-cultural experiential learning opportunities in various communities.

The most significant gap in the global literature this review has pointed out is the limited research on global content. Although there are a number of studies reporting the effects of various cross-cultural experiences on the development of preservice teachers' understanding of global education, there are only a limited number of scholars examining issues of integrating global content into different teacher education programs. This is especially important at a time when there is considerable disagreement about the meaning of global education itself and conflicting views about the nature of globalization with respect to its historical and cultural origins and its economic, political, and social consequences, as well as its implications for educational policies and practices (Zong, Wilson, & Quashigah, 2008). As early as 1991, in their urgent call for incorporating a global perspective into teacher education programs, Tucker and Cistone (1991) suggested that the content of teacher education must be re-examined, especially its general and professional education requirements, in light of the global realities that are fostering new scholarship in the disciplines. Sixteen years later, Paula Cordeiro (2007), professor and dean of the School of Leadership and Education Sciences at the University of San Diego, reiterated this urgency: "The curriculum of the teacher education programs must not only explore the diversity of our nation and its changing demographics but also the many global issues that impact our daily lives." She continued, "we, the teacher educators, must ask questions such as: What knowledge should be required of our graduates in order to be productive teachers in a global age?" (p. 153).

It is my strong belief that it is time that teacher educators work much more purposefully toward developing coherent global education programs to prepare teacher candidates in global perspectives teaching so that they can effectively prepare their students to become competent and humanistic citizens of their communities, their nation, and the larger world. I also strongly believe that it is urgent that systematic research on such programs be conducted to better guide future teacher education policies and practices.

Chapter 5

Teacher Education in the United States: A Retrospective on the Global Awareness Program at Florida International University

Bárbara C. Cruz & Pedro R. Bermúdez

It is very difficult to give up our certainties—our positions, our beliefs, our explanations. These help define us; they lie at the heart of our personal identity. Yet, I believe that we will succeed in changing this world only if we can think and work together in new ways. Curiosity is what we need. We don't have to let go of what we believe, but we do need to be curious about what someone else believes. We do need to acknowledge that their way of interpreting the world might be essential to our survival.

—Margaret J. Wheatley, 2002

Of the many political and financial challenges generally encountered by global education programs, sustainability may well be the one overarching dilemma faced in the field. Often, educational program initiatives barely have an opportunity for implementation when they begin to lose momentum or support or both and fail to achieve permanency. If global educators are to realize their goals from the lessons learned from successful and unsuccessful endeavors, programs must be analyzed and results shared with the education community. This chapter addresses the achievements and decline of the Global Awareness Program (GAP) located in the College of Teacher Education, Florida International University (FIU), in Miami directed by the late Jan L. Tucker, Professor of Social Studies Education. The program grew to become a major player in advancing the goals of global education in local, state, national, and international education communities. It was identified by Merryfield (1991) as one of six exemplary programs in globalizing teacher education in the United States that "stands out as a model of what can be done if there is commitment to global perspectives" (p. 13). This chapter provides a critical look at the program's contributions in the areas of teacher education; curriculum development; global pedagogy; education conferences; travel studies abroad; and the program's leadership in implementing global education programs in Miami's public schools. We also examine the significant internal and external challenges the program encountered over a 10-year period.

Coming to this task, we are not completely unbiased. While GAP began in 1979 with the creation of global pilot schools, our direct involvement in the program began in 1986 while we were graduate students at FIU under the tutelage of Jan L. Tucker. Tucker served as our major professor on our doctoral committees. We considered him our mentor (see chapter 12). More than two decades have passed since we were directly involved in the program as we moved on to our individual career paths. Although the passage of time will not guarantee neutrality in our analysis of the program it does provide us with a critical lens for an objective review of the effectiveness and decline of the program.

The Global Awareness Program: 1979–2004

History

The GAP began in 1979 as a response to a resolution issued by the Florida State Board of Education that urged development of school programs emphasizing global perspectives. The program garnered further support at the state level two years later when the Florida Advisory Council on Global Education was created. The Florida Advisory Board, consisting of representatives from a wide cross-section of universities, schools, and educational agencies throughout Florida created the State Plan for Global Education, a definitive document on what schools and teachers should consider when introducing global perspectives in curriculum and instruction. Citing trade statistics, the growing number of immigrants, and the general international character of the state, the plan provided a cogent rationale for the inclusion of global perspectives into curriculum and instruction in public schooling. The State Plan for Global Education (1981) stated that

> global education is the process which provides students and individuals
> with the knowledge, skills and attitudes that are necessary for them to meet
> their responsibilities as citizens of their community, state, and nation in an
> increasingly interdependent and complex global society. In addition, educa-
> tion for a global perspective includes at least the following components: (1)
> the ability to conceptualize and understand the complexities of the interna-
> tional system; (2) a knowledge of world cultures and international events;
> and (3) an appreciation of the diversity and commonalities of human values
> and interests (p. 5).

The plan was approved and endorsed by then Commissioner of Education, Ralph Turlington, and the Florida State Board of Education and became one of the guiding frameworks for GAP in its revision of the teacher education program at FIU as well as in the integration of global education programs in schools. The State Plan (1981) and the Hanvey (1976) conceptual framework for global education (described below) formed the foundation for the Global Education Leadership Training Program (GELTP) under the leadership of Jan Tucker of GAP.

With over one million dollars in funding from the Danforth Foundation, additional grants from the Hitachi Foundation, the U.S.-Japan Foundation, the U.S. Department of Education soon followed. Other sources of funding included the Dade County Public Schools, the Dade-Monroe Teacher Education Center, the Florida Department of Education, the Florida International University Foundation, the Joyce-Mertz-Gilmore Foundation, the Longview Foundation, Social Issues Resources Series, and the U.S. National Commission for UNESCO (Merryfield, 1992). Supplementary support from local agencies contributed to the program's success.

Global Education Supports Major Systems Goals

The school-university partnership forged between the Director of GAP at FIU and the Bureau of Education of the Miami-Dade County Public Schools (DCPS) was informed by the district's five systems goals to ensure student academic excellence in preparedness for life as well as effective school governance (Miami-Dade County Public Schools, 1989). Systems goals are revisited every six years. Dade County is a natural environment for global education. The philosophy and aims of global education were compatible with the system's goals within the context of the multiethnic, multicultural urban school communities of the DCPS and its efforts to achieve excellence in education, including school-based management; professionalization of teaching; the Quality Incentive Program (QUIPP); teacher ownership; school-university partnership; and critical thinking. The GELTP spearheaded by Jan Tucker to implement global education programs in schools encouraged and supported the system's goals:

Goal I: Prepare students for their life's work by providing germane curricula; methods by which students can address the basic issues of their own lives and interpersonal relationship; by rewarding creativity, and by instilling motivation for excellence.

GELTP recognized Miami as a living laboratory for the future that will be utilized to prepare Miami's youth with the competence and skills to (1) participate successfully in the global economy of the twenty-first century; (2) acquire a fundamental knowledge of the world, foreign languages, historical, geographical, and cultural understanding, critical thinking skills, and computer literacy; and (3) engage in international study travel.

Goal II: *Provide schools that are effective and safe community learning centers where family life is supported through afterschool care, homeschool cooperation and broad-based community involvement in the decision-making process.*

GELTP was very effective in providing building principals with an organization focus that enables the entire school community to pull together toward a common goal. Building principals, teachers, staff, students, and parents can all share in and make a contribution to the idea of global awareness. This collaborative leadership spirit is captured in the testimony of Von Beebe, Principal of Tucker Elementary School, "The program generated intense enthusiasm for learning about our world community; this was true not only for our students but also for teachers, staff and parents. In addition professional cooperation and teamwork emerged" (cited in Kirkwood, 1991, p. 147).

Goal III: *Utilize educational resources effectively and efficiently through adequate planning, careful budgeting and systematic monitoring of all capital and noncapital expenditures, and strengthened accountability measures.*

GELTP was a cost-beneficial program of proven value and stands as one of the most effective school-university partnerships in the nation according to Gene L. Schwilck, President of the Danforth Foundation. As a collaborative effort between DCPS and FIU, with strong support from the Danforth Foundation of nearly $500,000 since 1984, the various program resources were pooled to achieve maximum learning outcomes. FIU provided nearly $400,000 of real and in-kind support with significant faculty, staff, space, material resources, and overall program leadership. DCPS contributed outstanding administrative and teacher leadership in addition to an annual budget of $68,000. Through the coordinated resources of GELTP and the Dade-Monroe Teacher Education Center, teacher-training was conducted systematically and effectively. Evaluations have been consistently positive. It was reported by administrators and teachers in two inner-city schools that global education activities improved school attendance. Students were so interested in the global education content and activities that they attended school enthusiastically. In the special dropout prevention program at one of Miami's major technical schools, global education served as the organizational focus of the entire program.

Goal IV: Staff the public schools with employees who maintain the highest standards of performance, and are adequately remunerated and recognized for their valuable contributions to society.

GELTP made a substantive contribution to the professionalization of teaching in the DCPS. Approximately 300 classroom teachers, media specialists, and administrators have undergone training in GELTP. These teachers, over a four-year period, reached an estimated 50,000 students. The training received by the teachers resulted in increased student scores on global understanding surveys. The enthusiasm of teachers and administrators led to their participation at state and national conferences describing their efforts in GELTP and thus increasing their professional skills and bringing credit to their school district. GELTP provided leadership opportunities for teachers within their schools and at the area and district levels. FIU social studies teachers were placed for field experience and for their student teaching experience with experienced global teachers in DCPS thereby reinforcing their global training at the university. Many of these globally trained FIU social studies students have been employed in DCPS and continue to make significant contributions in the classroom.

Goal V: Engender ethnic, religious, and racial harmony in our community by using the schools as an open forum in which the rich and diverse heritage of our students can be shared.

GELTP received high praise for its contributions to this important multicultural, multiethnic goal of DCPS. Frank de Varona, former Associate Superintendent, Bureau of Education, DCPS, stated that global education made a significant improvement in the attitudes of students toward each other when he served as principal at Miami Edison High School. For this reason he mandated global education in all 62 schools in the South Central Area when he became Area Superintendent, as GELTP training encouraged teachers to recognize and celebrate the diversities of local communities (see chapter 5).

Major Goals of the Global Awareness Program

The primary purpose of GAP initiated by its director and approved by the program's advisory board—comprising a diverse community of university professors, members of community organizations (such as NGOs), and school administrators—was to achieve seven major goals in order to realize the director's long-envisioned dream of globalizing the teacher education program at FIU as well as offer the DCPS, the fourth largest school district in the United States, his expertise and service to implement global education programs in its schools. The major goals of the program were (1) to globalize the teacher education program at FIU; (2) to collaborate with the DCPS District and other university entities to train in-service teachers in global education; (3) to place student interns with globally trained cooperating teachers; (4) to offer teacher-training workshops; (5) to host local, state, national, and international education conferences; (6) to implement travel studies abroad; and (7) to link GAP with leading institutions in other parts of the world.

Teacher Education

In globalizing the teacher education program at FIU, existing education courses in social studies education were modified to reflect a global perspective. GAP's director believed that teacher preparation was the first priority that needed to be addressed in developing a global dimension in teacher education and urged university teacher educators to see themselves as change agents (Tucker, 1982a). The first and foremost accomplishment was the creation and introduction of a new course, *Global Perspectives in Education*, to be required of all undergraduate and graduate students in social science education. The course featured content, strategies, and assessment methods that promoted a global perspective in education. This course is still in effect and is offered today at major state universities throughout Florida's state university system. The course examines major issues, practices, and controversies surrounding global perspectives in social studies education with the aim of having teachers become more conversant with these topics. Moreover, the course offers appropriate and effective instructional strategies to help K-12 students develop a global perspective. The undergraduate and graduate program requirements were also revised to include a substantial amount of coursework in non-Western history, geography, and cultural studies. Tucker also instituted a computer technology course requirement; he was among the first professors at FIU to do so. Wanting his students to be computer literate, he had his classes telecommunicate with Canadian counterparts discussing persistent problems and issues between the two countries.

Placement of Student Teachers

A very important concern of the teacher education program was that prospective social studies teacher candidates be placed with cooperating teachers who had received training in how to effectively integrate a global perspective into the mandated curriculum and daily instruction. Tucker's tireless efforts in working in the schools of Miami resulted in the unique feature that student teachers were exclusively placed with cooperating teachers who themselves had undergone global education training. This was an expression of Tucker's explicit intent to increase teacher professionalism and build global leadership capacity in schools. A long-term consequence of this arrangement was the multiplier effect it had; that is, by placing student teachers with globally trained cooperating teachers, the practice resulted in additional cohorts of educators who were adept at infusing global perspectives and content into their teaching practice.

Partnerships

Acting on the belief that understanding a complex and interdependent world requires multiple perspectives and areas of expertise, Tucker actively cultivated and forged working relationships with a wide array of organizations and individuals both within the university and across the Miami community. Partnering with the local school system proved to be a critical component of the program and allowed the program to flourish. This emphasis on collaboration reflected the director's belief that global education is essentially a grassroots activity that necessitates a partnership among educators, community leaders, and parents (Tucker, 1982a). With the district's support, program staff had access to school personnel, were given time on the district meeting agendas, and were able to conduct teacher-training workshops in many schools. Principals were a key component of the program since they were the primary entities involved in the selection process of the teacher participants. They were asked to identify exceptional teachers who not only showed an interest in global education but also were willing to provide leadership in training their peers in implementing global education. In addition to teachers, program participants included media specialists, counselors, school building administrators, and district-level administrators. Recognizing that the tone is crucially set by high-ranking administrators, the program enjoyed close working relationships with principals, area directors, deputy superintendents, members of the school board, and the teachers' union.

GAP was also able to draw from the expertise of members of the advisory board. Of particular note was Jack Gordon, the Florida state senator who was the founder of the Institute for Public Policy and Citizenship Studies at FIU and with whom GAP partnered for several teacher education events. Alliances with the local United Nations–United States chapter, the consulates of Japan, Germany, Mexico, and the Asia Society resulted in stimulating, up-to-date content workshops. GAP's ongoing collaboration with the Russian Ministry of Education was a mutually beneficial partnership that resulted not only in U.S. teachers learning more about Russia, but in GAP becoming "an active player in the democratization of Russian education" (Kirkwood-Tucker, 1998, p. 206). FIU's Latin American and Caribbean Center, the Department of International Relations, and faculty from Sociology and Anthropology were also involved in including additional content expertise for training Miami's teachers in globalizing their respective schools.

Teacher-Training Workshops

The Global Education Leadership Training Model (GELTP, a six-phase teacher-training and program development model, informed the approach to the integration of global education in schools. One of the critical goals of GAP was the in-service workshops for teachers of the Miami public schools, which had chosen to implement a global education program as part of the district's initiative. The model consisted of conceptualization, inventory, design, implementation, networking, and assessment (described below). These teachers were either selected by their principal or volunteered to be among the global leadership teams responsible in the effective implementation of a global perspective in grade levels at the elementary and secondary schools in the four administrative areas of the district (see chapter 6). Although GAP was housed in the social studies education department of FIU's College of Education, a unique feature of the program was its embrace of interdisciplinary studies. The program's director and staff, recognizing the expansive nature of the field and the complex and interdependent makeup of global issues, incorporated other core content areas such as mathematics, science, language arts, and vocational education. This cross-disciplinary approach made global education a broad-based school reform effort; it also resulted in a broad range of curriculum materials. The program's director recognized the importance of a holistic approach in working with schools, involving teachers, media specialists, and administrators in global education training (see chapter 6).

The teacher workshops for in-service training were especially effective because they embraced a "teachers teaching other teachers" model at each of the participating schools, as participants in GAP workshops were expected to share their newly acquired content and skills with their peers, administrators, media specialists, and others at their schools. This model, with its inherent multiplier effect, allowed for the efficient and effective transmission of knowledge and teaching strategies to many others. Workshop content included global issues, controversial topics, and regional studies. Examples of topics examined include international trade and the global economy, food and population growth, immigration and naturalization issues (particularly relevant in Miami's international community), the environment, and international human rights. Experts on Africa, Latin America and the Caribbean, Asia, Russia, the European Community, and other regions and countries conducted seminars as well. Scholars with international experiences were asked to deliver content and perspective workshops on a number of topics and regions. For example, having facilitated Caiphas Nziramasanga's study at FIU as a Fulbright Scholar from Zimbabwe, Tucker asked him to lead a series of workshops on his homeland and on Africa in general. Merry Merryfield, among the leading global scholars in the United States, was asked to speak on her Fulbright experiences in Africa, complementing Nziramasanga's work. Among the many benefits of these workshops was that the number of African American teachers participating in GAP tripled (Kirkwood-Tucker, 2008).

Teachers who participated in GAP activities repeatedly spoke of their appreciation of "being treated like professionals." Rather than conducting the training sessions during teachers' "off" time (i.e., after school or on weekends), workshops were all-day or all-week programs for which teachers were provided substitute release days. In addition to content- and pedagogy-related sessions, cultural events and performances were also scheduled, which added an aesthetic component and complemented the awareness and information gained in the trainings. Private funds facilitated offering complimentary meals and receptions for participants. Teachers were also asked to share their ideas and resources with others, cultivating a collegial environment that participants appreciated and that fostered goodwill.

Education Conferences

Partnering with the College of Arts and Sciences, regional studies institutes, and the National Council for the Social Studies (NCSS), GAP played a major role in hosting conferences and key political figures. Being on the NCSS board and later its president, Tucker, along with his Canadian counterparts, founded the International Assembly (IA), an affiliate of NCSS with the distinct purpose of extending the NCSS conferences to international scholars from abroad, as he so strongly believed that the social studies are inherently global. He collaborated with the International Assembly and his Canadian colleagues to host NCSS' first international social studies conference in Vancouver, British Columbia, in 1987. Subsequent international meetings were held in Miami, Florida, Australia, and Kenya. Tucker was also involved in bringing political luminaries such as the Russian Minister of Education Edvard Dneprov to Miami to address educators.

One major conference, a three-day intensive global education leadership workshop in 1985 at FIU, brought together district administrators, area superintendents, school principals, teachers, and media specialists to deliberate on the direction of the Global Leadership Training Program. As more and more teachers and administrators were being trained, the program sought input on future priorities and implementation strategies. One meeting in particular, convened in Key Biscayne, Florida, was pivotal in several respects. The Russian education delegates in attendance were high-level administrators from the Ministry of Education. The conference was their first exposure to the concept of global education that provided them with a possibility for a viable transition from their existing educational practice. This visit resulted in a subsequent invitation from the Russian Minister of Education to Jan Tucker and Toni Kirkwood to give a presentation on global education at the first international conference in the new Russia. This conference, "The Process of Educational Reform in Russia," was held in Sochi, Russia, in September 1991 following the failed coup against Mikhail Gorbachev (see chapters 7, 8, and 9). Consequently, a Miami delegation composed of school board members, and the president of FIU (Modesto Maidique) attended the second international conference, held in Ryazan, Russia. The gathering resulted in FIU and the Miami public schools signing a partnership agreement for faculty and student exchanges and joint research involving the Russian Ministry of Education, FIU, and the DCPS.

Travel-Study Abroad

The director of GAP strongly believed that the opportunity to travel or study abroad results in seminal experiences for teachers who wish to teach from a global perspective. Wilson (1984; 1993a; 1993b; 1997) argues persuasively on the importance of experiential learning in promoting cross-cultural understanding. The exposure to other cultures and ways of life causes self-reflection and an expansion of one's worldview. For educators these international experiences can result in tangible effects in the classroom.

In the initial stage of the program in 1981, the director arranged for a series of international exposures for teachers and administrators in the Miami schools. *Bridges to the World* was the name given to GAP's commitment to facilitate travel and study abroad opportunities for educators. The first travel-study abroad trip, in 1981, took participants to England's Cambridge University, where they were housed on campus, attended class, and visited schools. Cultural and social activities included attending a Shakespeare festival, visiting Cambridge's unique farmers' market, and interacting with locals at the neighborhood pub. Participants were required to develop curricular units reflecting perspectives from the English point of view and to integrate the unit in their classroom upon their return. Other travel study trips to Japan, China, and Russia were made available to teachers and administrators; dozens of them participated in these programs. As with the England trip, participants were required to develop lesson plans based on their experiences and share them with their cohorts. Often the program staff made copies of these lesson plans for distribution to all participants of the trip. A second important feature of the travel–study trips was their active research and study component where participants attended lectures, engaged in discussions with fellow educators, and took part in cultural events. These engaging trips resulted in a number of educational ventures once the participants returned home. A three-year (1995–1997) travel program to Japan was funded by the U.S.-Japan Foundation and enabled the 60 educators who participated to infuse content about Japan into their existing curricula in Miami's schools (see Kirkwood-Tucker, 2002).

When taken in toto, what is striking about GAP and added greatly to its success was how the goals of the program were seamlessly interrelated, one reinforcing the other and often overlapping to provide multiple support. Undergraduate students often became master's students and several undertook doctoral study, all with an emphasis on global education. Preservice teachers attended workshops alongside in-service teachers, who later served as cooperating teachers for the interns. Participating teachers benefited from the travel study abroad trips, enriching their teaching practice and resulting in new curriculum units that were shared with others. All of these interconnected goals contributed to teacher professional development and growth, further supporting program objectives.

The Global Education Leadership Training Program

The GELTP under the auspices of GAP was the brainchild of Jan Tucker and became the foundation for all future in-service training of Miami's teachers whose schools participated in the implementation of global education programs. GELTP was first field-tested at a middle school in 1979 in Miami and disseminated in selected middle schools in the Miami-Dade, Broward, Collier, and Bay Counties in the state of Florida, reaching an estimated 1,000 teachers in 40 workshops. The dissemination of global education programs in Florida's schools coincided with the global developments in the Department of Education that led to a call by the Commissioner of Education to globalize schools. The components of GELTP comprise six stages: Conceptualization, Needs Assessment, Design, Implementation, Assessment, and Networking. This segment of our chapter will address the impact of this global education leadership training model utilized at the various content and pedagogy workshops held at the university for in-service training and the implementation of global programs in schools.

Conceptualization

During the initial *Conceptualization* period, participants learned about the meaning of global education and its different conceptualizations. Because the field does not espouse one definitive definition, participants examined a number of theories and concepts. However, as Kirkwood (2001a) points out, despite multiple scholarly perspectives an analytical comparison of the major definitions of global education that exist reveal that all share the same core concepts. After reviewing different definitions and models teachers were encouraged to construct their own, reflecting their understanding and teaching reality.

Table 5.1. The Teacher Training and Program Development Model

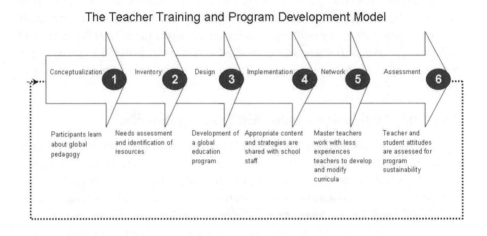

The Global Awareness Program

Teachers also examined the differences between international educa-tion and global education. It was during the conceptualization stage that teachers and school personnel were introduced to the conceptual frame-work of the Hanvey model outlined in *An Attainable Global Perspective*, a path-breaking work developed by Robert Hanvey in 1976 and chosen by the program director for its ease of application in the classroom. The seminal working model, along with the Florida State Plan for Global Education (1982) formed the foundation for teacher-training in global education (Kirkwood-Tucker, 1998). In fact, much of the global pedagogy espoused by the program staff and modeled in preservice courses and in-service workshops was derived directly from Hanvey's five-dimensional model that is briefed below.

Perspective Consciousness: the understanding that one's view of the world is not universally shared and that others have a view of the world that may be profoundly different from one's own; often, how these views were shaped escape conscious detection. Perspective maps, political cartoons from other countries, and even simple optical illusions can afford students the opportunity to see things from other vantage points.

State of the Planet Awareness: knowledge of the prevailing trends, conditions, and developments in the world and their cause-and-effect relationships. A class subscription to international newspapers or Internet news sites, music videos on global issues, and experiential activities related to world population can be used by teachers to address this dimension. Teachers often include reports of current events from around the world to expand students' limited knowledge about the world.

Cross-Cultural Awareness: an appreciation for the diversity of ideas and practices to be found in human societies. The concept of *transpection*, Hanvey's term for the ability to view one's own culture from the vantage points of others, is key for this dimension. Classic readings such as *The Body Ritual of the Nacirema* or *The Sacred Rac*, cross-cultural simulations, and role-playing exercises can all be useful in developing empathy toward others and heightening awareness of how one's own culture can be seen from others' perspectives.

Knowledge of Global Dynamics: awareness of the world as an interrelated, interconnected, and often unpredictable system and its unanticipated consequences; metaphors like "the world is a vast machine" or an "enormous organism" are useful in helping students grasp the enormousness of this concept. Simple exercises such as Global Bingo or keeping track of the international provenance of products used in a 24-hour period are helpful in underscoring our connection to the rest of the world.

Awareness of Human Choices: an understanding of the problems of choice that confront individuals, nations, and the human species as our knowledge of the global system expands and increases. Case studies of consumer boycotts (conscious decisions not to purchase certain products for political or environmental reasons) give students an opportunity to consider how increased knowledge can lead to action, but can also give them a sense of hope that personal action can result in global change.

While Hanvey's treatise did not advocate any specific pedagogy (although we think that implicitly it could be described as student-centered and constructivist), the dimensions are ideally suited to application in the classroom. GAP trainers developed a series of learning activities and strategies based on the framework that both develops global awareness and increases knowledge in regional studies (such as those on Africa, Latin America and the Caribbean, China, the European Union, Middle East, and Japan).

Needs Assessment

After conducting a needs assessment and identifying resources as part of an *Inventory*, members of a school's design team identified the strengths of their resources in supporting teaching and learning from a global perspective. School personnel also took stock of what funds were available for classroom resources, technology, and field trips. This process also revealed the gaps that would have to be filled in order to implement and sustain a balanced global education instructional program. The Hanvey model provided useful analytical lenses from which to conduct this self-assessment. Further, GAP developed a checklist that listed the following items as a "must have" in each classroom: world map; globe; class set of reusable desk maps; poster of Hanvey's five dimensions; class set of atlases; global perspective maps; world almanac; resource file maintained by teachers featuring current events, activities, and readings; global education catalogs (to earmark additional materials). Working with the school's media specialist, these materials were purchased to ensure that all classrooms were properly equipped.

Design

During this phase of the program teachers and other school personnel present at the workshop would sit in groups and *design* a global education *school plan* for their individual school, an important factor because of the implication for how schools might allocate resources and, above all, time. The school plans covered specific themes and global concepts for curriculum and instruction for schools in the entire feeder pattern and for the culminating activity at the end of the school year (see chapter 6).

Implementation

In the *Implementation* stage, content and strategies would be shared with school staff to help realize program goals outlined in their respective *school plans*. Global facilitators conducting clinical support would respond to requests to demonstrate a global infusion lesson, share materials, and respond to concerns. For content information, guest speakers would be invited from the Miami International Visitors Bureau as well as from local groups, nonprofit organizations, and cultural associations. In addition to the task of listening to concerns and addressing needs reported by other teachers at school site meetings, members of the global leadership team were invited to discuss successes of teaching from a global perspective (see chapter 7).

Assessment

In the final *Assessment* phase, teacher and student attitudes were reviewed to inform program development, maintenance, and revision. With input from the principals of participating schools, GAP developed a comprehensive measurement protocol. The evaluation procedure included (1) evaluation of university content workshops; (2) evaluation of school-site in-service training; (3) program and materials evaluation at school site; (4) pre-post tests of teacher attitudes and global knowledge gain; (5) pre-post tests of student attitudes and global knowledge gain; and (6) analysis of school plans and revealed effective results in realizing program goals.

Networking

Networking, often an afterthought or side effect of programs, comprised a critical and conscious aspect of the program. Networking was mainly designed for being connected with GAP, other teachers in other global schools, and the identification of new global materials and training possibilities. Members of the global leadership teams assisted each other in curriculum implementation, informed each other of professional development opportunities, and stayed connected with the program director and global facilitators. This support system enabled master teachers to work with less experienced teachers in developing and modifying curricula. Media specialists in particular took advantage of networking as they were the resource builders, buyers, and suppliers for their schools.

GAP also produced a newsletter that was issued twice a year. In addition to announcing global administrators of the year and global teachers of the year, it was a good source of disseminating information about new resources, program initiatives, and curriculum materials available through the program and other free or reduced-cost items. GELTP, in tandem with the GAP at the university, was instrumental for bringing a global perspective to the public schools of Miami. While it was phased out as part of a larger district restructuring, its core mission and goals are still palpable in the district's curriculum and teacher-training efforts.

Challenges to Global Education

Though the program had enormous success during its initial years with teachers, district-level supervisors in the DCPS, at the university level, and at the state, national, and international level, it failed to achieve permanency. As both a grassroots movement and curricular reform movement, GAP's long-term sustainability was hampered by a variety of powerful forces at the national, state, and local levels. Until the mid-1980s, global education in the country went unchallenged (Schukar, 1993), resulting in calls for global education of future generations. For example, the 1981 report issued by the National Task Force on Education and the World View declared an "urgent need" to reevaluate the preparation of teachers and ensure opportunities for the development of global perspectives (p. 3). Similarly, the Study Commission on Global Education (1987) published a report titled *The United States Prepares for Its Future: Global Perspectives in Education* recommending, among other things, changes in curriculum offerings and teacher education. However, by the mid-1980s, the global education movement began receiving criticism on the national level and found itself at the center of political, curricular, and pedagogical controversy. There were three major attacks on global education programs in the country (see chapter 1).

In addition to attacks at the national level, global educators in Florida were feeling the backlash at the state level as well. Although the state's education commissioner and board strongly supported global initiatives in 1979 and 1984 and passed Florida Statutes 229.6055 and 229.6054 (both encouraging international education programs), by the early 1990s, hostility toward international projects began to be felt. The antiglobal sentiments experienced at the national level, which were having negative impact on federal grants and foundation funding, were also palpable at the state level. As the political climate changed and global education came under attack, the Florida legislature removed both international education statutes (State of Florida, 2000), and funding from the state became increasingly difficult to obtain. Ironically, neither the GAP at FIU nor the implementation of global perspectives in curriculum and instruction in the Miami Public Schools came under attack. While it is difficult to determine exactly why GAP was spared the virulent criticism directed at other programs, we believe that the emphasis on materials that included a multiplicity of perspectives and the broad-base support the program enjoyed shielded it from assault.

Despite the national scene and the funding challenges, the program carried on by restructuring and attaining additional support from the DCPS (Merryfield, 1992) and continued the programs in Miami's schools. However, in a large-scale restructuring effort the DCPS closed the doors of the International Global Education Program in 1994 although global education objectives were integrated for each course in the K-12 social studies curriculum. At about the same time, Tucker appointed an assistant director to the program, Mohammed K. Farouk, a professor of social studies education at FIU. Tucker's unexpected death in 1997 left an immediate leadership void. One school administrator commented to Merryfield (1992) that GAP "could not have happened if it were not for Jan" (p. 36). Farouk assumed the duty of GAP's director and continues to oversee the program with limited support.

Another challenge to GAP was an internal one common to other global education programs. Because all preservice teachers in the social studies education program were required to take courses in global perspectives and infuse curricula and their teaching with global pedagogy, there were inevitable complaints from a minority of students that the global education focus was exhortatory. Some teachers also objected to the emphasis on tolerance for other cultures at the expense of addressing racism and prejudice in the United States (Merryfield, 1992).

In many respects, the challenges GAP experienced in the 1980s and 1990s merely reflected the growing conservative trend in American education that was being felt everywhere. As Hazel Greenberg (2008) pointed out in an interview, "The national context is vital for the success of global education. If the national consensus sees the U.S. in a parochial manner, schools and districts (and school boards) will not encourage learning and understanding about the rest of the world."

The national context would again come into play in 2001 in the aftermath of the terrorist attacks of September 11. While the terrorist attacks of September 11, 2001, could have had a galvanizing effect on global education, underscoring its vital necessity in schools, they seemed to have had the opposite effect. The questions raised by the event and their implications for citizens were quickly overrun by the need to punish the perpetrators. In the months that followed, attempts to hold teach-ins at colleges and universities around the nation met with a conservative backlash reminiscent of the earlier controversy, which accused individuals who questioned the motives and effects of past policies as being unpatriotic and un-American. As social studies teachers, we were trained to seize the teachable moment and push for deeper understanding. Clearly, the potential was there but, as the nation hunkered down for war—first in Afghanistan and later in Iraq—we failed to seize the moment.

By the time the No Child Left Behind (NCLB) Act (Public Law 107–110) was signed into law by President Bush on January 8, 2002, the prospects for a resurgence of global education grew even dimmer. The NCLB Act had four key elements: Accountability, Freedom, Research-Based Methods, and Choice. The most significant changes with respect to schools came from accountability. This system of public accountability gave rise to a high-stakes testing environment with a focus on test preparation and on instructional approaches and materials designed to increase test scores. When combined with B. Tye (2000) analysis of the "deep structure" of schooling in America, the prevailing sets of assumptions and patterns of behavior that appear to be at odds with bringing about substantive change in the way schools work, the prospects for global education to be once again a major force in school change appear bleak.

Lessons Learned

Ultimately, we come to this retrospective study not only as participant-observers who were enthusiastic supporters of a program but also as realistic analysts who wish to learn from the experience and determine how the lessons learned (both positive and negative) can inform future efforts. A rather obvious realization of our experiences as global educators is that *global education is complex, controversial, and vulnerable to external challenges*. The attacks on global education programs in selected states were a local manifestation of a much broader movement that sought to understand the nature of a rapidly changing, interdependent, and complex world. The changes associated with globalization raised questions about the kind of education that would help students understand the world both as American citizens and as global citizens. It drew on a multidisciplinary approach because it assumed that no one discipline would be able to fully explain such complex, dynamic, and interrelated forces.

Although instructional materials were developed to supplement the existing curricula as well as stand-alone elective courses, it was clear that the development of effective global approaches to teaching and learning would be highly dependent on the local efforts of teachers. This required time, support, and resources both at the state, district, and school level. GAP ensured that by arranging for substitute release days, teachers were provided with extended time to think, analyze, and produce lessons and units that explicitly infused global perspectives. Thus, another important lesson learned was that *infusing global perspectives into existing curricula requires time and high levels of teacher commitment and collaboration.* Today the time devoted to teacher collaboration is almost exclusively focused on diagnosing test data and adjusting instruction to increase test scores. In this context, few opportunities are left for teachers to work and learn together to design instructional approaches that effectively infuse global perspectives into the existing curriculum. Moreover, the current fiscal realities in Florida suggest that funding to support this kind of teacher collaboration is likely to be even more difficult in the coming years.

We know that *infusion curriculum approaches work best.* Much has been written about the cramped curriculum and teachers as curriculum decision-makers (see e.g., Thornton, 2005; Merryfield, 2007). Clearly, if teachers feel that a particular topic, issue, or approach is merely an "add on" to the already-crowded instructional day, they are unlikely to teach it. If, on the other hand, teachers are afforded strategies and encouragement to design practices that effectively infuse global content and skills into the mandated curriculum, there is a better likelihood they will integrate global perspectives into their courses.

Just as college courses cannot be solely dependent on one instructor if they are to become a standard offering, programs cannot be exclusively reliant on any one individual. Upon Tucker's death, the void in leadership was palpable, and the effects on the program were immediate. *Leadership for sustainability* means developing a cadre of individuals who work in concert and can guide the program on new or different paths as times change. In order for a global education program to achieve sustainability in schools these individuals must be embedded in the schools and function as "tempered radicals" — conscious change agents who are in it for the long haul and whose work inspires change as well as people in "big and small ways every day" (Meyerson, 2003).

Unlike the attacks at the national level, the GAP was able to avoid criticism regarding the political orientation or intent of curricular materials. Ensuring that *balanced curricular materials* are developed and used in teacher-training and in classrooms is just good practice. GAP's director searched tirelessly for a wide variety of resources that reflected the entire political spectrum and that examined a given issue from many different perspectives, what Merryfield (2007) calls "contrapuntal voices." While this generated healthy debate and discussion, it also modeled the belief that multiple viewpoints must be studied in order to fully understand a given topic or event. It also served as a reminder that thoughtful design and implementation of high quality, balanced, global instruction requires that schools have structures in place that support teachers as innovators rather than mere implementers of other people's ideas.

In Miami-Dade County as in many other parts of the world "local" issues are often global in nature. The relative fairness of the "wet foot/dry foot policy" with respect to Cuban and Haitian refugees, drug smuggling, the effects of sea level rise for small Caribbean nations, or the recent tensions between Venezuela, Ecuador, and Colombia, represent issues of vital importance to the local community that will spill over into classroom discussions. To properly address these complex and highly controversial issues, teachers need the time, support, and resources that will turn these concerns into powerful, rigorous, and relevant learning experiences for students.

Effecting School Reform through Global Education

The complex and interdisciplinary makeup of the issues that define both the challenges and opportunities of contemporary human existence requires that global education become a broad-based school reform effort. Global educators, in turn, will have to embrace the role of change agents. Fullan (2000) points out that in the complex process of school reform, "there is no magic bullet...and that, in fact, each group must build its own model and develop local ownership through its own process" (p. 582). Fullan calls our attention to the fact that any attempt to change the way adults work in schools has to start with an understanding of and appreciation for the context where the proposed change is to take place — for most of us, the primary context for change will be the school.

One way to understand this context is to view it as the interplay of a set of variables that manifest themselves along two dimensions of complexity (see figure 5.2). Some variables operate vertically and are visible in the bureaucratic command and control structures that generate a series of state and local mandates and accountability measures implemented at the school level. Currently, these mandates are heavily influenced by the national educational agenda driven by the NCLB Act. As a result, powerful accountability measures are being channeled vertically, that is, national-state-district-school-classroom, as a result of NCLB. The effects of these forces on principals, teachers, students, and parents are particularly visible in, but not exclusive to, low-performing schools. These accountability pressures emphasize compliance with state and district curriculum mandates specifically designed to raise test scores. As we have seen, these mandates have left little time and resources for the kind of interdisciplinary curriculum design work that would be necessary to implement and sustain teaching from a global perspective.

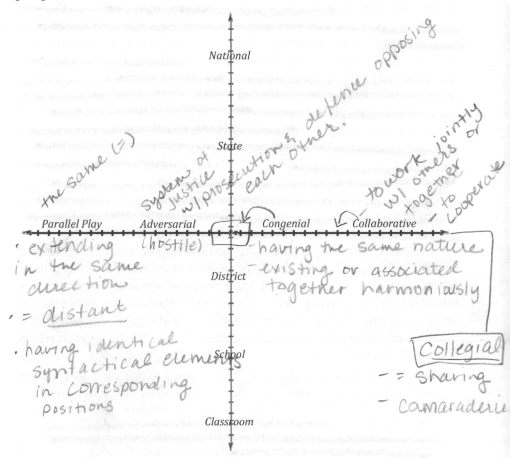

handwritten annotations:

opposing

system of justice w/ prosecution & defence. each other.

to work jointly w/ others or together to cooperate

the same (✓)

• extending in the same direction

(hostile)

having the same nature - existing or associated together harmoniously

• = distant

• having identical syntactical elements in corresponding positions

Collegial

-= sharing

- camaraderie

Table 5.2. Vertical and Horizontal Complexity

The figure above attempts to illustrate two interrelated levels of complexity that affect the prospects for school change. Vertical complexity involves factors associated with the command and control functions of hierarchical organizations that generate mandates and result in compliance-driven behaviors. Horizontal complexity describes the nature of interpersonal and professional relationships as affected by the prevailing district and school cultures. The interplay of these forces and the tendency for them to operate at cross purposes create formidable barriers to deep change in schools.

The second group of variables operates on the horizontal dimension of complexity and is visible in the existing culture of a school, what Barth (2002) has termed, "the way we do things around here" and the way school culture influences human social interactions and people's disposition to change. If the existing culture is "toxic," the challenge of transforming that culture is formidable. Horizontal complexity is characterized by patterns of interpersonal relationships influenced by the "norms, attitudes, beliefs, behaviors, values, ceremonies, traditions, and myths that are deeply ingrained in the very core of the organization." It's important to realize from the get-go that this is a "historically transmitted pattern of meaning that wields astonishing power in shaping what people think and how they act" (p. 212). Thus, the challenge of implementing and sustaining a global agenda in schools lies in understanding that, at any given time, powerful vertical and horizontal forces influence what, why, and how a particular reform initiative is implemented and how it is perceived and understood by the individuals who work there.

In Miami-Dade County the GAP and the implementation of a global education curriculum will have to navigate and contend with this powerful interplay of complex vertical and horizontal forces that maintain the status quo. Vertical complexity will no doubt continue to shape the life and change prospects in schools; however, global educators interested in a sustainable school-based model will have to take on the issue of school culture. As Fullan explains,

> We're talking about a change in the culture of schools and a change in the culture of teaching. We know that when we think about change we have to get to ownership, participation, and a sense of meaning on the part of the majority of teachers. You can't get ownership through technical means; you have to get it through interaction, through developing people, through attention to what students are learning (Fullan in Sparks, 2003, p. 58).

This suggests that global educators will have to pay much more attention to how change happens in schools and how teaching from a global perspective will enhance student learning and achievement—especially in the current regime of test score–driven accountability. Our own experiences with the GAP teach us that most of the initial change that brought global education into the DCPS was externally driven—from the university to the district and schools. A cadre of globally trained teachers emerged, but these teachers tended to see themselves more as having expertise in teaching from a global perspective than as change agents. We were out to change the curriculum, not necessarily to change the way adults worked in schools—despite the fact that the two are inextricably linked in a web of both vertical and horizontal complexity.

Final Thoughts

The revitalization of the GAP and the DCPS will continue to face formidable challenges. If, as some argue (Kennedy, 1987; Schell, 2003; Khanna, 2008), we are witnessing a decline in American hegemony, global education as a school reform movement may become even more difficult and vulnerable to external attacks. Given the complexity and rapidly changing nature of world events, teaching from a global perspective will continue to be a generative process dependant on extensive content knowledge, substantive collaboration across multiple content areas, and subject to peer review to assure balance, rigor, and relevance.

We believe that despite the many challenges facing global educators there are opportunities that bode well for the future of global education in schools. These opportunities exist in the need to continue to provide students with a reality-based education—one that enables them to understand the world as it exists, neither the world of the past nor the world that we wish it should be. This world will continue to be shaped by powerful forces resulting from the movement of goods, ideas, and people across national borders both in virtual and real terms. Interdependence among nations will continue to be a fact of life that will affect people in a myriad of ways and will make globalization critically relevant to the lives of individuals, regions, and nations of the world.

Heidi Hursh (2008), former director of the Center for Teaching International Relations (CTIR) at the University of Denver was, along with several other programs in the mid-1980s, charged with advancing leftist propaganda, radical political change, and student activism. In an interview she offers the following perspective, arguing that global education is now better understood by the general public and too much a part of mainstream education in the United States for it to come under similar attack again:

> The economic and political changes in the past 20 years have brought support from many other constituencies, some quite conservative. There are major global issues that affect each of the core subjects in our curriculum, and mainstream organizations such as the National Geographic have launched major initiatives for global education. As individuals, we are still somewhat vulnerable, but if we teach our students to question, if we use an inquiry model for instruction, and if we incorporate a broad spectrum of

points of view in our materials we should be able to deal with any criticisms.

Opportunities for global education can also be found in a growing consensus on the part of a variety of educational and business organizations on the need to build partnerships to support the kind of education that will enable students "to successfully face rigorous higher education coursework, career challenges and a globally competitive workforce" (Partnership for 21st Century Skills, 2008). Formed in 2002 by the U.S. Department of Education and a group of private business firms and organizations including the National Education Association, the Partnership for 21st Century Skills includes "global awareness" as one of their key components. Innovative global education programs in schools that are able to collaboratively and successfully design inquiry-based, project-driven, cross-disciplinary learning experiences for students will contribute significantly to this effort.

Resurgence of Global Education

Despite the ongoing financial stressors and the death of its founder, the GAP continues to have a significant presence at FIU. It offers a variety of undergraduate and graduate courses designed to provide social studies teachers with a global perspective as a platform from which to develop instructional approaches and materials that will develop a global perspective for students. In fact, the DCPS may be witnessing something of a resurgence since the district's superintendent, Dr. Rudy Crew, has identified global education as a district priority. Inspired by the work of Thomas L. Friedman (2005) in *The World Is Flat*, Crew (2008) reminds us that "poverty and limited language skills conspire against many of our students; as educators and as a community we have to lean hard against the trends of the flat world for our students to make progress in being prepared to flourish in that world." Crew recognizes that Miami-Dade County's schools must transform to a flat world. The district is also currently updating its curriculum with special attention to global education instructional objectives.

A third bright spot in the Miami context is the establishment of the Cambridge Global Studies Academy at G. Holmes Braddock Senior High School, one of the largest high schools in Miami. Led by one of the leading global teacher educators in Miami, Joseph I. Lamas, a protégé of Jan L. Tucker, the academy offers a rigorous, college-preparatory curriculum for high school students in global studies. The core values of the academy include global citizenship, personal integrity, individual leadership, passionate learning, defending human rights, valuing our common humanity, and compassion and altruism. Starting in the ninth grade and continuing through the twelfth grade, the program is affiliated with the International Center of the University of Cambridge, England. Perhaps the greatest opportunity for global education to develop and expand may lie in students themselves. In an interview with Heidi Hursh (2008) she responds to a question about the future of global education:

> Students today are taking the initiative to stretch their minds and their plans for the future in ways that we barely imagined in the 1960s. They have become actively involved in initiatives such as loaning money to micro-business projects in other countries, raising money for cyclone victims in South Asia, participating in landmine clearing programs, and teaching in rural schools in China. Their opportunities for travel have expanded and, with that, their visions of a variety of international careers. Global education is no longer just a part of social studies—it can be a foundation for their future lives.

More than three decades ago, Robert G. Hanvey wrote a seminal piece on global education. He defined a global perspective and argued that schools had a special responsibility to help all students attain a global perspective. For us, it was a revelation that provided a cogent and systematic framework for thinking about how to organize and develop instruction for global understanding. This framework played a central role in the work of the GAP. It suggests that forward-thinking ideas and vision can have a lasting impact in the education of future generations. Thirty years later, it reminds us of the good work of the past and it beckons us to the difficult work that is still to be done.

Tales from the Field: Possibilities and Processes Leading to Global Education Reform in the Miami-Dade County Public Schools

Toni Fuss Kirkwood-Tucker

I dedicate this chapter to the visionary administrators, school-site principals and assistant principals of the Greater Miami Public Schools and the extraordinary leadership of Frank de Varona.

This chapter seeks to capture a unique and momentous period in the life of the fourth largest school district in the United States between 1984 and 1994, the Miami-Dade County Public Schools.[1] I have decided to tell the tale as a firsthand account from the field, a tale often ignored yet critical to the processes of establishing democratic learning communities.

The story traces the historical development of the possibilities and processes that transformed almost three-fourths of Miami's public schools into global classrooms over a ten-year period. The partnership forged between the Bureau of Education of the Miami-Dade County Public Schools and the Global Awareness Program of Florida International University achieved national recognition as one of the leading school-university collaborations in global education in the United States (Merryfield, 1992; O'Neil, 1989). The planning, design, and integration of global programs were undertaken with an eye toward potential replication in high school feeder-pattern learning communities in Florida and the nation as the program serves as an exemplar for the development of global education for school districts in the United States and other nations.

My first-hand experiences in the field in our country's fourth largest school system are organized into two consecutive chapters. Chapter 6 focuses on the possibilities and processes leading to global education reform in the Miami-Dade County Public Schools over a ten-year period. Chapter 7 embraces the integration of a global perspective into curriculum and instruction in the Greater Miami's public schools over a ten-year period. This chapter is organized into seven major topics: (1) the Miami-

Dade County Public Schools in context and the district's organizational structure; (2) the school district–university partnership between the Miami-Dade County Public Schools and Florida International University; (3) global education as a systems objective; (4) the selection of global facilitators to provide training in global education and clinical support in schools; (5) the incremental selection of schools to be globalized; (6) identification and selection of school leadership teams by school-site administrators; and (7) my reflections on education reform in global education in the Greater Miami public schools and the golden research opportunities in the areas of school improvement through program implementation and administrative leadership opportunities.

Though I was the principal global facilitator in the district, training teachers, media specialists, and administrators to integrate a global perspective into curriculum and instruction, I am confident that I can tell this story from the field objectively. It is authenticated by Frank de Varona, school-site principal, area director, area superintendent, and associate superintendent of the Miami-Dade County Public Schools, who played a critical role in the ten-year global education reform in the Greater Miami public schools.

The Miami-Dade County Public Schools in Context

Metropolitan Miami is among the most diverse urban communities in the United States. It is a microcosm of the world, mirroring its multiethnic, multilingual, and multi-socio-economic communities. It is a vibrant, dynamic blend of the domestic and international, of retrenchment and change, of the past, present, and future. This vibrant megalopolis and its 27 municipalities are the home of almost 2.5 million residents.

Miami's tropical climate and eternal sunshine have attracted immigrants from every continent. Miami-Dade County ranks highest among the 776 counties in the U.S. with a 50.3% foreign-born population. The ten primary spoken languages other than English are Arabic, Chinese, Creole, French, Hebrew, Portuguese, Russian, Spanish, Urdu, and Vietnamese. Located at the crossroads of the Americas, it is not surprising that 61.5% of Miami's residents are of Hispanic origin. The remaining population consists of 18.4% African American, 18.1% non-Hispanic European American; the remainder is Asian, Indian and Pacific Islanders. The once-dominant Anglo-Saxon Protestant population has shrunk, affected by a consistent pattern of out-migration and a pattern of increasing in-migration of foreign peoples and their families (Metropolitan Miami Report, 2005). At the time of this study beginning in 1984, 20% of all business activities in the county were connected to the international economy (Birger, 1988), and the Miami-Dade County Public Schools boasted 274 schools, 12,500 teachers, 230,000 students of 122 nationalities (64,000 students were foreign born). At the conclusion of this study in 1994, the number of schools had increased to 353, 18,758 teachers, and the student population to almost 400,000, of whom 71,000 students were foreign born. Today, the school district has expanded to 392 schools and 22,393 teachers; due to out-migration there has been a decrease in the total number of students to 347,774 but an increase in the number of foreign-born students to 76,387 who speak a primary language other than English (Miami-Dade County Public Schools Statistical Highlights, 1984; 1994; 2008).

Table 6.1. The Miami-Dade County Public Schools Administrative Areas

North Area					
High School #1	High School #2	High School #3	High School #4	High School #5	High School #6

North Center Area					
High School #1	High School #2	High School #3	High School #4	High School #5	High School #6

South Central Area					
High School #1	High School #2	High School #3	High School #4	High School #5	High School #6

South Area					
High School #1	High School #2	High School #3	High School #4	High School #5	High School #6

On the average, there are six high schools in one administrative area. Each high school represents a typical feeder pattern of a designated number of middle and elementary schools.

District Organizational Structure

At the time of the global education reform the Miami-Dade County Public School district was organized into four administrative entities: the North Area (Region I), North Central Area (Region II); South Central Area (Region III); and South Area (Region IV). [2]

These four administrative areas included 24 senior high schools and their families of feeder schools, each area administering six senior high schools and their respective middle and elementary schools. Each senior high school was organized into a feeder-pattern configuration consisting of a specific number of middle schools and elementary schools headed by a lead principal who was also principal of one of the elementary or secondary schools. Each feeder pattern was, and still is, under the jurisdiction of an area director who supervises lead principals and building-level principals in the feeder-pattern configuration. The area directors report directly to the area superintendent who in turn reports to the District Associate Superintendent of Curriculum and Instruction or Deputy Superintendent for School Operations responsible to the Superintendent of Schools and School Board. The feeder-pattern configuration played a significant role in the implementation of global education programs during its ten-year duration, as it provided the ideal administrative structure for curricular reform.

Table 6.2. The Miami-Dade County Public Schools Typical Feeder Pattern Configuration

Typically, three elementary schools feed into one middle school, and three middle schools feed into a senior high school.

The primary purpose of a feeder-pattern configuration is to assure (1) effective management of schools within the family of feeder schools configurations, (2) uniformity of curriculum and instruction, (3) continuity of leadership, and (4) oversight and accountability. If an area superintendent introduces curricular reform, all high schools and their feeder schools within the administrative area are directly affected. And if an area director of a given high school feeder configuration proposes curricular reform, all schools belonging to the configuration are directly affected. Thus, the implementation of global education reform was driven by administrative decisions initiated either by school-site principals, area directors, or area superintendents.

The feeder-pattern concept has a powerful effect on the creation of an interdisciplinary global curriculum infusion program across grade levels. Granted that some students will not attend school in any one feeder pattern for the entire 12 years of schooling, many students do. From the administrative point of view, this longitudinal aspect is an incentive to consider long-term organization and planning. Building administrators frame their vision for students from the entering kindergarteners to graduating seniors. The specific environmental and demographic contexts of the feeder-pattern schools shape the building principals and assistant principals as they develop their mission statements, educational aims, objectives, curricular scope and sequence, and expectations for student learning outcomes. Teachers are able to meet their peers from sibling schools as they attend professional development workshops. The feeder-pattern configuration also provides a natural environment for friendly competition among schools, especially at the elementary levels. Most important, in light of the fact that school-site administrators in urban school districts are frequently shifted to other schools, the feeder-pattern concept provides greater administrative and instructional continuity for education reform as it is possible to rely on a critical mass of experienced administrators from year to year.

School District–University Partnership

This section describes a school district and a university partnered for the purpose of curricular reform in global education; global education as systems goals; the nature of the partnership, and the selection of globally trained facilitators assisting in teacher training and implementation of global programs in schools.

Numerous research scholars of school–university partnerships have concluded that such collaborative efforts work effectively when the partnerships are thoughtfully designed for success and include significant benefits for all participants, from preservice teachers to university faculty, and benefits for the schools themselves ranging from the effectiveness of their teachers in the classroom to becoming an increased part of the educational community (Castle, Fox & Souder 2006; Crocco, Faithfull & Schwartz 2003; Fang & Ashley 2004). In this study, the partnership was forged between the Bureau of Education of the Miami-Dade County Public Schools and the Global Awareness Program at Florida International University under the leadership of Jan Tucker, professor of social studies education and director of the Global Awareness Program supported by the Danforth Foundation. Its explicit purpose was to introduce education reform by implementing global education programs in the Miami-Dade County Public Schools. Essex (2001) points to the significance of school–university partnerships that

> given the unique challenges faced by public schools and colleges of education today, it is essential that they join forces in forming meaningful partnerships as one means of enhancing and improving instructional effectiveness and learning outcomes for students (p. 734).

The very essence of this program was to improve student achievement through global education. The Global Education Leadership Training Program (GELTP), a teacher training and program development model developed and spearheaded by Tucker under the umbrella of the Global Awareness Program, served as the foundation for teacher training and program development over the ten-year program duration in a variety of settings with relatively little modification (see chapter 5). After the global education program's official conclusion and the end of the school–university partnership in 1994, many of the Greater Miami schools continued their already well-established programs which had effectively led to desirable curricular independence and continuity of program (Warren & Peel, 2005).

Global Education as Systems Goal

On the basis of field tests of the Global Education Leadership Training Program model in selected Florida middle schools, Jan Tucker had worked tirelessly to convince Miami's administration of the urgency of preparing students for an increasingly interdependent and rapidly changing world. He was overjoyed when in 1981 the Miami-Dade County School Board included global education reform in two of its major systems goals. The first of these goals was to engender ethnic, religious, and racial harmony in the community by using the schools as an open forum in which the rich, diverse heritage of their students could be shared. The second was to prepare students for their life's work by providing germane curricula using methods by which students could address the basic issues of their own lives and interpersonal relationships and by rewarding creativity and instilling motivation for excellence. The philosophy and aims of global education were highly compatible with these goals, especially in the context of the multi-ethnic multicultural urban school communities of Greater Miami's public schools.

Subsequently the implementation of global education programs became a major objective of the performance appraisals of the area superintendents, area directors, and building principals. Frank de Varona (1987), who rapidly climbed the ladder of success from classroom teacher, school-site principal, area director, and area superintendent to associate superintendent in the district, stated that "global education offers tremendous opportunities to a community like Miami" (p. 3). Some senior high school principals and their counterparts in their feeder schools chose global education for the purpose of meeting their major objectives of the Quality Instruction Incentive Program (QUIIP), a merit school program instituted by the district to provide individual schools with choices for new initiatives to improve student academic performance, a desirable incentive program that offered teachers in the winning schools a $3,000 bonus. With the systems goals as their objectives, area administrators, school-site principals, teachers, and media specialists ventured into robust global education reform.

Selection of Global Facilitators

The Global Awareness Program at Florida International University assumed responsibility for teacher training in university-based content workshops, global pedagogy workshops, symposia and conferences (see chapter 5). The school district provided in-kind services, such as the release of two classroom teachers who were housed at the university and worked under the leadership of Jan Tucker. Burton and Greher (2007) call our attention to the important role of school–university partnerships as "a fundamental link to strengthen teacher education reform. The formation of new partnerships in which academic faculty and in-service teachers assume expanded roles holds promise as a primary avenue toward developing content and contextual expertise of teachers and strengthening pre K-12 students' learning" (p. 1).

My colleague Charlotte Christensen and I were the two classroom teachers assigned to the program, both of us Master's Degree graduates from Florida International University under the tutelage of Jan Tucker. Barbara and Ken Tye (1992) define the tasks of the global educator as helping school leaders see that their vision reflects the changing nature of the world and supporting them in every way as they work to bring a global perspective to the curriculum of the school. Our responsibilities were to (1) attend area and school-site administrative meetings; (2) respond to area directors, lead principals, and school-site principals who requested integration of global programs in individual schools and feeder pattern schools, (3) plan content workshops and global pedagogy training; (4) conduct in-service workshops at the university and school sites; (5) provide clinical assistance to schools; and (6) respond to requests and concerns from district administrators, the district's social studies supervisor, school-site principals, and teachers.

Initially each of us was assigned to one administrative area in the North Central and South Central areas (see Table 6.1). The rapid increase in requests for assistance in implementing global programs in schools from the other two administrative areas in the North Area and South Area of the district began to overwhelm us and, to our consternation, we were soon no longer able to meet the increasing demand for teacher training and clinical support. In response, in 1988 the district established the International Global Education Program under the direction of the social studies supervisor of the Dade County Public Schools and released two additional teachers from the classroom. All four of us were placed in a newly created district office in downtown Miami, where we continued to work closely with the Global Awareness Program at Florida International University on the design, planning, and implementation of content workshops, teacher training, and education conferences.

I remained in that position until promoted to social studies coordinator for the South Central Area and later to the Coordinator of the International Global Education Program, where I continued as the principal teacher trainer in the field.

Incremental Selection of Schools to be Globalized

In this section I address both the selection of schools for field testing the newly created Global Education Leadership Training Program model under the umbrella of the Global Awareness Program, Florida International University, and the subsequent incremental selection of schools to be globalized in the Greater Miami public schools over a ten-year period.

As trainers of teachers in global education, we were conscious of the advice of scholars such as Fullan (2000) who warned that any attempt to change the way adults work in schools has to start with an understanding of and appreciation for the context in which the proposed change is to take place. He cautions that "each group must build its own model and develop local ownership through its own process" (p. 582, cited in chapter 5). Tye and Tye (1992) suggested to interventionists that "if we are interested in real school improvement, not just cosmetic changes, a major focus of the outside agency is to provide assistance to school-sites, particularly the principal, clarifying the vision and meaning for their school, as such vision cannot be imposed from the outside" (p. 190).

Criteria for selection of a given high school and its feeder schools in the fourth largest school district in the country depended on four essential elements: (1) cooperation of area directors, building principals, and school faculty; (2) commitment to the philosophy and aims of global education; (3) geographic location of school sites (inner-city versus suburban); and (4) demographic representation of the student population. The fourth criterion weighed heavily in the selection process, as the Miami-Dade County Public Schools' inner-city schools struggled with societal issues such as students living in poverty, students as members of unemployed or underemployed families, high dropout rates, and low-performance schools.

Selection of Pilot School Sites

The implementation of global education programs in the Miami-Dade County Public Schools began in 1979 with field testing of the Global Education Leadership Training model over a three-year period in a single pilot middle school whose administrators and teachers felt strongly the salience of global education in preparing students for a diverse world. The program was first introduced in the social studies classes and integrated incrementally into all subject areas. By the third year of the pilot program, students across all grade levels and subject areas were taught from a global perspective. John Doyle, (2008) among the first globally trained teachers at this school, commented recently that the program had become "institutionalized after three years despite the fact that we experienced some low tides with changes in leadership. Teaching globally became second nature to us."

The following section sketches the historical development of global education programs in three chronological phases from their official beginnings in 1984 to their decline in 1994.

Phase I: 1984–1987

During Phase I, as the pilot phase of systematic program integration at a feeder-pattern level, area administrators and principals of the district's North Central and South Central decided to integrate a comprehensive global program into three of their most ethnically diverse high schools and their associated families of feeder schools (see Table 6.2). From these a total of 43 elementary and secondary teachers were recommended by their principals to form the global leadership teams (Tucker, 1985). Two of the high schools were characterized by predominantly Hispanic student populations of 62% and 87%, respectively, and the third high school by 84% African American students. In these three schools the white student populations had decreased to 19%, 3%, and 4%, respectively. Minority groups of Hispanic and African American students had become majorities in these schools, a pattern that continued in the Greater Miami schools with growing in-migration of foreign students and increasing out-migration of the white European American population.

North Central Area. The school in the North Central area in which African American students predominated was chosen in part because it had been the scene of frequent racial confrontations between them and the growing number of Haitian immigrant students. The suicide of a Haitian student who had concealed his national identity from his native-born peers sent shock waves through the district and its Cuban-born principal, Frank de Varona. Cognizant of the importance of retaining inner-city students in schools, he reorganized the schedule and the entire curriculum for incoming ninth-graders, creating "a school within a school," which he housed on the third floor of the building. He required all ninth-graders to take "global studies," a newly developed secondary course approved by the Florida Department of Education. This innovative arrangement lasted from 1979 to 1984, when he was promoted to Director of the South Central Area of the district. In 2008, looking back at his tenure as principal, de Varona reflected, "Global education emphasizes respect for equality and diversity of all human beings, which is critical for our students to understand in reducing the tension in our school. The idea was to open the minds of students that other groups are also making a contribution to our nation."

During the second and third years of Phase I, two additional high schools, two middle schools, and 25 elementary schools in the North Central Area undertook global education reform. My co-worker Charlotte Christensen was the global facilitator primarily responsible for serving the North Central Area; I worked in the South Central Area under the direction of Frank de Varona, by then promoted to area director.

South Central Area. It was in the South Central area where de Varona initiated the pilot program in the 87% Hispanic high school (mentioned above) and its feeder pattern schools. Located in that section of Miami called "Little Havana" for its large mostly Cuban population, it was the first high school in Miami, built in 1906, the building materials for its Norman-Sicilian architecture imported from Spain and Portugal. Surrounded by lush courtyards and fountains, it is the pride of the community. Cooperative leadership among its committed teachers carried over to the Homecoming Parade with bands playing international anthems, students dressed in native garments of the 23 nations represented in their school, and the department of home economics cooking international cuisine (Kirkwood, 1990). The high school represents a prototype of interdisciplinary integration of curriculum and instruction across grade levels. Its Spanish-born principal Diego Garcia (1990) observed, "The best single result of global education is the unifying effect on our students" (p. 1).

De Varona mandated implementation of global education in all schools in the South Central area as part of principals' performance appraisals, but already "almost all principals welcomed the idea and were enthusiastic and motivated to support global and multi-ethnic education in their schools" (de Varona, 2008). As area director he introduced me to every school-site principal in his area, greatly easing my interventions—and letting me sample some of the Cuban food prepared for his visit! By the third year of Phase I, all 62 schools in the South Central Area had implemented global education in curriculum and instruction and a total of 124 teachers, 62 media specialists, and administrators had been trained. Unexpected side-effects were the establishment in 1987 of the district's first elementary magnet school focusing on intensive language acquisition, followed by a magnet middle school emphasizing international studies and an international baccalaureate (IB) senior high school.

Phase II: 1987–1990

During Phase II the remaining schools in the North Central Area were globalized. By its completion, an additional 182 teachers, 64 media specialists, and administrators had been trained and all 64 schools in the area offered their mostly inner-city students a global education. One middle school principal observed, "We have made strides with regard to racial tensions since the introduction of the program" (Ladd, 1985, p. 3). Reflected Tucker (1990):

> In 1984 we initiated global programs in the social studies departments of 13 schools located in two administrative areas. In 1989, five years later, more than 500 teachers, administrators, and media specialists were trained in global education representing 155 schools. We estimate that over 50,000 students in the Miami schools have benefited directly from the training from a total of 245,000 students in the Miami schools at that time (p. 5).

Phase III: 1990–1993

In the three-year period between 1990 and 1993, four additional senior high schools and their families of 48 elementary and middle schools completed initiation of global programs. These schools (described below) stand out for the individuality of their needs, the enthusiasm and engagement of the local communities, and their ingenuity and creativity in program implementation. Some schools in both the North and South Areas of the district experimented with their own pilot programs, implementing the program in an individual school before engaging the entire feeder pattern in the process. For example, the principal directing the Center for Modern Languages in the North Area required all her faculty to be trained in global perspectives teaching in one academic year. In the same area, the lead principal of one senior high school and its feeder schools asked that the global program be established in a single school year. Although this presented a severe time challenge to the four of us, the use of global leadership teams (described in chapter 5 as the *teachers-teaching-teachers model*) saved us from failing to meet these requests for training from two of the finest principals in the district. Our training concerns became increasingly those of organization, planning, scheduling, and delegation of training to global leadership teams.

The following sections describe the four high schools selected during Phase III which distinguished them in exceptional program implementation.

School I. In September 1990, the School Board, with grant support of $165,000 from the Hitachi Foundation, approved implementation of the Global Inner-City Site Training (GIST) program in a low-performance senior high school and its feeder schools in the poorest section of Miami. Its focus was to create a model program that would meet the urgent need for global education in inner-city school communities to enable minority students to compete equally and successfully for employment in the most desirable sectors of the global economy. An important theme of the national effort to reform education was the growing recognition that all citizens must receive a global education if the United States wishes to remain a vital and creative force in world affairs (National Commission on Excellence, 1983). Tucker (1989) argued that

> it is unacceptable for our democratic nation to allow the development of a poorly educated underclass. During the 1980s this high moral standard has become an economic imperative as we begin to face up to the challenges presented by an independent and rapidly changing world (p. 2).

The GIST feeder-pattern configuration was selected on the basis of the deeply held belief that all children can learn. A rich interdisciplinary curriculum focusing on cultural areas of the world, conceptual themes, and intra- and inter-school "Global Knowledge Bowls" electrified parents and teachers. Two state-of-the-art technology features of the program included the Learning Link Project, which facilitated the connection of teachers in global schools with their peers, and the International Communication (ICONS) Project, a worldwide simulation network using the internet to teach international negotiation and intercultural communication in order to build cross-cultural understanding and promote global awareness. As Adler (2008) states, "the biggest change in research on social studies teacher education is the large increase in the use of technology in teacher preparation" (p. 338).

School II. The feeder-pattern configuration of the second senior high school was comprised of 17 schools, the largest in the district. Integration of global education here represented the program's most ambitious education project. The initiative came from teacher leaders, who had procured a grant, and chose teacher training by self-selection. In contrast to other feeder-pattern schools, "The Global Village," so named by its teachers, distinguished itself by a *six-year spiral program design* integrating a comprehensive interdisciplinary curriculum across K-12 grade levels that cycled twice through the world's major cultural and geographic regions. The overarching goal of this curricular innovation was to emphasize links, interconnections, and commonalties among major cultures of the world. Its area superintendent Eddy Pearson (1993) commented, "The best evidence of the success of the global inner-city site training program (School I described above) was the $100,000 funding for our program in October 1993 by the School Board" (p. 2). This senior high school is located in the Homestead area south of Miami, an area that was devastated by Hurricane Andrew in 1992 that killed hundreds of people and left tens of thousands without food, water, homes, schools, and employment. Ironically, the other day, one of the social studies teachers who was traumatized by the devastation contacted me. She had moved to Tallahassee 800 miles away to begin a new life in a Leon County public high school.

School III. This senior high school and its feeder schools excelled in organizational structure, utilizing the talents and commitment of its assistant principals, who created the first Global Advisory Council in the system. Fifteen of them met weekly at the crack of dawn to discuss interdisciplinary program development and implementation in their elementary and secondary schools. (I would eagerly have given up breakfast for another hour of sleep!) These schools implemented remarkably creative themes in the instructional process, based on conceptual themes such as commonalities of the human family across the world (e.g., international lullabies for kindergartners) which emphasized empathy for the Other; historical and cultural linkages between Latin Americans and European Americans in the United States; and cultural and artistic interconnections between African Americans and African peoples (e.g., the art of hair braiding, shared rhythms and jazz). Located in a Hispanic-dominated community in the city, the schools conducted bilingual elementary and secondary Knowledge Bowl competitions in a shopping mall, which turned into a well-attended annual community event.

School IV. The fourth senior high school and its family of middle and elementary schools, located in the trenches of poverty and crime, was embedded in the philosophy of the Nine Principles of the Coalition of Essential Schools (Sizer, 1984), offering its diverse inner-city student population specialized "Academies" which facilitated interdisciplinary teaching. Three teachers and the media specialist participated in an 18-day study-abroad program to Japan offered by the Global Awareness Program. This indelible professional experience motivated us on our return to integrate Japan studies as the focus of our global program (see Kirkwood-Tucker, 1996; 2002). I was one of those teachers. After the district closed the International Global Education Program in 1994 I had returned to the classroom in this high school, initiating the most rewarding experience in my professional life.

Of a 15-member interdisciplinary faculty in our "Academy of International Business and Finance," nine teachers endorsed the global program. With the beginning of the second semester we infused the geographic, cultural, economic, educational, and historical interconnectedness between Japan and the U.S. into the existing curriculum every Wednesday for the remainder of the school year. This Wednesday approach was unique to our school; all academies in the school joined in our enthusiasm and participated. On those momentous Wednesdays the building turned into a Japanese school; students wore *yokatas* and kimonos, took off their shoes before entering classrooms, bowed to their teachers with "*Ohayoo-gozaimasu*," used chopsticks in the cafeteria, made origami paper cranes, and much more; a hand-built wooden Japanese teahouse demonstrating authentic tea ceremonies was our exhibition. The program was one of the most successful in the district. At one of the Global Awareness Program Advisory Board meetings Tucker (1994) reported:

> The swift growth of global education in the schools can be attributed to the tremendous enthusiasm it has generated among teachers, administrators, media specialists and students. We in the Miami community have received extraordinarily strong support from the grassroots. The program has provided an opportunity for everyone to become meaningfully involved, to make a contribution, and to upgrade their professional skills (p. 2).

This brief account of some of the outstanding global high schools and their feeder pattern school cannot do justice to their distinct implementations of the program, which require a full and separate analysis.

Identification and Selection of Global Leadership Teams

This section examines one of the aspects of the program most fascinating to me: how school-site principals chose the global leadership teams for their critical role in integration global perspectives in their respective schools. Tye and Tye (1992) in their study of global program implementation in the Orange County Public Schools in California analyzed the leadership styles exercised in school districts. Oliva (2005) in his research in school management identified similar leadership styles inherent in large school districts. These scholars observed that most administrators in school systems operated in what they called the "X Theory" of management style and saw themselves "making the decisions that others carry out," a top-down, directive style that permeated the deep structure of schooling (p. 162). The "Y Theory" approach, by contrast, entailed a more flexible, democratic, cooperative style. In the Miami-Dade County Public Schools the X Theory seemed the pattern at the district and area (superordinate) levels. At the school-site level, however, both the X and

Y leadership styles were evident in the process of teacher selection as well as in approaches to curricular innovation. The difference in administrative leadership styles was most clearly manifested between elementary and secondary school-site principals.

Elementary Schools

Elementary school principals tended to be X managers. They generally appointed the grade-level chairs and several teachers to form the global leadership team. These chairs were frequently the administration's right hand in carrying out school-site training, disseminating textual materials and initiating interdisciplinary curriculum development. Principals invited their global teams to share their workshop learning experiences at the faculty meetings where they advanced plans with timelines for the implementation. The elementary school principals in the Miami-Dade County public schools were known for the close relationships among them and frequently shared ideas for program implementation. I strongly suspect they were also in friendly competition to surpass their sibling schools.

Middle Schools

In middle schools most principals tended to Y Theory approaches to team selection, but the process was also affected by the organizational structures in the schools. Those schools that were organized into interdisciplinary teams representing subject areas and grade levels chose their own team leaders and one or more teachers from each subject area. The common planning period, which is part of interdisciplinary team-teaching structures, facilitated team planning and discussion of the most effective ways to integrate the program. In traditional middle schools where teachers taught their courses independently, the global leadership teams were, at the direction of the principal, made up of the department chairs and two or three volunteer teachers from each discipline.

Senior High Schools

In senior high schools, principals delegated the selection of the global leadership team to the subject-area department chairs or interdisciplinary team leaders. In schools structured according to the model of the Coalition of Essential Schools (Sizer, 1984), where self-selection is the practice, principals have long recognized the value of equal faculty-administration relationships. Darling-Hammond (1988) reflects on the positive results in school reform when teachers have the opportunity to engage in collaborative discourse that benefits all participants: "It was the process of collective struggle that produced the vitality, the shared vision, and conviction that allowed schools to redesign education in fundamentally different ways" (p. 28).

The global teams experienced that very struggle when, returning from their content workshops, it was their responsibility to train their peers in how to infuse a global perspective into curriculum and instruction and how to integrate the global program. Despite enthusiastic endorsement by global leadership teams, not all teachers in global school communities participated in the program. That very enthusiasm resulted in resentment among those who already felt overburdened by the curriculum. I have learned that resistance to curricular reform comes predominantly from senior high school teachers. Tye and Tye (1992) also found this in their study in Orange County schools. Merryfield (2008b) cautions that "it is important to work at understanding the deeply-held beliefs and values of teachers if we are to understand why they make the decisions they do" and that we need to examine carefully why teachers resist innovation in curriculum reform, to focus attention on their ideology, experiences with reform, time constraints, and the pressure of other goals. Other researchers point out that "change in classrooms involves a process of mutual adaptation between the innovation and teachers" (McLaughlin, 1997; cited in Thornton, 2005, p. 1), a process which the reluctant teachers were not prepared to engage in. Since a sufficient number of teachers at the high school level were enthusiastic about global education, resisters did not seriously impede the program. We remained on friendly terms, smiling at each other in the hallways. In time, due to growing enthusiasm among students and teachers, some formerly reluctant teachers joined the global team and became belated believers in the program.

Discussion and Conclusion

In this chapter I have tried to tell tales from the field—a firsthand account of the possibilities and processes that led to global education reform in the Miami-Dade County Public Schools over a ten-year period. This account seeks to capture the district's contextual position and organizational structure, the school district–university partnership between the Greater Miami Public Schools and Florida International University, global education as systems objectives, the selection of global facilitators to provide global education training and clinical support in schools, the incremental selection of schools to be globalized, and the identification and selection of school leadership teams by school-site administrators.

Sarason in his classic discourse in *The Culture of the School and the Problem of Change* (1971) and *Revisiting "The Culture of the School and the Problem of Change"* (1996) describes the educational environment as the inseparable relationship between leadership and school culture, a relationship that the global programs were able to penetrate. The systematic training of over 1,000 teachers, media specialists, and administrators in three cycles of three years each affected over 100,000 students in almost 300 schools. The global intervention in schools was made possible with the extensive foundation-supported collaboration between the Director of the Global Awareness Program, Florida International University, the unfailing support of district administrators, area superintendents, area directors, school-site principals and the globally-trained, knowledgeable, caring, and committed teachers and media specialists. Jan Tucker (1994), who envisioned this life-long dream, rejoiced,

> The global education leadership training program achieved national recognition as a leading example of a successful global education partnership between a school system, university, and a philanthropic foundation (p. 3).

There are multiple reasons for the success of global education reform in the Miami-Dade County Public Schools between 1984 and 1994. This success is predicated on the constructive relationships built among district administrators, area administrative leaders, building principals, assistant principals, and teachers. But above all the success of global education reform was due to the strong and unflinching support of administrators at the district, area, and building levels. Far-sighted administrators recognized the necessity to globalize curriculum and instruction in the age of globalization in order to prepare students to become well-informed, open-minded, flexible, skilled, and critical thinkers in an increasingly interdependent complex world and may inspire school administrators in schools in other parts of our country and other nations. Though taxed with uncountable daily responsibilities these committed administrative leaders believed in the importance of a global education program, thoughtfully and democratically designed, planned, and implemented by all participants that would increase student academic achievement and a sense of bonding often lacking in the setting of schools. Relationships among administrators, teachers, media specialists and global facilitators were democratically enacted. All stakeholders were treated with respect resonant of the philosophy of global education. Diego Garcia (1985), principal of the oldest high-school in the Greater Miami public schools with the largest student body of predominantly 3,000 primarily Hispanic students, observed,

> Global education is not a course. It is more of a feeling that I am part of the world and the world is part of me, and we are all in this together. The training also encouraged teachers to recognize, compare, and celebrate the diversity of local cultures with the diversity of the world's cultures (p. 2).

A second principal reason for the success of global education reform in the Miami-Dade County Public Schools is the teachers. It is well known within university–school partnerships that administrators cannot command change in schools unless interested teachers are committed to the change; otherwise the results are dubious (Henderson & Hawthorne, 2000; Oliva, 2005; Tye & Tye, 1992). Despite serious time constraints and diverse curricular interests the globally trained teachers recognized the value and importance of teaching and learning about the larger world that leads to the discussion of multiple perspectives and the cultural, geographic, economic, and political interconnections of the world's people to identifying commonalties of the human family and were willing to give it their time and energy.

A third critical reason for this success story is the students, who were enthusiastic and felt in many instances that teachers really cared about their interests and how the broader world related to their worlds. And finally, not to be underestimated is enthusiastic community support for the program over its ten-year time span. I will address in more detail the active engagement of teachers, students, and community responsible for the success of the program in chapter 7.

Research Opportunities

The ten-year global education reform in the Miami-Dade County Public Schools lends itself to multiple research opportunities for the scholar-practitioner interested in the areas of school improvement through specific program implementation and in the administrative leadership opportunities during the possibilities and processes of education reform.

This study contributes to the field in several ways. There are at least ten possibilities for research which need attention to help create a rich database subject to peer review to assure balance, rigor, and relevance. Regarding research possibilities in school improvement through cutting-edge program implementation in global education, the researcher might embrace the following questions among others: (1) What are the long-term effects of Greater Miami's global school programs after their decline in the mid-1990s? (2) How many schools continued the program despite the encroaching high-stakes testing and public accountability movement sweeping the country? (3) How many schools that closed their global programs reopened their doors to global education after its decline—and to what extent? (4) Is the reopening of school doors to global education a result of leadership change or district policy changes? (5) To which distinguishing features do you attest the success of global education reform in the Miami-Dade County Public Schools? The field of global education requires research studies that are informed by individuals' direct involvement in schools and driven by first-hand experiences that define weaknesses and strengths in new program implementation.

A second genre of research possibilities in global education reform in the Miami-Dade County Public Schools lies in administrative leadership. Research questions might include the following topics, among others: (1) What are the definitive roles and responsibilities of area superintendents, area directors, and school-site administrators in implementing global education reform? (2) Do the roles and responsibilities of area superintendents, area directors, building-level principals and assistant principals change with the nature of intended reform? (3) What leadership styles are most conducive to educational reform? (4) Given educational reform in a particular school district, what opportunities exist for middle-level management administrators for promotion? What are the necessary skills to accomplish this? And finally, (5) what became of the global leadership teams after conclusion of the program in 1994? Did they simply return to their classrooms, or have some used their leadership opportunities to advance in the system? These inquiries lend themselves to qualitative research methodologies embedded in random selection in-depth interviews of appropriate administrators and teachers.

This tale from the field has brought the Miami-Dade County Public Schools to the cutting edge of the education reform movement in the late 20th century. I strongly believe that the intensity and vivaciousness of these programs so well received by students, teachers, and administrators have planted a deep curiosity about the larger world and its people in students and expanded their world view about the Other. Curiously, the global education programs of the Miami-Dade County Public Schools, which clearly consisted of a wide continuum of curricular creativity and innovation in its global education reform, were not attacked by the right wing during the late 1980s and early 1990s as was the case with other programs in the country (see chapter 1). We will never know whether it was an oversight (which I doubt) or simply that a system of such size, complexity, and diversity, and with such strong community support for a globalized curriculum that engaged hundreds of schools, enthusiastic administrators and teachers and parents, and thousands of students, all of whom embraced this process with such joie de vivre, was too powerful to attack.

A resurgence of interest by the new superintendent of the Greater Miami public schools in the necessity of global education teaching and learning, his quoting Friedman's (2005) *The World Is Flat* in public meetings, and recent revision of the Miami-Dade County Public Schools' global standard in the curricular guidelines may return the fourth largest U.S. school district in the nation, once more, to its earlier preeminence in global education reform and a new generation of students will be exposed to the cultures and peoples of the larger world.

What began with the implementation of one global program in one social studies department in one school grew into the integration of global programs in entire feeder pattern configurations in almost three-fourths of Greater Miami's public schools. There seems to be a magic and purpose to learning about the world's people with whom we share this planet—if you have an open mind.

Notes

1. I used Miami-Dade County interchangeably with Greater Miami and Metropolitan Miami.
2. In the 1990s, the district changed from four *areas* to four *regions*, eventually six regions and *two zones*: the school improvement zone and alternative schools zone. Today, the administrative boundaries have been reduced to four areas.

Chapter 7

From the Trenches:
The Integration of a Global Perspective in Curriculum and Instruction in the Miami-Dade County Public Schools

Toni Fuss Kirkwood-Tucker

I dedicate this chapter to the exemplary global teachers and media specialists in the Miami-Dade County Public Schools who with their deep commitment and love for their profession made the impossible possible.

This chapter traces the historical development of the integration of a global perspective in curriculum and instruction into the classrooms of nearly three-fourths of the Miami-Dade County Public Schools, the fourth largest school district in our country, between 1984 and 1994.[1] The process of planning, design, and integration of global perspectives into the reality of the trenches was undertaken with an eye to serving as an exemplar for its potential replication in high school feeder-pattern schools in Florida and the nation. I have decided to recount my own experiences from these trenches, the place where the accumulated knowledge, decision-making, pedagogy, and experiences of the classroom teacher are genuinely tested. This account is a response to some of the urgent calls for global education research in the multiple realities of our country's democratic learning communities, as teachers are the ultimate curricular and instructional gatekeepers of their classrooms (Thornton, 2005).

The basic principles of a global education comprise the abilities to see one's world from multiple perspectives, recognizing that others may have views of the world profoundly different from one's own; to see the causes and effects of globalization as they affect the lives of communities and people, of students and schools; to be able to analyze cross-cultural commonalities and differences and appreciate the contributions made by nations and cultures to civilization; to perceive the interconnectedness of cultural, economic, geographic, political, and technical phenomena with their often-numerous unanticipated consequences; and to perceive the ramifications of decisions made by individuals, groups, and entire nations and how they affect the future of the world (Case, 1993; Hanvey, 1976; Heilman, 2006; Kirkwood, 2001; Kniep, 1989). In our attempt to understand the world from the perspective of a post-Cold War orientation, Merryfield (2001) argues that the preparation of teachers has to be expanded to include the capacity to teach about the legacy of imperialism; formerly colonized people struggling with the inheritance of imperialism; increasing political polarization resulting in economic and technological inequities; cultural conflicts due to globalization; the interconnectedness of local and global intersections of power, discrimination, and identity; and the challenges in moving the center of global education from institutionalized divisions of people and ideas to the complexity of human interactions leading to hybridity and synergy of the human experience (see chapter 10). With the world becoming increasingly uncertain and unpredictable, teaching from a global perspective requires deepening complexity and sophistication to achieve equality and social justice for all members of the human family—a moral responsibility of the global educator.

During the ten-year program, I was the principal global facilitator (described in more detail in chapter 6) of the district training teachers, media specialists, and administrators to integrate a global perspective into curriculum and instruction. I am confident that I can report these tales from the trenches with objectivity, though with nostalgia, as it was a chapter in my life when I felt I made a real difference in the lives of the teachers in those trenches. My recollections are corroborated by Frank de Varona, school-site principal, area director, area superintendent, and associate superintendent of the Miami-Dade County Public Schools, who played a decisive leadership role in the ten-year global education reform in the Greater Miami public schools.

I have organized this chapter into seven major topics: (1) the integration of global perspectives in curriculum and instruction including program goals, administrative meetings global facilitators had to attend, and teacher in-service training; (2) program goals for years one, two, and three including content workshops, school site sessions, and culminating activities; (3) the professionalization of teachers, opportunities for their leadership, and their construction of interdisciplinary age-appropriate school plans; (4) an example of a feeder pattern interdisciplinary conceptual framework studying the world from kindergarten to twelfth grade; (5) program specific activities to enhance the integration of global programs in schools; (6) assessment; and (7) my reflections on the effectiveness of the ten-year integration of a global perspective in curriculum and instruction in the Miami-Dade County Public Schools offering alluring research possibilities for the field of global education.

The Integration of Global Perspectives in Curriculum and Instruction

This segment of the chapter embraces four aspects: universal program goals, administrative meetings that global facilitators needed to attend; teacher in-service training; and program-specific goals for three consecutive years of the program cycle.

Universal Program Goals

The global education program model implemented in the Miami-Dade County Public Schools between 1984 and 1994 was driven by the following goals: (1) to conduct intensive university-based and school-site-based leadership training in global education across disciplines and grade levels; (2) to develop globally oriented instructional materials, teaching strategies, and a K-12 curriculum relevant in scope and sequence to the needs of the high school and its family of middle and elementary schools and responsive to recommendations of national commissions and professional organizations; (3) to construct a school plan for each participating school consistent with the curriculum plan for its whole feeder-pattern configuration; (4) to create interdisciplinary units of instruction that capture the world's regions and those global issues and concepts consistent with the overall theme of the feeder schools; (5) to apply the conceptual framework of the Hanvey Model (1976) as a basis for curricular development and instruction; and (6) beginning in the second and third years, for each feeder pattern group of schools to enact culminating activities at the end of the school year based on their theme for the year and in which students and community from all feeder pattern schools participate.

Effective global education programs in schools require judicious and creative planning throughout the school year in each participating school and in each feeder pattern; thoughtful development of the scope and sequence of curriculum; training in knowledge of the world and open-mindedness toward its inhabitants; global pedagogy; and effective articulation across grade levels and schools to ensure that the K-12 program is effectively implemented, and that program aims, systems goals, district curricular standards, and specified student learning outcomes are achieved. Barbara Tye (2000) reminds us that in the process of introduc-

ing educational reform, the culture of the school directly influences human social interactions and people's disposition to change. If the existing
school culture is toxic, the challenge of transforming it is formidable. The
hundreds of hours that school-site administrators, teachers, and media
specialists spent to organize their school's program require democratic
learning communities where the relationship among participants is equal
and nonthreatening. Growing enthusiasm in students, teachers, and administrators may mitigate, if not prevent, teacher resistance (see chapter
6). Fullan (2003) explains:

> We're talking about a change in the culture of schools and a change in the
> culture of teaching. We know that when we think about change we have to
> get to ownership, participation, and a sense of meaning on the part of the
> majority of teachers. You can't get ownership through technical means; you
> have to get it through interaction, through developing people (cited in
> Sparks, 2003, p. 58).

Administrative Meetings Attended by Global Facilitators

Integrating global perspectives in curriculum and instruction from kindergarten to twelfth grade is a complex and time-consuming process.
Global facilitators (their role is explained in chapter 6) assigned to specific administrative areas, as I was, attended several types of administrative meetings. The first, at the beginning of each school year, was
conducted by the area superintendent and attended by area directors,
and school-site principals of a given administrative area (see Table 6.1 in
chapter 6). There the global facilitators were called upon to present possibilities for curricular reform for feeder-pattern schools in their schools'
programs during the school year and to answer questions from administrators.

The second meeting was conducted by the area directors of a given
region and attended by the school-site principals and assistant principals
for curriculum of the feeder-pattern schools under the direction of its
area director. Here we distributed the annual master schedule of content
and pedagogy workshops and school-site follow-up sessions, scheduled
faculty and departmental meetings, presented options for professional
conferences, etc. The third level of meeting was the first faculty meeting
at each of the individual feeder-pattern schools. Here we, as global facilitators, were invited to speak to the purpose of global education and the
most effective methods by which to integrate global awareness in curriculum and instruction. Principals explained release days for teachers

and receipt of Master Plan Points (MPP) or university course credit for recertification and asked for volunteers (or appointed teachers) to form the global leadership team. Usually the assistant principals for curriculum assumed the administrative leadership role, collaborating with their school's global leadership team in the planning and implementation of global perspectives in curriculum and instruction at their respective schools.

Teacher In-service Training

In this era of rapid cultural, economic, and technical globalization, in-service training is particularly critical because most teacher training does not include comprehensive preparation for teaching from a global perspective (Gaudelli, 2003; Merryfield, 1998; Tye & Tye, 1992). Yet empirical research clearly demonstrates that "teaching and learning can be improved by promoting the intellectual development of teachers" (Gaudelli, 2003, p. 140). In a study of teacher trainees in England, Holden and Hicks (2007) argue that if in-service training is to be effective "there needs to be time and provision to learn strategies for teaching about global and controversial issues; time for teachers to improve their own knowledge and understanding; and time for them to learn how to critically evaluate sources of information" (pp. 22–23).

The training of in-service teachers was a formidable undertaking and constituted the very essence of the program, as teachers are the ultimate curricular and instructional gatekeepers of the classroom (Thornton, 2005). Their empowerment is of the highest value and often underestimated in educational reform. Dewey (1901) says it best:

> The teacher is the most important figure in so far as the curriculum is concerned, and there is simply no point in attempting a reform of the curriculum without the active participation of the teacher and without taking into account the teacher's ability, interests, and desires.

The in-service training was offered in three components, each building upon the preceding one from a minimum level of competency to higher levels of global competence in the acquisition of knowledge and understanding of global perspectives and global pedagogy. These three, called the Introductory, Intermediary, and Advanced Components for Global Awareness, each required 12 hours of training and each was awarded 12 credit points offered as professional incentive points (PIP) and master plan points (MPP) for certification, recertification and/or professional development authorized by the Dade-Monroe Teacher Education Center. Participants could also earn three university credit hours.

What follows details the three-year Global Education Leadership Training Program Model (see chapter 5 for more detail), the teacher training and program development model used to shape teachers' attitudes about the world, to increase their global knowledge, and to develop their skills for infusing a global perspective effectively into curriculum and instruction in order to build a global program in their schools. In discussing the importance of teacher training in achieving education reform, Essex (2001) draws our attention to the fact that "if educational renewal is to occur, there must be a strong connection between school reform and reform of teacher education...as public school and college restructuring is essential for the improvement of instruction and educational opportunities, especially in urban settings" (p. 734). The content and pedagogy workshops and the on-site visits over a three-year period provided multiple educational opportunities for teachers to become more receptive toward global curricular reform.

Program Goals for Year One

The global leadership teams were trained according to the Introductory Global Awareness component of the Dade-Monroe Teacher Education Center. Global leadership teams, administrators, and university faculty collaborated to develop a comprehensive plan with a carefully considered scope and sequence of global education curriculum for the entire feeder pattern, including specific student learning outcomes, and an evaluation scheme that included measurement of the program on indices such as attendance patterns, student interest, and student achievement. The global leadership teams participated in the following sessions throughout the year.

Year One Content Workshops I and II. These were held in October and February at Florida International University and conducted by experts from the College of Education, College of Arts and Sciences, Department of International Relations, the Latin American Center for Caribbean Studies, the Gordon Center for Civic Education and Policy Studies, and the global facilitators. Workshop I activities addressed (1) the rationale for global education; (2) the multiple definitions of global education; (3) the application of the Hanvey (1976) conceptual framework; (4) development of lessons and interdisciplinary units to infuse global content into instruction, and issues and skills related to instruction; and (5) the development of school plans in feeder-pattern groupings. Requests for workshop content were prioritized. Workshop II activities (1) emphasized global content and issues consistent with the chosen feeder pattern theme, (2) demonstrated strategies for infusing a global perspective into instruction, (3) developed a global issues lesson on workshop content combining lesson objectives with the district's balanced curriculum objectives, and (4) brainstormed selection of a feeder pattern theme for the second year.

Year One School-site Sessions. To achieve Introductory Global Awareness competency, four separate two-hour sessions were held for elementary, middle, and senior school global teams at a centrally located school site. In Session I, teachers (1) shared ideas and concerns resulting from a previous workshop, (2) demonstrated a lesson based on the Hanvey (1976) conceptual framework, (3) observed a global facilitator demonstrating a lesson on *Perspective Consciousness* (dimension 1), which teachers were asked to teach in their classrooms. Teachers were also asked to collaborate with media specialists to conduct an inventory of print, non-print, audio-visual, and human resources in their schools.

In Session II, teachers (1) shared inventory with others in the feeder system and (2) compared experiences in teaching the perspective consciousness lesson. (3) A global facilitator demonstrated teaching lessons about *State of the Planet Awareness* and *Cross-cultural Awareness* (dimensions 2 and 3), and distributed activities to teach global concepts (e.g., interconnectedness, interdependence, and change) for classroom use; (4) teachers were asked to design a favorite infusion lesson for Session III.

In Session III, teachers (1) shared favorite lessons related to the State of the Planet Awareness and Cross-cultural Awareness dimensions, (2) a global facilitator demonstrated lessons on *Knowledge of Global Dynamics* and *Awareness of Human Choices*, (3) participants brain-stormed infusion techniques and were asked to teach a lesson on Knowledge of Global Dynamics and Awareness of Human Choices in their classrooms. (4) All worked in groups to design a school plan based on a mutually agreed-upon theme for Year Two to be used throughout the feeder-pattern group. Teachers were assigned to share a school plan with grade levels, departments, entire faculty, and an assistant principal from their own schools and to invite new interested teachers to the next session.

In Session IV, teachers (1) shared experiences in teaching lessons on Knowledge of Global Dynamics and Awareness of Human Choices in their classroom; (2) recommended best practices in implementing individual school plans; and (3) the global facilitator distributed goals and objectives for Year Two.

Program Goals for Year Two

Global leadership teams were trained according to the Intermediate Global Awareness component. These teams of teachers, administrators, and university faculty developed the comprehensive feeder-pattern school plan, carefully considering the scope and sequence of a global education curriculum for the entire feeder pattern including learning outcomes and an evaluation as in the year before. During the year the global leadership teams participated in a series of content workshops, department meetings, and school-site sessions, as detailed below.

Year Two Content Workshops I and II. These were held in October and February at Florida International University, as described in Year One, above. Workshop I focused on (1) delivery of new global content, (2) development of individual school plans for Year Two, (3) creation of lesson plans and interdisciplinary units consistent with the global theme, (4) more global strategies, (5) new curricular materials, and (6) brainstorming and decision-making for the first feeder pattern culminating activity in assignment of activities and roles to individual schools within the feeder pattern configuration. Workshop II focused on (1) delivery of new global content, (2) welcoming those teachers new to the global program and partnering them with existing global teams to discuss implementation of individual school plans, (3) working within teams on strategies for scope and sequence, (4) finalizing decision-making about what specific role each school would play in the culminating activity to be held at the senior high school of the configuration, and (5) strategizing the content workshops for Year Three. Reflects Merryfield (2008b) in an interview on her extensive work in the Ohio public schools:

> It seems much more difficult for teachers to teach about global content issues or global systems. It is difficult for all of us to gain the multidisciplinary knowledge base required to understand how the world works especially from the points of view of diverse people across the planet.

Year Two Department Meetings. In individual departmental meetings of participating schools in September and March, each individual feeder-pattern school addressed its progress and concerns. Here the assigned global facilitator informed teachers about administrative decisions made at district and area-level meetings. Grade-level chairs, department chairs, and interdisciplinary teams deliberated about how to bring uninvolved teachers into the program.

Year Two School-site Sessions. Held as before in November, December, March, and April, these two-hour sessions helped elementary, middle, and senior school global teams achieve Intermediate Global Awareness competency. Session I provided an opportunity for the global facilitator to work with the global teams and teachers new to the program on the effective infusion of school plans into their teaching and on preparations for the culminating activity at the end of the school year. The focus in these meetings was on the individual school site and was an opportunity for global teams and teachers new to the program to discuss their concerns. The school-based global teams dictated the remainder of the agenda. Sessions II, III and IV focused exclusively on the needs of the global teams and new teachers who had recently joined the program; here global teams told the global facilitator their concerns, priorities, or needs for materials, speakers, etc. At session IV, the global facilitator also distributed goals and objectives for Year Three.

Program Goals for Year Three

In the third year, global leadership teams were trained according to the Advanced Global Awareness component. As before, global leadership teams of teachers, administrators and university faculty developed a comprehensive feeder-pattern school plan specifying global education curriculum scope and sequence, specific student learning outcomes, and an evaluation scheme.

Year Three Content Workshops I and II. These were again held in October and February as described above. Workshop I focused on new content and issues tailored to global themes taught in schools. Global teams developed interdisciplinary lessons for each grade level consistent with the global theme. They created and shared school plans for Year Three. The global facilitator introduced teachers to new infusion strategies and curricular materials and explored the ideas for a culminating activity consistent with global themes. A global master teacher demonstrated best practices from the field. Workshop II welcomed new teachers who wanted to participate in the program, inviting global teams to work collaboratively with them on how to integrate school plans into their teaching. The group brainstormed on a future three-year global program. Teachers were introduced to new global content, strategies, and curricular materials, and the global cadre and master teachers shared best practices from the field.

Year Three Department Meetings. In September, January, April and May individual department meetings were held at individual school-sites where the global facilitator discussed the scope and sequence of program in the feeder pattern configuration and invited new teachers interested in the program to the training. Additional agenda at departmental meetings was determined by the school-site global leadership teams.

Optional Activities for Years One, Two, and Three.

All teachers at all levels were encouraged to attend and participate in the (1) Florida Council for the Social Studies Convention, (2) the National Council for the Social Studies Conference and (3) the Advanced *Newspaper in the Classroom* weekend workshop conducted by the *Miami Herald* to develop strategies in teaching from a global perspective with foreign newspapers printed in English, Spanish, and Creole (remember, this was Miami!), or (4) to enroll in a university content course specifically designed for Miami's global teachers, held at a school mutually agreed upon. These optional activities could be applied toward certification, recertification, or university course credit toward the Master's Degree. Many teachers took advantage of this opportunity.

Culminating Activity

From Year Two onward, it became established practice throughout the ten-year program to end the year with a culminating activity representing all schools of the feeder-pattern configuration. This event brought together students, teachers, administrators, parents, and the community to celebrate the annual theme outlined in school plans and agreed upon by the feeder-pattern global leadership teams. Uniting schools and community in an effort to bring the world into the classroom became one of the major accomplishments of the program. District administrators and school board members paid tribute to the event and the media frequently covered the events.

The Professionalization of Teachers

The next section of this chapter addresses the empowerment of teachers, their opportunities for leadership in their districts, and the fruits of their highly productive labor of love, the construction of interdisciplinary age-appropriate school plans.[2]

Teacher Empowerment

Teachers are the soul of the educational process. Their attitudes, knowledge, and skills shape those of their students for effective global citizenship in a troubled, increasingly interdependent world. The tales from the trenches are a tribute to their indisputable commitment to this work. The growing number of schools requesting training to implement a global program provided numerous opportunities for the globally trained teachers. As global programs spread like a brush fire throughout the district, sparked by the enthusiasm of students, teachers, and community, members of the global leadership teams were identified to help train new groups of teachers. In addition to being part of the global core group in their own schools responsible for training their peers and overseeing implementation of the program, these master teachers became an integral part of the district's cadre of teachers teaching teachers. Their enthusiasm and commitment led to presentations at state and national conferences describing their work, which increased their professional skills and brought credit to their individual school and district. Global team leaders exhibited the attitude, expanded knowledge base, and creative global pedagogy that exemplify what Giroux (2004) defines as the "transformative intellectual," the consummate professional teacher emerging from effective global perspectives training, professional experiences, and leadership in schools and districts.

Empowerment contributed to teachers' growing academic confidence, leading to leadership positions and professionalization. Darling-Hammond (1988) defines the professionalization of teachers as affirming three principles: "Knowledge as the basis for meeting unique clients' (i.e., student) needs, and welfare of the clients as paramount concern, and collective responsibility of the profession for definition, transmittal, and enforcement of standards" (p. 12). The professional development of teachers in the context of global education reform is also informed by Gaudelli's (2003) reflection on his work in the New Jersey schools: "When teaching and learning are viewed as intellectual endeavors, teacher professionalism becomes an essential characteristic of their career" (p. 141). These master teachers assumed a unique leadership role, which shaped their professional growth and development that formed the very root from which innovative global pedagogy sprang.

By the third year of program implementation, I observed an interesting unanticipated consequence: teachers' deepening concerns about the world. Whereas first- and second-year teacher trainees taught the interconnections of culture, geographic determinism, and global events affecting students' lives, the more experienced (and more frequently trained) teachers spoke to global inequities, e.g., violation of human rights, lack of education, and poverty-related issues, suggesting their inclusion in the school curriculum. These observations corroborate Merryfield's (1998) work in the Ohio public schools where her "exemplary" global educators utilized the more sophisticated elements of global pedagogy of social injustice, U.S. hegemony, and cross-cultural experiential learning as the principal themes for teaching and learning.

Construction of School Plans

The effective integration of global perspectives into curriculum and instruction is supported by interdisciplinary school plans at each grade level crafted by global teams of each school, reflections of the teachers' freedom to negotiate and implement a conceptual framework, collectively designed by compromise and agreement—a product of their own competence and creativity, making them critical decision-makers about what students should know about the world. Teachers as curricularists argue Oliva (2005) offer a wide range of skills and professional experiences often untapped in their confinement to the classroom. Creating these school plans required that they address a scope and sequence of global education curriculum for the entire feeder pattern, supporting a commonly agreed-on thematic framework while incorporating specified student learning outcomes. Teachers also provided a written compendium of specific knowledge and skills students are expected to possess at the completion of each nine-week grading period and, cumulatively, by the end of the school year (and, we hope, for life). In a sense, those handwritten school plans comprised a written contract between teachers, administrators and global facilitator, being a blueprint of activities taking place in their classrooms. I collected those plans from every school in the feeder-pattern configurations and presented them in handsome binders to the teachers' respective school-site principals, the lead principals, and area directors to demonstrate the fruits of their teachers' hard labors of love.

Elementary Schools. At the elementary school level, examples of content emphasis in school plans for the early grades predominantly focused on the third dimension of the Hanvey Model, Cross-cultural Awareness, learning about the commonalties of cultural traditions, folk tales, and children's way of life in Africa, Asia, Australia, Canada, the Caribbean, Latin America, the Middle East, and Russia, promoting knowledge across cultures. First and second graders were taught about the concept of empathy with lessons such as "Teardrops," which showed them how the children of the developing world walk five miles to go to school or fetch water for the family three kilometers down a dirt road. In grades four and five, school plans exhibited deeper explorations and comparisons, such as historical intersections with Florida and contributions of native people and immigrants, thus affirming the pioneer research by Tye and Tye (1992) in the Orange County schools. Bahamian-born assistant principal, Maude P. Newbold (2008) of one of the leading global elementary schools in Coconut Grove of Miami, firmly states:

> Children must have knowledge of the world beyond their immediate surroundings. The fact that things are different does not make them right or wrong. And do not call another culture exotic. Please say different.

Middle Schools. At the middle school level, teachers' global school plans predominantly concentrated on the first and second dimensions of the Hanvey Model (1976), Perspective Consciousness and State of the Planet Awareness. Teachers stressed the multiple perspectives of people across the world, critically interpreting the news including current events, their causes and their effects on local communities and students' own lives; how cultural practices are viewed differently by different cultures and are of equal value; how some of the world's great non-Western prose, poetry, dance, and music share commonalities with Western cultural contributions; and that cultures across the world have contributed positively and negatively to civilization. Merryfield (2008) in her interview supports these observations:

> Teachers usually begin to infuse global perspectives in their instruction through multiple perspectives and perspective consciousness rather than teach global issues or global systems as often teachers do not have courses on such topics in their initial preparation.

Senior High Schools. At the senior high school level, the global school plans displayed a diversity of imaginations working with selective dimensions of the Hanvey Model (1976), emphasizing concepts of interdependence and the consequences of human choices as a comparative approach to discuss conflict as, for example, relationships between segregation in the U.S. and apartheid in South Africa; Japan's growing militarism and attack on Pearl Harbor with the U.S. internment of Japanese Americans during World War II; comparison of the violation of human rights (genocide) by Nazi war criminals with the violation of human rights in the U.S. in its near-annihilation of First Americans and of the deaths and injuries on both sides in times of war, the "enemy" and the conqueror. Peacebuilding discussions included the role of the United Nations and nongovernmental organizations (NGOs), challenging students to reflect on their own level of activism to improve the human condition. Contrary to the study by Merryfield (1991), who found that "most teachers in the United States learn to teach global perspectives through brief in-service education programs and professional conferences" (p. 1), in this three-year period of training in knowledge about the world and infusion pedagogy workshops, these teachers reached extraordinary sophistication in teaching global perspectives in a mandated curriculum.

Clearly these teachers demonstrated the characteristics of a globally minded teacher: the ability to work cooperatively with others; the ability to understand, accept, and tolerate cultural differences; sufficient problem-solving knowledge; and the capacity to think in critical and systemic ways (see chapter 11). In their common cause to expand students' attitudes and knowledge about the larger world, teachers of different ethnicity, backgrounds, and philosophies of education collaborated and produced the curricular foundation necessary to operationalize the global program in their classrooms. The knowledgeable, complex, and skilled performances of teachers in their teaching and learning about the world, argues Gaudelli (2003) in his seminal book *World Class: Teaching and Learning in Global Times*, are greatly enhanced through professional development in global education and are a testimony to the teacher as the community intellectual.

Example of a K-12 Interdisciplinary Conceptual Framework Studying the World

This next section provides an example of an interdisciplinary conceptual framework for studying cultural regions of the world, reinforced with global concepts taught in all elementary, middle, and senior high schools belonging to a specific feeder-pattern configuration in the Miami-Dade County Public Schools. The curriculum was taught in age-appropriate strategies from kindergarten to the 12th grade and repeated for the designated three-year program cycle.

Table 7.1 Studying the World Conceptual Interdisciplinary
Framework K-12 Three-Year Cycle

Grade levels	Nations/Regions/Themes/Issues/Concepts	
	1st Nine-Week Grading Period	2nd, 3rd, and 4th Nine-Week Grading Period
Kindergarten	United States	Australia
First Grade	United States	Central America and the Caribbean
Second Grade	United States	South America
Third Grade	United States	Africa
Fourth Grade	United States	Florida
Fifth Grade	United States	Canada and Mexico
Sixth Grade	United States	Europe and Russia
Seventh Grade	United States	East Asia
Eighth Grade	United States	South and Southeast Asia
Ninth Grade	United States	Linkages of Cultures
Tenth Grade	United States	Middle East
Eleventh Grade	United States	Cultural, Economic and Political Interconnectedness among Nations
Twelfth Grade	Conflict, War and Peacebuilding	

Year I: Implementation of global program begins with the third nine-week grading period. In the first nine-week grading period teachers are trained in global perspectives teaching, curricular design, and planning the entire academic year how to most effectively integrate global education into curriculum and instruction. During the second nine-week grading period the United States is studied for a basis of comparison with other regions of the world.
Years II & III: Implementation of global program begins with second nine-week grading period. Only K-11grade levels study the United States during the first nine-week grading period.

I now want you to imagine the realities of classrooms in the Miami-Dade County Public Schools in which globally trained teachers implement this framework in six elementary schools, two middle schools and its senior high school (the average size of a feeder-pattern configuration) with approximately 10,000 students simultaneously exploring the specific cultural, interdependent, issue-driven world on a consistent basis. Whereas the first grading period of the academic year was devoted to the study of the United States (except in the 12th grade), during the subsequent three grading periods annually for three consecutive years teachers integrated the interdisciplinary conceptual framework in the instructional process. Teachers chose their own global pedagogy to accomplish the task with different methodologies: (1) infusing the new content and concepts into the daily instruction of their given subject areas (most teachers), (2) teaching daily the new content and concepts during a 30-minute homeroom period (some teachers), or (3) teaching the new content in their given subject areas on the same day each week (some teachers). With effective teaching and administrative support we can assume that students are learning something about the world. Granted, some students will learn more, others less, others very little. But as Hanvey (1976) states in his cogent discourse, "An Attainable Global Perspective," collectively students *will* acquire knowledge and understanding about the world as

> global education is a loose assemblage of modes of thought, sensitivities, and intellectual skills. Any one individual may be relatively strong in some aspects, weaker in others. While schools need to strive to achieve a standard level of these traits in individuals, they can look to moving students as a group in the general direction (p. 1).

As many teachers in the global program taught about multiple perspectives in interpreting various worldviews of different people and nations, they were cautioned as to the difficulties the global educator encounters in the struggle for cross-cultural knowing. Heilman (2006) in her chapter "Critical, Liberal, and Poststructural Challenges for Global Education" supports the notion that we will never fully know who the Other is, and "coming to know across difference is an acutely difficult process when advocating appreciation for multiple perspectives denies or underestimates the discomfort of real difference" (p. 196). She reassures us, however, that "active tolerance and cross-cultural knowing does not require complete and nonjudgmental acceptance" (p. 197). This is a tall order for global facilitators to convey during in-service training.

Program Specific Activities to Enhance Global Pedagogy

The topic of this part of my chapter offers a glimpse into program-specific activities which enhanced the integration of global perspectives in curriculum and instruction in schools: the annual awards ceremony; the International Visitors Bureau; the Model United Nations; the U.S.-Russia Student Exchange Program; and the Miami-Moscow Hunger Project initiative.

Annual Awards Ceremony

Global facilitators came to realize that the members of the global leadership team, teachers, media specialists, and administrators alike, working tirelessly for hundreds of additional hours throughout the school year to implement the global programs in their schools must be publicly honored for their contributions to their school and district. Every year, one elementary teacher, one middle school teacher and one senior high school teacher and one media specialist were honored as the Global Teacher of the Year and Global Media Specialist of the Year. Of equal importance was the selection of outstanding Assistant Principals of the Year, who had been delegated the ultimate responsibility for effective implementation of the program. By the third year of implementation, we realized that the gatekeeper for successful programs in schools lies in the critical leadership of principals and lead principals who from that time on were honored as Distinguished Global Leaders. The joy and happiness exuding from the recipients remind the author of the critical importance of honoring the work of tireless educators in the trenches so often neglected if not forgotten, burdened with high public expectations and accountability.

The annual ceremony was held at the district's school board auditorium for maximum effect. Its central location made it easy for school board members, the superintendent, and high-level administrators attend the awards ceremony, enhanced by the leading elementary, middle and high school symphonic orchestras or jazz bands contributing to the festive atmosphere.

International Visitors Bureau

Since learning about the world and openness to the Other require as much firsthand exposure to international visitors as possible, the invaluable support of the International Visitors Bureau of the City of Miami became an integral component of the program. Students were seldom aware of the elevated status of the occasional visitors who represented their governments to the United States as well as our schools! But two distinguished themselves. A high-level representative of the Peruvian government clad in the attire of the Incas spoke of their civilization and their struggle for renewal. A visitor from Sierra Leone dressed in layered earth-colored gown and a turban spoke of the civil war and of the very young who were forced to fight as child soldiers. Visits of this nature require teachers to prepare students in the geography and culture of the visitor and to debrief their impressions. Merryfield (1997) and Wilson (1984; 1993a; 1993b; 1997) argue forcibly for the importance of such experiential learning in promoting cross-cultural understanding.

Model United Nations

Simulating the United Nations (UN) became an effective activity in the Miami-Dade County Public Schools in 1984. This was a dream of mine, recalling that Jim Becker, honored as the Father of Global Education, was the first teacher in the country to simulate the UN with his high school students in the early 1960s. I had visited the United Nations in New York observing no less than 2,000 high school students from the U.S. and other nations simulating the body politic discussing global issues. I never dreamt that I would have the opportunity to implement the simulation in my own school district.

In the Miami-Dade County Public Schools, with every year, the program expanded from schools in the district to neighboring Broward and Monroe Counties with as many as 25 high school teams participating in the simulation made possible with the collaboration of the Global Awareness Program, the Colleges of Arts and Sciences, Department of International Relations, and the Latin American Caribbean Center of Florida International University. At the two-day simulation held every spring, as many as 250 young ambassadors and their sponsoring teachers representing nations around the world swarmed the FIU campus and performed admirably in the various committees developing resolutions to be brought before the General Assembly. Throughout the two days, evaluators—parents, school administrators, and members of the local United Nations Association—sat incognito on committees and in the General Assembly to select the three best performing schools in this increasingly competitive endeavor.

One unanticipated aspect of the simulation was the intermingling of high school students of great diversity and from various socio-economic backgrounds, such as the emergence of the much-respected ambassadorial team from a high school near Lake Okeechobee, one of the poorest farm-worker communities in South Florida. The Model UN of the Miami-Dade County Public Schools was one of the most successful activities during the ten-year period and is still in place today—after 25 years. The simulation today also includes middle school students.

Miami-Moscow Hunger Project

After the fall of the Berlin Wall and the end of the Communist regime in Russia, Dr. Edvard Dneprov, Russian Minister of Education under the Yeltsin government, called upon the U.S. for assistance in the hunger crisis that had caused pervasive malnutrition of children and the elderly, particularly in rural areas. Miami's global schools embraced the urgent call with their hearts. Placing milk cartons on students' cafeteria dining tables, teachers encouraged students to drink water and place their milk money (a quarter) into the container "For Russia's Hungry Children." The successful project, thanks to Miami's generous administrators, teachers, and students, collected thousands of pounds of flour, vitamins, nuts, raisins, and basic medicine, which Delta Airline cargo planes shipped to Moscow free of charge.

Russia's cry to Miami for help came in response to the close relationship established between the Miami education community and the high-level delegation of the Russian Ministry of Education which attended the 1991 Key Biscayne invitational conference "The United States and the Soviet Union: Education Innovation and Reform" arranged under the leadership of Jan Tucker, Director of the Global Awareness Program, Florida International University, and Frank de Varona, Associate Superintendent of the Dade County Public Schools. In response to the Ministry's invitation, Jan Tucker and I attended the first international conference held in the new Russia in 1991 after the coup d'état against Gorbachev and the rise of a democratic Russia under the leadership of Boris Yeltsin (see chapter 9). It was there that hunger came to our attention as a permanent condition in many Russian communities (see Kirkwood & Tucker, 2001). [3]

The U.S.-Russian Student Exchange Program

The U.S.-Russian Student Exchange Program, sponsored by the American Forum for Global Education with a grant from the U.S. Department of Education, initiated a high-school student exchange program between 10 U.S. and Russian schools all of which were implementing global education programs. Russian and American schools were paired; the parents of students hosted each other's children. My high school, Turner Technical Arts High School in Miami, paired with a high school in Cheboksary in the autonomous region of Chuvash nestled along the Volga River and in a high school in the university city of Ryazan, 150 kilometers southeast of Moscow. Two of us classroom teachers accompanied four students each to our cities in Russia, a three-week stay in the midst of a cold winter that forever changed our students' lives and the attitudes of the hospitable Russian families who became parents to our inner-city youth of color. To this day I am in touch with some of "my children" who have carved out their own lives in admirable ways (see Kirkwood, 2001b). [4]

Assessment

In close collaboration with the principals of global schools the Director of the Global Awareness Program developed a comprehensive measurement protocol of the ten-year program that included (1) evaluation of content workshops held at the university; (2) evaluation of in-service training at school sites; (3) program and materials evaluation at school site; (4) pre- and post-tests of teacher attitudes and global knowledge gain gathered at the school site; (5) pre- and post-tests of student attitudes and global knowledge gain administered at school-site; (6) and analysis of school plans. As the principal global facilitator as well as a doctoral student at the university, I conducted the following unpublished research: a qualitative study of one high school (Kirkwood, 1989) and two middle schools (Kirkwood, 1992), and a content analysis of 45 elementary school plans (1987). My dissertation in 1995, *Teaching from a Global Perspective: A Case Study of Three High School Social Studies Teachers*, examines in situ how three social studies teachers integrated a global perspective in American and world history classes. The evaluation results were utilized for the purpose of requesting additional funding and to provide the knowledge base needed for program maintenance and revision.

The evaluation of program was a constant concern for Jan Tucker, Director of the Global Awareness Program, which he considered instrumental in the integration of global perspectives in curriculum and instruction in Greater Miami's public schools. The research results of student and teacher attitudes towards the world and acquisition of new global knowledge were one of the most important components of the program. However, the assessment of teachers and students presented the greatest challenge to school-site administrators, global leadership teams and global facilitators as the systematic administration of test materials had to be scheduled during school hours. Moreover, the program steadily grew in the number of schools, teachers, and students, and newly arrived students needed to be identified and exempted from the assessment. Chapter length constraints and the wealth of assessment information available require a separate publication.

Discussion and Conclusion

This discourse has attempted to capture the integration of global perspectives in curriculum and instruction in three-fourths of the Greater Miami's public schools over a ten-year period. The chapter addressed program goals, administrative meetings global facilitators had to attend, and teacher in-service training; program goals for three consecutive years including content workshops, school site sessions, and culminating activities; the professionalization of teachers, opportunities for their leadership, and their construction of school plans; an example of a feeder-pattern interdisciplinary framework studying the world from kindergarten to twelfth grade; specific activities to enhance the integration of global programs in schools; and assessment. This section will express my reflections on the effectiveness of the ten-year integration of a global perspective in curriculum and instruction in the Greater Miami schools offering alluring research possibilities for the field.

The Global Awareness Program of Florida International University was the principal setting for building an in-service education prototype in global education in the fourth largest school district in the U.S with thousands of teachers and over one hundred thousand students exposed to global perspectives over a 10-year period. The program's effectiveness led me to deduce three principal reasons for its indisputable success. The validity of attributing this success to that program is informed by the experiences of Frank de Varona, the district's principal leader in global education and by my own experiences in my roles as the global facilitator, social studies coordinator of the South Central Area, and coordinator of the International Global Education Program.

The first principal reason for the program's success in the effective integration of global perspectives in curriculum and pedagogy in the Greater Miami Public Schools is a direct consequence of the deeply held belief systems of teachers, media specialists and administrators in the philosophy of global education grounded in the inalienable equality of the human family, inclusion of marginalized people, and social justice. Heilman (2006), in her two cogent conceptualizations of human equality, reasons that

> there are two inclusive conceptions of humanity that underlie the duties of democratic citizenship: One is that all people are equal. From this point of view, whatever the important elements of human well-being are these elements belong to all human beings: nutrition, health, shelter, security or more broadly, happiness, autonomy, and cultural freedom…. Another conception of humanity…is the idea that all people are capable of reason and decency to justify government of, by, and for the people and…to arrive at suitable compromises to work with others to create a more just society (p. 194).

In democratic global dialogue and decision making there is no place for exclusion. Global education teaching is synonymous with making education equal. The notion of social justice resonates with the divergent groups in the Greater Miami community and schools. Global education is also generic, embracing all disciplines and age groups without boundaries, which led to interdisciplinary school plans in teaching and learning about the world.

A second principal reason for the success in the effective integration of global perspectives in curriculum and pedagogy in the Greater Miami Public Schools is unquestionably the teachers and students (of equal importance with the visionary administrators discussed in chapter 6). Despite serious time constraints and diverse curricular interests, these teachers recognized the salience of teaching and learning about the larger world that leads to the discussion of multiple perspectives and the cultural, geographic, economic, and political interconnections of the world's people to identifying commonalties of the human family. The infusion approach in integrating a global perspective in the existing curriculum was most frequently used and is considered the least time consuming methodology in global perspectives teaching (Merryfield, 2007; see also chapter 5). However, in this study, some teachers also chose the teaching of global perspectives and global concepts during a 30-minute homeroom period or on a designed day each week as that was their prerogative. Classrooms became dynamic, enthusiastic learning communities and improved attendance rates on Wednesdays (remarkably at Edison Senior High School and Turner Technical Arts High School), the day that was reserved for global teaching and learning and mitigating racial tensions inherent in urban schools (Christensen, 1993). Teachers increasingly observed the growing enthusiasm of their students, growing participation in class discussions, and frequency of questions asked about the world's people invigorating their teaching, renewing their energy, and validating their authenticity as teachers.

Students learned to appreciate the diversity among cultures and their contributions to humankind and to relate to their own heritage which resulted in ancestral pride. Culturally relevant pedagogy (Ladson-Billings, 1994) "elicits student knowledge as cultural experts encouraging students to speak about their social identities and making personal connections" (cited in Gaudelli, 2003, p. 104). Any school climate of caring administrators and global facilitators extended to caring teachers who are affecting students builds an ongoing dialogue about moral issues challenging for "a humane center for emotional and cognitive development built on relationship and nurture" (Gaudelli, 2003, p. 131).

In constructivist pedagogy frequently employed in global perspectives teaching, students enjoyed the active role in the exploration of cultures and peoples. They worked in cooperative teams conducting research on specific topics; presented their findings to class in a professional manner; conducted in-school interviews on a global issue; prepared multi-audio-visual exhibitions; and demonstrated enthusiasm about the constructive approach to learning. According to Gaudelli (2003) in his study of global programs in three New Jersey high schools,

> students are interested in global education because of the novelty inherent in the content...which offers them a unique opportunity to make personal meaning from novel experiences and knowledge (p. 64).

I also believe that creative pedagogy of culturally responsive teaching embraces students in an inviting, warm classroom community in which they are able to share meanings of culture and identity issues in open nonthreatening dialogue.

A third principal reason for the effective integration of global perspectives in curriculum and pedagogy in the Greater Miami Public Schools is community support. The annual bilingual Knowledge Bowls across grade levels and the culminating activities performed by student representatives from each feeder-pattern school which were held at shopping malls or senior high school provided ample opportunities for parents, extended families, and friends to attend activities deliberately scheduled at convenient times. When compared with approaches to education that emphasize cultural uniqueness, the overarching bonding power of global education is noted by parents, teachers, and students, who all see it as an effective context for learning about the world. There is an innate desire to appreciate and value one's own cultural and ethnic heritage. It appears that many parents, like the students, and teachers, wanted to recognize their own cultures in the context of the many cultures presented; it tends to increase the strength of any given culture when it is viewed as an important part of the larger, integrative whole of humanity. Lead Principal Day (2008), whose quiet firm leadership was instrumental in getting parents to attend school functions, reflects, "Not in my entire career have I observed such enthusiasm among parents. They were openly proud of their performing children."

The continuity of global education programs in the Miami-Dade County Public Schools is bittersweet. With new leadership and in a large-scale restructuring effort in the mid-1990s, the district closed the International Global Education Program office in 1994. Consequently, some global programs have stopped entirely; others have continued on a smaller scale. Still others continued to teach from a global perspective after the program officially ended and was absorbed into the culture of the school. As the functioning roles of university faculty and global facilitators were removed from overt support to global schools, Warren and Peel (2005) suggest that "administrators and teachers rely on their own talents and expertise...the university partner has achieved success if the school is better able to achieve independently...as university partners should create leaders not dependency" (pp. 346–352). Although increasing numbers of schools succumbed to the growing pressure of the high-stakes testing and public accountability movement sweeping across the country and the arrival of the Florida Comprehensive Assessment Test (FCAT) mandated by Governor Jeb Bush, many globally trained teachers have continued to carry the torch of global perspectives teaching according to de Varona (2008).

Research Opportunities

The Miami-Dade County Public Schools represent a goldmine for research in global education embracing the purpose that "global education should prepare teachers to build bridges across cultural boundaries and citizens to be able to communicate and collaborate with those whose attitudes, values, knowledge, and ways of doing things differ significantly from their own" (Cushner & Brennan, 2007, p. 6). There presently exists limited research in the global education literature regarding the teaching of global perspectives in the reality of public school classrooms in our nation. Of the many studies of global education programs (often self-reported), few individual inquiries have contributed to the strong empirical base called for by the community of global scholars to provide the firm empirical foundation of its curricular history which is necessary for readers of the research to consider broader generalizations (Gaudelli, 2003; Merryfield, 1998; Ochoa, 1986; Zong, 2008; also see chapter 4). Yet this paucity of empirical research persists despite years of advocacy and rich experiences of programs engaged in transforming global education theory into practice in our nation's schools.

This study provides at least four alluring research opportunities for the scholar-researcher-practitioner: First, one study might address whether (or how many) globally trained teachers have continued to teach from a global perspective after the official termination of the program in the district. Secondary questions might include: Why did these teachers continue integrating a global perspective in instruction? Why did the high-stakes accountability movement and mandatory statewide assessment not hinder these teachers from continuing their global pedagogy? A second inquiry may investigate teachers who refused to participate in the global program, chose only reluctantly to participate in the program, or who changed their minds and joined the program at a later stage. This study would provide insight into these teachers' deeply held beliefs and the environmental contexts that led to their continued resistance or to their eventual conversion and would greatly benefit the research community.

A third qualitative inquiry conducting content analyses of the hundreds of interdisciplinary school plans designed by elementary and secondary teachers, which provided the blueprint for the integration of a global perspective in individual schools and feeder schools can shed light on the question whether these documents attest to effective global perspectives teaching. Finally, an oratory ethnographic inquiry into the U.S.-Russian Student Exchange Program offers opportunities to examine attitude formation and attitudinal changes, acquisition of global knowledge, and cross-cultural experiential learning critical in understanding the Other in both the Russian and American student populations participating in the program, as well as parental and home care concerns on both sides of the Atlantic (Merryfield, 1997; Wilson, 1984; 1993a; 1993b; 1997). Studies of this nature can contribute greatly to the global education field.

At the time of this study beginning in 1984, the Miami-Dade County Public Schools boasted 274 schools, 12,500 teachers, 230,000 students of 122 nationalities (64,000 students had been born in countries other than the U.S.). At the conclusion of this study in 1994, the number of schools increased to 353, 18,758 teachers and almost 400,000 students of whom 71,000 students were foreign born. Today, the school district has expanded to 392 schools, 24,308 teachers, 347,774 students (a decrease of students due to out-migration), and an increase to 76,387 foreign-born students of whom 219,851 speak a primary language other than English (Miami-Dade County Public Schools Statistical Highlights, 1984; 1994; 2008). Do such staggering numbers of students of diversity and varying socio-economic backgrounds in communities benefit from a global education? You are the judge.

The preparation of teachers for the 21st century is of critical importance in meeting the challenges of the global age. I am convinced that global education can make a difference in the perception and acceptance of the Other. Americans have made a giant step towards equality and social justice reflected in the 2008 presidential election with a divided country selecting the first African American to the most powerful office in the modern world. Americans of the 21st century have demonstrated that they *are* capable of transcending Du Bois' (1903) tragic pronouncement that "the problem of the twentieth century is the problem of the color-line." With renewed hope for social justice, educators in the United States and other nations may consider integrating global perspectives in curriculum and pedagogy in the schools of their nation.

Notes

1. I use Miami-Dade County interchangeably with Greater Miami and Metropolitan Miami.
2. All school plans are stored in my house. Upon Jan Tucker's untimely death in May 1997, I placed his meticulously organized materials on the Global Awareness Program, the Global Education Leadership Training Program, and his work in schools in boxes which have traveled with me to my new destination in Tallahassee. They are waiting to be shared with the research community.
3. The globalization of Russian schools and teacher education programs are addressed in Kirkwood, T. F. & Tucker J. L. (2001). "Global Education: Catalyst in the Russian Education Reform Movement." *The International Social Studies Forum,* 1(1), 63–75. Copyright: Information Age Publishing, Inc. ISSN 1531-2763.
4. Our visit to Russia and my students' changes in how they perceived the Russian people before and after the visit is published in Kirkwood, T. F. (2001b). "Building Bridges: Miami Ambassadors Visit Russia." *Social Education,* 65(4), 236-239.

Chapter 8

The Russian Experience in Integrating Global Perspectives in Primary, Secondary, and Tertiary Education

Jacob M. Kolker, Irina M. Sheina, &Elena S. Ustinova

> Education makes a people easy to lead but difficult to drive; easy to govern but impossible to enslave.
>
> —Lord Brougham

The philosophy of global education attracted scholars and teachers in Russia because its ideas are not alien to the philosophical foundations of Russian academic tradition. Global education, with its democratic approach, gave new impetus to what is associated with school reform after the fall of the Berlin Wall at a period of romantic expectations in Russian society. American educators who brought global education to Russia at that time were not only scholars and visionaries but enthusiastic implementers who spared no effort in achieving what they thought to be feasible at a time of profound change in our country

Global Visionaries

A global vision has always been part of the Russian mentality. The idea of the world as a common home of humankind, the spirit of togetherness (*sobornost*), has passed down to us from the works of Russian philosophers and theologians since medieval times. As far back as the twelfth and thirteenth centuries in pre-Mongol times Russian scholars such as Kliment of Smolensk and Kirill of Turov drew from inexhaustible sources of the antiquity of philosophy and literature when they laid the foundations for a humanist pedagogy to glorify the spiritual values of man (Liferov, 1994). During the tragic times of discord among principalities of the Old Russia, Serapion of Vladimir saw the root of all evil not only in the invasion of the Mongols but, above all, in the ill feelings that brought about strife and caused fratricide. He stated: "Evil overcame reason, brother turned against brother...denounce evil, let goodness prevail."

The concept of cross-cultural awareness was promoted by fifteenth-and sixteenth-century Russian scholars, Epiphany the Wise, Maxim the Greek, and Ivan Fyodorov. They traveled far and wide and absorbed West European and Byzantine cultural experiences, which were reflected in their scholarship. A holistic approach to the world can be seen in the works of Karion Istomin (2004), an outstanding Russian poet and educator of the late seventeenth and early eighteenth centuries who adopted the ideas of Western pedagogy (above all those of Komensky) to contemporary Russian life. Another eighteenth-century scholar, Dmitry of Rostov, placed the virtues of the individual above his or her rank and ethnicity (Liferov, 2004). The idea of the Earth as a common dwelling place of humanity was advocated in the philosophy of early nineteenth-century Russia. Humankind and virtue were treated as two pivotal axes of the new model of existence. Humankind was viewed as a field to be cultivated by the ennobled heart and virtue was seen as the seed and plough.

The Russian School of Orthodox Theology was equally based on the idea of preserving national cultural identity and aspiration to the Absolute Good. Pavel Florensky (1990) asserts that one cannot be an individual if one does not feel an inseparable part of humankind. At about the same time, our famous writer Lev Tolstoy expressed the idea that every individual can contribute to promoting peace, understanding, and mutual forgiveness among nations. Dmitry Mendeleyev (1991), the author of the periodic table, believes that civilizations cannot develop successfully unless people find "a way of harmonizing their personal actions with the common good of humankind" (p. 408).

Synergy of Minds

Considering our indebtedness to U.S. global scholars, we would like to refer to them as a "constellation" because they represented a constellation of educators-philosophers-practitioners, each of them a star in his or her own right. Each of them proposed his or her own vision of global education as they all were attracted (as stars in a constellation should be) by the idea of an education reform to bring about a truly democratic world community. They have taught Russian educators why and how to teach "living with diversity."

The notion of perspective consciousness or multiple perspectives advanced by Hanvey (1976) provided us with a foundation for a new philosophy of global education. Hanvey's ideas might sound somewhat abstract if it were not for global scholars and their concepts grounded in an identity-centered vision of oneself within a framework of world community (Tucker, 1986; 1991a; Tucker & Cistone 1992); a framework for interdisciplinary and measurable student outcomes (Kniep, 1994); the application of theory into practice in case studies of teaching from a global perspective (Kirkwood, 1990; 1991; 1995); ideas of school reform in the information age (Mehlinger, 1995); the studies of school change as a result of implementing a global perspective (Kirkwood & Tucker, 2001; Tye & Tye, 1992); the presentations of our Canadian colleague Ronald Case on methods of integration and alternative assessment (1991; 1994); and ideas of conceptual themes as an instrument of integration (Kniep, 1987; 1989). Every one of these studies is invaluable to Russian scholars in developing their own vision of global education. We have learned a great deal from our North American colleagues and, in turn, have conceptualized the meaning of global education for lifelong learning in Russian education.

True, the ideas of global education have also met with opposition on the grounds that Russian culture is becoming "Westernized." But its opponents forget that no country can "import" foreign models of development without adjusting them to the sociopolitical and culture-specific conditions that can make these adaptations work. That is why the Russian concept of global education is a natural blend of Western experience and deeply rooted native tradition.

International Collaboration

Global education in the New Russia gradually took shape in the course of long-standing cooperation with U.S. and European scholars. Extensive communication and interaction occurred during international conferences held in the United States and Russia during the 1990s. It is necessary to mention the spirit of academic research and cooperation that reigned at these conferences.

The first international conference, "Global Education: A Multicultural Perspective," held in Sochi in 1991, treated the issues of global dimensions and perspectives as a vehicle for school and university education reform. A second conference, in Ryazan, "Global Education as a Vehicle for Humanizing Schools," focused on issues of school management and school-community relationships as tools in reforming education. The third conference, also held in Ryazan, in 1995, under the aegis of the International Network of Global Education (INGE), brought together scholars from nine countries. The scope of issues it encompassed included national policies, legislative revision, reduction of chauvinism, language policy, and the ethnic component of education as a means of releasing ethnic tensions. Participants were deeply involved in discussing such urgent topics as "Education Promoting Peace," "Human Rights Education and UNESCO," "The Work of the European Council," and "Education Promoting Democracy." Later conferences treated issues of curriculum and syllabus design, alternative assessment, integration as a tool of globalizing classes across the curriculum, and planning globally oriented classes and modules.

These conferences, supported by the Ministry of Education, were used by U.S. and Russian scholars as a basis for implementing a system of global education in many regions of Russia. The selection of regions was made by the Ministry of Education in its specific interest in education reform and development of a global vision in multiethnic communities. As a result, numerous global schools were organized in locations ranging from St. Petersburg in the west, Siberia in the east, to Sochi in the south. The experiences in Russian global schools have demonstrated that the transition to global education is a gradual process that can be successful only if a countrywide network of global institutions is established in order to develop and disseminate the achievements as well as share concerns in global education both in Russia and abroad. The functions and responsibilities of the participating institutions are effectively summarized by Kniep (1996).

Participating institutions consisted of regional centers, centers for inservice education, affiliated schools, and pedagogical universities.

Regional Centers

The establishment of the first regional center in the Russian education reform movement was the Ryazan Center for Global Education located at Ryazan State University, Ryazan, Russia, in 1992. The center established a global network for scholars, teachers, teacher educators, and administrators across a vast region of Russia. In the same year, 12 public schools from different regions expressed their commitment to embark as pilot schools on the path toward global education. The purpose of the Ryazan Center for Global Education was to (1) provide leadership in the development of global education in Russia; (2) acquaint the Russian communities with the philosophy and achievements of global education to garner public support; (3) coordinate the activities and networking of partnerships; (4) organize consultations and workshops for regional centers; (5) publish materials on global education; (6) translate foreign language textual materials into the Russian language; (7) maintain relationships with foreign partners; and (8) offer technical assistance to regional centers.

The first volunteers for a global program were schools in Moscow, St. Petersburg, Ryazan, Krasnoyarsk, Sochi, Voronezh, and Volsky. Three more schools joined subsequently in Barnaul, Samara, and the Chuvash Republic. By 1996, additional schools and higher educational institutions applied for admission to the network and were put on a waiting list. The demand necessitated a restructuring of the network and the implementation of nine additional regional centers to be located in St. Petersburg (northwestern region); Vladimir (central Russia); Cheboksary (Chuvash Republic); Rostov (southern region); Sochi (north Caucasian region); Volzhsk (Volga region); Barnaul (Altai region); Krasnoyarsk (Siberia); and Irkutsk (Siberia). The purpose of regional centers was to function as integrated partnerships and coordinate the endeavors of three or four pedagogical universities, affiliated pilot schools, and a center for in-service education within the region. Each regional center developed its own research priorities proceeding from its own needs and strengths (e.g., the Chuvash, Altai, and Dagestan regions focused on interethnic cultural contacts; the Ryazan region emphasized teaching foreign languages with a global perspective; the Vladimir region focused on social studies). This kind of "specialization" made it easier to combine teams of university professors, teachers, and administrators to collaborate and assist each other with their expressed interests and needs and effectively channel international cooperation to global educators in Russia, the United States, and other countries.

Centers for in-service education were responsible for training teachers, promoting global education throughout the region, and cooperation with other partners. Affiliated schools served as laboratories for research, demonstration centers, and sites for practical training of in-service and preservice teachers. The pedagogical universities were charged with preparing global teacher educators, coordinating activities within their region, conducting, publishing, and disseminating research in global education, providing expertise and identifying funding sources to support the center.

Global Pedagogy in Teacher Education and Syllabus Development

One major goal in the implementation of global perspectives in teacher education programs was to develop new courses, creating globalized curricula and instruction for the preparation of our future teachers. The

Ryazan Center for Global Education continues to lead in supervision of the research that has led to the development of new globally infused mandatory and elective courses, which include, among others, Introduction to Theory of Intercultural Communication, Competence-Oriented British and American Studies, and Theory and Practice of Global Education.

Common Goals

The global nature of these courses manifests itself in their content and range of issues as well as in their competence-oriented syllabi, measurable globally infused outcomes, and alternative assessments. The courses have common goals: forming an unbiased worldview, presenting information about the world as vital to the survival of humankind in the social and natural environment, and teaching to think globally and act locally.

We believe that at the pedagogical university (and schools) it is possible to delineate *three levels of globalization* of instructional courses informing the development of corresponding syllabi. All three levels have "equal rights," that is, they are equally important for the development of a global world outlook in preparing preservice teachers for the profession.

On *the first level*, the formation of a global perception of the world is accomplished basically by gathering information concerning humankind's current problems. It is the level of *attitude formation* related to global issues. *The second level* of globalization is concerned with the development of *universal intellectual skills* necessary for communication with people, for independent research, and for making decisions. This level, like the first, promotes interdisciplinary integration. Thus in studying any subject it is important to be able to classify objects, compare facts and events, generalize about information received, draw conclusions, and so forth. The third level of globalization of instructional courses informing the development of syllabi is what we tentatively call the *inherent global potential* of a given subject (discussed in more detail below). It is here that "the language" of the subject (vocabulary, grammar, theorems, formulas, equations) stops being merely form but is treated as content.

Any academic course is called upon to (1) lay the foundations of a holistic perception of the world; (2) establish the preconditions for seeing the world through the prism of the given subject; (3) teach students to learn, that is, to form scholarly habits and skills; (4) establish a system of interrelationship between the people involved in instruction; (5) develop, through the subject material, the intellectual operations fundamental to the development of universal intellectual skills; (6) teach the distinctive meta-language of the subject that aids communication on specific topics; and (7) ensure a sufficient level of competency in the given discipline.

Furthermore, the syllabus of a globally oriented course is required to (1) lay the foundation of a *humanitarian worldview* to teach students to act according to the rules of the global society and to be aware of himself or herself as an individual in interrelationships; (2) define the logic of the course design, that is, the sequence and consistency of its parts, so that the global approach does not contradict but rather promote the systematic assimilation of the bases of the subject; (3) define the nomenclature of the most effective strategies of conducting a lesson; (4) identify alternative methods of qualitative and quantitative verification of the results of instruction and of the level of learning and "teachability"; (5) designate time frames for the study of specific sections of the syllabus; and (6) offer a list of alternative texts and study aids that can be used with specific sections of the syllabus.

Moreover, a globally oriented syllabus for a subject should describe the role of the given course among other disciplines of the curriculum both "across" (interdisciplinary integration) and "down" (the linear or concentric continuity of different disciplines). The conception of the holistic perception of the world does not negate but, on the contrary, affirms that each course of instruction participates in the creation of a picture of the world from a definite point of vision as outlined in the Hanvey (1976) conceptual model (see chapter 5).

Blending Tradition and Innovation

Forming an unbiased view of the world depends not only on facts but also on the ways these facts are acquired and processed. In this respect, the concept of global education has much in common with the ideas of developmental education suggested by twentieth-century Russian scholars. For example, Vygotsky (1978) discovered "zones of proximal development," the distance "between the actual developmental level as determined by individual problem-solving and the level of potential development as determined through problem-solving under adult guidance or in collaboration with more capable peers" (p. 86). Davydov (1981) points out that it is possible to teach elementary school children the basics of theoretical thinking, which he considers the foundation of man's creative attitude toward reality. The principles of problem-solving education treated by Matiushkin (1987) proceed from an approach that takes into account a conscious algorithm of decision-making. That is, "learning occurs as a by-product of searching for a solution" (p. 395).

The blend of global innovation by North American scholars and the Russian pedagogical tradition makes it possible to define global education and the qualities of a global individual. Global education, which treats the world as a complex, ever-changing entity with its intensified problems and crises, can be defined as education that is systemic by nature, holistic in approach and structure, using integration as a strategic basis and modern pedagogical technology as a tool for imparting knowledge, skills, and attitudes. The aim is to create a global individual who

- possesses a multi-perspective and multidimensional vision of the world as a unity composed of interdependent factors, phenomena, and processes
- applies critical and creative thinking in everyday life
- is committed to and has the necessary skills for lifelong self-propelled learning
- has a capacity for self-knowledge and self-adjustment
- has a capacity for empathy and altruism, tolerance, and an appreciation for diversity in human viewpoints, beliefs, and customs
- is prepared to challenge chauvinism in all its forms
- has a sense for responsible citizenship, extending from his or her immediate community to the whole world; and
- is ready to make informed decisions and take actions after considering long-term consequences (see chapter 11).

The essence of each aspect of the definition is specified below to show how the idea of global education is implemented in Russian global education.

The Essence in Implementing Global Education in Russian Education

Making Education Systemic and Holistic

This approach views the phenomena studied as part of a variety of paradigms. Within a systemic approach the phenomena studied overlap and reveal their innermost connections. This approach, by definition, presupposes viewing the world in its entirety as a kind of meta-system that consists of a number of overlapping perspectives. Kniep (1987) speaks of four kinds of global systems consisting of economic, global political, ecological, and technological as the domains of the human experience that comprise its substance. But each academic discipline or branch of knowledge can also be regarded as a system. What matters is that *no discipline is viewed in isolation*. Rather, discipline-related facts can be viewed like fragments of colored glass in a kaleidoscope that gives us a different picture when it is turned, though the construction blocks are the same.

A holistic learner establishes numerous logical and imaginative associations, observes similarities between diverse processes and facts, and notices a variety of ways in which the same phenomenon can be approached. A holistic worldview helps to bring together things that at first sight seem to bear no visible resemblance to each other. This connection is effected by discovering certain organizing principles such as symmetry. A picture of an antique vase is like a math equation or a butterfly insofar as each, by being symmetrical, illustrates the same law of nature. This defies the existing philosophy of education based on the world vision introduced by Ptolemy: the world is static and not liable to change; therefore it can be sliced into segments. This perspective accounts for education being sliced into different disciplines.

A holistic vision of the world is impossible without critical thinking: that is, the ability of the mind to process information, evaluate it, compare facts, and draw conclusions. Critical thinking makes learning a more democratic process, since dissent is encouraged instead of being censured. On the other hand, taking sides and standing one's ground should be balanced by tolerance for views and attitudes different from one's own. Critical thinking can be regarded as a basis for creative thinking. Both require a flexibility of mind. A rigid mind cuts itself off from the solution of a problem by imposing limitations on one's self. These limitations come from previous experience that shapes our decision-making and often sets blinders on our minds (Kuliutkin, 1995, p. 11). For instance, if a student is asked to take six matches and make four triangles of them without breaking the matches, he will never cope with the task as long as he assumes that it must necessarily fall into a two-dimensional pattern. Flexibility of mind encourages unorthodox solutions and multiple perspectives—so important in our rapidly changing world.

Skills for Lifelong Learning

Skills related to lifelong learning or self-education can be said to fall into three categories. The first category includes discipline-related skills that have little bearing on global education. The second category comprises cross-cultural skills of looking for information (using the Internet or reference libraries, etc.), and processing that information (making a resume, comparing texts for similarities and divergences, collecting and classifying data, etc.). The third category falls within the philosophy of global education with emphasis on the following competences:

- predict plausible cause-effect chains (e.g., better roads—more cars—more traffic jams—more air pollution)
- examine the same phenomenon from different perspective (e.g., "rain" as part of the water circulation system; as part of landscape; as a literary symbol)
- establish associations between seemingly unrelated phenomena (e.g., a planetary system and the structure of an atom; a beehive and a human community; a math formula and a haiku). If extended too far, however, the analogy becomes false. If judiciously balanced it helps to draw subtle inferences.

Immunity to Chauvinism

Immunity to chauvinism, whether ethnic, racial, religious, gender-based, cultural, or linguistic, is just as important an aspect of survival as environmental balance. Chauvinism can be prevented in two ways. First, we select representative samples of content that instill respect for cultural diversity. The learners come to appreciate contributions of various ethnic groups to the national or world culture; they realize that every cultural tradition is meaningful. They learn that a pattern of behavior that appears entirely wrong in the context of one's own culture can make sense in the context of the culture of another. Second, classroom management encourages independent thinkers to be tolerant of views and values different from their own. A classroom becomes a microcosm of society where other people's options and preferences, habits and ideas have as much right to exist as do your own views, and becomes a place where you discover that hardly any opinion can be entirely right or entirely wrong and learn to come to terms with the concepts of others.

Responsible Citizenship

Responsible citizenship means caring about what is taking place in your community, state, nation, and world, and feeling that you, too, have a voice in the matter and can influence the way things happen, no matter how insignificant your social role might be. Global awareness does not in any way diminish one's patriotic feeling for one's country. Patriotism is no longer opposed to the so-called cosmopolitism in education, as both represent an ever-widening circle of belonging and personal participation in your family, your neighborhood, your city, your country, your planet.

Integration of Knowledge

Although the qualities of a global individual can be analyzed separately, they "synergetically" form an ever-developing entity. The latter can hardly be ensured unless teaching is largely based on *integration.* Integration is basically related to two notions: wholeness (a holistic vision) and economy. *Holistic* is a synonym of *integral.* But what kind of integration do we suggest? Is it integration of education as a process of learning and socialization? Or is it integration of school into the life of the community, or integration of individualized and generalized human experience? Answers to these and similar questions can outline the social aspect of integration in education. We are mostly concerned with integration as a basis for curriculum, syllabus, and lesson design and are going to discuss how learning shapes consistent pictures of the world in which every phenomenon is seen as part of a larger whole, a form of learning that deepens self-cognition.

The integration of knowledge is multifunctional. It saves time and eliminates redundancy. It makes knowledge personally meaningful when what appears to be abstract theory is applied to everyday problems and issues. It fosters a more holistic vision because the same phenomenon is regarded from different perspectives. Integration develops the habit of looking for all kinds of associations when one studies a phenomenon on one's own; it prevents chauvinism and rigidity of thinking because it helps us to assess the same fact from various and sometimes unexpected perspectives. Even such a hateful thing as war turns out in the historical perspective to have its positive side-effects, having encouraged from time immemorial the development of myriad technologies that were later employed for peaceful purposes. And conversely, extermination of dangerous diseases, certainly a blessing for humankind, has led to overpopulation and global hunger. So integration means bringing together the scientific and ethical aspects of cognition.

According to Case (1994), "a study is integrated when the bringing together of the parts contributes to a better understanding of the individual elements and a clearer picture of the unit" (p. 2). We strongly agree with the Case definition because it shows that integration is much more than a simultaneous study of the same fact from different perspectives. One often hears of team-teaching as a vehicle for integration. Team-teaching is a useful approach as long as its value is not exaggerated. But a lesson does not automatically become integrated if the phenomenon under discussion is presented by two or three teachers of different subjects.

Pre-Integration versus Integration Proper in Lesson Planning

Pre-Integration

In this section of the chapter we address the notion of pre-integration versus integration proper in the attempt to teach a lesson from a global perspective. The following is an example of integrating physics and literature in School 14 in our town of Ryazan.[1] The lesson focused on the study of lightning and thunder. It was team-taught, and neither the scientific nor the literary aspect was a mere background to the other. The students analyzed the physical properties of these phenomena, attempted a laboratory experiment, quoted Russian poetry and prose, tried to account for the impressions they convey, discussed why a thunderstorm gives a feeling of such wonderful freshness, and so on. And yet such lessons can hardly form an important part of a global curriculum: the links between physics and poetry are too fragile and occasional, and a team-taught lesson of this kind with all the effort it must have taken is rather a brilliant curiosity than a living part of a global curriculum. The extra effort required by team-teaching is justified when the two or three subjects do not just work smoothly alongside each other but when *each one really works for the benefit of the other(s)*. If poetic analogy ensures a deeper insight into the essence of a natural or social phenomenon or if background knowledge of natural or social phenomena helps to attain a better understanding of a short story, then integration really works. In the lesson in question, poetry and physics "looked nice together," but they did not enhance each other.

The definition offered by Case (1994) sets high standards for integration. Anything falling short of its requirements is no more than a prelude to integration, a kind of pre-integration. With such lessons the disciplines brought under the same roof may have the advantage of creating an emotional background for each other. This lesson on thunder and lightning exemplifies this kind of pre-integration.

Another interesting example of pre-integration is a class in math and literature for six-year-old kindergarten children, "A Visit to Fairyland," taught at the Ecol Kindergarten School in Moscow. At the very beginning of the lesson the children operate with numbers to find out on what page the fairy-tale begins. On the teacher's desk stands a cardboard model of an enchanted palace and inside the enchanted palace dwell characters from well-known fairy-tales of different nations. The children listen to short episodes and identify each tale. As soon as they guess which story it is, a window opens and reveals a picture of the main characters (Snow White, Sleeping Beauty, etc.). Then the children do more math tasks that are for them part of the game they are playing: for example, the teacher shows the class pictures of the seven dwarfs and the children think up a number of criteria by which to classify and count the dwarfs. The little folk have brought more tasks with an "invisible" number (3 + the invisible = 5). Thus six-year-old children become acquainted with simple equations: $3 + X = 5$.

In this lesson, the cross-cultural aspect of Hanvey's (1976) conceptual third dimension was clearly emphasized. While identifying the fairy-tales, the children named the country the fairy-tale came from or the author of the tale. They also compared the situations in which the characters found themselves and came to the conclusion that different fairy-tales can be very similar. The children exercised their imaginations by trying to guess what tale is represented by a symbolic picture (with its conflict depicted metonymically, e.g., an apple and a mirror in Alexandr Pushkin's (1983) tale, "The Dead Princess and Seven Knights." Of course, the study of literature did not bring about an insight into the logic of mathematics, or vice versa. But the shifting of attention from literature to math was easy and joyful: the students learned as naturally as they breathed.

Integration Proper

The conception of integration proper works for classes designed as a blend of two or three subjects. An attempt at true integration was a lesson in geography and literature, "A Journey with a Fairytale," taught at School 44 in Ryazan. The study of fairy-tales belonging to different ethnic groups made it possible to detect and analyze the similarities of both conflicts and attitudes and also of cultural peculiarities. The latter, as the students discovered, depend upon the natural environment in which the story is couched, and the geographical position of the country (and therefore its climate, flora, fauna, etc.) conditions the culture and lifestyle of the ethnic group revealed in its fairy-tales. In this case the two components of the unit, geography and literature, blend into one body. Classes of this kind often necessitate team-teaching.

Let us examine how integration can be achieved. Case (1994) distinguishes between *integrating principles* and *modes of integration*. The former represent the content or type of activity around which integration occurs. The modes of integration show how integrated disciplines are related to one another and what role they play respectively in a course, unit, or lesson plan.

Integrating Principles

In the first category, identified as integrating principles, Case (1991; 1994) includes the following: themes, issues, inquiries, problems, and projects. In turn, each group can be further subclassified. For example, themes can be subdivided into places, events, eras, concepts (e.g., friendship, harmony, time, creativity); generalizations (e.g., Man is a social animal or History repeats itself); phenomena (biological change, war, growing old); and entities (bears, atoms). An inquiry, according to Case (1994), further identifies a specific question whose answer is a description of how things actually were or are likely to become (What will my life be 30 years from now?). The difference between issues and problems is that an issue identifies a question about what is most desirable or what ought to be the case (Should further technological innovation be encouraged?) while a problem identifies a question whose answer is a course of action (How can our school be made more personal?). As to projects, they require a definite product whether verbal or nonverbal (a research paper, a dance performance, a mural, or a multimedia presentation).

Not all of these integrating principles appear to be equally valid. Most of the principles are dynamic by their very nature and therefore intrinsically presuppose reasoning or creative activity: a project to implement, an issue to debate, a problem to solve, an inquiry to carry out. As to narratives, unless their purpose is specified, they don't seem to have enough point for an integrating principle: what do we narrate for? And as far as themes go, this unifying principle appears too static and even devoid of purpose: people do not communicate "on a topic" as there must be an intention behind any oral or written discourse! A theme's gravitational power is too weak to turn the module into a unified whole: there is no inner connection between any two classes, and the knowledge gained remains a number of isolated facts.

Modes of Integration

In addition to principles of integration, Case (1994) speaks to four modes (strategies) of integration in developing a global perspective in curriculum and instruction: (1) *Fusion*. Integration occurs by fusing elements of the curriculum into a new single entity (e.g., joining the history and language curricula to create a new humanities course); (2) *Insertion*. Integration is achieved by fitting one element into the framework of another. For example, in a translation class, students are faced with the following context: *Churchill did not cause Soviet domination of Eastern Europe: that was unstoppable once the German army was crushed. The sea was not Canute's fault.* The obvious challenge is the historical allusion: hardly any Russian student knows the name of Canute and the story attached to it. The phrase seems to have no sense: how can the sea be anybody's fault, anyway? So we need to insert a brief glimpse of early medieval British history. Canute, a pre-Norman English king of Danish origin, began to rule with fire and sword. But, once his power was firmly established, he appeared to be so fed up with flattery that one day, when walking along the shore in the company of his courtiers, he ordered the tide to stop rising in order to show that he was *not* omnipotent. This story makes the meaning of the phrase transparent and enables students to decide on the best translation strategy. Actually, the none-too-familiar name can be dropped altogether, and the translation may go like this: "Churchill might just as well have told the tide to stop rising."

The third mode of integration is *Correlation*. Integration is achieved by synchronizing and drawing connections between discrete elements (e.g., having teachers in various subjects deal with a common theme at the same time); and (4) *Harmonization*. Integration occurs by making disparate elements compatible or promotive of each other (e.g., getting all teachers in a school to agree to a common form of research and writing essays). *Fusion* as a mode of integrating "a new entity" may be attributed to separate lessons as well as to short units or longer courses. A good example of fusion on the level of a whole course is, for instance, The ABC of Theatre (School 14, Ryazan). It is hard to identify the specific subject that is taught as the course represents a unity of rhetoric, ethics, aesthetics, music, and lots of other things. *Insertion* is likely to be applied more widely than fusion at least during the transition period from a traditional curriculum to a global curriculum. Fusion is harder to attain and requires more creative and organizational effort, especially in team-teaching. Insertion, like fusion, promotes a multi-perspective vision of the world. For instance, if a lesson in rhetoric hinges on the topic of ethnic conflict and racial prejudice, it can draw from a lesson of anatomy where children have just discussed not only how people of various races differ in appearance but *why* they differ: what conditions of life brought about these differences (this lesson was taught in a private school called The Voices of Spring in Volzhsk of the Volgograd region (post-communist state supported schools no longer were referred to by a number; principal and community could choose their own name for their new school). Another advantage of inserting elements of knowledge into other subjects is an opportunity to unify an emotional and an intellectual appeal. Thus, when discussing political, environmental, or scientific issues it is most useful to appeal to poetry, which by means of imagery gives us condensed and multilevel meaning to fit to the situation under analysis. It is a stimulus for generalization and for looking at things in a new, unprejudiced way. Scientific cognition is closely connected with poetic thinking because both require precision and economy. It is also possible to speak about *insertion within the same discipline.* For instance, a math teacher (School 8 in Sochi) helps students to discover a new math formula (a) by asking them to recollect a familiar one (b) which deals with different notions but logically is the same: for example, (a) the amount of work done equals work productivity multiplied by the time required; (b) the total sum of money paid equals the price of one item multiplied by the number of similar items bought. Integration of this kind helps one to think systemically, and to discover the familiar in the strange when applying mental operations.

 Correlation as a mode of integration (also referred to as *synchronization)* depends on the connections between various facts, phenomena, and regularities studied at more or less the same time. This mode of integration is hard to achieve because syllabi for different disciplines possess their own logic of grading difficulties that may be ruined when synchronizing the cross-curricula study of certain components. Teachers of physics are often heard to complain that the math syllabus lags behind and does not provide them with the necessary tools. Ideal correlation is unattainable if treated on the level of facts. But as soon as we use such an integrating principle as a metaconcept (discussed later in the chapter), correlation reveals almost unlimited possibilities. It also requires cooperation among teachers. When planning a syllabus for the year, every discipline teacher ought to be aware of what will be taught in the other subjects. The metaconcepts of change, symmetry, movement, and the like may be an ideal ground for synchronizing the study of disciplines whose subject matter has little or nothing to do with that of the others.

Harmonization as a mode of integration aims at turning incompatible components into compatible elements so that the results obtained in one class can be helpful in another. It is this very mode of integration that can rely on such organizing principles as universal cognitive and communicative skills (see in the section that follows). Teachers can negotiate about a certain group of interrelated skills that can be pursued as a set of benchmarks throughout a term or an entire year. In summary, the various principles and modes of integration advanced by Case (1994) offer unlimited opportunities to school and university teachers provided they possess enough enthusiasm and willingness to cooperate. Integration is more than a means; it is a way of viewing the world. It is the very heart of a truly holistic perspective.

Epistemes and Metaconcepts as Organizing Cross-Disciplinary Principles

Perhaps it was the amorphous status of a "theme" that brought Kniep (1987) to differentiation between phenomenological, conceptual, and persistent problem themes. Concepts can be on different levels of abstraction; a tree is a less concrete notion than an oak tree but it is more concrete than a plant, which is generic for a tree. But to attain a global, integrative vision, we need a different kind of systematization. An issue, inquiry, problem, or project is likely to draw from varied sources in order to have an interdisciplinary perspective. For instance, the problem of increasing medium life expectancy requires an examination of medical, biological, environmental, social, cultural, and political factors that affect the human life span. The disciplines across which integration occurs will be united by a single purpose. That is why conceptual and persistent problem themes outlined in Kniep's classification system are a more effective base for integration than are phenomenological themes.

We believe it is possible to speak of two kinds of cross-disciplinary notions. One is the so-called *episteme* that is derived from a Greek word meaning knowledge. Lysenko (1994) believes that studies can be organized around such epistemes as war, tree, mother, conscience, home (pp. 66–72). The second is what can best be defined as a *metaconcept*, such as system, equilibrium or balance and hierarchy. At first sight these notions seem to possess an equal degree of generalization. But we find a great difference between the two. An episteme is an external, thematic unifying notion. But if we look back on the definition of integration suggested by Case (1994) we clearly see that one group of facts we establish may have little or nothing to do with another. What is more, the episteme violates the natural course of a syllabus for a given subject. If "pushed into" a lesson, it feels like a splinter in your palm.

A metaconcept, unlike an episteme, is not a theme. Rather, it is a mechanism of cognition, a tool for discovering the way things work. A metaconcept reveals the intrinsic unity of general laws of thinking and perceiving the world around. Compare the notions of friendship and balance. The former belongs exclusively to the sphere of ethics and has nothing to do with math or science. The notion of balance, on the other hand, ranks in our opinion as a metaconcept. In fact, friendship can be one of its manifestations. But balance does not occur in human relations only. We observe balance in nature where it regulates the population of certain species in a region. When studying science, we observe balance between nuclear particles in the structure of an atom, or balance as valence in a molecule. In social studies, balance ensures stability and lack of tension. In terms of ecology, balance reveals itself as sustainability. Other notions that can be called metaconcepts are change, interdependence, conflict (Kniep, 1987), or algorithm and symmetry (introduced by the authors of a series of school textbooks under the general heading Ecology and Dialectics supervised by Tarasov & Pushkareva [1993; 1994]). A list of metaconcepts remains to be developed. But the main criterion for testing a metaconcept can be given now: it must be *applicable to all spheres of knowledge, concerning the laws of nature, and man and his ways.*

From our experiences in classroom observation we have learned that if a cross-curricular unit is based on a metaconcept, integration occurs smoothly and naturally, and a student can pass from a literature class to a science class feeling that it is all part of one global lesson. But when integration is attempted around a theme (an episteme), even such a broad one as "home," it sometimes works and sometimes fails to function as a unifying principle because it is not an instrument of cognition but simply a topic for discussion that may be quite foreign to the normal course of a lesson.[2] We have no intention, however, of denying the value of phenomenological themes, or epistemes, as an organizing principle in creating a globally integrated lesson. In fact, it can be a marvelous idea if the notion to focus on is personally relevant to the students. But curriculum planners should not insist that for a certain period of time every lesson of the curriculum should be based on a definite episteme.

Communicative Skills and Intellectual Cognitive Skills

There are two other unifying principles in establishing an integrated global lesson: communicative skills and intellectual cognitive skills based on mental operations. Years ago it was customary to believe that communicative skills were really relevant only for language studies or at best for the humanities, whereas in a math or chemistry class one could allegedly communicate by nonverbal signs. Today, the all-permeating relevance of communicative skills is no longer questioned and one can observe a music or geometry class in which emphasis is laid on verbal perfection.

For all the differences in the subject matter, classes in different fields of knowledge will be perceived as closely connected if we teach students to perform similar intellectual functions, for instance, to give definitions to notions or to classify various phenomena. Cognitive skills are an outward manifestation of mental operations. Psychologists are not unanimous as to the total list of mental operations, but they all mention at least the following: identification, classification, generalization, comparison, selection, grouping, arrangement, transformation, substitution, analogy, abstraction. The more attention we give to developing cognitive skills and mental operations in one academic subject, the more effectively students will function in another subject.

Nonglobal and Global-by-Nature Academic Subjects

There are disciplines that are global by nature (e.g., geography, history, economics, and ecology) and disciplines whose content is at some remove from the urgent global issues such as the native and foreign languages, mathematics, logic, computer literacy, and others. Mathematics, for instance, does not have a clearly defined global coloration. Its language is a universal code, in itself indifferent to the content that is put into it. But on the other hand, the universality of the language of mathematics makes it truly indispensable for the resolution of practically any global problem.

Nonglobal Academic Subjects as Form and Content

We start with an assumption that subjects like mathematics serve to increase global awareness in two ways. First, they act as form to be filled with relevant global content; math formulas, as mere form, make it possible to discuss urgent issues. Like mathematics, spoken languages represent an ideal form to contain global content. The practical objective of mastering communication in a foreign language, or literacy and rhetoric in a native language, can be achieved in the context of the most vital and varied contemporary problems: from ethnic tensions to ozone holes, from demographic processes to the extinction of rare species of plants and animals. However, teachers of seemingly "less global" disciplines should not regard their subjects as empty vessels that must be filled with globally significant content. Otherwise, we will not be able to develop a subject-oriented picture of the world, and without that the worldview of the student will be considerably poorer.

The language of an academic course (formulas, equations, vocabulary, grammar, etc.) can be treated as content when language itself is brought into the focus of discussion. We do not mean the purely formal tasks, like choosing the right tense or finding roots. We mean all kinds of tasks that may contribute to the shaping of a discipline-focused picture of the world. For instance, students may be asked to discuss the basic principles uniting the decimal and the binary codes as compared with other numerical systems and to find the merits and shortcomings of each. Similarly, a foreign language course may include many types of globally oriented tasks contributing to a linguistic picture of the world. For instance, a student may be encouraged to discover that words that seem at first sight to be absolutely different in meaning are conceptually related (e.g., *inspector, specter, spectacles, respect, prospect* all come from the Latin root "to behold"). Comparing equivalent proverbs across languages, students discover the similarity of meaning beyond different systems of imagery: "Too many cooks spoil the broth" in English is equivalent to the Russian "Seven nurses leave the child unattended"; moreover, the imagery of proverbs and sayings betrays the peculiarities of everyday life, the economics, the culture of the countries, and the languages that are being studied: the English *"carry coals to Newcastle,"* whereas Russians *"go to Tula with their own samovar."* An even more important thing is to learn that any language can express any idea, but our vision of reality is "packaged" a bit differently (e.g., English: "*My name is Anna*"; Russian: "*Me they call Anna*"; German: "*I am called Anna,*" and in French: "*I call myself Anna*"). Such observations demonstrate that linguistic relationship to reality is simultaneously universal and unique for each language. This awareness breeds respect for other languages, however strange they may seem at first sight. It can be a useful antidote to "linguistic chauvinism" so brilliantly illustrated by Mark Twain in the episode where Huckleberry Finn is trying to explain to Jim why the French talk in a different way.

It was more than 80 years ago that Thomas Huxley (1952) defined education as learning the rules of the game of life. To him, it meant "instruction of the intellect in the laws of nature." By "laws of nature" he understood "not merely things and their forces, but men and their ways" and the stimulation of "an earnest and loving desire to move in harmony with these laws" (pp. 464–467). Using the analogy of a game, Huxley pointed out that if our life and fortune depended on losing or winning a game of chess, no father would allow his son and no state would allow its members to grow up without knowing a pawn from a knight. We presume that the rules of survival as Huxley understood them can be embedded in the content of a foreign language as an academic discipline and the way it is taught. What matters here is the palate for research, the spirit of intellectual adventure, and the never-ceasing curiosity that foster linguistic discoveries in foreign languages and in one's native language.

Some rules that one can deduce from the aforementioned assumptions are as follows: (1) No language is better or worse, richer or poorer, less expressive or more expressive than others; (2) every language reflects the culture of the country where it is spoken and explains its peculiarities; and (3) every cultural tradition makes sense. The outcomes that emerge from these rules are profound and include:

- respect for ethnic minorities who have to and are able to master several other languages in order to survive (the development of this kind of empathy is especially important for countries with an "imperialist" linguistic outlook);
- linguistic curiosity; the sheer joy of being able to say and understand at least a few things in the language of the host country; and
- tolerance for people of other cultures who are not fluent in your native language, and so on.

Thus, Huxley's metaphor of life as a game based on a set of rules can be applied to goals and outcomes of language education within a global perspective. These rules may be viewed as broad goals leading to a hierarchy of outcomes that are specified in a list of objectives. They boil down to skills that are measurable, types of behavior that are observable, and attitudes that prompt predictable reactions.

Global versus Traditional Classes

The three levels of globalizing education and the pre-integration versus integration proper discussed earlier make it easier to bridge the gap between "global" classes and "traditional" classes. A class can be "traditional" insofar as its subject matter is discipline related and does not concern the urgent problems of survival, yet it can be global in the sense that it can develop critical and creative thinking, undermine stereotypes, or breed tolerance.

On the other hand, global content does not automatically guarantee the success of a lesson. It is not enough to identify the problems facing humankind. One ought to be able to suggest a course of action and to see its possible consequences. That is why global education as a whole and a global lesson as its integral unit can be seen as a process of deducing the rules of survival in an interdependent world where every individual is a part of four systems: (1) people and nature, (2) individual among others, (3) humankind and technology, and (4) people and semiotic systems.

Some of the school disciplines fall within the framework of one group; others embrace more than one group. Thus, mathematics, languages, logic, music, and painting belong to the fourth group of "people and semiotic systems" as they are all systems of meaningful signs. History, political science, sociology, and ethics represent the "individual among others" group. But ecology cannot be pinned down exclusively to the "people and nature" group. The study of environment cannot be divorced from political issues such as piling up outdated chemical weapons or dumping one's nuclear waste on the territory of another country.

Not every lesson can focus on global problems. Many lessons aim at providing students with factual material as a basis for further integration seen from a global perspective. Thematically, they may seem very insignificant and irrelevant for a global vision. But it seems a grave misconception to subdivide lessons into "global" and "traditional." Rather, they can be classified into "global" and "globally oriented" (i.e., "globally focused" or "globally infused") lessons depending on the intent of the teacher or the mandate of the curriculum. Both types answer the following requirements:

- correspond to didactic principles of teaching and learning;
- teach how to learn;
- stimulate freedom of self-expression;
- aim at emotional and intellectual involvement;
- stimulate cooperative skills, alongside with a sense of personal responsibility;
- employ specific integrating principles and modes of integration (cognitive universals being one of the main integrating principles) so as to make cognition a more profound and economic process;

- use alternative assessment contributing to the development of self-esteem and creative abilities; and
- create a discipline-related perspective of the world.

Moreover, a truly "global" lesson should possess a number of distinguishing features that a globally oriented lesson may not have. No matter whether it is part of a traditional curriculum or part of a cross-disciplinary course, as we believe that a global lesson is a blend, a place where two or more disciplines meet and are equally relevant, none serving as a mere background to the other, is based on one or more metaconcepts; contributes to the shaping of a multifaceted view of the world; and teaches students to establish connections between interrelated systems (economic, ecological, etc.) and make informed decisions concerning issues vital for the survival of their community and the community of nations.

Global Education in Russia Today

Today, global education programs in Russia operate as separate entities and do not form a holistic and unified network. The continuity of systematic implementation of global perspectives in teacher education programs and schools of the mid-1990s and the flourishing of their development was interrupted for several reasons: a lack of resources to organize Russian conferences and to provide on-site expertise; political unrest that could not be quenched by education alone; and changes in leadership in the Ministry of Education resulting in a different vision of the contemporary world—not as a comprehensive whole but as a set of specific global issues that had to be addressed immediately, such as tolerance, conflict resolution, environmental pollution, drug trafficking, and other immediate concerns challenging the new Russia. The term "global education" acquired a negative connotation owing to activities of antiglobalists and far-right thinking individuals. However, the idea of global education, whether it is called "global education" or "education for the future," has never been abandoned by Russian educators and still forms an integral part of curriculum and pedagogy in selected teacher education programs and schools. In some Russian universities elective courses in global education have been implemented, books on global perspective in education have been published (one of them in English), and textbooks based on the global vision of culture and ethnic issues were written and disseminated in schools.

From our years of experience in teacher education and schools we have found that the global perspective gives education a chance to escape two extremes; the first is that of narrow specialization (whether university research or apprenticeship in a manual trade), and the second extreme is that of broad general education that so often vanishes with no visible imprint on the learners' minds. Global education bridges the gap between the pragmatic and the ethical. "The more I give to thee, the more I have" becomes more than a paradox of selfless love and emerges as one of the basic rules of survival in an interdependent world. What is more, the philosophy of pragmatic empathy extends beyond human relationships. It also embraces nature and brings us to the attitude of Robert Burns's "of mice and men" or John Donne's idea of "for whom the bell tolls" that humankind is diminished by the extinction of any species.

Notes

1. Ryazan is located approximately 150 kilometers southeast of Moscow.
2. Some of the "epistemes" enumerated by Lysenko (1994) can be considered metaconcepts (e.g., time, energy, movement).

Chapter 9

Historical and Sociopolitical Context in the Development and Implementation of Global Education in Russian Education Reform

Lena Lenskaya

You must be the change you wish to see in the world.

--Mahatma Gandhi

In December 1991, the Soviet Union of the Socialist Republics ceased to exist. Mikhail Gorbachev resigned from his post as President of the Soviet Union after a failed coup d'état. Boris Yeltsin was elected by an overwhelming majority to the Presidency of the Russian Federation and Dr. Edvard Dneprov was elected Minister of Education by the sitting Parliament (Verkhovny Sovet) from a group of alternative candidates. Dneprov's (1991) cogent public policy statement on education reform still reverberates with me today:

> It is education that is to destroy old-fashioned stereotypes and that will change the psyche of the nation; it is education as well that is to lead the way in developing people's democratic world outlook, their acquiring a new political culture and an economic awareness (p. 2).

Dneprov's commitment to the Russian people would set in motion a major education reform movement that resonated around the world—a daunting task. This chapter describes one of the momentous events in the history of Russia with the leadership of Mikhail Gorbachev: the Soviet system of education; processes leading to education reform; the coup d'état against Gorbachev and social revolution; turbulent winds of change blowing over my country in our education reform efforts; the birth, processes, and implementation of global education as a priority in the Russian education reform movement; and the Beslan tragedy.

Listen to the Winds of Change

In April 1985 when Mikhail Gorbachev became Secretary General of the Communist Party and head of the Soviet State I was a single mother with two children aged 13 and 5 just returning to Moscow from the Far North of the country to resume my academic career. I have a PhD in psycholinguistics and have published several English language textbooks. My family survived the harsh climate of the Far North living in a small town populated by families of the navy. I did not have any hope that life in my country might change in any significant way. In his very first speech to the Communist Party, Gorbachev mentioned the atrocities committed by Stalin and the compassion he felt for the families who lost their relatives during the reign of one of the worst tyrants the world has ever known. The Russian people, used to reading between the lines, could tell that the time for change had arrived.

The Gorbachev Era

The Gorbachev era became known for three concepts: *perestroika* (transformation), *uskoreniye* (economic development), and *glasnost* (access to information). They became known internationally, as they were the source of hope for other nations waiting for the collapse of the Soviet regime. Under Gorbachev, more and more victims of the Stalin regime were rehabilitated. Not just Nicholaí Bukharin, one of the most liberal minded right-wing communists whose popularity Stalin had envied, but Leo Trotsky, whose works had been strictly forbidden. More important, academician Sakharov, our famous dissident and one of the sharpest minds of the century who had been exiled to a closed provincial city by Leonid Brezhnev's administration, was released and escorted back to Moscow where Mikhail Gorbachev welcomed him.

The Gorbachev era permitted publication of books that had previously been forbidden including works of Bukharin, Trotsky, and Sakharov. The entire nation was desperately trying to catch up, reading Boris Pasternak, Anna Akhmatova, and Mikhail Bulgakov as well as the philosophers who dared to contradict communist dogmas and political leaders of the past. One could put together a very nice library just by collecting the books read by passengers on a morning metro train in Moscow. TV programs became diverse; foreign newspapers and magazines were sold openly; and critique of the decisions of party leaders could now be open. Public meetings and demonstrations were allowed. The first groups of foreign visitors were moving freely across the city, and the Russian people were no longer afraid to greet them. The basic right of religious choice was given back to the people, and new churches, mosques, synagogues, and Buddhist temples were built. Old church buildings previously converted into Soviet institutions, cinemas, and shops were returned to the church. Small businesses could reopen their doors. Private restaurants, shops, theatres, and tourist shops appeared. State enterprises could now elect their own leaders, and if dissatisfied with their performance, could elect new ones. The workers during Soviet times had been sick of incompetent leadership and could not wait for new leaders to emerge.

In the Gorbachev era, the Central European States and members of the Warsaw Pact started flying out of the Soviet nest one by one heading toward EU membership. The Berlin Wall had fallen and people were crying and cheering at its ruins. For the first time in the history of Russia, the Communist Party and Parliamentary Congresses became great fun and people were watching them on television into the night. One of the continuing big debates was the fate of the Soviet Republics of Latvia, Lithuania, and Estonia. They had been annexed before World War II and they consistently appealed to regain their freedom from the Soviet Union, but this was one change for which Mikhail Gorbachev was not ready. Unlike Lenin, who easily traded territories and granted independence to survive as a Soviet state, Gorbachev believed that losing territories symbolized failure of a political leader. He also might have had other considerations such as not being able, under the economic circumstances, to afford repatriation of millions of Russian families who resided in the Baltic States. For Gorbachev, it would have not only constituted a territorial loss, but a betrayal of the Russian people, and the uprisings in Lithuania (Vilnius) and later in Georgia (Tbilisi) were stopped by Soviet tanks.

The freedom of demonstration also had its dark side: Nazis, anti-Semitic and pan-Slavic groups paraded in big cities shouting slogans hardly to be associated with a democratic state. As a consequence, as soon as Soviet citizens were allowed to travel internationally, two to three million of the intellectual elite, university professors, teachers as well as vulnerable ethnic groups of the Russian population started leaving the country.

The Soviet System of Education

The Soviet system of education had reasons to be proud of the outcomes of schooling it had offered. Secondary education was mandatory for all and free. Higher education was also free, and its 600 institutions of higher education could not accommodate all those willing and eligible for university studies. The country was 100 percent literate and Russian school teams always won the World Olympiads in mathematics and physics. However, if you had looked deeper, the harsh reality would have surfaced. Yes, the country had universal literacy but the literacy taught was not necessarily functional for a considerable proportion of the population and was divorced from critical thinking. Most people believed anything they had read in the newspapers or seen on the TV screen. The math curriculum was demanding, but only a small proportion of the school population mastered it to the expected standard. The international TIMMS reviews suggest that although many Russian schoolchildren possessed a solid knowledge base they could not apply this knowledge across the curriculum, let alone outside the school context.

Standardization during the Soviet era was one of the peculiar things about the education system. Everything had to be standardized: the curriculum, timetables, textbooks, even school buildings. And this was in a country that stretched across 11 time zones! I remember visiting schools in the tundra where local children have never seen trees. Yet they were assigned to color autumn leaves of the trees they had never seen. The only aspect of the Soviet education system that was not standardized was the exams. They were administered by the schools themselves and although there was a list of prescribed questions, there was no guidance on how to grade answers that were mostly oral. Since teachers wanted their students pass the exams to demonstrate the effectiveness of their teaching, they would give students better grades than they deserved. As a consequence one could not compare results of one school against another, with the result that universities had to administer their own exams for admission. The degree of corruption at the university entry stage was embarrassing.

Other major concerns during the Soviet era were brainwashing and hypocrisy. The curriculum, particularly in the humanities, was politicized to an extent that when studying great Russian writers of the nineteenth century students had to speculate whether Leo Tolstoy would have participated in the Great October Socialist Revolution had he lived long enough. If the history could not be twisted to satisfaction of socialist *bonzes*, it had to be invented. It was not just the twisting of history that was a problem; it was the twisting of students' lives. Schools were run by party committees. Every high school student was supposed to join the Young Communist League (YCL). Those unwilling to do so were risking their academic careers. Once an YCL member, you were not allowed to cross a church door step, be critical of anything the Communist Party did or said, and were supposed to stand by any decision that the party made including the exile of Sakharov and his wife, the Afghan war, and tank attacks on peaceful demonstrators.

The Soviet Union was a very multicultural state: Russia alone had more than 120 ethnicities, mostly indigenous, and 15 ethnic republics different in language and religion. Half of the world's families of languages were spoken in the Soviet Union. In theory, the education system responded to this challenge well, as 37 local languages were taught at schools across the Soviet Union. However, none of these was the language of instruction even in the primary grades, since Russian was taught to all students as if it were their mother tongue, and no support was given to nonnative speakers.

During the Soviet era, schools were supposed to preach internationalism. In reality, however, what was taught was the concept of the melting pot. Although it was deemed nice to have all those ethnicities, everyone was supposed to speak impeccable Russian without any accent, know Russian literature and history in as much detail as any student of Russian origin, and never question Russian dominance. My family is very multicultural, but more than a half of my blood is Ukrainian. I was always proud of being Ukrainian and when I was competing to enter a school that specialized in teaching English as a foreign language I was nearly denied access because of my Ukrainian accent. My ability to speak Ukrainian was the source of incessant jokes.

In the second half of the 1980s it became obvious that something should be done about identity issues and the recognition of languages and cultures of indigenous and non-indigenous Russian people. The Baltic and Caucasian republics were campaigning for the reintroduction of their ethnic history and literature into the prevailing school curriculum. More and more ethnicities living in the Russian territory wanted their languages to be the language of instruction. Summer language schools were opening for ethnic minorities and their children. Yet chauvinist slogans penetrated classrooms from street meetings of the Neo-Nazis. Schools teaching Hebrew were targeted by the Nazis who painted swastikas on their doors or shouted insults into the windows.

As Mikhail Gorbachev's government was returning representatives of ethnic groups exiled earlier to Siberia by Stalin to their original homes (e.g., Chechens and the Crimean Tatars) and their children began to attend schools in their hometowns, they found unfriendly and unwelcoming classmates at these schools. Some attitudes were inspired by labels such as "traitor," which had been given to whole nations by Stalin during World War II as he looked for scapegoats to blame for military failures during the first years of the war. No one knew what to do about those issues. Skilled teachers were the only hope. Committed teachers have always been the unsung heroes and heroines of Russian education. Yet in the late 1980s they found themselves in such a state of poverty and neglect that even the best were beginning to consider leaving their schools. It was clear that Russia needed reform of its education systems.

Processes Leading to Education Reform

In the summer of 1987 I was invited to a conference in Sochi, the southernmost city of Russia. This conference was intended to be a long brainstorming session after which a select group of the conference participants were to draft a concept paper for education reform. The participants in the conference were also supposed to form a temporary research team (VNIK). The conference was probably the most impressive gathering I have ever seen. Every educational guru—researchers whose works I admired, famous teachers, and school principals whose names were familiar from the press, and federal, regional, and municipal education leaders—was in attendance. The main convener of the conference was Dr. Edvard Dneprov, a historian who had published extensively about education reforms in tsarist Russia and was known for his sharp critique of the Soviet education system. The conference resulted in a salient concept paper that addressed educational reform as summarized below:

Ten Principles of Education Reform

1. *Democratization of Education.* The strategy proposed to decentralize the system previously hierarchically managed; to introduce public governance in educational institutions to counterbalance state control; to remove brainwashing through making schools politics-free zones by law and allowing no political parties on their premises; to demilitarize schools and abolish military training, which had been a must for people of both genders in upper secondary schools

2. *Multiplicity of Sources of Funding.* The proposal was to make the education system more entrepreneurial; to allow it to raise funds to complement an insufficient state budget, and to combine federal resources with regional and municipal ones and invest those into better quality education. Private schools that were previously strictly pro-

hibited could now exist provided that they reached the standards prescribed by the state.

3. Regionalization. To continue decentralization, the leadership in education had been shifted from the federal to the regional level and regional leaders had been trained in planning and sustaining their systems of education. The regions were to get full control over their systems of education including some control over the curriculum. They could add up to 30 percent of the content they thought was important for the employability of their graduates.

4. Cultural Identity. The diverse ethnicities across the then-Soviet Union were longing for greater recognition of their languages and cultures in the school curricula and the indigenous population of the country felt it was their right to emphasize their identity in schools. However, striking a proper balance between national and ethnic identities was a challenge, and the concept paper only recommended introducing more languages into language blocks of disciplines and more languages of instruction into primary grades though it also suggested that the regions could introduce courses of local history, art, and culture.

5. Humanization. The Soviet system of education was highly teacher-centered and authoritarian. The concept paper emphasized child-centeredness, interactive learning, and diversified methods of teaching. It encouraged recognition of individual learning styles and multiple intelligences as well as individualized curricula based on each child's needs. It was also calling for inclusion of children with special needs who were largely segregated within the Soviet system.

6. Humanitization. The Soviet schools were well known for their high quality of teaching math and science. However this high quality was available only to a relatively small percentage of school children whereas the rest of the student population could not cope with the demanding curriculum. As regards the humanities, those were politicized to an extent that even literature and languages were taught through the texts full of Marxist dogmas. The emphasis here was to completely reshape curriculum in humanities, to diversify the content, to invite new textbook writers, and ultimately to increase the ratio of the humanities in the curriculum.

7. Openness. This concept suggested that schools should be open to parents, the community, and the larger world. They were to become accountable to their real clients, students, and their parents. Schools were encouraged to analyze the needs of the employment market and the best practices of countries recognized for their educational excellence. Schools were to find international partners and set up school exchanges. Teachers also needed to become internationally mobile. An open school was seen as a prototype of an open society; therefore, this principle was of particular importance.

8. Diversification. This concept implied diversifying school patterns and types as well as school curricula available to students. Options and choices were to be introduced more broadly into school curriculum for students to design their own educational trajectories and learn more autonomously, pursuing their own goals and objectives. Textbook markets were to be de-monopolized and diversified so that teachers could choose a textbook best suited for the goals of the curriculum.

9. Developmental Character of Education. Some tendencies in Soviet educational psychology were very much in line with the modern approach to child-centered teaching, encouraging every student to reach his or her full potential and to set tasks to challenge them into the proximate zone of their development. In the early 1980s, several followers of Lev Vigotsky set up pilot schools in Moscow and in Siberia that were calling themselves *developmental* (the closest analogue is probably *constructivist*) that have restructured the entire school curriculum to meet the effective development of a child's thinking skills. Those were highly successful, challenging, and child centered. Teachers were teaching competencies rather than factual knowledge and simple skills. The concept paper called for wide dissemination of this concept.

10. Lifelong Learning. It was clear to the developers of the concept that in the fast-changing world of today one can no longer hope to get an education that will be sufficient for one's lifetime. Therefore, the emphasis was on encouraging learning throughout one's lifetime and creating conditions for smooth transition from one type of educational institution to another, avoiding redundancy and repetition.

The policy paper presented at the Sochi conference was discussed across the education community. Strong opposition came from the Russian Academy of Pedagogical Sciences leadership, the hub of Soviet pedagogy, which took the position that the Soviet system was the best in the world and therefore was not to be touched by any reforms. The all-union Congress of Teachers convened in 1988 and voted for the new concept, which was then officially endorsed. VNIK was to continue its work for another two years to produce a detailed plan of the reforms in every sector of education, to draft a new "Law of Education," and a series of diversified school curricula. Shortly before this work was completed, the leader of the team, Dr. Edvard Dneprov, was elected Minister of Education of the Russian Federation.

I was appointed his personal advisor for International Relations. My mission was to develop relationships with lead countries of the world and to identify tendencies and trends in their education systems that should be studied and explored. The United States was one of the first countries we wanted to study and explore.

Ministry of Education Delegates Visit the United States

In April 1991, at the invitation of Howard Mehlinger, Indiana University, four members of the ministry team, Drs. Mihail Kuzmin, advisor in ethnic and interethnic issues in education; Victor Bolotov, head of teacher-training; Vladimir Sobkin, head of sociological services; and I were invited to visit the United States. Our first destination was the American Education Research Association (AERA) conference in the city of Chicago to be followed by a second conference on Global Education in Key Biscayne, Florida. The AERA conference was truly overwhelming for us.

We did not have much hope for the conference in Key Biscayne. As we arrived at the Miami airport, we were met by a man who presented himself as Professor Jan Tucker, a social scientist and global educator with a deep interest in history, who was our escort to the Key Biscayne conference venue. In the car Professor Tucker asked me about some Russian movies he had recently seen. Those movies were new and my colleagues and I had not seen all of them. Jan was asking about some details of our life he had observed in the films that were indeed very typical of the current setting in Russia, and his questions made us all reflect upon his observations. I was convinced that Jan was a Russian historian specializing in Russian cinema, and I was surprised he did not speak Russian. To my amazement, Jan denied any prior knowledge of the Russian cinema. He had borrowed several Russian movies just to learn more about his Russian guests who were about to arrive. This was our first induction into the global education community. Jan was communicating the spirit of the global education movement even then: respect for diversity.

Key Biscayne Conference. The first day of the conference showed clearly that we had found what we were looking for to take home: an idea and a concept. This idea and concept were the very image of Edvard Dneprov's visions for school reform to be "open to global problems of the world, capable of recognizing diverse faces of other ethnicities, other cultures, and preparing students for a dialogue between them, thus enriching themselves and improving communities around them" (1991, pp. 92–93). The concept of "respect for diversity" was particularly useful for us. This was not an abstract internationalism that called for universal similarity. Global education was genuine rejoicing in putting together mosaics of different cultures and teaching children to admire this wonderfully diverse world. Education for global citizenship should clearly presuppose such an attitude to diversity unless one wants to live in a totally uniform and standardized world, which we had experienced in our Soviet past. While at the conference, we met people who were passionate about the concept and who had invested their lives and energy into global education. We agreed with Jan Tucker and others that we needed to meet in Russia and invited our new friends to our first international conference in Sochi in August of the same year. History *almost* interfered with our plans.

Coup d'état and Social Revolution

After our exhausting but productive trip, very early in the morning on the 19th of August 1991 a friend called and yelled into the phone, "Turn on the TV set," and hung up. The television was broadcasting "Swan Lake" from the Bolshoi Theatre. Must be another channel, I thought, but that channel was also broadcasting "Swan Lake," and so did another and another. It became clear to me that something sinister was happening in the country. When I learned that Mikhail Gorbachev is seriously ill and could not perform his functions as the president of the Soviet Union it was clear: this was a coup d'état. My first thought was, "The international conference will be cancelled and all my efforts to invite over 100 foreign educators will now be in vain." But my second thought was,

"What will happen to my country and to all of us? Edvard Dneprov may be arrested, as he is one of the most radical voices in Russia. Well, they may arrest all of us." I also was worried about my two sons. I had left my 11-year-old son at home with strict instructions to keep calling me in the ministry. If he could not reach me I instructed him to go to our summer house to be with my parents. On the same day, my 18-year old son was returning from a hiking tour and I knew if he did not find me at home, he would go to our dacha. Since I feared that my older son would join the protest marches, I had instructed my younger son *not* tell his older brother of the crisis. I did not learn until much later that my older son and my brother-in-law were standing in the Live Ring just several meters away from me in the huge crowd.

The Ministry of Education was full of anxious people, as the August planning session with representatives from all regional education authorities was about to take place. We waited for the minister to arrive from the White House where he had been summoned by President Yeltsin. I received a call from the Norwegian colleague helping me organize the international conference in Sochi. "What is going on in Moscow? You have tanks entering the city!" Edvard Dneprov arrived, informing us that the autumn planning session would be postponed until "this madness is over." He then convened the leadership team of the ministry and told us that the situation was serious: Gorbachev was probably arrested; tanks were in the street clearly to arrest President Yeltsin; and the new government of the Russian Federation had decided to disobey the coup. The ministry was to become one of the strongholds of resistance.

Our first task was to call all the teachers of Russia on strike. Several representatives of the ministry were sent to other cities to communicate the government's decisions to resist the coup. We learned that all the newspapers were shut down and all television and radio stations still kept broadcasting "Swan Lake." The entire country was left without information. We started printing leaflets and distributed them in the streets.

The Live Ring

On the first night of the coup I headed for the White House where a "Live Ring" of people was assembling. The people were determined to stand by our Russian White House where the new government was sitting to protect them against the coup organizers. The crowd was not very large yet. Nobody carried weapons, but the people sang and recited poetry. There were many foreigners in the crowd; some Spaniards were waving their flags and crying "Venceremos!" Some English-speaking students were singing: "We Shall Overcome." For the first time in my life I saw my nation standing side by side with representatives of other nations to protect our newborn democracy. At night on our way home the churches were open and, as I entered, I found that the prayer was for Gorbachev's recovery and rescue. The tanks were parked along the streets and I heard an old woman feeding the soldiers with some home-made soup say, "Why are you here, sons? Go home! We do not need your guns and tanks here."

Arriving at the ministry the next day I observed the Live Ring becoming bigger and bigger as there were rumors that tanks were going to attack the White House. There was one radio station not shut down by the coup organizers, *Echo of Moscow*, which kept on broadcasting while every other station was closed or "Swan-Laking." Finally, the ministry put a loud speaker into the street so that the growing crowd could hear the news that President Yeltsin has declared the coup regime unconstitutional and that a part of the army was now supporting him as the newly democratically elected leader. In the meantime a whole division of tanks headed by General Lebed decided to advance to the White House to protect the Yeltsin government. To show the army's support, Yeltsin stood on one of the tanks to address the nation. The world famous cello player Rostropovich, exiled by the former Soviet government, had returned from abroad to protect democracy at the White House walls. His picture holding his cello in one hand and a gun in the other was published across the world.

Teachers' Voices

In the evening of the second day of the coup d'état, the men in the ministry were leaving one by one to join the Live Ring growing larger outside the White House. By midnight, Edvard sent us home: the coup leaders had announced curfew. At home I was glued to the radio. The *Echo of Moscow* was still broadcasting the latest news informing us that the tanks were moving toward the White House and several people had been killed. Then I heard a voice on the *Echo of Moscow* that was strangely familiar—my son's history teacher, his favorite teacher who taught his students to work with reliable sources of information and examine history from multiple perspectives, who was addressing his former and current students, saying in effect,

> While teaching you history I was trying to teach you values of an open soci-
> ety and the basics of democracy. Now the time has come to stand by this
> democracy and to behave like citizens who care about the future. I cannot
> guarantee you safety, but if you come to the White House walls I can guar-
> antee you the respect and gratitude of your nation.

Many people came to the Live Ring because they heard appeals from
their teachers who were broadcasting from the *Echo of Moscow* radio station that night. Several years later I learned that *Echo of Moscow* was not
shut down like all the rest of radio stations because they were broadcasting from the school where my sons were studying, which the hardliners
failed to shut down.

For the first time during these tragic days my eyes were full of tears.
But then I began to feel guilty: I had protected my children by sending
them to their grandparents while at least the older one should have been
here protecting democracy. My motherly instincts were stronger than my
citizenship. I decided I must go to the White House myself and participate in the Live Ring. Approaching the White House, I passed the place
where three young people had been killed earlier by the tanks. It was
covered with fresh flowers. A burnt trolley bus was standing nearby as a
horrid monument. The Live Ring around the White House was filled
with hundreds of thousands of people. At first we stood in a chain block-
ing the bridge from the tanks. At one point the tanks started approaching
and came very close. No one left the chain, but my neighbor's hand in
mine began to shake. The tanks were very close—then suddenly they
made a U-turn. The huge crowd starts cheering. A true national reunion!
Rockers on their motorbikes were doing reconnaissance in front of the
tanks; punks appeared with their interesting hairdos; drunkards brought
their last supplies of vodka while people were soaking wet from the rain.
Women who brought food organized to distribute it. Many English-
speaking, German-speaking, and French-speaking people assembled.
They had been here with us during our most difficult hours.

The last day of the coup dawned. The Russian Parliament met in the
White House. The coup leadership did not attack. The crowd was enormous. Many famous actors and singers had arrived to express their solidarity with the people in the Live Ring. They sang and talked from the
White House balcony and the crowd sang, laughed, and cheered with
them. When I could access the phone I dictated some texts for the leaflets
to my colleagues in the ministry, and my *Appeal to Mothers of Russia* was
sent back to me in printed form. In the evening the Russian government
sent its emissaries to the Crimea to return Gorbachev to Moscow. It is

clear that the coup d'état had failed. The crowd stayed up for another long night to greet their president. We had learned that his plane had landed but Gorbachev never came to the White House to thank the Live Ring for supporting him. This was a big mistake or an unfortunate set of circumstances. Had he done so he would have had all the support he needed to remain president of the new Russia. His reason for not going before the people was that his wife had had a stroke.

On the morning of August 21, we left the White House walls. I looked at the barricades one more time to be sure I would carry this picture in my heart through my entire life. *Democracy won. Our Soviet past is dead and buried.* Complete strangers embraced each other in the streets. The heroic decisions made inside the walls of the ministry during the coup period are described in *Education and Politics: Chronicle of Resistance* (Dneprov, 2006). The next day I received notification from conference participants including more than 100 educators from abroad confirming their attendance at the Sochi conference. Jan and Toni were coming from Florida.

Birth of a New Idea in Education

The first international conference in a free Russia began on the 7th of September, 1991 in Sochi. It was organized jointly by the Russian Ministry of Education and the nongovernmental organization headed by a Norwegian educator, Per Dalin. Sochi, a very multicultural city sitting right on the Russian-Georgian border has always been perceived as the best recreation spot in the country: warm subtropical climate throughout the year, the Black Sea, high peaks of the Caucasus Mountains in the background and only a one-hour drive to a skiing place in the mountains where the snow never melts completely. There were at least 250 educators at the conference.

The conference agenda was comprehensive, as we were looking for opportunities to generate international projects in almost every sector of education: setting up facilities for training leaders of education to decentralize education management, producing new legislation in education, diversifying schools and training school leaders, designing new educational standards, revising curriculum, mainstreaming children with special needs, creating family homes for orphan children, creating child-centered systems of pre-school education. Our Sochi hosts and leaders in education kept reminding us of the needs of their city. They wanted a project which could reconcile the needs of their diverse population and offer a curriculum to their students which would be common and yet diversified in accordance with the needs of different ethnic groups.

The conference was organized in sections, and the global education section was one of the best attended. The reason Russian participants were so enthusiastic about the concept was twofold: global education addresses the concept of openness in the best possible way and global education curriculum suggests becoming familiar with the way of life of all major nations of the world and that of your immediate neighbors as well as being an integral part of the world community. Representatives of the various regions attending the conference felt that their regional multicultural contexts were different from those of any other part of Russia and wanted this specificity to be recognized in a new school model. However, teachers and administrators recognized a need for an integrative framework within which their diversity could flourish. Global education offered such a framework, as it is all-encompassing.

Advancing Global Education in Russia

The idea of developing a global education program was to create a hub for global education in Russia to advocate the concept to be endorsed in schools and teacher education programs throughout the Russian Federation as a model of schooling. As a result, the Ryazan Center of Global Education was established at Ryazan State Pedagogical University, which possessed the capacity and interest to lead the project (see chapter 7). The purpose was to design suitable models of global education for each of the participating schools and to partner them with schools in United States. The U.S. schools were to support Russian schools in the implementation of global education. This plan was discussed in detail and approved by the Minister of Education. Dr. Dneprov put together a portfolio of projects supported at the federal level and decided to pursue the concepts by planning to visit Florida International University (FIU) and the Miami-Dade Public Schools in spring 1992. His speech centered on the following message:

> Innovations in education pave the way for innovations in the society and in the economy. The humanitarian, child-centered approach in education is a prerequisite of social cohesion, democratic development, and economic growth. The way we model our school is the way we want to model our society. Global education is a model which I would like to see developing in our society. (Dneprov, 1992, p. 7)

Native Language Retention and Culture of Minorities

The policies developed and brought before the new government of Russia by Edvard Dneprov were approved, and global education became a priority. Moreover, an analysis of the vast multicultural issues in education was undertaken in order to target the project properly. Russia has more than 120 ethnicities indigenous to its territory, mostly living compactly, though not exactly in enclaves, because there was not a single territory where Russians and other large ethnicities did not prevail. There are at least 40 ethnic groups that were largely scattered around Russia and whose majority resided in other countries: ethnic Koreans, Chinese, Germans, Jews, Poles, and so on. Despite their numbers, their ethnic rights in the times of the Soviet Union were largely neglected.

Within only six years of Gorbachev's *perestroika* there were many changes in education. Schools became free to choose languages they wished to offer, including their language of instruction. The recommended pattern was to begin primary school instruction in the local language but for Russian to be dominant in school curriculum and the language of instruction by the end of schooling; the local language could be taught as a school discipline. However in 1991 there were already at least 20 languages of instruction in primary schools and several of them remained the language of instruction in secondary school as well. This was a problem because children whose parents sent them to ethnic schools were made less competitive in the education market. Schools were now teaching more than 90 languages of local ethnicities as a discipline and, again, there was an extreme scarcity of trained teachers and teaching materials, the methodology was outdated, and the motivation of students in many cases was very low. One could feel, however, how passionately people felt about their languages and cultures and that they wanted their children to know them at all costs as a result of the previous discrimination against them.

Results of the Ten Principles of Education Reform

Some of the results of the Ten Principles of Education Reform announced by the Minister of Education in 1991 were clearly visible as the context for multicultural education changed in our country. For example: (1) political activity in schools was prohibited in the sense that no party officials, no matter what party they represented, were allowed to intervene with school life. They could not set up any party committees or involve students into their political activity. Military training was abolished and schools had become weapons-free; (2) the system was rapidly decentralizing: autonomous ethnic republics had been given full autonomy in the way they ran the system of education; (3) schools could mobilize resources from multiple sources of funding: federal, regional, and municipal budgets; sponsorship and donations; sale of services outside the prescribed curriculum; the only thing they could not do was to rent space, which prevented private schools from developing in much greater numbers; (4) schools were much more open to the world around them; school exchanges were expanding; Russian education leaders were rapidly learning from their Western colleagues; the first Montessori and Steiner schools had opened; and new approaches to managing education and curriculum design had been piloted.

However problems were beginning to surface as well. The regions now had control over 30 percent or more of the curriculum and many of them had introduced courses of local studies: ethnic histories, ethnic culture (in some regions these were even courses of pagan religion camouflaged as local culture, as religious studies were not to be allowed as mandatory disciplines within school curriculum, unless it was a private religious school). History courses in particular began to contradict one another and almost all of them were in conflict with the textbooks of the history of Russia. Apart from all the issues mentioned above there was a direct threat to national identity coming from schools segregating their students on the basis of ethnicity. Private Muslim, Orthodox, or Jewish schools were growing in number and were escalating existing conflicts. Ethnic Armenian school teachers for instance often reminded their students about the recent war in Nagorno-Karabakh, making them hostile to Azeri students whose families and parents mostly had nothing to do with the conflict. And vice versa; Azeri schools were labeling all Armenians as aggressors.

It was becoming more and more clear to the members of the Ministry of Education team that they needed a concept for education reform that would serve the needs of social cohesion; advocate antibias and antiracist; promote cross-cultural dialogue to bring Russia into the world community mainstreaming global education development; and open schools for parents and community. Their major responsibility was to accommodate the interests and needs of different ethnicities while bringing them closer as a nation, stimulating their interest in and respect for the needs of their neighbors and other nations in the wider world. Moreover, the desegregation of schools and making public schools inclusive for students with special needs and interests were critical. There was need to learn from the best practices existing in the country. Since global education could respond to these challenges, the Ministry of Education made the decision to implement global education as a priority to develop a prototype of countrywide education reform. The decision was made to hold a series of international global education conferences at Ryazan State University in Ryazan, Russia.

You Must Be the Change

The first Cabinet of Ministers of the new Russian government inherited an economy in shambles. The salaries of workers in the state sector including those of teachers were badly delayed and the amount was so small that in some regions they were below the survival level—the savings from over decades were gone as a consequence of prime minister Pavlov's reform in 1991, and pensions, if paid at all, were so small that they were eaten by hyper-inflation before they were paid. The government envisioned more hardships as a new liberal market reform was introduced for economic revival in a country that had never been so poverty-stricken in the past 40 years.

Famine Crisis

At the time of these changes, Russia faced a serious danger of famine. The new government was concerned that those who would get the worst of it would be old people in small towns and rural settings as well as the lowest paid categories of the population. The world community was quickly sensitized to this threat and the first shipments of food and medical supplies began to arrive into Russia. Yet the distribution chain was set up in haste and did not function well. Many needy people were not served, and some families were on the verge of starving. It was then that Minister Dneprov asked me to visit the United States for the purpose of fund-raising. His idea was to organize direct supplies of food into the most poverty-stricken regions and to distribute these supplies with the help of Russian schools and schoolchildren who knew their communities and could identify those in real need more effectively than foreign charities.

Many educators I had met in the United States responded positively to our request: some suggested immediate monetary donations; some to form famine relief committees. Under the leadership of Toni Kirkwood, coordinator of the International Global Education Program, the Miami-Dade Public Schools proposed a most straightforward plan. They received a commitment from Delta Airlines to fly the emergency supplies into the Ryazan region near Moscow, which had an aging rural population and where businesses had shut down from lack of raw materials and energy. The first shipment was to arrive in autumn of 1992. Unfortunately, Hurricane Andrew struck the coast of South Florida that same fall and destroyed large residential areas in Miami. It now was our turn to support our friends in Florida, even if only morally. But to our amazement, the first plane of food supplies sent to Russia came from Miami just two weeks after the hurricane (see chapter 6). Many families received help from this shipment. The global education ethos is best illustrated by this story.

Leaving the Ministry

In 1996 the Ministry of Education was merged with the State Committee on Higher Education in Russia. This was a good idea considering that many aspects of secondary, general, and vocational education could not be reformed in the absence of similar or matching changes in tertiary education. School graduates were badly in need of fairer university entry exam systems; vocational students could not make sense of their qualification in the absence of a transparent national qualifications framework; and so on. I had just returned from a semester at Northeastern Illinois University in Chicago in 1995 where I assisted graduate students with a track record in inner-city Chicago schools identifying projects they could implement in their schools. As I was listening to one story after another it was becoming clear to me that global education was the answer. I was amazed by how little American students knew about global education.

Upon my return to Russia, I was energized to begin work on our global education projects, a priority approved by the Minister of Education at the Sochi conference in 1991. I soon discovered that the top leaders in the new ministry were not interested in global education reform and that secondary education was not a priority for them. They focused their attention on the decentralization of school systems management so that they could fully delegate responsibilities to the regions and did not have to be concerned with the needs of schools and vocational colleges. As a result, many reformers eager to globalize the education systems in schools and universities left the ministry because their interest had lost priority, and they felt their skills were not needed. I was one of the first to leave, and after careful consideration of where I could continue with many of my unfinished projects I accepted a position with the British Council because it practices the best spirit of a true global partnership.

The Case of Textbooks

One of the first projects I undertook addressed English language textbooks. We selected a group of our best-trained practicing teachers who were child centered and skills based. These teachers were trained by British English language methodology specialists and were to design a new textbook series that would best suit the needs of English language learners in a Russian classroom. One of the key principles that had been agreed from the very beginning was the emphasis on global English. It implied that in the globalized world the user of the English language could function most effectively when they could understand different accents, and knew the vocabulary coming from a variety of "Englishes" including European English, which belonged to no particular nation. Now that the series is completed and is the best seller in a free textbook market, we can see how much it has contributed to global understanding. The graduates who learned from this series have no problems understanding their global neighbors, no matter which country they come from and are not taken aback by the diversity of forms of expressing the same meaning. Another principle that is close to global education principles is teaching global awareness through an issue-based discourse that young people consider important: sharing resources, global warming, youth groups and movements, conflict resolution and military service, diversity and identity, and the like. From the very first pilot textbook we had almost unanimous support of students who felt that the English language lessons were one of the few places where they had an opportunity to discuss important issues.

Search for Identity and Ethnic Conflicts in Schools

Another effort to a similar end has been made jointly with the Open Society Institute. Teachers in big cities, which were beginning to experience in-migration on a massive scale, were suddenly confronted with problems they had never experienced before. The appearance of nonnative language speakers whose needs were not properly addressed was followed by ethnic conflicts in their classrooms that were often provoked by much bigger conflicts in the country. The search for identity in a diverse society whose diversity had previously been suppressed by ethnically segregated schools was becoming a pressing issue for many students and for the teachers themselves, who often did not know how to respond. Therefore, we decided to launch a new teacher-training program in the city of Sochi. A new institution was established: the Sochi Multicultural Teacher Training College. It consists of several departments, and the global education curriculum was our inspiration. Future teachers were learning critical thinking and conflict resolution skills, the art of negotiation, and civilized debate that was never part of the teacher-training curriculum before. The skills teachers were beginning to acquire were so precious that the city authorities asked us to design a similar program for in-service teacher-training.

Cry in the Night: The Beslan Tragedy

On the 1st of September 2004, the day when school starts in Russia, teachers and students of School 1 in the small town of Beslan (North Ossetia in the North Caucasian region) gathered in their school yard to greet new first graders to celebrate the beginning of a new school year. Russian schools are comprised of kindergarten to eleventh grade and have children of all ages from 6 to 17 or 18 years of age. Many parents with their toddlers and babies in their festive dresses were gathered in the school yard. Suddenly the yard was surrounded by armed men who told them that they were now hostages until the federal authorities released prisoners of the Chechen war and stopped the war. The hostages were made to sit in the gym where bombs and explosives were installed. More than 1,000 people were kept in the small school building for three days without food and water and constantly abused; those who were trying to protest were shot mercilessly; and the heat was unbearable and many children collapsed from exhaustion. After three days of unsuccessful negotiations and poor planning, the federal authorities attacked the terrorists when a big explosion occurred. Many hostages were killed. Those rescued were injured physically and psychologically. The terrorists were identified as ethnic Ingushi who were Ossetians' closest neighbors with whom they had conflicts before on religious grounds.

Almost 300 children were disabled. The youngest ones, particularly primary graders, were so scared that they refused to go to anything that even looked like a school. Many parents, particularly those who lost all their children, were on the verge of starting a war with the neighboring Ingushis and great efforts were undertaken to prevent more bloodshed. As the whole world was watching the Beslan tragedy on their TV screens, many people around the world showed support and solidarity, donated large sums of money for medical treatment, showered victims with presents and sponsored them to visit Russian health resorts and rehabilitation centers in other countries. Gradually, however, the donations dwindled and by the end of the year, other world catastrophes replaced the Beslan images of half-naked children running from a burning school.

Call for Help Answered. Educator and former advisor to the British Secretary of State Michael Barber watched the live broadcast of the tragedy. Having been to Russia many times raising money for several projects he decided to respond to the tragedy through education and a long-term program of support and assistance to the North Caucasian region. With approval of the Russian Minister of Education, Andrei Fursenko, the new initiative was planned with four sets of goals: (1) to improve youth employment opportunities through identifying needs of local markets, restructuring the vocational education system, and making it competence based; (2) to expand English language skills of all graduates of schools in three republics; (3) to mainstream the victims of Beslan tragedy into regular secondary schools and offer them long-term support; (4) to develop a pan-Caucasus network of schools with a multicultural tolerant ethos to offer quality support to migrants, to prevent bullying and harassment, to involve their communities in social projects aimed at restoring peace and tolerance in the region, and to form a multicultural community of students possessing skills needed for life and cooperation within a multicultural society.

Three republics were chosen as pilot sites for the initiative: North Ossetia, Ingushetia, and Kabardino-Balkaria. The British Council was asked to become the coordination unit. The three regions proposed strategies for their vocational education development and developed a modular competence-based curriculum piloted in nine colleges that have become centers of Vocational Excellence. Special support has been given to children at risk, mostly victims of conflicts in the region, and they were coached through the first stages of their career paths. In-service centers were created for English language teachers and trained as trainers of peers. A textbook titled *Tolerance through English* was produced with an accommodating global education program concentrating on developing respect for diversity and skills needed for life in a multicultural community.

All Beslan victims were included into mainstream schools. It took us a special effort to help primary school children adapt to a school setting, but after two years of study in the Rainbow Centre they managed to make the transition to a regular school. Those children who remain disabled (almost 230 children have been rehabilitated) receive special care, are socially active, and form communities supported by nongovernmental organizations. Parents have formed a special association and many of them see support to Beslan victims as the only way of survival after the loss of their own children. An important precedent has been created: parents in the region now believe in inclusion and send their disabled children to a mainstream school.

The results of the school network component of the program are perhaps the best demonstration of the relevance of global education ideas. Each school was asked to analyze its context and identify major issues and concerns that they wanted to address. Some schools decided to design policies directed toward better integration of migrants and their families; others looked at bullying and conflicts in their schools and were seeking ways to minimize those; still others taught their students how to make responsible choices in life and equip them with leadership skills, preventing dependency and addictions; another school celebrated diversity by moving out of its enclave and opening up to the outside world. Every teacher in the network received training in emotional competence; critical thinking; school rules; conflict resolution; pedagogical support; negotiation skills; multicultural dialogue; leadership; and classroom research.

Many students were engaged in projects that challenged stereotypes and learned more about their neighbors. One of our most successful projects has been one where children wrote books about their ethnicities, based on the concept of a popular series *Those Strange Armenians* (*Russians, Ossetians, Ingushi,* etc.). This series encouraged students to look at their backgrounds with good humor, and the project gradually helped them to realize that they had more commonalties than differences (Khasan, 2007).

One of our best experiences has been a multicultural summer camp when some children would not share rooms with those of some other ethnicities; however after interactive training, simulations, and games, conflicts stopped and by the end of their camp days children were complaining about being sent back home in a bus separated from their former "enemies." The best news about the project is that it will continue even if the funding ceases completely.

Can Education Make a Difference?

I strongly believe it can, and the most vivid example for me of how it has made a difference is Northern Ireland, which we have visited twice in a course of a decade to look for partners for our projects in the North Caucasus region. While in 2000 schools were segregating Catholics and Protestant students, the major tension in the region resulted from the declining economy and subsequent desolation in the region. As soon as the first integrated schools began to appear and a dialogue with neighbors was established, the situation began to improve. Today the number of integrated schools has grown to 56 and not all the children of families wishing to enroll them can be accommodated. The schools have opened up to the larger world and the implementation of global education is on the rise, which has reduced the tension existing for centuries to such a considerable extent that the economy is now booming and the number of tourists visiting the country is growing each year.

Conclusion

Global education created a significant paradigm shift in the early beginnings of the Russian education reform movement. Many schools and teacher education programs included global perspectives in curriculum and instruction. With change in leadership and priorities, particularly those of language issues, the priorities shifted. Now our global education network is needed more than ever. The early 1990s were a time when many people thought Europe and the United States had learned their lessons, that there would be no more armed conflicts. There were also many economies in transition and not delivering.

Global education in those days was felt to be something that, while it might enhance Russian education, was not a necessity. It is different now, and there is an enormous need for global education not only in Russia and in other transitional countries but also in the post–9/11 United States. When the generous American philanthropist, George Soros, asked me what could benefit American education most, I responded, "global education." Clearly, I am not the only person who thinks global education is a necessity in the global age. At the Organization for Economic Co-operation and Development conference held in Santo Domingo in 2008, the Austrian Minister of Education said in her opening speech, "I would like to draw your attention to two education issues that are important in relation to globalization: Global education and education for sustainable development. Global education means that no student should leave school without having a grasp of global relationships."

We in Russia understand this message profoundly. With the economy improving and more funds available, global education continues to be integrated into Russian schools, teacher education, and youth camps. The new school curriculum now under debate must be built around global understanding, skills required in the global market place, and, most importantly, the values of global education. As Russia is rapidly becoming a globalized community, this need will become greater. Today, scholars, administrators, and teachers who have experienced global education principles in their institutions continue to teach these principles to improve the quality of life in Russia and the world community.

III. Pedagogy and Possibilities in the Postmodern World

Moving the Center of Global Education: From Imperial Worldviews That Divide the World to Double Consciousness, Contrapuntal Pedagogy, Hybridity, and Cross-Cultural Competence

Merry M. Merryfield

> We need to learn again how five centuries of studying, classifying and or-
> dering humanity within an imperial context gave rise to peculiar and pow-
> erful ideas of race, culture, and nation that were, in effect, conceptual
> instruments that the West used both to divide up and educate the world.
>
> ---Willinsky, 1998

It is time for social studies educators to move beyond the global education conceived in the Cold War. In the 1970s the seminal work of Lee
Anderson (1979), Chadwick Alger (1974), James Becker (1979), and
Robert Hanvey (1976) contributed greatly to the social studies by conceptualizing citizenship education for a global age. Global education developed world-mindedness by expanding the social studies' Eurocentric
curriculum with more content on Africa, Asia, Latin America, and the
Middle East and infusing voices from people in these world regions to
develop skills in perspective consciousness (Becker, 1979; Hanvey, 1976).
Globally oriented social studies curricula added to the traditional U.S.
foreign policy view of the world by examining how non-state actors such
as individuals, multinational corporations, and nongovernmental organizations (NGOs) (as diverse as CARE, the International Monetary
Fund, the Grameen Bank, Greenpeace, the National Council of Churches,
the Palestinian Liberation Organization) were interacting globally and
changing the world (Alger, 1974; Alger & Harf, 1986; Anderson, 1979).
Teachers began to teach concepts such as globalization, economic interdependence, and global political systems and situated environmental
and human rights issues in a world context so that students would learn
how they and their communities influence and are influenced by the ac-

tions and beliefs of people around the planet (Merryfield, 1998). Adopted by the National Council for the Social Studies in 1982, elements of global education have been integrated into the social studies curriculum in many states and school districts to help young people understand their increasingly interconnected world.

In the 1980s and 1990s while Americans witnessed the fall of the Berlin Wall and the breakup of the Soviet Union and felt the effects of global labor markets, computer technology, and the spread of AIDS, global educators taught young people to understand these and other unprecedented changes through dimensions of global education: local/global connections, perspective consciousness, cross-cultural awareness, global history, and global economic, political, ecological, and technological systems and issues. Social studies educators have often used popular metaphors such as the global village or spaceship earth and slogans such as "think globally, act locally" to help their students envision their place and choices in a global age. From the 1970s to the early 1990s there were criticisms and occasional attacks on global education, usually from religious or conservative groups that were concerned about biased instructional materials or points of view they perceived as detrimental to American education (Buehrer, 1990; Lamy, 1991; Nash, Crabtree, & Dunn, 1997; Schukar, 1993). However, few have questioned the assumptions implicit in the seminal scholarship in global education that (1) globalization is neither good or bad, it is simply the result of long-term trends in technological progress; (2) globalization demonstrates the superiority of Western capitalism, free markets, and democracy over communism; and (3) if schools educate young Americans in the dynamics of globalization, their generation will be able to sustain the American way of life and the role of the United States within the world system (Alger & Harf, 1986; Anderson, 1979; Becker, 1979; Lamy, 1991; Leetsma, 1979; Pike, 2000; Werner, 1990).

Recently these and other assumptions have been challenged by a tidal wave of popular protest and scholarly literature questioning the meaning, inevitability, and outcomes of globalization. Most common are fears that people and countries are losing political or economic control as seen in *The Global Trap: Globalization and the Assault on Democracy and Prosperity* (Martin & Schumann, 1997) and *Losing Control? Sovereignty in an Age of Globalization* (Sassen, 1996) or dilution of cultural identity as written about in *The Clash of Civilizations and the Remaking of the World Order* (Huntington, 1998) and *Globalization and Identity* (Meyer & Geschiere, 1999). Crossing many disciplines and paradigms, writers are concerned that globalization is increasing political polarization, economic and technological inequities, and cultural conflicts in such works as *Capitalism in the Age of Globalization* (Amin, 1997), *The Lexus and the Olive Tree* (Friedman, 1999), *Jihad vs. McWorld: How Globalism and Tribalism Are Reshaping Our World* (Barber, 1995), and *Articulating the Global and the Local* (Cvetkovich & Kellner, 1997).

Other writers, such as Robert Kaplan (2000) in *The Coming Anarchy*, Cameron McCarthy in *The Uses of Culture* (1998), Saskia Sassen (1998) in *Globalization and Its Discontents*, and Edward Said (1993) in *Culture and Imperialism*, have addressed the paradoxes of divergent, even conflicting local and global forces that are occurring at the same time, even in the same places, and the resulting hybridity of ideas, experiences, and cultures that increasingly characterize the human experience. In the past few years people engaged in new electronic technologies have begun to ask how the Internet and World Wide Web are affecting people's worldviews and the felt realities of globalization. Scholars raise critical issues about the power of electronic media and communication in globalization and changes in culture, community, work, politics, education, and identity in works such as *Communication and Global Society* (Chen & Starosta, 2000), *Electronic Literacies* (Warschauer, 1999), *Culture of the Internet* (Kiesler, 1997), "Telecommunication in the Classroom: Rhetoric versus Reality" (Fabos & Young, 1999), and *Women@internet: Creating New Cultures in Cyberspace* (Harcourt, 1999). The effects of globalization on education may mean moving from national to global curricula for world citizenship as in *Educating World Citizens: Multinational Curriculum Development* (Parker, Ninomiya, & Cogan, 1999) and *Reconnecting from National to Global Curriculum* (Pike & Selby, 1995). Or globalization may necessitate fundamental restructuring and innovation to avoid a worsening of educational inequities and educational irrelevance as noted in *Globalization and Education* (Burbules & Torres, 2000) and *Education and the Rise of the Global Economy* (Spring, 1998).

The argument of this chapter is that it is time to reconceptualize global education. Although some of the seminal work of global educators from the 1970s is undoubtedly still relevant, we need to globalize global education through literature, theories, and diverse perspectives that reflect the complexity of the planet in the early twenty-first century. The field needs to be informed by interdisciplinary and multidisciplinary scholarship from many cultures and the issues and concerns of people currently invisible in the curriculum in the United States. However, the task does not end with inclusion—an addition of perspectives is required so that students understand the felt needs and realities of the majority of the world's peoples. More important, students must examine the origins and assumptions that underlie the mainstream, Eurocentric, Cold War framework that divides the world into "us" and "them" and analyze alternative frameworks for understanding people and the planet past and present. The challenge is in moving the center of global education from institutionalized divisions of people and ideas to the complexity of the interaction and syncrety of the global human experience.

I have organized this chapter into three pedagological processes that I believe are particularly relevant for teachers who want to decolonize social studies content and prepare young people to interact in a variety of contexts with people different from themselves. Within each section I discuss both theoretical work and ideas for application in social studies classrooms. The first process examines the pedagogy of imperialism. Students inquire into relationships between empire-building and knowledge construction and examine how the educational legacy of imperialism shapes mainstream academic knowledge today (Willinsky, 1998). Unlike the global education of the 1970s, this process requires that students identify how imperialist assumptions frame knowledge and information in their lives and analyze how this framework limits their ability to understand many of the world's people, changes, and conflicts. Second is the process of illuminating worldviews of people on the planet who are usually omitted, marginalized, or misrepresented in mainstream academic knowledge. If global education is to be truly global, it is critical that students learn from the experiences, ideas, and knowledge of people who are poor, oppressed, or in opposition to people in power. Unlike the global education of the 1970s, this process brings to the center of the curriculum concerns for equity in representation and pedagogy for social justice (Freire, 1995; Gioseffi, 1993; Harding, 1998; Ladson-Billings, 1994; McCarthy & Crichlow, 1993; Ngugi, 1993; Said, 1993). Students learn from people whose experience and knowledge differ from dominant discourse (Ashcroft, Griffiths, & Tiffin, 1989; Chavez & O'Donnell, 1998; Gioseffi, 1993). The third process is cross-cultural experiential learning within different contexts of power. Unlike the cross-cultural awareness conceptualized by Hanvey (1976) cross-cultural experiential learning goes beyond the academic study of differences to place people in real-life situations in which they experience the complexities of deep culture, the tangible privileges that come with the power of the mainstream, and the frustrating inequities of marginalization or outsider status. Cross-cultural experiential learning requires students to demonstrate their ability to use cultural knowledge and skills in actual cross-cultural communication and conflict management (Brislin & Yoshida, 1994; Cushner, McClelland, & Safford, 1992; Gochenour, 1993; Slavin, 1992; Sleeter, 1995). These three processes can be integrated and developmentally sequenced within K-12 social studies.

Process One: Analyzing How the Educational Legacy of Imperialism Shapes Today's Mainstream Academic Knowledge

> We need to learn again how five centuries of studying, classifying and ordering humanity within an imperial context gave rise to peculiar and powerful ideas of race, culture, and nation that were, in effect, conceptual instruments that the West used both to divide up and educate the world. (Willinsky, 1998, pp. 2–3)

In order to recognize the effects of imperialism on today's mainstream academic knowledge and identify how it limits understanding of the world, students must delve into relationships between empire-building and the development of what we call today mainstream academic knowledge, the normative knowledge validated by educational institutions as the objective truth (see Banks, 1995, for a multicultural critique of mainstream academic knowledge in the social studies). In *Learning to Divide the World*, John Willinsky (1998) examines how histories and literature written under imperialism "live on, for many of us, as an unconscious aspect of our education" as mainstream academic knowledge (p. 3). Willinsky (1998) builds upon the postcolonial theory of *Orientalism* (Said, 1978) to demonstrate how the "educational legacy of imperialism" shapes mainstream knowledge through its framework of opposition, its priorities for learning, its divisions and constructions of the world's peoples, and its "scientifically underwritten racism" (p. 4). Whether the dichotomous terms are The Orient/The Occident, First World/Third World, free/communist, or industrialized/developing nations, there is an "us"—usually the white middle-class descendants of Western Europeans who are said to have developed democracy and today make the world safe—and "them," the Others who are divided from real Americans by their culture, skin color, language, politics, or other differences. Others have noted the legacy of imperialism in Anglophone countries in the teaching of "European diffusionism," racialized identities, and reliance upon American and European constructions of other peoples and the world (Blaut, 1993; Freire, 1995; Harding, 1998; McCarthy, 1995; 1998; Omi & Winant, 1993; Pratt, 1992; 1996).

An analysis of the legacy of imperialism could begin with students examining the European struggle from the fifteenth to eighteenth centuries to make sense of the unprecedented sights that they came into contact with in their explorations of Africa, Asia, and what they named "the new world." At first mythical creatures from Pliny's *Historia Naturalis* filled the navigators' maps, and biblical prophecies were used to explain new lands and phenomena. Eventually the contrast between accepted knowledge of the world and their own experiences led the early European explorers and colonizers to recognize that "much of their learning had been shaken, if not undone, and they needed to rebuild that world anew" (Willinsky, 1998, p. 23). Rabasa's (1993) chapter "Allegories of Atlas" in *Inventing A-M-E-R-I-C-A: Spanish Historiography and the Formation of Ethnocentrism* offers insights into the construction of Mercator's (1636) *Atlas*, his world maps, and their impact on education. Students can analyze maps, histories, literature, and visuals to trace early changes in European thinking about other places and cultures and juxtapose constructions by the people they were interacting with in Africa, Asia, and the Americas. Instructional materials that pull together literature, primary sources, and critiques are available from Rethinking Schools, The Network for Educators on the Americas (NECA), and many of the African, Asian, and Middle Eastern Title VI area studies centers in the United States. Numerous scholars have produced collections that are especially pertinent to the social studies, such as *Prejudice: A Global Perspective* (Gioseffi, 1993), *The Africa That Never Was: Four Centuries of British Writing about Africa* (Hammond & Jablow, 1992), *The Post-Colonial Studies Reader* (Ashcroft, Griffiths, & Tiffin, 1995), and the CITE series of primary sources that illustrate national or regional cultures' diverse perspectives, such as Clark's (1997) *Through African Eyes*.

As exploration led to empire, the interpretation of these new worlds developed into a vast scholarship that provided new explanations and a reordering of both past and present knowledge. "Like architects after an earthquake many lettered Europeans saw a chance to rebuild the world" (Willinsky, 1998, p. 24). Over five centuries, knowledge was generated in the name of imperialism's intellectual interests by scientists, naturalists, ethnographers, historians, geographers, journalists, painters, and poets. This "research and development arm of imperialism" informed its "educational project" and made "the whole world coherent for the West by bringing all we knew of it within the imperial order of things" (pp. 10–11). The extensive literature from "the colonies," visual images from sketches, paintings, and photos, and the incredible physical acquisitions brought back to Europe provide fertile ground for an examination of how Europeans interacted with and made sense of their new environments. Willinsky's meticulous details and references are rich resources in themselves for the social studies classroom. In "The Imperial Show and Tell," he provides many examples of how not only animals and artifacts were exhibited for European edification, but also people of color. For example, in 1810 a Xhosa girl of 16 was brought to London where she was exhibited nude as the "Hottentot Venus." Her body became the subject of cartoons and vaudeville plays and, as she became famous, the show moved to Paris. When she died at 25, her body was dissected by Georges Cuvier, the founder of comparative anatomy, who took this opportunity to compare her organs to those of orangutans and then prepare and present her genitalia to the Academie Royale de Medecine to demonstrate the "African perversity, deformation and pathology" said to be caused by Africans' primitive sexual appetites and lack of moral turpitude (Gilman, 1985, as quoted in Willinsky, 1998, pp. 59–60; see Gilman, 1985, for an in-depth examination of this case of using science to define moral differences as well as other characteristics in colonial Europe). To examine hybridity and make connections across time and place, students could analyze examples of Europeans' depictions of both white and African women, African women writers own descriptions of their lives and the whites they knew, white American literature about white and African American women, and African American women's writing, such as Michelle Wallace's (1993) "Negative Images: Towards a Black Feminist Cultural Criticism."

Willinsky (1998, pp. 23–87) vividly illustrates how the roots of Western education are embedded in European dedication to describing, organizing, labeling, and interpreting everything they perceived of interest as they "discovered" new worlds. New academic disciplines of anthropology and sociology were developed and old disciplines of history, geography, and anatomy were revised so that these new bodies of knowledge could be pursued and taught. "There was an effective blend of administrative and educational strategies for regulating and ordering the other" (Willinsky, 2000). Colonial rule and trade gave rise to many structures for knowledge about the world: experimental agriculture and the import of "exotic" plants and animals for botanical and zoological gardens, lectures before learned societies on theories of race, encyclopedias, ethnographies of "primitive peoples," and museums in which to view their artifacts, and travel literature, plays, and fiction that take the reader into different cultures through European eyes (Willinsky, 1998, pp. 23–87).

In analyzing the effects of museums, exhibitions, zoos, and other collections from the empire, Willinsky illustrates how enduring these "instruments of public instruction" have been in teaching as scientific truth European constructions of the cultures, geographies, and histories of Africa, Asia, and the Americas. In chapters such as "History and the Rise of the West," "Geographies of Difference," and "Science and the Origin of Race," he details the imperial framework of knowledge production and its legacy in today's schools. It was the best anthropological, geographical, and historical knowledge that Europe could offer that defined the differences between civilized and uncivilized, East and West. These instruments were also cast as training the West (and its students) to look out at the world as if from its center, to seek new horizons and adventures in learning, all of which still informs how we can situate students as imperial tourist-adventurers in their learning about the world" (Willinsky, 2000).

Has the imperial framework survived to shape education on the world today? Students can test Willinsky's ideas by examining the mainstream academic knowledge of their school or community. They could also compare scholarly publications or texts from previous generations with those of today. In deciding what should serve as data for analysis of mainstream academic knowledge, teachers and students could choose to focus on academic scholarship (textbooks, journals) in libraries and museums or include popular knowledge through trade, business, or government documents, cultural or leisure attractions (theme parks, plays, exhibitions, fairs, circuses), and media (newspapers, TV, films, music, cartoons). How can one judge if an imperial framework lives on in our accepted academic or everyday knowledge? Here are some questions to consider: Is there a portrayal of "the Other" (people of color in the United States or peoples in Africa, Asia, the Middle East) based only on European or American perceptions and scholarship? Is there a focus on differences between peoples who are like "us" and people who are different from us? Is there attention to differences that make the Other appear as ignorant, amusing, violent, exotic, or bizarre? Do whites dominate discourse and set the agenda with people of color given less attention, voice, or complexity of character than the whites? Do whites interact on exotic backdrops with people of color serving minor roles? Are there omissions of discrimination or justifications of inequities or oppression? Does culture or nationality equal racial differences or ethnic purity? Is there more interest in the "pure" or traditional that the realities of dynamic cultural change? Is there use of colonial language, literature, or points of view, such as a rationalization for imperialism (as in manifest destiny)? Are there assumptions that Americans or Europeans know what is best for people in African, Asian, or Latin American countries?

An inquiry into the imperial legacy could also focus on a particular group of people or a world region. Work across 30 years demonstrates that ignorance, stereotypes, and incomplete knowledge continue to characterize what Americans teach and learn about Africa and African peoples (Beyer & Hicks, 1968; Brantlinger, 1986; Crofts, 1986; Merryfield, 1986; 1989; Osunde, Tlou, & Brown, 1996; Ukpokodu, 1996; Wiley, 1982; Wilson, 1968; 1980; 1995). In a recent action research project (Merryfield, 2001), 21 classroom teachers worked with students to evaluate educational materials in their school on their African content and interview people in their neighborhoods about their knowledge of Africa. They found that the complexity of more than 50 countries of the continent and the diversity of its hundreds of cultures and languages was almost always simplified or reduced to "African." More than 10 negative examples of differences (poverty, ethnic conflicts) between Africans and Americans were found for every positive difference (strong family bonds). An inordinate amount of attention was given to people who are the most different from Americans (e.g., the Masai, the San) instead of more representative African ethnic groups. Europeans' pejorative language (such as "bushman" and "witch doctors") and stereotypes ("jungles," "huts," "tribal warfare,") are still used (see Crofts, 1986; Merryfield, 1986, on pejorative language and imperialist assumptions). African animals and artifacts are often given more attention than people (especially at the elementary level), and it is only when white people have explored, settled, traded, or sent in troops that people know anything about African history or geography. There were also some findings indicative of changes from an imperial framework, such as the identification of library books, instructional materials, and media that teach about Africa through authors, primary sources, and websites from the continent (Merryfield, 2001). In the next section we look beyond the educational legacy of imperialism and examine theories and practices that take students into the lives, voices, experiences, knowledge, and theories of people who have postcolonial worldviews.

Process Two: Understanding the Worldviews of People Underrepresented in Mainstream Academic Knowledge

If global education is to be world centered, it is critical that students learn from the knowledge and experiences of people who, because of their race, gender, class, culture, national origin, religious or political beliefs, are ignored, stereotyped, or marginalized in mainstream academic knowledge. Unlike the global education of the 1970s, this process brings to the center of the curriculum the voices of people past and present who were silenced because they had little or no power to be heard. As students analyze this new knowledge and synthesize its connections with the legacy of imperialism and mainstream academic knowledge, new global understandings begin to emerge that have less to do with divisions among people or nations than they do with the borrowing of ideas, the evolution and hybridity of cultures, the syncrety of shared experience, and enduring human conflicts. In this section I have focused on three ideas that can contribute to a postcolonial pedagogy.

Developing a Double Consciousness

Challenging the imperial legacy of racism in American life, the great African American scholar W. E. B. Du Bois (1989) wrote about its effects on identity and worldview:

> It is a peculiar sensation, this double-consciousness, this sense of always looking at one's self through the eyes of others, of measuring one's soul by the tape of a world that looks on in amused contempt and pity. One ever feels his twoness—an American, a negro: two souls, two thoughts, two unreconciled strivings; two warring ideals in one dark body, whose dogged strength alone keeps it from being torn asunder. (p. 3; the first edition was published in 1903).

Unlike the perspective consciousness of global education (Hanvey, 1976) that teaches students to become aware that other people may have views of the world profoundly different from their own, double consciousness is an act of survival in coping with the institutionalized violence and pervasive discrimination of racism. In early twentieth-century America, black children grew up conscious not only of their own culture that they learned from family and community but also the white culture that oppressed them as inferior because of their race. White people did not need to develop a double consciousness as they were never in the position where their survival depended upon their understanding of how blacks perceived them. The work of Du Bois (1965; 1989), which

spans many decades and world regions, is an example of seminal literature that illuminates the worldview of people struggling with the inheritance of imperialism in dividing people by the color of their skin into
superior and inferior categories. In his own famous words, "the problem
of the Twentieth Century is the problem of the color-line" (1989, p. 29).

The realities that create a double consciousness are a global phenomenon. Understanding two worldviews develops when people are
separated or discriminated against because of their race, language, religion, national origin, or other differences (Gilroy, 1993; Narayan, 1988). In
conceptualizing *The Black Atlantic* as black consciousness that is intercultural and transnational for people of the African diaspora, Paul Gilroy
(1993) was drawn to the work of Jewish thinkers as they have also struggled with identity, a double consciousness, slavery, and diaspora. Writers have used other terms to describe the multiple perspectives that
people develop to deal with oppression. In writing about the effects of
the ultimate oppression—genocide—Anna Newman (1998) describes
how her father's "double visions, a double knowing of sorts that infil-
trates every corner of his life" paralleled his view before Auschwitz and
his experiences afterward (p. 430).

The ramifications of double consciousness can be examined across
many contexts through biography and other nonfiction. Manthia Diawara (1998), a professor of Comparative Literature and Film at New York
University, tells of his return to Guinea after 32 years in the book *In
Search of Africa*. To work on a commentary on Sekou Toure and to better
understand Negritude, a topic central to his teaching and scholarship,
Diawara visits Guinea, looks up old friends, explores old neighborhoods,
and reflects upon his own and Guinea's psychological changes. He ex-
pects to be welcomed back as an insider but finds himself treated as a
tourist, an American, a foreigner. At one point he becomes lost in the city
only to realize he has walked into Camp Boiro, "Sekou Toure's infamous
prison, from which no one had ever come out alive" (p. 37). The flash of
fear he experiences triggers reflections on William Sassine, a Guinean
writer "whose novels describe the loneliness and ineptitude of people in
the face of the crushing force of Afro-Pessimism" through "wordplay
that draws on Mandinka idioms to bend the meaning of French expressions" (p. 40). Diawara uses his experiences in returning to Guinea to inform his rethinking of Sassine's work, especially Camara, a character
who returns to Guinea to be "berated by an acquaintance who accuses
him of loving white people more than his own brothers and of scorning
the things that Guineans accomplished" (p. 40). Throughout the book

Diawara captures the disconcerting experience of seeing old friends and places through the consciousness of childhood memories at the same time as through the eyes of a New Yorker, an outsider, and recognizing that neither Americans nor Guineans see him as one of them. He uses these insights to re-examine diaspora themes in African and African American literature such as return narratives and Richard Wright, resistance literature, and Malcolm X (Diawara, 1998).

The ability to see one's world both from the mainstream and from the margins is one of the shared characteristics of multicultural and global educators (Merryfield, 2000a, b). In analyzing profiles of the lived experiences of 80 American and Canadian teacher educators who were recognized by peers as exemplary in the ways in which they prepare teachers in multicultural and global education, I found that most identified experiences that led to a consciousness of what it is like to be considered inferior, to be placed on the periphery of society, to be looked at as an outsider who does not and will never belong. For people of color in the study, these experiences happened early in life as part of growing up in white America. Many of the white educators, however, did not develop this consciousness until they left North America and lived overseas. In order to make sense of these experiences, they looked critically at fundamental assumptions about reality, truth, power, and culture that they had before taken for granted. By highlighting dissonance between identity and contexts of power, the experiences became milestones in the development of a consciousness of multiple realities. For many educators, there were parallels in recognizing that the multiple realities that exist in a community or country also exist globally. This recognition is what has led many people concerned with domestic diversity and social justice to make connections with people supporting global diversity and human rights and become interested in how global perspectives can inform multicultural education. For others in the study, the recognition of the interconnectedness of local and global intersections of power, discrimination, and identity has turned their attention to multicultural education to pursue local ramifications of globalization (Merryfield, 2000a).

Synthesizing Differences through Contrapuntal Literature and Histories

The work of Edward Said has much to offer in understanding the hybridity that comes from the conflict, accommodation, borrowing, and rethinking across diverse people's experiences, knowledge, and worldviews. Said (1978; 1993) grew up within the conflicting realities of being a Christian Palestinian in a British and French colonial world. His study of colonialism and imperialism led to the development of *Orientalism*, a theory to explain the "Western style for dominating, restructuring, and having authority over the Orient" (p. 3). Said analyzed the characteristics of European literature and history from the Enlightenment onward to understand how and why Europeans had assigned particular meanings to the part of the world they called "the Orient," when those meanings were in conflict with the ways in which Asian and Arab peoples perceived themselves. Among his many works, I have found *Orientalism* (1978), *Culture and Imperialism* (1993), and *Covering Islam* (1997) particularly relevant because of extensive attention to geographical divisions, language, people, books, and events that we teach about in the social studies. His analyses are thought provoking as he reminds us that many of the terms we use to divide the world—The Middle East, The Far East, The Third World—are man-made constructions that Europeans developed to situate the Other. *Orientalist* divisions (e.g., East is East and West is West), perspectives (Europeans are civilized, and Orientals are barbaric), phrases (the mysterious East), and images (a scantily clad oriental woman as courtesan in an Egyptian harem) define the "Orientals." It is a colonialist presumption that Europeans were the experts and the peoples they colonized were not able to define themselves (1978, pp. 26–28, 216).

Through *Orientalism* Europeans have projected their perspectives (and myths and misinformation) not only upon the Western world but also upon the peoples of Asia, Africa, and elsewhere whom they have oppressed. As in double consciousness, those colonized by the Europeans had to contend with the colonizer's reality. Said saw Europe's Orientalist perspectives dynamically interacting with the cultural identities of peoples who were colonized and that interaction continuing to influence identity and thought after independence. "Indeed all culture as hybrid (in Homi Bhabha's complex sense of that word) and encumbered, or entangled and overlapping ... strikes me as the essential idea" (Said, 1993, p. 317). Teaching about hybridity of cultures counters the imperial legacy of dividing the world and provides complex and dynamic knowledge about two major characteristics of globalization: increasing cultural hybridity and the fusion or syncrety of political, military, health, economic, or religious ideas that once were isolated or opposed to each other (see Bhabha, 1986; Parry, 1987, for other postcolonial constructions of hybridity).

In *Culture and Imperialism,* Said articulates a pedagogy for countering *Orientalist* history and literature that apply to the social studies. Students can "look back at the cultural archive" and "reread it not univocally but *contrapuntally,* with a simultaneous awareness both of the metropolitan history that is narrated and of those other histories against which (and together with which) the dominating discourse acts" (1993, p. 51). By adding new perspectives and knowledge to American or European constructions of history, culture, political or economic systems, contrapuntal writing and reading can illuminate other worldviews and provide insights into how identity, power, and history interact. Contrapuntal pedagogy in the social studies is not simply the provision of different perspectives. Instead the focus is on the interaction and integration of cultures, the dynamic process in which the colonizer and the colonized were changed as they experienced each other's lifestyles, technologies, goods, and ideas about the natural world, community, spirituality, and governance.

> An example of the new knowledge would be the study of Orientalism or Africanism and, to take a related set, the study of Englishness and Frenchness. These identities are today analyzed not as God-given essences, but as results of collaboration between African history and the study of Africa in England, for instance, or between the study of French history and the reorganization of knowledge during the First Empire. In an important sense we are dealing with the formation of cultural identities understood not as essentializations ... but as contrapuntal ensembles, for it is the case that no identity can ever exist by itself and without an array of opposites, negatives, oppositions: Greeks always require barbarians, and Europeans Africans, Orientals. (Said, 1993, p. 52).

By organizing contrapuntal history or cultural studies by events or ideas valued by the Other, students can identify the power that comes with who frames the questions and recognize the limitations of knowledge that focuses on differences. In *Uses of Culture,* Cameron McCarthy (1998) criticizes multiculturalists, who in their efforts to view the world through the "gaze of the subaltern," "stack African Americans, Latinos, and Native Americans against Polish-Americans, Italian Americans, Jewish Americans, etc." (p. 156). Instead of continuing the colonial division of the Other, he encourages educators to "study the historical and contemporary heterogeneity of human interactions and lives" (p. 160). Thus, a postcolonial curriculum does not focus on or try to reconstruct "pure" or authentic" cultures that may have existed before imperial contact. The myth of the noble savage comes to mind as a part of some people's efforts to romanticize so-called untouched primitive cultures. Postimperial global educators might even question whether such cultural isolation or ethnic purity has ever existed as global history documents the continual movement, diffusion, and metamorphoses of cultures (Crofts, 1986).

Decolonizing the Mind

A third scholar whose work can inform global education within the social studies is Ngugi wa Thiong'o, a Kenyan writer who experienced the Gikuyu liberation movement (the Mau Mau rebellion in colonialist language) against British colonialism. As a young teacher and writer, Ngugi was jailed when his plays and books were perceived as subversive by the postindependence government. He examines the effects of racism and oppression on identity and language and looks closely at the role of schools in perpetuating what he calls a colonized mind. In *Decolonising the Mind*, Ngugi (1986) explores how the identity developed during the dehumanization of colonization has lived on in many Kenyans' minds a generation after independence. He illustrates how a colonial mentality deeply permeates many people's thinking today because it is not only embedded but unexamined. Thirty years after independence, many Kenyans do not question the colonialist assumptions that Kenyan languages and literature are appropriate for lower levels of learning such as primary education or basic literacy while English and British literature are prerequisites for higher education (Ngugi, 1986).

Decolonizing the mind, as in transformative multicultural education (Banks, 1995), helps people become conscious of how oppressors force their worldviews into oppressed peoples' lives in such ways that in later generations people may never realize that their ideas and choice are affected by colonialist or neocolonialist perspectives. It is not only subjugated peoples who have a colonized mind. When white students assume they are superior to others because of their race, they are exhibiting similar colonialist assumptions. The pedagogy of decolonizing the mind is congruent with Willinsky's examination of the educational legacy of imperialism described above as it focuses on examining where norms, assumptions, and underlying beliefs came from and what effect they have on people's lives.

In *Moving the Centre*, Ngugi (1993) offers a solution to the postcolonial inheritance of cultural imperialism, especially, the imperialism of the English language, by "moving the center." Not unlike the use of "margins and mainstream" written by Grant (1992), center and periphery denote geopower relationships. Ngugi's goal is to "shift the base from which to view the world from its narrow base in Europe to a multi-plicity of centres ... from Asia, Africa and South America" (Ngugi, 1993, p. 6). He is concerned with moving the center within countries and glob-ally to include all cultures so that none is excluded or, as he describes third world literature in American universities, "treated as something outside the mainstream" (p. 10).

Du Bois, Said, and Ngugi are some of the growing number of writers whose ideas can open minds and help young people better understand the diversity and conflicts of the human experience past and present. If we move the center of the social studies curriculum to include the ex-periences, knowledge, and worldviews of people who are now ignored or underrepresented, young Americans will have a broader, more com-plex understanding of global realities.

Process Three: Sustained and Reflective Cross-Cultural Experiential Learning

Although cross-cultural interaction and immersion are mentioned within the social studies by some multicultural and global educators, there is little evidence that most K-12 social studies teachers or teacher educators have had sufficient training in theories of cross-cultural psychology or methods of intercultural education to put these ideas into practice (Mer-ryfield, 1995; Powell, Zehm, & Garcia, 1996; Wilson, 1982; 1983; 1993b; Zeichner & Hoeft, 1996; Zeichner & Melnick, 1995). On one hand there is a plethora of rhetoric about the need to prepare students to work with diverse people, and on the other a paucity of scholarship on the ability of teachers or teacher educators to do so. In this section I identify work that can inform the social studies on cross-cultural and intercultural learning. Due to space constraints and the complexity of these theories, my over-view serves as an introduction with recommendations for further read-ing and resources. I begin with literature on understanding lived experiences.

Reflecting upon Lived Experiences in Culture Learning

Cross-cultural experiential education builds upon the lived experiences that students and teachers bring with them into the classroom. What is lived experience? Max Van Manen (1990) describes the temporal nature of lived experience:

> Various thinkers have noted that lived experience first of all has a temporal structure: it can never be grasped in its immediate manifestation but only re-

flectively as past presence ... Lived experience is the breathing of meaning ... Thus a lived experience has a certain essence, a "quality" that we gain in retrospect (p. 36).

Van Manen also points out how reflective writing interacts with experience and "teaches us what we know, and in what way we know what we know" (p. 127). Through a poststructuralist perspective, Deborah Britzman (1994) suggests that a person's experiences and identity interact in a complicated construction of self and experience. One's identity shapes how experiences are seen and how they are interpreted over time. This perspective challenges conventional assumptions that experiences have some essentialist effect or meaning (Britzman, 1994; Brodkey, 1987; McCarthy, 1990; 1998; Scott, 1991). They argue that power undergirds the construction of identities and interpretation of experiences. This area of research is informed by Foucault's (1980) discourse of experience. It is in creating narratives of one's experience that who a person is and what the person experienced becomes one.

This interaction across identity, power, and experience is central to understanding how cross-cultural experiences create meaning in people's lives. It is especially critical to keep in mind when cross-cultural experiential learning places people in different positions of power than they normally experience. Think of the change in the context of power when an African American male student leaves his Afrocentric school near his home to work in a service learning project with the city's mostly white businessmen. Another type of change in power would be from the periphery to the center when a white female teacher returns to her middle-class suburban school after a year of teaching English within the Muslim culture of Northern Nigeria. The dynamic nature of reflection and discourse over time is very complex as people and their narratives of experience may change. When adults or even high school students look back upon their lives and identify those experiences they now see as significant in shaping their worldviews they may see meaning that differs from how they made sense of those events at the time when they were actually experiencing them. The retrospective meaning-making quality of reflection upon one's lived experiences means that the significance of cross-cultural experiences may change over time and contexts. Teachers need to reflect upon their own lived experiences with people who are different from themselves and analyze how they have developed their perspectives and knowledge of others before they begin such processes with their students (Dillard, 1996; Ford & Dillard, 1996; Hoffman, 1996; Merryfield, 1993; Sleeter, 1993; 1995).

Writing about Lived Experiences in Culture Learning

One of the fundamental steps in becoming an effective educator is understanding the cultural background and experiences of one's students so that content and pedagogy are connected to their lives (Ladson-Billings, 1994). Many teachers use writing assignments to identify what students already know or assume about culture or history or to explore their family heritage, their interaction with other people, experiences in other places, or with immigration or migration. The act of writing about cross-cultural experiences may complicate reflection and meaning. In a collection of essays titled *"Race," Writing and Difference*, Henry Louis Gates (1986) raises issues about writing by the Other (whom "the European defined as African, Arabic, Chinese, Latin American, Yiddish or female") as he examines the history of written texts and their portrayal of people of color around the world, a portrayal that is challenged when the Other also writes (p. 2). Historically, writing has served as a powerful tool in creating European "truths" about Africans and Asians, and the ability to write has been considered to be a skill that separated Europeans from the Other (Gates, 1986; Said, 1978; 1993). For more than 200 years white Americans tried to prevent Africans and African Americans from writing at all as they recognized its power:

> By 1750, the chain had been minutely calibrated; the human scale rose from "the lowliest Hottentot" (black South Africans) to "glorious Milton and Newton." If blacks could write and publish imaginative literature, then they could, in effect, take a few giant steps up the chain of being in an evil game of "Mother, May I?" (Gates, 1986, p. 8)

For people of color, the act of writing about cross-cultural experiences may draw on different goals or epistemologies in the tradition of the Other writing as social or political action against oppression. Because of the interconnectedness of identity, power, lived experience, writing, and reflection, the learning from cross-cultural experiences may differ considerably across a group of students who differ in race, class, gender, language, or national origin. Today postcolonial literature can supply a rich diversity of ideas, experiences, and perspectives on what it means for people of color as "the empire writes back" to the European canon (Ashcroft, Griffiths, & Tiffin, 1989).

Cross-Cultural Experiences in Culture Learning

Within the seminal work in cross-cultural psychology and sociology (Allport, 1954; Cole & Scribner, 1974; Dasen, 1992; Hall, 1959; 1976; Kelly,

1955; Secrest & Flores, 1969; Triandis & Berry, 1980) and intercultural experiential education (M. Bennett, 1993; Brislin, 1986; 1993; Brislin & Yoshida, 1994; Gochenour, 1993; Paige, 1993) scholars have developed theories of cultural interaction, communication, and learning and applied them to educating people to live and work with people of diverse cultures either within their own country or in countries different from their own. Kenneth Cushner (1999) has written extensively on intercultural education for social studies classrooms. His work provides insights into conceptualizing, planning, sequencing, and evaluating cross-cultural learning. *Human Diversity in Education* (Cushner, McClelland, & Safford, 2000) and *Intercultural Interactions* (Cushner & Brislin, 1996) are especially significant resources for social studies educators in developing an understanding of how cross-cultural experiential education integrates the goals of global education and multicultural education to address prejudice, ethnocentrism, and discrimination while teaching skills in cross-cultural communication and interaction and knowledge of diverse cultures. Besides practical suggestions on intercultural activities, Cushner, McClelland, & Safford (1992) explore the phenomenon of culture shock within as well as across national boundaries and its implications for American classrooms. Experienced by nearly everyone who adjusts to a new culture, culture shock is the "disorientation that occurs whenever someone moves from their known, comfortable surroundings to an environment which is significantly different and in which their needs are not easily met" (p. 44). They conclude that culture shock is a stress that happens every day in American schools when children leave their homes and enter a different culture from the one in which they have been socialized (Cushner, McClelland, & Safford, 1992). Insights from this literature are relevant to teachers and students who enter new cultures within their school or community and experience disorientation, confusion, or discomfort in dealing with people different from themselves or unfamiliar situations. The emotions and stress that result from encounters with human differences are cumulative. Considering the magnitude of these emotions–the stresses of dealing with the ambiguity of wanting to belong yet being an outsider, the discomfort and insecurity of being treated as different–one can understand how experiences with people different from oneself would be magnified when a person's experiences with diversity are always characterized by being positioned on the margins of society or dismissed as inferior (Collins, 1990; Cushner, McClelland, & Safford, 2000).

There are two frameworks in the intercultural education literature that are especially relevant for the social studies. First is Milton Bennett's (1993) developmental model of intercultural sensitivity that provides insights into how people move from stages of ethnocentrism toward intercultural competence and how teachers can enhance this process. The ethnocentric stages include (1) denial (either from accidental isolation or deliberate separation); (2) defense as evidenced by denigration (derogatory attitudes, stereotyping, overt hostility), superiority (seeing those who are different as inferior), or reversal (denigration of one's own culture and assumptions of the superiority of another culture); and (3) minimization from either physical (all people have the same physical needs) or transcendent (we are all God's children) universalism. The ethnorelative stages include (1) acceptance of behavioral and value differences (cultural differences are seen as neither good nor bad; they are acknowledged and respected); (2) adaptation of skills for interacting and communicating are enhanced (development of empathy and understanding of pluralism through multiple cultural frames of reference); (3) integration, which includes both contextual evaluation and constructive marginality in which a person is "always in the process of becoming a part of and apart from a given cultural context" (Alder, 1977 as quoted in M. Bennett, 1993, p. 59).

In discussing each of the six stages, Bennett describes the psychology of peoples' thought processes and identifies educational strategies and activities that meet the needs of people in that stage. For example, if students are at the denial stage ("there are no cultural differences I need to know about"), activities such as holding an international festival or visiting an exhibit of Chinese art would help people develop recognition of some differences without overwhelming them with profound cultural contrasts. However, if they are at the stage of minimization where cultural differences are recognized but trivialized (the "one worldview" of "we are really more alike than different, so I don't have to worry about all those differences") activities are needed to help students recognize the significance of cultural contexts. To give a practical significance to cultural differences, Bennett recommends using simulations and shared experiences with people from other cultures that reward people's recognition of both profound cultural differences and the need to learn how to interact differently because of them. It is important that people learn that there are times when "just being themselves" with people of other cultures may mean their behaviors are inappropriate, even insulting (M. Bennett, 1993).

In the same book, Janet Bennett (1993) expands on cultural marginality, the experience of many students today who are on the margins of two or more cultures. Her work on encapsulated marginals (people who are troubled or alienated by the ambiguity of their identity) and constructive marginals (people are never not "at home" and find advantages in "dynamic in-betweenness") is very useful for understanding the connections between teaching cultural content and teaching diverse student populations.

The second framework, called "The Culture-General Framework," can inform both teaching about different cultures as well as communication and interaction across cultures. Developed through the research of Brislin, Cushner, Cherrie, & Yong (1986), its 18 themes are grouped into 3 categories—emotions, knowledge, and cultural differences. Emotions that often develop with cross-cultural experiences include (1) anxiety over unfamiliar demands; (2) disconfirmed expectations when situations differ from what was expected; (3) the need to belong but being unable to do so as an outsider; (4) the ambiguity of not understanding messages being sent in the new culture, yet having to respond; and (5) confrontation with one's own prejudices.   The five emotions can be examined by teachers and students as they are immersed in different levels of cross-cultural learning from a service learning project with a local mosque to a study abroad project in rural Mexico, or especially when five Kosovar refugees join a fifth grade global history class. These emotions are also very relevant for professional development programs as most educators these days find themselves (and their students) coming into contact with people from cultures that they may know little about.   For example, when more than 5,000 Somali immigrants were resettled in Columbus, Ohio, in the 1990s, not only did the Somalis experience such emotions in dealing with the schools, but many American teachers and students also developed the same feelings as the Somalis were different in many ways from other immigrants they had known. Recognizing the power of these emotions is the first step in improving teaching and learning.

Knowledge areas that incorporate many cross-cultural differences but are difficult to understand include work, time and space, language, roles (based on gender, age, religious beliefs, inherited position, etc.), the importance of the group versus importance of the individual, rituals versus superstition, social hierarchies/class/status, and values (Brislin, Cushner, Cherrie, & Yong, 1986). These areas can provide teachers with a structure to move beyond the superficiality of dress, holidays, and food or a focus on the exotic and bizarre. (I once observed a fourth-grade teacher's *one and only* lesson on Botswana titled "Why Africans Eat Bugs.") A Columbus middle school teacher I work with applied this part of the Culture-General Framework to her teaching of India. In the previous year, the students had read a section in their cultural geography book, watched a video on Hinduism, mapped different ethnic groups and religions and visited a local Indian grocery store and restaurant. Now the class became involved in researching patterns of belief and behavior. Groups of two or three students selected a concept from the list above and collected data from the library, the Internet, and Indians living in the community to learn how beliefs affect behavior. By the end of the project the students not only understood some of the diversity of contemporary Indian cultures better than ever before, they also recognized how their own cultural patterns are transmitted and changed over generations, yet rarely examined. Interest and motivation were sparked by the focus on beliefs and Indians became more than "school work." They were real people, key-pals, friends they wanted to visit someday. When fighting broke out in Kashmir later in the school year, the students were eager to find out what was happening because one of their key-pals in New Delhi had grown up in Kashmir and had shared with them some photos of his village when explaining his family's place in the social hierarchy. Using the events as a teachable moment, the teacher invited five Indian students from a local university to work with her students and prepare some instructional materials for some other middle school students to learn about cultural conflicts in India. But first she had her students develop cross-cultural handouts on "making our Indian visitors comfortable" based on their research on beliefs and behaviors.

Third, the Culture-General Framework describes bases of cultural differences, those ways that people in different cultures think about and evaluate information: the differences in how people (1) categorize, (2) differentiate, (3) make ingroup/outgroup distinctions, (4) distinguish the differences in learning styles, and (5) highlight differences in how people attribute or judge the causes of behavior. This work can be used to develop culturally relevant pedagogy as well as cross-cultural understanding (Brislin, Cushner, Cherrie, & Yong, 1986). Several publications of Intercultural Press focus on instructional activities and cross-cultural assignments that clarify these differences or demonstrate their significance in everyday interactions. *Experiential Activities for Intercultural Living* (Seelye, 1996), *Living with Strangers in the U.S.A.* (Archer, 1991), and *Cross-Cultural Dialogues* (Stori, 1994) provide insights into cross-cultural interaction and help K-12 and university educators recognize the power of cultural differences in the way people make judgments, ask questions, make sense of body language, develop expectations, and so forth.

Finally there is some research on how cross-cultural experiences contribute to the development of multicultural and global educators. Teachers' narratives, stories, and theories take us into the process of educators' thinking about events, how experiences lead to insights, and the dynamic processes of constructing or deconstructing meaning (Day, 1993; Deering & Stanutz, 1995; Finney & Orr, 1995; Gomez, 1996; Schubert & Ayers, 1992; Wilson, 1998; Wolk & Rodman, 1994). Angene Wilson (1982; 1983; 1986; 1993a; 1993b; 1997; 1998) has written extensively about how their cross-cultural experiences positively affect how social studies educators think and teach about the world and its people. Her article, "Oburoni Outside the Whale: Reflections on an Experience in Ghana," provides powerful insights into the contexts of power and how identity can be transformed through immersion in another culture (Wilson, 1998). Within narratives of classrooms and schools are compelling stories of experiences in social studies and global education. Martha Germaine's (1998) *Worldly Teachers* takes us into the lives of six American teachers as they leave their teaching positions in the Midwest or East Coast, move to either China or Japan to teach, and then return home and resume their teaching here. Other research describes the intersections of lived experience, cultural diversity, equity, and education through the perspectives of teachers and students in urban schools (Fine, 1991; Kozol, 1991; Meier, 1995), African American and African Canadian teachers (Foster, 1997; Henry, 1998), and immigrant students (Olsen, 1997).

Teachers and students come to schools with lived experience that inform their understanding of identity, human differences, power, hybridity, cultural change, and other constructs of social studies. These lived experiences provide the foundation for specialized cross-cultural experiential learning in social studies classrooms, in the community, in service learning projects and experiences within and across different cultures. Few people forget the lessons learned when they experience firsthand what it feels like when one's human differences are the basis for being welcomed into the center or pushed toward the periphery of a society.

Conclusions

Last week I returned to Ohio from a conference in Seoul in which several Korean historians, representatives from the Ministry of Education, and five American social studies professors pondered over the teaching of world history, content on Korea in American classrooms, and global education for both American and Korean students. We met in the wake of the historic June 2000 meeting of the leaders of North Korea and South Korea and in the anticipation of 100 North and South Koreans crossing the border to visit family members they had not seen or heard from in almost 50 years. There is no more profound example of Cold War divisions than the two Koreas today. Since curriculum guides, standards, textbooks, and other social studies materials were on the agenda, the Korean professors puzzled over evidence that Americans are teaching that the Cold War is over, that it ended with the fall of the Berlin Wall and the breakup of the Soviet Union. Americans are teaching that they have won the war with communism—yet what about North Korea? Do Americans know troops are facing off on the border? They queried American use of "Third World" and wondered why their highly industrialized, well-educated, democratic country is categorized as though it has more in common with Burma or Nigeria that it does with the United States.

As we drove past the U.S. Army base in Seoul, my Korean colleagues described the anger of some Koreans who see the soldiers as American imperialists and the differences in how the older generation remembers the war. At the King's palace, a colleague shared with me how Korean social studies teachers teach about the Japanese occupation from 1910 to 1945, about being forced to give up their Korean names and take Japanese ones, about the King's home being turned into a zoo, and about Japanese "use" of Korean women. With evidence everywhere of American multinationals, food, fashion, services, websites, and media (films, rock videos, CNN, and Armed Forces Network-Korea, to name a few), one Korean colleague shared her concerns that economic development and globalization mean Westernization of Korean culture and values.

As I rode the subway, talked with Korean teachers at a social studies conference, experienced teenage hangouts with a former student, I faced a very unpleasant reality that is at the heart of this chapter. The issues, ideas, and lifestyles on the minds of Koreans today (and most other people in Asia, Africa, Latin America) are not being taught in American classrooms. Yes, American students will study the Korean War, and they may even learn about reunification talks if they happen to have a social studies teacher who values current events.

But unless things change, young Americans will continue to be taught to place Korea in certain categories defined by imperial and Cold War frameworks: Asia, World War II, Cold War/containment, the Korean Conflict, anticommunist allies, and perhaps trading partners or "emerging" democracies. None of these categories will lead to understanding what is important to Koreans today, their changing culture and values, their concerns and issues, their complex connections to China and Japan, their Koreanization of American and Japanese pop culture. The assumption that we need to understand Korean culture only in the context of the Korean peninsula, not Koreans in Japan or the United States is another imperial habit of defining culture by national boundaries.

Here is where a reconceptualized global education can make a difference. Social studies students examine the construction, assumptions, and legacy of imperial knowledge that leads Americans to place Koreans and others in such categories, analyze the perspectives and ideas of Koreans and other underrepresented people and the hybridity of their ideas and experiences. They learn from face to face, online, and simulated cross-cultural experiences with Koreans in Asia and Koreans in their neighborhood. They place the vast changes over the past 50 years within a global perspective of issues facing other people and the planet. They come to understand the complexity of globalization, *the* defining issue of our time.

Note

The italics or references in quotations are the author's own throughout this chapter.

Permission to publish this chapter was granted by George F. Johnson, president and publisher, IAP-Information Age Publishing, Charlotte, NC 28277, September 13, 2008.

Chapter 11

Characteristics of Globally Minded Teachers: A Twenty-First Century View

John J. Cogan & David L. Grossman

The world has become a more crowded, more interconnected, more volatile, and more unstable place. If education cannot help students see beyond themselves and better understand the interdependent nature of our world, each new generation will remain ignorant, and its capacity to live confidently and responsible will be dangerously diminished.

—Boyer, 1985

Globally Minded Teachers: The Gap between Policy and Practice

Ernest Boyer's warning of nearly a quarter century ago sadly still rings true today. Even if we accept this as a mantra for achieving authentic global education, we are still confronted by a number of continuing challenges. Twenty years ago a report of the U.S. National Governors' Association (1989) advocated that international education should become part of the basic education of all our students, and teachers must know more about international issues. About the same time, Lambert (1989, cited in Schneider, 2003) conducted a comprehensive review of the international content of undergraduate education and was disturbed to find that education majors had relatively light exposure to courses with an international focus. At the comprehensive institutions of higher education—the type of institution where most teachers are trained—the average education major took only 1.5 such courses compared to an average of 2.4 courses for all majors. The situation for education majors differed little between research universities and four-year colleges. A 1980 survey estimated that less than 5 percent of teachers had any academic training in global or international topics or issues (Council on Learning, 1981, cited in Merryfield, 1991).

A more recent study (Heyl & McCarthy, 2003) of the transcripts of 690 graduates of teacher education programs in three U.S. states showed that compared with students in other degree programs these students had a significant lack of exposure to international subjects, foreign language study, and overseas experience. Teacher preparation students rarely pursued foreign language study at the college level beyond two semesters (6 percent), a relatively small number studied abroad (3.5 percent); the somewhat loosely construed international content of their courses was highly variable (from 8 to 26 percent). From a two-phase study of internationalization of teacher education programs that involved more than 500 teacher and university respondents, Schneider (2006) reports that about half of the teachers reported having met a general education requirement of one or more non-U.S. courses, and less than a third remembered any international or comparative modules being included in their courses. In the same study, about two-thirds of the responding teachers reported that recently modified certification and subject standards do *not* reflect increasing globalization. Less than a quarter reported that they were required to take any course oriented to regions other than North America as part of their major.

Therefore preparing teachers who have the knowledge, skills, and attitudes to be effective purveyors of global education is a major challenge. Despite increasing demands for teachers to teach for equity, diversity, and global interconnectedness, colleges of education are not producing teachers with such knowledge and skills (Merryfield, 2000a). What is the difficulty in producing and nurturing globally minded teachers?

The difficulty does not seem to be a lack of rhetorical commitment. In 2006, the Council of Chief State School Officers issued policy statements on global education (CCSSO, 2006a). They noted that "our teachers are not sufficiently supported and trained in global content" (p. 2). A report from a Phi Delta Kappa summit on global education reports that only one American university, the University of Wisconsin, requires all teachers to take some kind of international qualification (Young, 2008). In a study of global education practices in 52 countries, Tye (1999) reported an overall impression that there were only a small number of teacher-training programs anywhere in the world, particularly at the preservice level directed specifically at developing globally minded teachers. When asked about the barriers to global education, most participants simply stated a lack of adequate training of teachers. The National Coalition on Asia and International Studies in the Schools reports that school administrators and policy-makers invariably point to the shortage of teachers with mastery of international knowledge, skills, and perspectives as one of the biggest obstacles to achieving global education in the schools:

> While many states have come a long way toward making international knowledge and skills a significant policy priority, they have done very little

to train teachers to be competent in global issues. Nor has much attention been paid to reforming licensing and certification requirements or providing incentives for teachers to focus on international themes (Asia Society, 2006, p. 10).

Barriers to Formation of Globally Minded Teachers

As a preamble to discussing the characteristics necessary in a globally minded teacher there are substantial barriers to the process of developing such a teacher that must be addressed. To begin with, global education is not completely accepted within the educational or broader communities that schools serve. It is often contrasted with patriotism, and the events of 9/11 have only heightened and renewed these kinds of attacks. Schukar (1993) asserts that there are at least three reasons for these attacks:

- The inherently controversial nature of global education
- Struggles to control the agenda in both content and instructional strategies
- The failure of some global educators to provide balance in curriculum development, the selection of resource materials, and classroom instruction (p. 52).

Attacks on Global Education

In the late 1980s and early 1990s there were three notable challenges to global education programs in Colorado, Minnesota and Iowa (see chapter 1). It became apparent as these three controversies unfolded that the attacks were clearly a carefully and well-articulated political agenda driven by the conservative political right and fundamentalist Christian groups. The same people were contacting the directors and key financial supporters of each global education program under attack. Editorials and letters to the programs and local and national news organizations used basically the same wording; only the name of the program under attack changed.

Hicks (2003) reports that England in the 1980s experienced similar attacks from the Right on world studies, peace education, and multicultural education. Critics said that these educational initiatives were being used for political ends, were a form of indoctrination, used improper teaching methods, and lowered educational standards. Hicks concluded that these attacks reflected a wider international shift toward neoconservative and neoliberal forms of education, which opposed and marginalized initiatives such as global education.

Lessons were learned in the global education community. First of all, the attacks had the impact of making state departments of education, school district administrators, teachers in those districts, and teacher educators much more cautious about offering programs under the name of global education. All were quickly reminded of the highly charged political arena that is public education in the United States (Schukar, 1993). In a recent study, Parker and Camicia (2007) report that of nine educational activists in international education whom they interviewed, four chose not to use the term "global education" in communicating their work to other stakeholders. One preferred "world studies" and three preferred "international education."

National Standards Movement and Teacher Education

The national standards movement has also impacted global education programming in schools as the focus in the social studies standards is on traditional history, geography, economics, civics, and government curriculum content and not on material that is more global in nature. Further, the No Child Left Behind legislation of the Bush years in the first decade of the twenty-first century and its orientation toward high-stakes testing further eroded any hope of including more global content in the social studies specifically and the overall school curriculum in general. What was to be tested was more traditional discipline content, and no room was left for global content.

Finally, these same issues impacted what was happening in initial teacher education professional development programs in colleges and universities. New and in-service teachers were schooled in the national standards and prepared to meet the rigors of the new national high-stakes tests that focus on traditional content in the disciplines of history, geography, economics, civics, and government. The content was and still is decidedly nonglobal. Thus the relative lack of preparation for globally minded teachers is not surprising.

Definitional and Conceptual Issues

Another ongoing problem is that there is considerable diversity in defining just what is meant by global education. Tye (1999) points out that many fields related to global education (e.g., peace education, development education, environmental education, and intercultural education) have their separate identities. Bales (2004) reports that partly because of the various conceptions of international education that abound, the

American public lacks a well-defined image and does not see it as essential. This makes it a challenge to frame a conception of what characteristics a globally or internationally minded teacher might require.

This confusion or debate about the usage of the term *global education* is not new of course. In the early years of the global education movement—the 1960s, 1970s, and early 1980s—most of the attention was placed on definitions of the field and the kind of curriculum that was required to offer students a global education (Anderson & Anderson, 1977; Anderson, 1982; 1968; 1979; Bailey, 1975; Becker, 1975; 1979; 1982; Becker & Anderson, 1980; Hanvey, 1976; Hicks & Townley, 1982; Morris, 1977; Richardson, 1976). However, in these early decades little or no attention was given to the kind of teachers who would be needed to teach this curriculum to children and youth in schools. There was an early exception. Cogan in 1979, in the *Journal of the Florida Council for the Social Studies* in an article titled, "Characteristics of Globally-Minded Teachers," listed 10 characteristics essential to the formation of such a teacher: the globally minded teacher, he says,

- is empathic, sensitive, and self-assured
- has a worldview
- is able to tolerate and work within a changing world
- values the processes of scientific inquiry
- is knowledgeable and well informed
- is knowledgeable about and appreciative of other cultures
- is strongly rooted in his own cultural heritage
- is an active participant in global society at all levels
- sees learning as a lifelong process
- is concerned with continued professional growth (pp. 25–27).

Cogan later reiterated these same characteristics, or versions thereof, in invited conference papers and journal articles (1982a, 1982b). Others, too, have put forward their ideas about the qualities of globally minded teachers over the years (Case, 1993; Hicks, 2003; Gilliom, 1993; Johnston & Ochoa, 1993; McFadden, Merryfield, & Barron, 1997; Urso, 1991; Osler & Vincent, 2002). One of the most insightful contributions to how we might conceptualize the qualities of a globally minded teacher is Case's (1993) essay, in which he distinguishes between

> two interrelated dimensions of a global perspective, the substantive and the perceptual. The substantive dimension refers to knowledge of various features of the world and how it works. The perceptual dimension, reflected in contrasting spatial metaphors such as narrow or broad, provincial or cos-

mopolitan, and parochial or far-reaching, describes an orientation or outlook (p. 318) .Table 11.1 illustrates the components of each of these dimensions.

Table 11.1. Key Elements of a Global Perspective

Substantive Dimensions	Perceptual Dimension
Universal and cultural values and practices	Openmindedness
Global interconnections	Anticipation of complexity
Present worldwide trends and conditions	Resistance to stereotyping
Origins and past patterns of world affairs	Inclination to empathize
Alternative worldwide futures	Non-chauvinism

Case contends that it is this substantive dimension that most global educators (including all of the authors cited above except Hanvey) are talking about when they describe the field. Case (1993) asserts, and we believe rightly so, that *without* the parallel development of the *perceptual* dimension, one cannot be said to have truly developed into a global citizen. Case believes that the substantive dimension is fairly easy to impart to teachers in service and those preparing for a career in the profession, but that developing the perceptual dimension is far more difficult. This makes the task of preparing the globally minded teacher all the more challenging. As insightful as many conceptions of global education and descriptions of globally minded teachers are, by and large they have tended to be conceptually based and lacking in supportive empirical evidence. Notable exceptions include studies by Merryfield in the 1990s (1991; 1992; 2000) and Kubow (1995). So before we list our own set of characteristics of the globally minded teacher, we believe it is important to consider more recent work in the field of citizenship education, where we see a body of research literature based on evidence from empirical studies.

Selected Empirical Studies of Citizen Characteristics

The empirical research reported here is based in citizenship education, but it speaks in some relevant way to the kind of teacher needed to develop active, participatory citizens in an increasingly globalized twenty-first century. Modern political systems depend upon a concept of citizenship that embodies certain principles or understandings of the knowledge, skills, values, and dispositions that citizens should possess. These may be explicitly noted in a constitution, a bill of rights, or some such document, or be implicit in national traditions and institutions, but generally the idea of citizenship includes both explicit prescription and implicit practice. Drawing on Marshall's (1950) work in the mid-twentieth century, the study (in the Citizenship Education Policy Study [CEPS] reported on below) drew up a list of key dimensions of citizenship. Though the particulars may vary from system to system they can usually be grouped into one of five categories:

1. A sense of identity
2. Enjoyment of certain rights
3. A set of corresponding obligations
4. Interest and involvement in public affairs
5. An acceptance of basic societal values (Cogan, 1997, p. 4)

From curricular and pedagogical perspectives, what are the characteristics teachers need to instill in those in their care to create these conditions for global democratic citizenship? How would they develop these five attributes of citizenship? To answer these questions, we first draw upon three research studies in which both authors of this chapter were key participants.

The Citizenship Education Policy Study I

The first such foundational study is the Citizenship Education Policy Study (CEPS I) (Cogan & Derricott, 1998; 2000). This investigation involved interviewing and surveying 182 policy shapers from nine nations from Japan and Thailand in Asia; Canada and the United States of America in North America; and England, Germany, Greece, Hungary, and the Netherlands in Europe. These policy experts, from a broad range of fields, were invited to identify (1) the global challenges, issues, and trends that citizens would have to cope with and manage during the first two decades of the twenty-first century; (2) the characteristics required of citizens to meet these challenges and trends; and (3) the educational strategies that would be necessary to develop these citizen characteristics. The findings with respect to global trends suggested that these policy shapers believed that there would be growing economic disparities between peoples, a rapidly deteriorating state of the global environment, inequities with respect to access to and use of information technologies, increased regulation and control by governments over the lives of people, increasing consumerism, and difficult issues of an ethical nature that would continue to impact societies (Cogan, 1997, p. 1). From an initial list of 20 citizen characteristics, they agreed upon 8 that they believed were essential to cope with or manage these global trends. These are found in table 11.2.

The second empirical work, CEPS II, builds upon the original CEPS I project. This time, however, the respondents were 285 students preparing to be teachers of social studies and civic education, the very individuals who would be responsible for implementing the 8 citizen characteristics outlined in table 10.2. The respondents were primarily from Asian societies (South China, Hong Kong SAR, Japan, Taiwan, and Thailand), Europe (The Netherlands), and the North American continent (the United States of America). These social studies teacher education students responded to the original CEPS Delphi instrument in a straightforward survey. The future teachers and the policy shaper experts had six characteristics in common; four characteristics that were unique to this sample are found in the second column of table 10.2 (Karsten, Cogan, Grossman, Liu, & Pitiyanuwat, 2002, p. 175).

The six characteristics on which the two groups agreed and the four differences were telling. These future teachers evidenced more concern with *applied skills and abilities* (problem-solving knowledge and adapting to rapid change) and on *personal development* (meaningful relationships and spiritual development) than the policy shapers. They seemed less concerned with universal understanding and more concerned with what applies to the here and now. This is instructive given that these students will be classroom teachers responsible for the development of citizens in the first three decades of the twenty-first century.

Table 11.2. Consensus Citizenship Characteristics from Three Studies
in Rank Order by Study

CEPS I	CEPS II	Global Concerns Study
Ability to look at and approach problems as a member of a global society**	Ability to work with others in a cooperative way and take responsibility for one's roles/duties within society***	Ability to work with others in a cooperative way and take responsibility for one's roles/duties within society***
Ability to work with others in a cooperative way and take responsibility for one's roles/duties within society***	Ability to understand, accept and tolerate cultural differences*	Possession of sufficient problem-solving knowledge that can be implemented in every day life**
Capacity to think in a critical and systemic way**	Possession of sufficient problem-solving knowledge that can be implemented in every day life**	
Willingness to resolve conflict in a non-violent manner**	Willingness to resolve conflict in a non-violent manner**	
Willingness to change one's lifestyle and consumption habits to protect the environment**	Capacity to think in a critical and systemic way**	
Ability to be sensitive towards and to defend human rights*	Willingness to change one's lifestyle and consumption habits to protect the environment**	
Willingness and ability to participate in politics at local/national/ international levels*	Ability to look at and approach problems as a member of a global society**	
	Values spiritual development*	
	Ability to actively adapt to rapid, unpredictable change*	
	Ability to create and sustain meaningful personal relationships*	
Key: * = Consensus within one study; ** = Consensus within two studies; *** = Consensus within all three studies		

The Citizenship Education Policy Study II

Global Concerns Survey

The third empirical work was part of the University of Minnesota-Hong Kong Institute of Education Partnership Program (EPP) funded through a three-year grant from the United States Department of State. This program focused on areas of civic values and environmental education and was designed to strengthen the capacities of both partner institutions in these areas. The initial project activity was to conduct the Global Concerns Study (GCS), a baseline inquiry into in-service teachers' perceptions of necessary citizenship characteristics and their environmental concerns. A total of 405 of 559 sampled in-service teachers (a response rate of 72 percent) from the Hong Kong Special Administrative Region of China, Guangdong Province in South China, and Minnesota, United States, responded to the survey. The GCS used the list of 20 citizen characteristics from the original CEPS project to which were added 20 environmental concerns identified by leading global environmental experts as likely to be important for citizens to understand during the first 25 years of the twenty-first century. Let us compare the citizen characteristics selected by each of the three groups of in-service teachers (Paige & Cogan, 2002).

Similarities

All three groups of teachers agreed that *cooperation with others* and *problem-solving skills* were the most important citizen characteristics. Teachers in Minnesota and Hong Kong shared two more: *the ability to understand, accept, and tolerate cultural differences*, and *the willingness to change one's lifestyle and consumption habits to protect the environment*, both of which concur with the characteristics selected by the policy experts. Teachers in Hong Kong and Guangdong shared another characteristic: *spiritual development*, also a characteristic chosen by the future teachers in the CEPS II study but not by the policy experts in CEPS I.

Differences

There were also differences in these preservice teachers' perceptions of desirable citizen characteristics. The Hong Kong preservice teachers valued critical thinking highly, more so than either their Minnesota or Guangdong peers. The Hong Kong preservice teachers also placed a high value on spiritual and moral development while this ranked very low for Minnesota teachers. The Guangdong teachers rated loyalty to one's nation very high while Hong Kong and Minnesota teachers did not see this as important at all.

Comparison of Findings across the Three Projects

This comparison will be critical in understanding what role schools must assume for the development of these characteristics and what form education must take to prepare teachers in the twenty-first century. The first question to consider is which of these characteristics can be developed within the formal curriculum and the context of the schools, and which require a broader base of implementation. In each of the three studies, participants chose three of the same characteristics from the top five. These are

- ability to work with others in a cooperative way and to take responsibility for one's roles/duties within society (42 percent of experts, 47.4 percent of future teachers, and 65.2 percent of in-service teachers)
- ability to understand, accept, and tolerate cultural differences (38 percent of experts, 39.4 percent of future teachers, and 45.9 percent of in-service teachers)
- willingness to resolve conflict in a nonviolent manner (34 percent of experts, 35.3 percent of future teachers, 29.6 percent of in-service teachers).

These overlapping choices would therefore all be considered key attributes of global citizens and globally minded teachers in the twenty-first century.

The policy experts and future teachers also shared another characteristic, *the capacity to think in a critical and systematic way* (37 percent of experts, 32.7 percent of future teachers), while both future teachers (38.5 percent) and in-service teachers (38.5 percent) in the EPP Study valued the *possession of sufficient problem-solving knowledge that can be implemented in everyday life*. Finally, both policy experts in the CEPS project (31 percent) and the in-service teachers (30.4 percent) in the GCS study chose *willingness to change one's lifestyle and consumption habits to protect the environment* as one of the important citizen characteristics for the twenty-first century.

However, of the top five, the citizenship characteristic that was identified as first importance only by the group of policy experts (but by 44
percent of that group) is *the ability to look at and approach problems as a
member of a global society.* This suggests that policy experts, given their
roles and responsibilities, take a more global view of citizenship than future or in-service teachers. On the other hand, it could suggest that what
is often said about those who go into teaching—that teachers are very
conservative—is validated by the findings from these three empirical
studies.

While each of these critical characteristics of citizens identified across
the three groups can in part be developed within schools and the stated
curriculum, all of them also require arenas outside the formal schooling
structure where they can be applied and refined. That is to say, schooling
for democratic citizenship will in the future require a much closer working relationship among schools, their leaders, teachers, and—most assur-
edly—the students and the wider communities in which they exist. All of
these citizen characteristics identified by the three research groups require a more holistic approach to learning. It would seem that teachers in
these schools need to be prepared in ways that are very different from
those that are current practice and need to be educated to be more active
in their pedagogies and more deliberative in their interaction with their
students.

Implications for the Development of Globally Minded Teachers

If these empirical findings were to be used to influence curricula and
pedagogical best practice, we would need to develop teachers who
viewed cooperative learning opportunities, problem-solving, conflict
resolution, development of tolerance toward others, and changing one's
lifestyle and consumption habits to a sustainable lifestyle as imperative.
And although this was cited only by the policy shapers, we would also
urge that problems and issues should be approached from a global perspective. In summary then, the globally minded teacher should possess

- the ability to work with others in a cooperative way and to take responsibility for his or her own roles and duties within society
- ability to understand, accept, and tolerate cultural differences
- willingness to resolve conflict in a nonviolent manner
- capacity to think in critical and systematic ways
- command of problem-solving knowledge that can be implemented in
  everyday life

- willingness to change his or her lifestyle and consumption habits to protect the environment
- ability to look at and approach problems and issues as a member of the global society

When we compare these 7 characteristics drawn from the empirical research literature with the 10 characteristics required of globally minded teachers Cogan identified in 1979, we find some overlap, some new elements, and some characteristics found only in the earlier list. Worldview, tolerance, cultural appreciation, and scientific inquiry are included in both listings; cooperation, resolving conflict in a nonviolent manner, problem-solving ability, and reducing consumption to protect the environment are new; characteristics of empathy, knowledgeable, lifelong learning, and continued professional development appear only in Cogan's 1979 list.

Reviewing these characteristics from the present perspective, we would expect to see some changes in both the list and rank order. First, we might expect more concerns to be expressed about national and global security in the post–9/11 world, though from another point of view this might be represented as greater concern for nonviolent resolution of conflict. There might also be increased concern for more emphasis on the ability to understand, accept, and tolerate religious as well as cultural differences.

Preparation of Globally Minded Teachers

Earlier in this chapter we cited the challenge of preparing globally minded teachers. The study by Tye (1999) of 52 countries identified only a small number of teachers that had training programs (32) around the world that had significant global content. His study also found that there is more in-service than preservice education related to global education. There are exemplary programs, however, as well as evidence that the number is growing at least in Canada, the United Kingdom, and the United States (Holden & Hicks, 2007; Asia Society, 2006; Council of Chief State School Officers, 2006a; Development Education Association, 2004).

In a study of teacher trainees in England, Holden and Hicks (2007) argue that it is vital that initial teacher education programs (and professional development programs as well, we might add) find ways of broadening their scope: "There needs to be time and provision for students to learn strategies for teaching about global and controversial issues; time for them to improve their own knowledge and understanding;

and time for them to learn how to critically evaluate sources of information" (pp. 22–23). This requires attention to a pedagogy that matches the needs of globally minded teachers. In another empirical work that uses the CEPS model and focuses on young people in Canada, England, and the United States, findings by Kubow (1999) suggest "the need that increased attention be given to global issues within teacher preparation programs. Discussion of global issues can increase preservice teachers' awareness of different cultures and problems shared worldwide" (p. 62). Kubow concludes that a deliberation-based curriculum is the means to implement the findings of this study (Cogan & Derricott, 1998; 2000; Parker, Ninomiya, & Cogan, 1999). It is Kubow's view, and we wholeheartedly agree, that democratic dialogue is a necessary part of one's preparation to be a teacher for a global age.

Students, whether they are in a teacher-training program or in a primary or secondary classroom, must in the end see their teachers as living examples of what they are professing. Teachers must be seen as people who are personally involved in their communities, working on projects of a civic or public nature, knowledgeable about developments in other parts of the nation and the world, and able to debate key civic issues in local, national, and world communities. As Kissock (2002) points out, though we live in a post–9/11 world in which countries halfway around the world can impact our lives, many educators act as if they are in isolation, as if they are part of a local trade. Though much has been written about the need for teachers to have and act upon a global perspective, little action has been taken to change individual and institutional structures to accomplish this. Kissock (2002) and others (e.g., Asia Society, 2006; Development Education Association, 2004; Heyl & McCarthy, 2003; Kagan & Stewart, 2004; Schneider, 2003; 2006; 2007) suggest lists of policies programs to bring the rhetoric of producing globally minded teachers closer to reality. As we have seen, it will not be an easy task. In a study of teacher educators, Merryfield (2000a, b) found that their lack of experiential knowledge of diversity and equity is a significant barrier to developing new teachers competent to deal with diversity, equity, and global interconnectedness. The Development Education Association (2004, p. 11) in the United Kingdom warns that embedding a global dimension in teacher-training

- may involve creative reorganization, for example, extending courses over four years, running additional optional courses and/or working with subject specialists to identify possibilities

- requires a willingness to think outside traditional subject boundaries and explore deeper moral issues through subject teaching
- may involve a steep and challenging learning curve for trainees, but can also provide motivation and a richer curriculum.

Policy Recommendations

Based on an exploratory study that involved interviews with some 400 administrators, faculty, and students at 41 institutions in the United States over a five-year period, Schneider (2007) has an extensive list of policy recommendations for state and local governments; accrediting agencies; institutions of higher education; professional associations; and outside funders. For schools, colleges, and department of education, she makes the following recommendations:

- Review all courses for possible addition of international content
- Integrate study and internships abroad into the professional training of teachers
- Emphasize and increase the options for observation and practice teaching in bilingual and international magnet schools
- Require that prospective foreign language teachers have at least one semester of overseas experience in an area where the target language is spoken
- Strengthen the international components of academic and career advising services, in cooperation with other university and community college advising services
- Offer an effective introductory course, even observational internships and a minor in education, open to all undergraduates, to reinforce advising about teaching career option
- Include international orientation in the criteria for selecting cooperating teachers for students

These policy recommendations comprise an impressive list as they are drawn from empirical research. To date, much of the research on the preparation of globally minded teachers is primarily conceptual in nature. Much of the research agenda on teacher education for global perspectives proposed 25 years ago by Johnston and Ochoa (1993) has yet to be realized.

In conclusion, we offer our own list of research-derived key approaches to nurture and support globally minded teachers. From the empirical studies cited we can draw eight key recommendations that clearly speak to those critical characteristics teachers need to possess to be effective globally minded teachers in an increasingly interdependent and rapidly changing global age:

- Support the teaching of subject matter in a manner that encourages students to think critically
- Emphasize students' ability to assess information critically in an increasingly media-based society
- Increase attention to global issues and international studies in the curriculum
- Establish extensive liaisons and joint projects among schools and other social institutions (e.g., industry, NGOs, churches, community groups) to support education
- Require that opportunities for community action and involvement be an important feature of the school curriculum
- Promote schools as active centers of community life and as agents for community development
- Increase opportunities for students to be involved in cooperative learning activities
- Ensure that all social institutions (including the family and educational and religious institutions) have an abiding respect for the basic rights of children and contribute to their well-being (Cogan, 1997, pp. 10–11).

These strategies strongly suggest both the need to learn how to work cooperatively toward common goals that serve both individuals and communities and the need to learn that the concept of community has broadened to include not only the particular place where we live but the entire planet.

Note

1. The studies we reported here predate 9/11 and, therefore, do not take into account the significant impact of the events of 9/11 and the aftermath on the global scene. This factor should be considered in any final analysis of teacher characteristics that we generate here.

Chapter 12

The Power of One: Continuing the Dream

Bárbara C. Cruz & Pedro R. Bermúdez

I expect to pass through this world but once; any good thing, therefore, that
I can do or any kindness that I can show to any fellow creature, let me do it
now; let me not defer or neglect it, for I shall not pass this way again
--Stephan Grellet (1773-1855)

There is much discussion of late of the role and importance of mentorship both in and out of academia. In global education, it may be especially critical because of its controversial nature, its unique and often contested place in the curriculum, and the dearth of dedicated educators. Graduate students and new faculty in global education frequently find themselves isolated from mainstream colleagues for their ideas on how to best prepare the current young generations for the future. Having a trustworthy mentor who can guide, provide support, facilitate networking, and direct protégés toward meaningful and realistic career choices can greatly alleviate the disconnect many global educators often feel as they endeavor to advance the movement.

This chapter discusses the complexities and significance of the mentor-mentee relationship in academia, explores the critical attributes of a mentor, describes the phases of mentorship, and analyzes the best practices in mentoring. We will also discuss our own mentor, Jan L. Tucker, and the impact he had on his graduate students and others in the field. Our discussion also demonstrates how our mentor's passion in social studies teacher education, international studies, and global education influenced the lives of his graduate students professionally and personally, and strengthened their own work in education in general and in global education particularly. Having been his graduate students at Florida International University (FIU) as well as participants in the Global Awareness Program (GAP) that he directed (see chapter 5) we come to this reflection as mentees of Jan L. Tucker more than a decade after his death. During this time we have experienced relationships with other mentors and served as mentors ourselves. We begin first with an overview of mentorship in academia to frame our examination.

Mentorship in Academia

Given the interest in mentoring, it is surprising that this has surfaced as a field of research only since the 1980s. The earliest existing treatment of mentoring is Levinson, Darrow, Klein, Levinson, and McKee's (1978) study of 40 young adult men. In addition to providing one of the earliest working definitions of mentoring—a process that involves older, more experienced sponsors providing novices with guided learning experiences—their study found that true mentoring relationships are exceptional. But by most accounts, it was Kram's 1985 work *Mentoring at Work: Developmental Relations in Organizational Life* that was most influential in launching systematic research studies on this topic. In this book, Kram examines the workplace relationships that can advance individuals' careers, boost their performance, and help them in their development at all stages of their professional life. Although the book has a focus on the business sector, its message cuts across all professions. Its effect began to be felt almost immediately in academia. Since then, a number of scholars have looked more closely at the phenomenon and, as a result we now have a noteworthy body of research that can provide insight on the functions, phases, best practices, and benefits of mentoring in education. While the research literature on mentorship tends to be overwhelmingly positive, there have been a number of potential problems cited such as lack of time, personality mismatch, and mentors who are overly critical (Ehrich, Hansford, & Tennent, 2004). The research by Long (1997) cautions that an ill-matched mentor-mentee pairing can be detrimental to both parties, as can a lack of time to devote to the relationship and a misunderstanding of what effective mentoring entails. Of greatest concern, perhaps, for those who are interested in global education is personal or professional incompatibility, lack of commitment, and lack of time to devote to the mentoring relationship. Despite these potential drawbacks, the literature is clear: mentoring relationships offer valuable benefits for both parties that result in both personal and professional gains.

Attributes of Effective Mentors

It is important to realize what is *not* mentorship. It is not role modeling (although that can certainly be a characteristic of a good mentor) nor does it exclusively entail academic advising. While the effective mentor is deeply vested in the protégé's academic success, preparing protégés for success in their profession often involves fulfilling a psychosocial function that "may acculturate a graduate student toward a specific professional career" (Campbell, 2007, p. 327). More than being just a supportive relationship (Mertz, 2004) that often starts as an advisor-advisee association, it is "when the advisor begins to offer a range of both career-enhancing and emotional or psychosocial functions" that the relationship has become a true mentorship (Johnson, 2007, pp. 190–191). Effective mentors are also described as being "intentional"; that is, they are purposeful and deliberate in their approach to mentorship (Johnson, 2002; see Mertz, 2004).

Mentors are people who nurture less experienced individuals in their professional and/or personal development (Anderson & Shannon, 1988). In addition to counsel and advice, mentors often provide support and sponsorship as well. They also help to immerse "new members into a community of practice and ensuring their professional success" (Koro-Ljungberg & Hayes, 2006, p. 389). "The business of education" as Mertz (2004) notes "is developing people" (p. 544). In its finest incarnation mentorship can also be transformative, in that mentors can facilitate "the mentee's experiences of transformation through the development of a unique bond, the promotion of self-discovery, and the belief that mentor and mentee are kindred spirits" (Koro-Ljungberg & Hayes, 2006, p. 391).

Personal characteristics of effective mentors include intelligence, caring, patience, flexibility, empathy, kindness, and competence (Johnson, 2002). Mentoring relationships between faculty and student can extend beyond the typical relationship that a student may have with his or her professor or advisor. As Lentz and Allen (2007) explain, "The faculty mentor is a source of learning, guidance, and influence. For the student, the faculty mentor may represent how the student perceives the profession and how he or she fits into it" (p. 159). And unlike other mentoring relationships, faculty-student mentorships are often characterized by sustainability—that is, that the benefits "continue to impact the protégé long after graduation" (Lockwood, Evans, Carr, & Eby, 2007, p. 235). Scholars in mentoring research have found that effective mentoring relationships have certain characteristics in common. Researchers report that informal mentoring relationships are believed to be more satisfying and effective than assigned mentoring partnerships (Johnson, 2002; Johnson & Ridley, 2004). It is also important to match mentors to protégés, since not all pairings automatically lead to a successful or productive relationship (Jackson et al., 2003). Effective mentors also know to establish appropriate boundaries, basing their relationships with their protégés on respect and they regularly schedule meetings that provide support and structure for the protégé (Campbell, 2007). Ultimately, the hallmarks of an effective mentor include showing care and concern for the mentee's professional welfare and clear signs that the mentorship originates from an organic need and desire for the relationship.

Phases of Mentorship

In her early work Kram (1985) names the phases that evolve during a mentoring relationship: initiation, cultivation, separation, and finally, redefinition. O'Neil and Wrightsman (2001) have further clarified the stages. During the initial stage, as a potential protégé makes the critical entry decision, the relationship begins formally with topics of conversation limited to the participants' clearly delineated roles. The second phase is marked by the gradual and reciprocal development of confidence, self-disclosure, and reliance as mutual trust is built. As the relationship develops, both mentee and mentor take professional and personal risks that can result in either loss or gain. The next phase is noted by role modeling by the more experienced mentor, who imparts valuable teaching skills, both formal (in the classroom) and informal (via dialogue, social events, etc.). As the relationship deepens, the mentor helps to develop, clarify, and transmit the standards and expectations of the profession. Finally, a certain degree of independence from the mentor must be achieved; as such, it is typical that the relationship dissolves or changes as the protégé gets ready to enter the profession. For many, positive mentoring relationships often evolve into long-term professional and/or personal friendships.

Benefits of Mentoring

It is clear that mentoring can provide significant benefits, both short term and long term, in a number of ways. Researchers are careful to differentiate between academic-career mentorship and the psychosocial functions that mentoring fulfills, although they often overlap. In very skilled mentors, these functions tend to intermingle and are difficult to distinguish. In addition to the academic support that faculty mentors provide, other less obvious outcomes include scholarly productivity, professional skill development, networking, securing employment, and identity development (Johnson, 2007). Those who receive effective mentoring also later report higher career satisfaction, increased income, and a higher likelihood of mentoring others. Some experts feel that effective mentoring is so valuable that it should be regarded as of utmost importance in the early developmental stages of an individual's career (Russell & Adams,

1997). Providing the protégé with visibility, access to networks, exposure to learning experiences, and assignments that can promote growth are invaluable in establishing the neophyte's professional identity and career path.

Scholars have also pointed out that mentoring relationships can also benefit the mentors. Much-needed assistance on projects or in teaching can be a boon to the mentor's productivity. Murray and Owen (1991) found that in addition to increased productivity on the part of mentors, mentoring programs also resulted in improved motivation, enhancement of services, and better recruitment. The mentor is also likely to experience increased confidence and personal fulfillment (Douglas, 1997). By helping protégés in their careers, mentors often find that they experience rejuvenation of` their own (Levinson, Darrow, Klein, Levinson, & McKee, 1978).

Mentorship in Global Education: A Case Study

As we reviewed the literature in mentoring, it became obvious to us that Jan Tucker satisfied the roles and functions of a mentor to a great many of his students and colleagues. In particular, he seemed to emphasize his roles as an academic advisor, his personal orientation with his mentees, his intentional mentoring, his sensitivity to other cultures, and his passionate advocacy of global education. It is surprising how many of his students continued in his footsteps, working in the field of global education in a wide range of capacities and to varying degrees. He was a "primary" mentor (Russell & Adams, 1997) for most of his students—that is, that the relationship was between one mentor and one protégé and the relationship endured for several years even after graduation.

The Interviews

In addition to reflecting on our own academic and professional development under Jan Tucker's tutelage, we contacted, either via telephone or e-mail, 12 of his former protégés, mostly graduate students who studied under him and graduated from the social studies education program in FIU. We were able to interview eight; the others could not be reached or did not return our request to contact us. Former mentees are presently scattered around the country in varied educational positions, all connected to global education in one way or another. Most have gone on to become university professors, school administrators, and curriculum specialists.

To guide our interviews, we asked all former mentees the following questions but allowed them to reminisce and reflect as they wished:

1. Describe your mentor/mentee relationship with Jan Tucker.
2. Do you believe that having a mentor was an important factor in your education? If consequently, to what extent? In what way(s)?
3. Did you encounter any academic barriers or challenges with which he helped you?
4. Can you provide any specific examples of Jan's mentorship?
5. In what ways did Jan's mentorship have an impact on your work?
6. Do your mentee experiences influence you as a professional to serve as a mentor to others?

As we conducted the interviews, several themes began to emerge, commensurate with the best practices in mentoring that we had found in the literature. They are: academic decision-making; psychological-personal orientation; intentional mentoring; multiple roles; advocacy for global education; and mentoring others. We hope that by considering these themes we can shed some light on the importance of mentorship in global education.

Academic Decision

For most of his graduate students, Tucker was a de facto mentor since he was the only one at his institution who identified himself as a global educator and who had developed a research and teaching agenda along those lines. In this capacity, he was enormously influential in guiding his students to matriculate in courses that had global studies content. One of his students, now a university professor of social studies education, credits our mentor's guidance as imperative in helping her identify her professional and research interests and focus. Because Tucker's scholarship, teaching, and research focused on three areas (teacher education, social studies education, and global education) through role modeling and academic counseling, these emphases greatly influenced her in her studies and scholarship and continue to do so to this day. The two met at an international academic conference at which Tucker made a presentation on global education—a new field in China—and exchanged contact information. He sought her out about a year later, when he was asked to review an article for *Theory and Research in Social Education* on textbooks in China) and sent her the manuscript for feedback. She recalls:

> He also sent me Tye's 1991 book *Global Education from Thought to Action* and other materials on global education; these further piqued my interest in the field. At about the same time, I decided to pursue my doctorate and applied to several universities in the U.S. As I reviewed my options, they all seemed to have more of a theoretical focus. By now I was recognizing the importance of an applied, more practical approach. Under Dr. Tucker's influence, I realized that my real interest was in curriculum development, teacher education, and global education.

It was then that she decided to matriculate at FIU and study under Tucker's tutelage. As a teacher educator herself now, she weaves both the theoretical and the practical aspects of global education into her work.

Another former student, now a professor of social science education, recalls her mentor's influence in determining her course of study:

> My program of studies was greatly influenced by him. I had quite a few electives for both my master's degree and for my Ph.D. cognate. Every semester when I sat down to plan my enrollment; Jan gently guided me towards the courses with international content. Some examples are "World Religions," "Latin American Politics," "Gender in the Contemporary World," and "Global Perspectives in Education." This last course I have modified and now offer at my current institution where it enjoys a healthy enrollment every semester.

Despite his passion for global education and his interests in growing local talent for the GAP, our mentor encouraged his students to explore all possibilities and make their own choices. One former student recalls being offered a tempting fellowship to pursue his doctoral studies at New York University in an Area Studies Program. Tucker encouraged him to consider the program and travel to New York for the interview, providing him with a strong recommendation. He was accepted in the program and while in New York had an opportunity to talk with Andrew Smith, president of the American Forum for Global Education, who helped him to consider the benefits and opportunities of the Area Studies program against those of the GAP at FIU. After doing so,

> I decided to do my doctoral work under Jan Tucker's direction. I never once felt any pressure from Jan to stay in Miami. I respected the fact that he allowed me the time and space to make my own decision about my future.

Psychosocial/Personal Orientation

As was noted in the literature, many mentees expressed the importance of the psychosocial function that Tucker's mentorship played. In the case of international students, helping them to negotiate the student visa and immigration process, navigate a new culture, and acclimate to a new system of education was especially crucial in their success. One protégé recalls:

> Although I was already an accomplished professional in my homeland of China, arriving in the U.S. and learning a whole new system—both academically and culturally—was new to me. Dr. Tucker helped me not just with education but in acclimating to a new society.

Another international student remembers the additional assistance that our mentor provided, especially with respect to cross-cultural differences:

> When I was an international graduate student, Dr. Tucker was my professor in one of the required courses in education. Sometimes I was confused about certain concepts and methodology of American education and research. He was extremely patient in explaining the concept of the course's tasks and cultural differences and similarities in education. He had a special talent in helping people stay focused. As a result, I was able to excel in the course.

Having a personal orientation toward students is an important characteristic for a mentor, especially for students who are equivocal in their goals or who do not have a high degree of self-confidence. One of his former doctoral students who had almost completed her master's degree remembers Jan asking her what she was planning to do next:

> I shrugged my shoulders, saying that I had not really given it much thought. He told me that I needed to think about going on for my doctorate. As a first generation college student, I wasn't even very sure or clear of what a doctoral degree entailed or what it prepared one for. Also I was not at all certain that I had the intellectual skills needed for an advanced graduate degree. Jan was earnest and convincing in his response: "I have had you in class, I have read your writing, and I have seen you present — you can do this." I applied that day.

Intentional Mentoring

As Johnson (2002) advocates, effective mentors are "overtly invitational, asking their protégés to watch them perform specific professional tasks...and encouraging them to try these activities as well" (p. 93). One of his protégé's experiences well illustrates this:

> Whether it was going on a study trip to Japan or asking me to teach one of his classes, I always sensed that each of these "invitations" was a carefully calculated move on his part to get me to stretch, grow, and develop.

On that same trip, the former protégé remembers how our mentor would model desirable behaviors and then step aside to let his mentees take center stage:

> I distinctly remember during our study trip to Japan how he coached us with the gift-giving ritual that usually preceded our visit to a Japanese firm or government office. He modeled one or two visits and then gave us opportunities to represent our group during the initial gift-giving ritual with our Japanese hosts. These were among my most memorable and authentic cross-cultural experiences.

Our mentor was also highly involved in professional organizations, attending conferences, publishing, teaching, and networking. When asked to provide an example of his mentorship, one protégé's immediate response was:

> Conferences...attending them, getting involved in professional organizations. He literally handed me membership and registration forms to fill out and submit. In some cases, he found funding for me to attend. Jan is the primary reason why I became involved with our state's council for social studies education and began attending the annual conference of the NCSS.

The importance of conference participation was echoed by another protégé who added

> He made sure that I got to NCSS and presented my work. He opened up the world for me. He affirmed my work, supported it, and encouraged me to share it with others.

Another mentee, already interested in global education but not having many opportunities to develop his expertise in the field, appreciated Tucker's intentional guidance:

> He channeled to a colleague and me the opportunity to develop *Dade County in the Global Community*, a resource guide for teachers that was published by Jan's Global Awareness Program at FIU. He also sent our way the opportunity to develop the global studies course for the Florida curriculum. It gave my work structural integrity and inner cohesion. It provided institutional credibility for our school administration and also motivated me to continue to develop in the field of global education.

Multiple Roles

Depending on the needs, talents, and goals of the protégés, Tucker fulfilled a number of roles as a mentor: academic advisor, career counselor, education recruiter, networking facilitator, and cultural ambassador, to name a few. Johnson and Huwe (2003) point out that mentoring relationships are idiosyncratic and flexible. His responsibilities to his mentees were, as Koro-Ljungberg and Hayes (2006) put it, "multifaceted." Being able to recognize and encourage individuals' unique talents is a hallmark of an effective mentor. A former mentee, now retired, remembers her first experience as a graduate student in his class:

> He noticed me right away, recognized my interest and potential, and encouraged me to develop the theme of "political action" in my teaching. He noticed others' strong points as well. He had a real talent for identifying people's unique strengths and encouraging their development.

This was especially true because of the large numbers of ethnic minority and international students our mentor actively recruited, advised, and sponsored. As Davidson and Foster-Johnson (2001) found, to be an effective mentor a faculty member must have sensitivity to and understanding of various cultures. Our mentor embodied cross-cultural understanding, a key design element of the GAP, by actively recruiting individuals who would bring their unique cultural and regional perspectives to the program. One of his mentees, a Nigerian tennis pro with a newly acquired doctorate in social studies and global education and currently a social studies teacher in the Miami-Dade County Public Schools and Adjunct Professor at FIU, recalls how Tucker welcomed him into the program and connected him to a network of global educators:

> He introduced me to a countless number of individuals including governors, professors, teachers, and other graduate students. He encouraged me to correspond with a professor in Canada to express my views on contemporary economic and political issues in Africa. Despite our cultural differences he believed in me from the start and had the ability to see who I really was at the human level, the goodness, and the talent. He was able to guide me and help me realize that talent.

Tucker not only learned about the cultural backgrounds of each of his mentees, but also engaged in a certain amount of self-disclosure, so that his students could better understand his own history and background. A former mentee relates this experience:

> I learned about the necessity and importance of self-disclosure from him. One day (it was 1986), Jan told me about a movie that was in the theaters called *Hoosiers*. He said, "If you want to know a little more about me, my background, and the kind of childhood I had, you should see this movie." The story takes place in a small town in Indiana and centers on the high school basketball team. It was Jan's way of sharing with me his cultural background, the values with which he was raised, and the experiences that shaped him as an adult.

His cultural roots from a small town in the American Midwest did not inhibit his embrace of Miami's Latino community. In the words of a colleague,

> He did not want to isolate himself in the Anglo community. He related to all cultures and actively involved many Cuban American teachers into his program. We welcomed the opportunity to participate. I believe that because we came from an island, it was easy for us to embrace it. We were a minority and as such we were allies. On a host of issues that were affecting our community—immigration, bilingual education, and multiculturalism—I always felt, as a Cuban, that Jan was an ally, especially during a time when we did not have the political power that we now have on the school board.

Jan was also instrumental in facilitating networking and introducing his protégés to key professional contacts. One associate remembers how he assisted him in his goal of entering the publishing world. After receiving counsel, he scheduled a meeting with publishers in New York and was able to secure two lucrative writing contracts. The importance of that research (on the Hispanic contributions to U.S. history and culture) resulted in the introduction of a resolution to both the Florida Council for the Social Studies and the National Council for the Social Studies, both of which were passed.

Advocacy for Global Education

As a scholar, our mentor's most striking attribute was our mentor's allegiance to and advocacy of global education. Literally all of his conference presentations, publications, and curriculum work centered on global content and pedagogy. He modeled the importance of good scholarship and advocacy when, in the late 1980s, attacks against global education began to be felt around the nation. As scathing reports and defamations were published (see chapter 1), one former mentee remembers how he gathered the GAP staff to review policy and strategize:

> I learned the importance of both thinking ahead and of taking a stand. First, he had us review all our curricular materials, making sure that everything we were distributing and promoting provided a balanced, multiple-perspective view. But he also modeled for us that we needed to speak out against narrow thinking and he quickly penned several op-ed pieces, essays for professional publications, and, of course, in the address he delivered as President of the National Council for the Social Studies, a clarion call to social studies educators to pay attention to what was happening in the country and to adjust our teaching and curriculum accordingly.

Another protégé, a curriculum expert now involved in school reform efforts, believes that in addition to his professional activities, Jan was a global education advocate in a more direct way:

> He was a living example of Gandhi's idea that one had a responsibility to "be the change you want to see in the world." He modeled what it meant to be a "global citizen" by simply and forthrightly behaving as one.

This same mentee credits his mentor with his emphasis on collaboration and collegiality:

> Cultivating long-term mentoring relationships with colleagues is the second way that Jan's work has influenced my own. This is a priority for me because as these relationships evolve over time, they influence my learning as well.

One of his students who is now a professor of art education underscores how his mentor's influence continues to impact his work:

> Jan's passion and compassion clearly came across as he talked about multicultural and global education. His profound knowledge and rich experience always impressed me and consequently had a significant impact on my work as an artist. My work still reflects such focus. For example, many of my paintings still focus on people or scenery of various cultures.

Mentoring might be especially critical in a field such as ours where global educators can sometimes feel isolated and disconnected from mainstream educational movements. As one mentee noted,

> Teaching can be very insular. He plucked me out of that little school and showed me that there were others who were like-minded and with whom I could work in global education.

Mentoring Others

In all cases, our mentor's mentees have gone on to serve as mentors to others, echoing past research that indicates that those who had mentors of their own are more likely to have mentees themselves (Busch, 1985). In some cases it is because the individual recognizes that Jan's mentorship was critical in their present-day success:

> Because of these positive experiences as a mentee, I became more aware of the importance in professional mentorship. I have successfully mentored many students and junior faculty members in achieving their professional goals.

In other cases it is because he provided the protégé with a valuable experience that developed that individual's skills and led to increased self-confidence. One of his mentees, now a public school administrator in charge of curriculum and instruction, explains:

> My involvement in the global awareness program, especially my involve-ment with the training of other teachers gave me an increased level of confi-dence in my ability to assist other teachers with their professional growth.

In almost every case, our mentor's mentees became mentors for oth-ers and these relationships continue to be informed by their initial rela-tionship with him:

> I have several long-standing mentoring relationships with several col-leagues. I'm always cognizant of how important it is to model "the change you want to see happen in the world." I know how much I learned from Jan this way and I hope to influence others in the same way. I believe I have been able to support others the way I was supported by Jan.

Another protégé describes how her long-term relationship with her mentor has influenced her present-day mentoring relationships:

> I learned that a mentor-mentee relationship does not end upon the mentee's graduation, or achievement of tenure, or some other terminal event. After I graduated, Jan continued in his role, encouraging, supporting, and celebrat-ing as the occasion called for. I will never forget when I had my first bit of writing published (as I look back on it, a not very good piece, published in a small regional journal). He made copies for his students and mailed them with a note attached: "An incoming tide lifts all boats." It was incredibly af-firming to have his support and encouragement even after I was no longer officially his student.

Final Thoughts

In many ways this tome is a *Festschrift*[1] to our mentor. Every contributor to this collection was touched or impacted by his work, friendship, or mentorship. His protégés continue in his footsteps, spreading the pur-pose and meaning of global education through their professional posi-tions and educational activities. As Johnson (2007) asks, "Do mentorships really make a difference in the life of a protégé?" (p. 189). If the personal and long-lasting effect of Jan Tucker's mentorship is any indication, the answer is a resounding "yes." His mentees in all cases not only remem-ber a mentor who was supportive and instrumental to their academic success, but are also cognizant of the tremendous impact their mentor had and continues to have on their professional and personal lives. One of his mentees captures this quality best when he states that once in a life time you meet an individual who has genuine compassion for people. Jan was one of these individuals, and he made me feel that I could contribute to that vision of making a better world. If I'm a good person it is because he supported me. Through him, I reinforced my commitment to serve humanity. I carry out this commitment by bringing people together to solve problems. That motivation is still strong in me. He was one of the most influential individuals in my life.

As Levinson and his colleagues (1978) noted, one of the most important functions a mentor can have is to facilitate a protégé's "realization of the dream" (p. 98). They explain that an effective mentor recognizes the protégé's goals, confirms that they can be achieved, and provides an encouraging environment in which to achieve the "dream." Jan L. Tucker facilitated his protégés' dreams and serves as a model in the mentoring of global educators.

Note

1. *Festschrift* (fest-shrift): a collection of articles, essays, and so on, written by several authors in honor of a colleague, usually published on the occasion of retirement, an important anniversary, or the like.

Chapter 13

Global Education to Build Peace

Kathy Bickmore

> In order to combat the culture of violence that pervades our society, the coming generation deserves a radically different education—one that does not glorify war but educates for peace and nonviolence and international cooperation.
>
> —The Hague Agenda for Peace and Justice for the 21st Century, 1999

North Americans became aware on September 11, 2001, of an experience many other citizens around the globe already knew firsthand: we live in an era of accelerated global interdependence and terrorism. The two systems are intricately interconnected. Nation-state militaries are more obsolete than ever. Neither national borders nor military buildups are capable of ensuring security; they are entangled in transnational problems and contain the violence they spawn. On September 11, for example, the perpetrators were people living in the West, and they mounted their devastating attack with consumer goods (box cutters and passenger airplanes), not conventional weapons. As Franklin (2006a) explains, citizens are both the funders of and justification used for the arms race, yet this system of threats cannot make us secure. In today's world more than ever, people's lives, the resources and natural systems upon which we depend, and our security are completely interrelated. Therefore, peace is indivisible: "either there will be peace for all and all gain, or there will be no peace, and all will lose" (p. 97). Only a radically different education can adequately speak to the world our young people already live in, and the roles they can play to ensure a sustaining peace today and tomorrow.

Most North American youth know a great deal about the rest of the world than others. The omnipresent mass media flash before their eyes images of conflict and violence from around the world almost continually. Many of these images are gripping and gruesome. Even young children frequently hear, watch, or overhear acts of violence and other physical, ecological, and human disasters. When asked, children make clear that they are emotionally engaged with the partial information they receive, are interested, and sometimes afraid (Elkind, 1995; Macy, 1983;

McDonnell, 2005). They are also observing the responses of adults to this global news—what is ignored or denied, what is decried only in private, what provokes collective action or approval or disapproval of political leaders—thus learning implicitly about the roles of global citizens. Given the informal education children have already received, the question, therefore, is not so much whether to teach young people about global peoples, problems, and processes but how school curriculum and teaching should intersect with and speak to these transnational phenomena.

Unchallenged and unexamined, mass media images are bound to generate stereotypes and misunderstandings. What makes something newsworthy is its unusualness. Peaceful relations are taken for granted and thus ignored in news and consciousness. However, a steady diet of violent news can give the impression that the world is a terrifying, alienating place, and that certain people (usually people of color) are especially dangerous. Many parts of the world (such as Rwanda, Somalia, or Kenya) appear in North American public consciousness only when there is sensational violence. News of them disappears from media reports as soon as attempted peacemaking begins. Like coverage of violence closer to home or house fires, typical media representations are voyeuristic and pacifying, offering no information about how people either caused or are trying to resolve the problems underlying the tragedies. Unfortunately, formal curriculum coverage, though less gripping, is no less misleading, focusing on wars and patriotic masculine heroes instead of on governmental and nongovernmental systems attempting negotiation toward problem-solving and transnational decision-making. If the causes and effects of these conflicts are not taught or discussed in school, this null curriculum may implicitly teach passive or unconscious consent and disengagement. The impression presented to our youth is that problems are there (and in them), not here (or in us) and that we cannot do much of anything about them. Thus the basic citizenship principle of informed consent continues to be violated in the next generation. As Alger (1995) argues, teaching about a range of "peace tools" would challenge both the damaging stereotypes and the reinforcement of hopeless passivity: "Educators must overcome the partial view of the human condition propagated by bad news in the headlines and by histories that emphasize battles and wars" (p. 128). Clearly, not all conflicts can be completely or even partially resolved, but all can be illuminated through careful study. In all cases, resolution processes to prevent or reverse escalation can be facilitated. Here is the challenge I see for educators: What if school curriculum and pedagogy effectively developed young people's capacity to understand conflicts and facilitated skills for peacemaking?

Curriculum for Global Peace-Building Citizenship

In many North American jurisdictions, official curriculum mandates already ostensibly require a significant amount of global and conflict-related content linked to such key concerns as environmental protection and human diversity (e.g., Bickmore, 2005a). However, the curriculum as it is actually implemented, in combination with the standardized testing that helps to shape it and the limitations on learning opportunities for teachers, is more likely to marginalize the teaching of international content and potentially controversial issues (e.g., Bickmore, 2007). Good resources for teaching global and conflictual curriculum certainly exist (e.g., Claire & Holden, 2007; Evans & Reynolds, 2005; Wood, 2007). However, most teachers are not adequately supported in their work environment with interactive learning opportunities and mentorship. For example, in an English research project about participants' perspectives on global citizenship education mandates in that country, English scholars interviewed students between the ages 8 and 16 and teachers. Unprompted, the students in overwhelming numbers expressed their wishes to study and discuss questions of conflict, peace, and war, including related issues such as weapons manufacture, impact on interethnic relations, and the earth's environment in school. In direct contrast, their teachers said that global citizenship education and especially discussion of current war-related events was "their least confident area of teaching" (Yamashita, 2006, p. 32). While students and official curricula are ready for global peace-building education, the challenge is in implementation. In particular, teachers need support and academic freedom to develop competence and confidence for their forays into uncertain curricular territory.

What needs to be included in a globalized education (and teacher education) that would better contribute to peace-building citizenship? No global education would be adequate that did not directly address violence, both large scale and domestic, raise problems presented by the representation of violence in mass media, and look beneath the surface of the news for the causes, effects, and factors that exacerbate and sustain it—in short, examine the spaces where action can be taken to resist that violence. Violence is a symptom: a result of all other serious global problems as well as a problem in and of itself. The fear and restrictions caused by violence limit many people's exercise of all human rights and freedoms. Norwegian peace scholar Johann Galtung (1969) argues that systemic factors (such as gender-based or political repression, or poverty arising from inequitable trade relations) are themselves structural forms of violence that can be just as harmful as visible, overt violence. Further, he describes the subconscious attitudes and values that support and assume the legitimacy of such structural and overt violence as cultural violence (Galtung, 1996). Ross's (1993; 2007) analysis of anthropological evidence and case studies from many cultures substantiates Galtung's theory: human conflicts are rooted both in relatively tangible socially structured interests (access to resources for fulfilling wants and needs) and in less tangible culturally shaped narratives and interpretations (beliefs and values, fears and concern: what matters to people and why). An excellent global education for peace-building would address both structural and psychocultural causes of conflict and alternatives to violence for managing those conflicts at transnational, national, and local levels. This requires transformation of curriculum, not mere addition to it. As British comparative education scholar Davies (2004) argues, peace education is about creating a degree of turbulence in the system by challenging what is accepted as reality about difference and about the ways to solve problems.

Feminist Perspectives

Feminist movements have taught us that "the personal is political." Individual private actions have ramifications for the large-scale public distribution and exercise of power, and this is certainly an important principle at global as well as national and local levels. A major goal of citizenship education for peace-building must be to develop young people's understanding of the consequences that their daily choices and habits have for the sources or escalation of global conflicts. For example, ecosystem interdependence means that environmental degradation and overuse of natural resources cause harm and scarcity for people around the globe. Economic interdependence and neoliberal globalization of trade mean that purchase of consumer goods produced far away where companies pay low wages and contribute little tax to local infrastructures contribute to forces that deprive workers of their human rights to safety and adequate sustenance. Globalized culture disseminated by mass media reinforces ideologies of sexism and racism, which in turn reinforce perpetuation of gender-based violence and institutionalized inequalities. Gender socialization is a key element of the culture of conflict and violence; much individual as well as military violence is perpetrated by males and wrapped up in assertions of masculinity and heterosexuality. Given this context of patriarchy, real inclusion of girls' and women's concerns, problems, viewpoints, and cultures inevitably raises conflict. Constructively handled conflict is the essence of democracy and peace-building. Thus, global citizenship education is designed to encourage students to imagine the future, to notice and predict effects of today's actions on tomorrow's lives, and to recognize, respect, and care about diverse other problems.

Dilemmas

Here is my worry: caring and individual choices are not sufficient to re-dress the transnational causes of destructive conflict and violence. The problems are big and, by far the most powerful actors in the global arena are still nation-states. Although the world has a very significant nongov-ernmental system of independent international organizations and a weak but still important intergovernmental system through the United Na-tions, its sister agencies, and international treaties (Boulding, 1988), su-perpower and middle-power national governments are still the locus of most large-scale collective decision-making, and they are the interna-tional actors most able to mobilize resources on a grand scale. Although many middle-class North American young people today are engaged via the Internet in politically relevant actions facilitated by nongovernmental organizations (NGOs) with global reach (Torney-Purta, Lehmann, Oswald, & Schultz, 2001), certain kinds of choices are inherently large scale and collective and cannot be made on an individual basis. For ex-ample, individuals can choose to cycle or to ride the bus, and they have a huge range of consumer goods to choose from, but by no independent personal choice can they fund public transportation or public education systems adequately, create a decent and accessible health care infrastruc-ture, or bring about effective regulation of the employment and envi-ronmental practices of business. Only governments can do that.

Thus young people's frequent disengagement from governmental poli-tics (Torney-Purta, Lehmann, Oswald, & Schultz, 2001) is a problem for global peace-building. Based on a study of schools' relationships with local NGOs, Kahne and Westheimer (1996) argued that an emphasis on charity (as opposed to critical study and change) in service learning ini-tiatives implicitly teaches ethnocentric superiority and reinforces incorrect stereotypes about the causes of social problems. It locates problems out there rather than here and often ignores the role of government policies (as well as concentrated economic power) in shaping both conflicts and routes toward resolution. This argument applies equally to the global arena. Well-intended global education that teaches students to care, to make responsible individual consumer choices, and to contribute to charity efforts does not adequately address the causes or the likely implementable solutions of destructive transnational conflict and war.

A Partial Solution: Developing Conflict Competence

One aspect of addressing these causes and solutions that public schools and teachers can address more effectively and equitably than any other social institution is the development of competence in understanding and handling all kinds of conflicts and controversies including questions of global and local justice (Davies, 2004; Hess & Posselt, 2002). Both teachers and students need learning opportunities that will help them overcome the fear of conflict and marginalization of dissent that is common in relatively peaceful societies such as North America (Merelman, 1990). It takes practice to develop familiarity with the dynamics of conflict and the avenues for mitigation and resolution. Since problems and disagreements are inevitable in human life, paradoxically we will never develop peace by avoiding conflict. Peace and nonviolence are not states of quiet stasis, but dynamic environments characterized by the absence of fear, the presence of justice, and the continual use of resourceful conflict management and problem-solving processes (Franklin, 2006b). Public classrooms are relatively safe laboratories for guided practice to develop such resourcefulness; challenging the ways they are not yet sufficiently safe for all voices can be item one in the learning process (Bickmore, 2008).

Simon (2001) demonstrated that moral and existential questions (about how people should act and one's role in the world) are barely discussed in many high school classrooms even though such discussions are generally regarded by students to be their best learning experiences. On the rare occasions when these questions were confronted in her study classrooms, the discussion was typically uninformed by academic evidence. Open, equitable classroom discussion of important political and moral issues is a necessary element of students' development of peace-building citizenship capabilities and motivations.

In teacher education as well, learners need diverse explicit models of real-world uncertainty and the thinking processes by which to address them in local, global, and governmental contexts. People need to hear multiple perspectives expressed out loud. For example,"this is what I think is going on, and here is how I'm searching for a resolution." People need practice in critical thinking and respectful listening across difference as well as in participation and creation (agency). In addition to traditional spaces for a democratic voice such as letters to government officials, teachers and students can conduct inquiries and communicate their views through the Internet and independent media, thereby not just demanding but contributing to more coverage of global issues relevant to peace and justice.

For example, Werner (1997; 2002) recommends addressing media reports of scary subjects such as sectarian violence in the classroom. He offers practical strategies for guiding such discussions: resist stereotyping by contextualizing the event in relation to time and place and identifying diverse real participants, investigate less immediate causes and subsequent events including attempts to resolve the problem, predict and evaluate consequences, take a stand on the various solutions advocated, and apply these globally gleaned insights to relevant actions in participants' own lives. Clearly, this kind of teaching requires teachers to have (and to know how to keep acquiring) substantive knowledge about world systems and spaces for action as well as procedural skills to facilitate open and cogent discussions. These are the very kinds of preparation that Yamashita (2006) found teachers to feel insecure about. Currently, typical teacher-development opportunities do not seem to have these global and conflict-facilitative dimensions (e.g., Bickmore, 2005b). The support and learning system for teachers will have to be changed before most teachers, most of the time, can be expected to facilitate global peace-building citizenship education effectively.

What I am arguing for here is consistent with long-standing proposals for actively democratic, critical, and problem-posing education, including those of John Dewey (1916) and Paulo Freire (1970).

> Problem-posing education involves a constant unveiling of reality....[It] strives for the emergence of consciousness and critical intervention in reality. Students, as they are increasingly posed with problems relating to themselves in the world and with the world, will feel increasingly challenged and obliged to respond to that challenge (pp. 80–81).

The danger, however, is that critical, conflictual pedagogy may inadvertently silence or exclude at the same time that it generates interest

(Ellsworth, 1989). When a teacher tries to engage a class in discussion of discrepant information or divergent viewpoints, often only the more confident students are directly involved in practicing elements of democratic conflict management. Other students remain invisible or outsiders, "alien and separate within" the classroom (Metz, 1978, p. 81). How many young females, in particular, still enact the old lesson, "If you can't say something nice, don't say anything at all"? Laissez-faire confrontation of conflictual topics, in which social exclusion is not confronted, can cause students to withdraw and reinforce closed-mindedness. In a long-term observational study of four high school classes that I conducted many years ago, both female and male students responded in varying ways to conflictual discussions in the social studies classroom (Bickmore, 1993; 1997). While more students were more engaged when there was conflict on the table, compared to more traditional pedagogies, many of the students (disproportionately females) remained silent. When the conflictual topic was framed as a competitive debate, the disparity between the stars and the "silent majority" was even bigger. Gendered roles of docility and aggression are still perpetuated in many classrooms.

However, there are real alternatives to competitive, exclusionary approaches to conflict pedagogy. The discipline of constructive silence—respectful and open-minded listening across difference—can be taught and practiced in classrooms.

> In the process of speaking and listening, the discipline of silence, which needs to be developed with serious intent by subjects who speak and listen, is a sine qua non of dialogical communication. ...Those who have something to say should know that they are not the only ones with ideas and opinions that need to be expressed. Even more than that, they should be conscious that, no matter how important the issue, their opinion probably will not be the one truth long and anxiously awaited for by the multitudes. In addition, they should be aware that the person listening also has something to say and that if this is not taken into account, their talking, no matter how correct and convincing, will not fall on receptive ears (Freire, 1998, pp. 104–107).

More explicit and consistent incorporation of transnational, multicultural, and gendered perspectives and conflict communication skills would deepen the peace-building relevance of critical democratic education. Sources of and solutions to conflict are deeply rooted within cultures and social identities, and deeply ingrained in transnational social structures, so practice with multiple perspectives only within an ethnocentric and gender-ignorant bubble is unlikely to apply to complex global problems. Teachers as well as students need lots of opportunities and lots of support to develop competence and confidence in listening and acting in the global arena.

Ideas for Teachers

Peace-Building Citizenship

Conflicts are inevitable. They present choices because they can be handled in many different ways. Violence is learned behavior, reinforced (or restricted) by norms, sanctions, and procedures in social contexts such as schools. Equally, nonviolence is both learned by individuals and encouraged or discouraged by social contexts. To try to explain a problem or to seek alternate solutions is not to excuse a violent act. Peace-building citizenship education includes vocabulary, examples, discussion, and reflection on the ways conflicts may arise, evolve, escalate and deescalate, and on the ways participants, bystanders, advocates, third-party peacemakers, and institutional changes can help to move conflicts away from violence and toward resolution. All this can occur in the daily practice of human relations and discipline in school as well as in explicit subject matter lessons.

Human relations and discipline teach by modeling, guiding students to practice, and reinforcing particular norms for interaction. For example, punitive approaches to school safety focus on blaming and excluding alleged perpetrators rather than meaningful problem-solving. Unfortunately, teachers sometimes reinforce status hierarchies by dividing in-groups (such as athletes or those designated as good students) from out-groups (such as newcomers, cultural minorities, or people who don't fit gendered body ideals) through laissez-faire classroom facilitation that does not challenge aggression, by engaging with or ignoring certain students, facilitating win-or-lose competitions, and so forth. Aronson (2000) shows how such competitive and dehumanizing environments can make severe violence more likely and how; in contrast, teachers and whole school staffs can build equitable, inclusive, and cooperative environments that discourage violence by encouraging healthy relationships.

Thus peace-building education can take place through transformation of punitive or competitive climates into participatory problem-solving environments. For example, students may be taught and empowered as peer mediators to help resolve disputes in classrooms or at recess and before school. Some teachers use peacemaking circles, class meetings, and other dialogue processes regularly in their classrooms to facilitate students' practice in caring, communicating, and problem-solving (including deliberating together to create fair and widely under-stood progressive discipline expectations). School staffs may work to cre-ate gender-equitable environments that broaden the social space and acceptance for nonviolent expressions of masculinity, to counteract bias and human rights violations such as homophobia and racism, and to de-normalize aggression. School-wide meetings and community activities also may facilitate opportunities for diverse students and staff to voice, understand, and handle disagreements and feelings on sensitive issues.

Subject-Matter Lessons

As for explicit subject-matter lessons, most of the elements of peace-building education are already included in North American curriculum guidelines, although these tend to emphasize component skills more than putting these together into practice with conflictual topics (e.g., Bickmore, 2005a). For example,

- English language arts: effective listening, speaking, and discussion, and comparing one's own responses to those of characters in litera-ture
- Social studies: critical thinking and media literacy, such as recogniz-ing bias, assessing reliability of sources, and appreciating social and cultural differences; familiarity with issue negotiation and decision-making processes of governmental and nongovernmental systems; simulation of the United Nations, Security Council, and the General Assembly's decision-making processes for negotiation and compro-mise rather than exclusionary measures, sanctions and retribution
- Health and physical education: participation, cooperation, respectful interaction, decision-making for healthy relationships
- Math and science: application of conceptual tools to real local, na-tional, and global problems, such as formulating questions, data management and probability, summarizing and assessing evidence, and describing the consequences of human actions on ecosystems
- Drama education and role-playing pedagogies: speaking or writing in role, creatively addressing multiple perspectives on controversial issues
- Fine arts: recognizing how elements of design communicate feelings and ideas.

Conflict Competency Pedagogy

Conflict competency includes capacities of the heart as well as of the mind. Below, I give examples of learning activities, applicable across various subject areas, to achieve three basic ingredients of conflict competency: critical inquiry and reasoning about conflict; conflict communication processes; and skills and values for inclusion and equity.

Critical Inquiry and Reasoning about Conflict

- Collect photo images depicting conflict from recent news media. Invite students in small groups to discuss each image: What does the conflict seem to be about? What viewpoints are represented? What kind of conflict is this? How might participants be affected by what is going on? Who else, not in the picture, might be affected? What might have happened to bring about this situation? What might happen as a result? How do you feel about the conflict depicted, and why? When groups report back to the class, compare results to discern common and contrasting features and causes of conflict. Discuss potential positive effects of conflict (such as change, redress of unfairness, or learning) as well as negative effects.

- Describe the symptoms and clues of conflict escalation and actions by participants and bystanders that can help to create safety and deescalate problems. Practice by role-playing scenarios, having actors "freeze" at key moments for the group to debrief. Distinguish behavior (what people do—which presents potentially resolvable problems) from identity (which addresses only what people are—which results in blame).

- Examine questions of resource scarcity, contamination, development, and other conflicts rooted in exchanging of space or capital, such as deciding where to locate a subway line or a landfill, or identifying patterns of energy consumption and consequent oil trade interests. Apply geographic and economic concepts such as population density, comparative advantage, and human-environment interaction. Facilitate conflict analysis by using geography skills such as thematic mapping and math skills such as graphing, patterning, and prediction.

- Practice identifying the wants, needs, and concerns motivating each party's position in a conflict (known as interests) including basic human rights such as clean water, nourishing food, adequate health care, access to quality education, work that confers a sense of dignity and worth, opportunities for rest and leisure. Examine situations in which parties have shared as well as competing interests. Study conflict persuasion strategies such as the use of symbols. Apply these concepts to interpret, compare, and create political cartoons about historical and current issues.

- Use various role-play pedagogies such as readers' theater and simulations, combined with thoughtful preparation and debriefing of roles and concepts, to illuminate diverse perspectives and interests, sources of power, and opportunities for addressing inequity problems. For example, have students research and then assume the roles of delegates at a community council, task force, or the UN Security Council or General Assembly, researching the positions of their constituencies or countries on a topic agreed upon, and then coming together to enact one or more meetings. The United States Institute of Peace has produced complete teaching guides and materials on peace settlements and human rights violations in Cambodia and Sri Lanka as well as a general Guide to Using Simulations (www.usip.org, 2004). Build in opportunities for all students to speak up as active participants, to take turns acting as observer and reporter, and to debrief afterward.

Conflict Communication Processes

- Nearly all literature plots and news stories involve some kind of conflict and characters with different perspectives, so reading and writing are natural places for conflict education. Engage students' imagination by discussing the viewpoints, fairness concerns, and alternative frames of reference embodied in literature, poetry, art, drama, and news. Select stories in which social justice problems are acted upon by the characters, to stimulate discussion, and to offer models of possible ways to resist injustice. Invite students to practice speaking for themselves, orally and in writing, using feelings-related vocabulary to articulate what I believe, want, and need, instead of blaming, and to respond respectfully to the feelings of others by discussing sensitive issues arising in various kinds of texts.

- Reflective listening and paraphrasing exercise: Divide students into two lines representing different viewpoints. Simultaneously (to reduce shyness), all those in line A state and explain their views on a contentious question while their partners in line B listen silently, then ask nonjudgmental questions to elicit further clarification and understanding. Next, person B summarizes (reflects) what he or she has heard including feelings expressed through body language. Person A offers feedback about what they understood or missed. Switch roles and repeat. Debrief as a group: summarize types of questions and listening behaviors that facilitated effective communication, and distinguish these from argumentative or inhibitive behaviors.

- Brainstorming creative thinking exercise: First, establish context expectations: set a time and place for voicing creative, incomplete, or potentially risky ideas, encourage a large number of ideas including ones that might seem silly or unworkable, have every idea recorded and visible, build on prior ideas by suggesting related ideas and alternatives (do not evaluate or discuss any idea during the session). Practice first with a fun topic such as imagining alternate uses for a familiar object, then practice again with potential responses to a problem in the school or in course material. After the brainstorming session, guide the class to categorize the suggestions according to types of solutions, different actors, or timing, and so forth. An optional second round of brainstorming may add categories or ideas that become apparent in this process. Have students predict the consequences of each action idea. Last, choose together a few promising ideas to combine, refine, and develop further: small groups may develop these into proposals to bring back to the class.

- Negotiation exercise: First, students discern, substantiate with evidence, and prepare to explain their own perspectives on the proposals above or on a topic linked to course content. Members of each side have a turn to explain their understanding of the problem and what they want. Participants ask each other open-ended questions and analyze the situation to identify interests that they have in common or that are compatible (interests that dovetail) as well as opposing interests and concerns, and consider the interests of other stakeholders not represented. Next, they brainstorm to invent win-win ways of meeting each party's interests and concerns. After brainstorming, they constructively express evaluations, predictions, and concerns about each potential solution; they articulate areas of agreement, and design a plan and timeline to address areas of continuing disagreement. Students also may be trained to act as third-party mediators to facilitate such negotiations (resources include the School Mediators Field Guide, www.schoolmediation.com/books).

- The constructive academic controversy format (Avery, Johnson, & Johnson, 1999; Stevahn, Johnson, Johnson, & Schultz, 2002), in contrast to traditional debates, supports universal participation and constructive conflict management rather than competition in addressing contentious topics. Students work in groups of four, composed of two pairs who adopt opposing points of view. First, partners investigate background information, planning how to organize and defend their perspective persuasively (collect preparation notes for assessment). Next, each pair presents its position to the other half of the group of four. The group of four discusses the issue, with both sides working to clarify facts, identify shared interests, and improve understanding of the problem. Pairs switch sides and repeat the first three steps while representing the opposite viewpoint. Last, the group of four tries to reach a consensus decision, using principled negotiation strategies, and prepares a report outlining the interests of each party and how they were satisfied in their agreement.

Skills and Values for Inclusion, Diversity, and Change

- Compare examples from literature, news media, history, and personal experience to describe what ridicule and social exclusion (such as cliques, teasing, and put-downs) look and sound like, and their consequences. Distinguish such aggressive behavior from the underlying conflicts or problems.
- Practice inclusion through community-building games. For example, in one name game, each person in a circle has a turn to say their name while doing a simple gesture; the group repeats each name and gesture. In concentric circle interviews, half the group forms an inside circle facing outward, the other half forms an outside circle facing inward; participants interview the person across from them about a question posed by the facilitator, then the outer circle moves one person clockwise for the next interview. Line-up games can be social, in which students arrange themselves according to things like birthdays or favorite types of food, or more substantive, in which participants locate themselves according to their perspectives on a problem, and later explain why they hold that viewpoint.
- Investigate characteristics by which people are identified or stereotyped as belonging to different social classes, and how social class is part of social identity. Use real estate and business advertisements to compare housing types and social facilities in local communities. Consider how social class may impact various life opportunities, such as consumption of basic and luxury goods, access to informa-

tion and travel, health and life expectancy, personal security, relationship to the police and justice system, and educational success.

- Fairness is a particular interest of young people, which can be linked
  to domestic and international human rights standards. Have students
  create public awareness posters regarding Millennium Development
  Goals that address extreme poverty on a global level, including hunger, disease, lack of adequate shelter, exclusion, and promoting gender equality, education, and environmental sustainability (Resources:
  www.un.org/millenniumgoals; www.unmillenniumproject.org/facts;
  www.savethechildren.org.uk/scuk/jsp/resources; www.oxfam.org.uk
  /coolplanet).

- Diversity awareness: In an exercise sometimes called inside and outside, or power shuffle (Yarrow, Lazar, Roerden, & Lantieri, 2000, pp.
  75–79), participants are invited to step forward in a circle or to place
  themselves on a continuum across the room, to identify themselves
  in relation to each characteristic given by the facilitator. The facilitator begins with low-risk identifiers such as family size, age, or gender
  and proceeds to identifiers such as levels of wealth, sexual prefer-
  ence, or experiences with violence or discrimination. A crucial element of this exercise is the opportunity for participants to speak out
  about their experiences. Debrief questions of social diversity and
  bias.

Conclusions

Conflicts show us who we are. As young people grow up, they develop
their identities in relation to their agreements and disagreements with
what others around them want, believe, and choose to do. As they live in
a permeable, densely interconnected world in which democracy is at risk,
they need to develop capacity to handle such questions at global and
governmental as well as personal levels. They are not really free unless
they know what their choices are, and how to predict and shape the consequences of those choices. For example, when students are left to choose
project topics autonomously and to seek information by themselves, they
are unlikely to choose projects that question official knowledge or ethnocentric perspectives unless teachers have made them aware of those possibilities (Vibert & Shields, 2003). Thus, the teacher's role is crucial in
facilitating students' awareness of and open-mindedness to alternative
global and local contexts and perspectives.

Sometimes, with the best of intentions, teachers try too hard to avoid
or resolve conflicts in the classroom. Our attempts to build consensus

and create comfortable learning environments may inadvertently silence the least powerful voices and viewpoints. The increasing system-level demands for efficiency, massive curriculum coverage, and accountability also discourage teachers from implementing content and pedagogies that are faithful to the real world's uncertainty and complexity. Yet the examples above show that it is entirely possible, within this context, to facilitate learning opportunities that encourage nonviolent coexistence among multiple identities and viewpoints, thereby contributing to building peace. In this era of insecurity, nothing is more urgent.

Global education is a crucial element of education for peace-building citizenship because it responds to the global dimensions of conflict and insecurity that already affect the lives of diverse young people in North America and worldwide, and prepares them to make responsible and effective choices in light of those global dimensions. At its best, global education addresses intersections among diverse identities, perspectives, cross-cultural sensitivities, needs and solutions at global, governmental, and local levels. It highlights spaces for well-informed engagement in constructive conflict and change. In our intimately interdependent and fragile world system, only creating a secure and just quality of life for all people everywhere will address the sources of conflict and violence at their roots and, thereby establish a secure foundation for sustainable peace. Global education is a major part of the preparation young people need so that they can help change the world toward a more peaceful future.

Epilogue

Toni Fuss Kirkwood-Tucker

As we arrive at the final stage of our analysis of the globalization of curriculum and pedagogy in teacher education and schools, I remind the reader of the disconcerting findings by the Pew Research Center (2003) in its survey, *Views of a Changing World*. Measuring the strength of nationalism among wealthy nations of the world, the survey found that the country with the highest proportion of the population that believed that "our culture is superior to others" was the United States. Similarly, the same study shows that in the venues of environmental protection and international courts, a majority of U.S. citizens favor national sovereignty over international authority, in contrast to the Europeans, who strongly support international governance and environmental sustainability. What, then, are the contributions in these chapters to education for a global perspective that might support a widening of that worldview?

A particular value of this book lies in the timeliness of its unpublished research, which addresses matters of great concern barely touched upon in the global education literature to date: first, the historical development of the global education movement from its inception to the present and the attacks on global education in the mid-1980s and early 1990s; the distinctions, points of contention, and commonalties between global education and multicultural education, a topic long begging to be addressed but bypassed on the basis of political correctness; and the overdue movement toward development of a philosophy of global education embedded in the confluence of the principles of human rights and the foundations of global education.

A valuable contribution is the chapter offering a critical analysis of the literature on teacher education in global perspectives. Its significance stands out in contrast to recent omissions of existing research in global education by prominent social science educators — a highly unfortunate occurrence in the academy where the implementation of global education in teacher education programs and schools has increased over the last fifty years in a world of globalization and growing interdependence.

The illuminating retrospective on one of the leading collaborations between a university-based global education program and one of the largest school systems in the nation captures the significance of school-university partnerships par excellence.

A most honored contribution, here made public for the first time, are the experiences of my Russian colleagues in implementing global education as the catalyst for radical educational reform in post Soviet Russia, as they engaged in the staggering process of replacing communist-centered curriculum in teacher education and schools across vast regions of the largest nation in the world.

Another contribution of great value is the discussion of what it means to be a competent global teacher in the twenty-first century. The chapter captures the research-based recommendations for the characteristics that globally oriented classroom teachers need to prepare their students to be internationally informed citizens, competent and active in the affairs of the world. Of critical importance is the salient proposal for a postmodern, poststructural conceptual pedagogy of thinking within which to transform the ways students learn about the world, a conceptualization that moves beyond Cold War mentality toward a paradigm shift into a global pedagogy that addresses the pervasive human events of imperialism, neocolonialism, injustice, poverty, and war. The chapter underscoring the significance of the art of mentoring, which illustrates the career paths chosen by mentees in the global education field as a result of effective professor-student mentoring relationships provides unique insight into our professional world. A final contribution of this book is the empirical discourse on the successful 10-year implementation of global education programs in the Miami-Dade (Florida) Public Schools in collaboration with one of the leading university-based global awareness programs in the country. This brings long overdue recognition to the previously unpublished experiences in global education in the fourth largest school system in the United States. The book's journey aptly concludes with the chapter that proposes strategies that convey the very essence of the purpose of global education: the integration of peace-building pedagogy to create a world of sustainability, respect for the dignity of all members of the human family, and social justice.

What Have We Learned?

Global pedagogy, according to Burbules and Torres (2002), "provides transformative knowledge and skills and offers a reconstruction of education to avoid a deepening of inequities and educational irrelevance" (p. 5). So, what elements of global pedagogy can be extracted from our chapters and integrated into the classrooms of the world in our efforts to promote cross-cultural understanding, international cooperation, and a world of equity and justice? If we had to choose only the most salient insight from each chapter, what would it be?

From the first segment of our book, *Historical and Theoretical Foundations* (chapters 1 through 3), the Tye chapter addresses the systematic integration of the concepts of nationalism and patriotism into our lessons. Einstein's position that "nationalism is an infantile disease,...the measles of mankind" is a critical reminder in the post–9/11 world to distinguish in our classrooms between a healthy, caring, and loyal patriotism embedded in pride in national virtue and responsibility and the dangers of nationalism and simple-minded ideas of superiority of a country laced with murky, ill-defined ideals and emotions. The difference is illustrated by incidents during the campaign of President Barack Obama, when his patriotism was attacked by allegations that he did not love his country because he did not wear a flag lapel pin—as if loyalty to country lay in outward demonstration.

From the Elizabeth Heilman chapter we are now cognizant that global education and multicultural education must be viewed in the context of power, ethnicity, and race; we are aware of their historical origins and distinctions and now should consider joining the forces of the two competing fields to work toward confluence rather than divergence. In particular I ask teacher educators in their programs with our future teachers to clarify misconceptions of the two fields and to demonstrate effective ways to choose from each field those elements that are best suited to the realities of the classroom.

From Hilary Landorf's discourse we recognize that the field of global education, formerly without a coherent philosophy, is moving toward a definitive, clearly articulated philosophy of global education embedded in the moral underpinnings of human freedom, equality, social justice, and respect, as clearly demonstrated in the logical intersection of global education and human rights. An added value in her chapter is that she recommends use of the Universal Declaration of Human Responsibilities, which charges citizens to fulfill their societal obligations in a world of selfishness and materialism. I call on teachers to integrate the Universal Declaration of Human Rights, the Convention of the Rights of the Child, and the Universal Declaration of Responsibilities into their classrooms and make their application to students' lives, their communities, and the communities of the industrialized and developing nations a permanent feature of their global pedagogy. The United States' refusal to sign the Convention of the Rights of the Child provides a particular teachable incident for critical debate.

An occasion for pride is the analysis by our Chinese-American colleague Guichun Zong of the growing research base of theoretical and
empirical studies in teacher education in global perspectives over the
past two decades. The reader might be alarmed by her findings that none
of the theoretical, conceptual, and empirical research in global perspectives education has been acknowledged either in the 2008 *Handbook of
Research on Teacher Education: Enduring Questions in Changing Contexts* or
in the highly publicized AACTE (American Association of Colleges for
Teacher Education) award-winning book on teacher education research,
*Studying Teacher Education: The Report of the AERA Panel on Research and
Teacher Education* (2005) authored by respected scholars in education.
This poses a perplexing challenge to global educators and clearly should
lead to an open dialogue among scholars of different persuasions.

The powerful messages of the second segment our book, *From Theory
to Practice* (chapters 5 through 9) relate to what is taking place in global
education in teacher education programs and classrooms in Russia and
the United States. In chapter 8 our Russian colleagues Jacob Kolker, Irina
Sheina, and Elena Ustinova analyze their years of involvement in the reform of Russian education. They detail their involvement in and the
transformation across the vast regions of their nation from a communist-
based curriculum to a curriculum integrating open-mindedness toward
and knowledge about the larger world. In Elena Lenskaya's chapter 9 we
are given a gripping narrative of the historical and sociopolitical context
during the dissolution of the Soviet Union leading to the coup d'état
against Gorbachev in the early dawn of Russian democracy and the rise,
fall, and rebirth of global education in Russian education. We obtain insight into the challenges Russian teachers face in multi-ethnic classrooms
that resulted as minority children and their families returned to their
home regions after years of forced displacement to Siberia under Stalin.
Other school-site principals and teachers may have reasons of their own
to be interested in these challenges mounted by ethnic minorities claiming rights to equity in education. Teacher educators and district and
school-site administrators around the world can learn from the Russian
experience of adapting global education in curricular reform under sociopolitical and culture-specific conditions that embraced Western experience and deeply rooted native tradition.

Continuing with the movement from theory to practice on the
American continent (chapter 5) we learn from our Cuban American col-
leagues, Barbára Cruz and Pedro Bermúdez, in their retrospective of the
Global Awareness Program at Florida International University and the

critical importance of both leadership in school-university-foundation partnerships and of the procurement of grants to maintain viable program development. My chapters (chapters 6 and 7) written from the German-American perspective, provide new information about the organization, planning, and incremental selection of schools during the 10-year education reform movement in global education in almost 200 elementary and secondary schools in the Miami-Dade County Public Schools in Florida, the fourth largest school district in the United States. Hey offer one answer to the paucity of empirical scholarship regarding the training of in-service teachers in the trenches of our public schools in global education in one of the most diverse international communities in our country and how to integrate global perspectives into mandated curriculum and instruction

These chapters are specifically intended for district-level and area-level administrators and school-site principals interested in curricular reform in global education. They provide a blueprint for effective school-university partnership and descriptive step-by-step processes of the training of teachers and the implementation of global education programs in the schools of feeder pattern configurations. The narratives demonstrate how global education theory translates into classroom practice that can transform human dispositions, how behaviors traditionally shaped by ethnic chauvinism or nation-centered parochialism can come to embrace a global perspective of open-mindedness, cross-cultural understanding and appreciation, and the increasing interconnectedness of the world community.

In the third segment of our book, *Pedagogy and Possibilities in the Postmodern World* (chapters 10 through 13) Merry Merryfield provides a seminal piece on twenty-first century teaching and learning in global education. If there is one idea we should take from one of the leading scholars in the field, it is this: global scholars, teacher educators, and classroom teachers trained in the classic Hanvey Model (1976) and other traditional frameworks are challenged to examine their own practice and to discard habits of mind shaped by traditional models of global perspectives teaching. They are invited to embrace a new twenty-first century postcolonial pedagogy that confronts the multiple ways the educational legacy of imperialism has shaped today's mainstream academics, a pedagogy that addresses the knowledge and experiences of people who have been ignored, stereotyped, or marginalized because of their race, gender, class, culture, national origin, religious, or political beliefs. This charge for "Hanveyites" can result in a revolutionary paradigm shift, as many of us—like me—are deeply shaped by the traditional frameworks that have guided our practice for decades.

The John Cogan and David Grossman chapter advances a comprehensive research-based list of qualities that globally minded teachers ought to possess for the development of an internationally knowledgeable citizenry of future generations. If we take this message to heart, the classrooms of our world could be transformed into true democratic learning communities embedded in open-mindedness, social justice, and peace-building activities moving the learner toward shaping a better world. Therefore, I call on global educators, globally minded teachers, traditionally trained teachers, and school-site principals to examine the characteristics of the globally trained teacher. Administrators and curriculum specialists weighing the possibility of implementing curricular reform in global perspectives can assess the need for in-service training in global perspectives teaching and learning. Moreover, traditionally trained teachers are provided a golden opportunity to compare their own teaching competencies with the desirable competencies of the globally trained teacher.

The central message of a second chapter (chapter 12) by collaborators Barbára Cruz and Pedro Bermúdez is their critical call for mentorship in global education pedagogy at the primary, secondary, and tertiary levels of schooling, a master-apprentice model driven by the reciprocity of teaching and learning that provides desired continuity for the profession. I call on graduate students as well as professors, teachers, and school administrators to seek out mentorships with their promising candidates. Whether in school settings or at the university, effective mentorships often result in promising careers for the apprentice and satisfaction as well as assistance for the mentor. I believe that global educators have a moral responsibility to engage in mentorship relationships to further the cause and purpose of global education.

The final chapter of our book is the passionate call by our Canadian colleague Kathy Bickmore for a global pedagogy as an integral part of global education curricula. The peace scholar calls for a transformative pedagogy grounded in strategies for peace-seeking and peace-building, for conflict resolution, community dialogue on social conflict and public controversies, and environmental ecological education to empower young people with a globalized efficacy. I urge all teachers, administrators, and global educators of the world to respond to this call in our life-long efforts to create a safer and more equal world for all humanity. In order to combat the culture of violence pervading societies across the globe, future generations deserve a radically different education—one that does not glorify war but educates for peace, nonviolence, and international cooperation and reminds us all that "peace begins with you."

Reflections

The process of globalization is ubiquitous and inevitable. It will continue its relentless course across the world with or without believers or assent. As multinational corporations and international business, finance, and commerce race to promising markets in the farthest corners of the world, a new class of citizens and corporations are seizing the moment to create new possibilities, penetrate cross-cultural boundaries, collaborate with their counterparts of different nations, and reap profits. The result is the widening gulf between industrialized and developing nations and two-thirds or more of the world's people sinking deeper into poverty and despair. Political scientists contend that we are witnessing a decline in American hegemony (Kennedy, 1987; Schell, 2003; Khanna, 2008). This phenomenon of decreasing U.S. political power and influence in the world brings even greater challenges for education, as education and commitment can make a long-term difference in the future of the world and in the lives of those on the edge of starvation and desperation.

It is my belief that the powerful triumvirate of teachers, teacher educators, and administrators is indispensable in the preparation of students as these can make a difference in shaping a more equitable, just, and harmonious world. Collectively their planned and deliberate collaboration can move learners across this planet to higher levels of perspective consciousness and global cognition. Motivated by their teachers, starting on the local level, students can engage in active participation toward solving the ills of their communities. Moving to the global level, students can engage in constructive, meaningful dialogue with their peers in other cultures, participate in student exchanges, and adopt schools in developing countries to build bridges across our fragile world.

It is the classroom teacher on whom the greatest responsibility falls in the attempt to make a difference in the lives of students, community, and society. Even without the explicit endorsement of the principal, the teacher is the ultimate gatekeeper what is being taught in the classroom (Thornton, 2005). Our teachers need to perceive themselves as accomplished intellectuals and an integral part of far-reaching democratic communities (Giroux, 2004) and proudly present themselves what Gaudelli (2003) defines as the community intellectuals.

Our Future

Among the qualities that globally oriented teachers should possess is a willingness to change their own lifestyles and consumption habits to protect the environment—a most demanding sacrifice. Education for sustainability embraces both the welfare of the planet and the welfare of people (Wade, 2007). The United Nations Conference on the Human Environment and other earth summits acknowledge that education must be the principal player in changing unsustainable practices. Finding solutions to this problem presents the most difficult challenge for global educators, as it requires active participation in local, national, and global communities. Noddings (2002) in her place-based education approach argues for a biocentric pedagogy to prepare our youth to become global citizens who will protect the earth, accept pluralism, and promote peace. Teachers are our greatest hope for promoting equality and respect for all people, teaching about the commonalties of humankind and the interconnectedness of humanity.

I predict that traditionally trained teachers and globally oriented teachers are willing to move toward becoming cosmopolitans "whose allegiance is to the worldwide community of human beings" (Nussbaum, 2002, p. 4) as the diversity of the world's people is represented in their classrooms and the acknowledgment of their students' origins and traditions is integral to their teaching. I predict that teachers are willing to move forward to become universalists because an essential purpose of global education is to deliberate "in reasonable perspectives in forums well-designed for deliberations" (Gutmann, 1993, p. 198) in order to promote a moral citizenship in students that facilitates respect for the Other, the world, and the planet (Nussbaum, 2002; Gutmann, 2003). The care theory (Noddings, 1984; 2002) of global education proposes a foundation for our actions of rethinking moral issues from a position that focuses on affective and emotive capacities rather than on judgment of the Other whose culture and values we do not understand. I dare suggest that in our world there are many teachers skilled and committed to their cause who are already engaging in such practices, teachers who are—as Lena Lenskaya observes from Russia—the unsung teacher heroes and heroines of the world.

My appeal for the globalization of curriculum and pedagogy in teacher education and schools is directed to all teachers, teacher educators, district-level administrators, school-site principals, curriculum specialists, and chief state school officers. The process of education lies in your hands. If you decide to prepare our youth in competent, humanistic, caring, and active citizenship, you will join what Jim Becker calls the "coalition of the willing," taking the first giant step into the future.

As we continue on our hazardous journey into the unknown, I am hopeful that we will continue to promote compelling programs in our schools and train globally competent teachers willing to implement them in the world's classrooms. The contemporary Russian philosopher Dmitry Mendeleyev (1991) believes that civilizations cannot successfully develop unless people find "a way of harmonizing their personal actions with the common good of humankind" (p. 408). The Russian scholar Dmitry of Rostov believes that we must value the virtues of individuals above their rank and ethnicity (cited in Liferov, 1994). Ronald Takaki (cited in Shea, 1993) responds simply with, "We can all get along and function as a community if we take the opportunity to learn about each other."

I know that you will.

References

Abdullahi, S. (2008). Personal communication. May 23.

Adler, S. A. (2008). The education of social studies teachers. In L. Levstik & C. Tyson (Eds.), *Handbook of research in social studies education* (pp. 329–351). New York: Routledge.

Alger, C. F. (1974). *Your city in the world—the world in your city*. Columbus: Mershon Center, Ohio State University.

Alger, C. F. (1995). Building peace: A global learning process. In M. Merryfield & R. Remy (Eds.), *Teaching about international conflict and peace* (pp. 127–162). Albany: State University of New York Press.

Alger, C. F., & Harf, J. E. (1986). Global education: Why? For whom? About what? In R. E. Freeman (Ed.), *Promising practices in global education: A handbook with case studies* (pp. 1–13). New York: National Council on Foreign Language and International Studies.

Allport, G. W. (1954). *The nature of prejudice*. New York: Addison-Wesley.

American Association of Colleges for Teacher Education (AACTE) (1996). *Best practices award*. Retrieved March 18, 2008, from http://www.aacte.org/Events/Awards/practice_awards.aspx

Amin, S. (1997). *Capitalism in the age of globalization*. London: Zed Books.

Anderson, C. C. (1982). Global education in the classroom. *Theory into Practice, 21* (3), 168–176.

Anderson, C. C. (2008). Personal communication. March 15.

Anderson, C. C., & Anderson, L. F. (1977). Global education in elementary schools. *Social Education, 41* (1), 34–37.

Anderson C. C., Niklas S., & Crawford, A. (1994). *Global understandings: A framework for teaching and learning*. Alexandria, VA: Association for Supervision and Curriculum Development.

Anderson, E. M., & Shannon, A. (1988). Toward a conceptualization of mentoring. *Journal of Teacher Education, 39* (1), 38–42.

Anderson, L. F. (1968). An examination of the structure and objectives of international education, *Social Education, 32* (7), 639–647.

Anderson, L. F. (Ed.). (1976). *Windows on our world*. Boston: Houghton Mifflin.

Anderson, L. F. (1979). *Schooling and citizenship in a global age: An exploration of the meaning and significance of global education*. Bloomington, IN: Social Studies Development Center.

Anderson, L. F. (1982). Why should American education be globalized? It's a nonsensical question. *Theory into Practice, 21* (3), 155–161.

Anderson, L. F. (1991). A rationale for global education. In K. A. Tye (Ed.), *Global education: From thought to action* (pp. 13–34). Alexandria, VA: Association for Supervision and Curriculum Development.

Anderson, L. F., & Anderson, C. C. (1979). A visit to Middleston's world-centered schools: A scenario. In J. M. Becker (Ed.), *Schooling for a global age* (pp. 33–58). New York: McGraw-Hill.

Anderson, L. F., & Becker, J. (1968). *An examination of objectives, needs and priorities in international education in U.S. secondary and elementary schools*. Foreign Policy Association. Washington, DC: U.S. Department of Health, Education and Welfare.

Appiah, K. A. (2006). *Cosmopolitanism: Ethics in a world of strangers.* New York: W. W. Norton.

Archer, C. M. (1991). *Living with strangers in the U.S.A.* Englewood Cliffs, NJ: Regents/Prentice Hall.

Arkansas International Center (2008). Retrieved March 1, 2008, from http://ualr.edu/aic.

Aronson, E. (2000). *Nobody left to hate: Teaching compassion after Columbine.* New York: Worth.

Asante, M. K. (1992). Afrocentric curriculum. *Educational Leadership, 49,* 28–39.

Asante, M. K. (1998). *The Afrocentric idea* (rev. and exp. ed.). Philadelphia: Temple University Press.

Ashcroft, B., Griffiths, G., & Tiffin, H. (Eds.). (1989). *The empire writes back: Theory and practice in post-colonial literature.* London: Routledge.

Ashcroft, B., Griffiths, G., & Tiffin, H. (Eds.). (1995). *The post-colonial studies reader.* New York: Routledge.

Asia Society (2006). *States prepare for the global age.* Retrieved March 18, 2008, from http://www.internationaled.org/statespreparefortheglobalage.htm

Associated Schools Project (2008). UNESCO. Retrieved March 1, 2008, from http://portal.unesco.org/education.

Avery, P. G. (2004). Social studies teacher education in an era of globalization. In S. Adler (Ed.), *Critical issues in social studies teacher education* (pp. 375). Greenwich, CT: Information Age.

Avery, P. G., Johnson, D., & Johnson, R. (1999). Teaching an understanding of war and peace through structured academic controversies. In A. Raviv et al. (Eds.), *How children understand war and peace* (pp. 260–280). San Francisco, CA: Jossey-Bass.

Ayton-Shenker, D., & Tessitore, J. (Eds.). (2002). *A global agenda: Issues before the general assembly of the United Nations.* New York: Rowman & Littlefield.

Bailey, S. K. (1975). International education: An agenda for global interdependence. *College Board Review, 97,* 3–5.

Bales, S. N. (2004). How Americans think about international education and why it matters. *Phi Delta Kappan, 86* (3), 206–209.

Banks, J. A. (1981). *Education in the 80s: Multiethnic education.* Washington, DC: National Education Association.

Banks, J. A. (1989). Multicultural education: Characteristics and goals. In J. Banks & C. Banks (Eds.), *Multicultural education: Issues and perspectives.* Boston: Allyn & Bacon.

Banks, J. A. (1993). Integrating the curriculum with ethnic content: Approaches and guidelines. In J. A. Banks & C. A. McGee-Banks (Eds.), *Multicultural education: Issues and perspectives* (pp. 189–207). Boston: Allyn & Bacon.

Banks, J. A. (1995). Transformative challenges to the social science disciplines: Implications for social studies teaching and learning. *Theory and Research in Social Education, 23* (1), 2–20.

Banks, J. A. (2004). Teaching for social justice, diversity, and citizenship in a global world. *Educational Forum, 68,* 289–298.

Barber, B. R. (1995). *Jihad vs. McWorld: How globalism and tribalism are reshaping the world.* New York: Random House.

Barth, R. S. (2002). The culture builder. *Educational Leadership, 59* (8), 6–11.

Becker, J. M. (1973). *Education for a global society.* Bloomington, IN: Phi Delta Kappa Educational Foundation.

Becker, J. M. (1975). *Guidelines for world studies: Mid-American program for global perspectives in education.* Bloomington: Indiana University Press.

Becker, J. M. (Ed.) (1979). *Schooling for a global age.* New York: McGraw-Hill.

Becker, J. M. (1982). Goals for global education. *Theory into Practice, 21* (3), 228–233.

Becker, J. M., & Anderson, L. F. (1980). Global perspectives in the social studies. *Journal of Research and Development in Education, 13* (2), 82–92.

Becker, J. M., & East, M. (1972). *Global dimensions in education: The secondary school.* New York: Center for War/Peace Studies.

Becker, J. M., & Hahn, C. (1976). *The wingspread workbook for educational change agents.* Boulder, CO: Social Science Educational Consortium.

Belz, J. A., & Muller-Hartmann, A. (2003). Teachers as intercultural learners: Negotiating German-American telecollaboration along the institutional fault line. *Modern Language Journal, 87,* 71–89.

Bennett, J. M. (1993). Towards ethnorelativism: A developmental model of intercultural sensitivity. In R. M. Paige (Ed.), *Education for the intercultural experience* (pp. 21–71). Yarmouth, ME: Intercultural Press.

Bennett, M. J. (1993). Cultural marginality: Identity issues in intercultural training. In R. M. Paige (Ed.), *Education for the intercultural experience* (pp. 109–135). Yarmouth, ME: Intercultural Press.

Bermúdez, P. R. (2008). Personal communication. May 12.

Beyer, B. K., & Hicks, E. P. (1968). *Image of Africa: A report on what American secondary school students know and believe about Africa south of the Sahara.* Pittsburgh Project Africa: Carnegie Mellon University.

Bhabha, H. K. (1986). Signs taken for wonders: Questions of ambivalence and authority under a tree outside Delhi May 1817. In H. L. Gates (Ed.), *Race writing and difference* (pp. 163–184). Chicago: University of Chicago Press.

Bickmore, K. (1993). Learning inclusion/inclusion in learning: Citizenship education for a pluralistic society. *Theory and Research in Social Education, 21* (4), 341–384. ERIC Document EJ 482 399.

Bickmore, K. (1997). Preparation for pluralism: Curricular and extra-curricular practice with conflict resolution. *Theory into Practice, 36:1* (Winter), 3–10. ERIC Document EJ 546 684.

Bickmore, K. (2002). Education for peacebuilding citizenship. Canada and the World: One year after 9/11. *Canadian Issues/Thémes Canadiens* (September), 19–23.

Bickmore, K. (2005a). Foundations for peacebuilding and discursive peacekeeping: Infusion and exclusion of conflict in Canadian public school curricula. *Journal of Peace Education, 2* (2), 161–181.

Bickmore, K. (2005b). Teacher development for conflict participation: Facilitating learning for difficult citizenship's education. *International Journal of Citizenship and Teacher Education, 1* (2). Retrieved April 14, 2008, from www.citized.info.

Bickmore, K. (2007). Linking global with local: Cross-cultural conflict education in urban Canadian schools. In F. Leach & M. Dunne (Eds.), *Education, conflict and reconciliation: International perspectives* (pp. 237–252). Oxford: Peter Lang.

Bickmore, K. (2008). Social studies for social justice: Learning/ navigating power and conflict. In L. Levstik & C. Tyson (Eds.), *Handbook of research in social studies* (pp. 155–171). Mahwah, NJ: Lawrence Erlbaum.

Bigelow, B., & Peterson, B. (2002). *Rethinking globalization: Teaching for justice in an unjust world*. Milwaukee, WI: Rethinking Schools Press.

Birger, L. (1988). The internationalization of South Florida's economy. Business Monday. *Miami Herald*. Presentation to the Advisory Board, Global Awareness Program, Florida International University, October 28.

Blaut, J. M. (1993). *The colonizer's model of the world: Geographical determinism and Eurocentric history*. New York: Guilford Press.

Blumer, H. (1969). *Symbolic interaction: Perspective and method*. Englewood Cliffs, NJ: Prentice Hall.

Boulding, E. (1988). *Building a global civic culture: Education for an independent world*. Syracuse, NY: Syracuse University Press.

Boyer, E. (1985). Common ground. In J. Mangieri (Ed.), *Excellence in education* (pp. 15–36). Fort Worth: Texas Christian University Press.

Brantlinger, P. (1986). Victorians and Africans: The genealogy of the myth of the dark continent. In H. L. Gates (Ed.), *Race writing and difference* (pp. 185–222). Chicago: University of Chicago Press.

Brislin, R. (Ed.). (1986). *Applied cross-cultural psychology*. Beverly Hills, CA: Sage.

Brislin, R. (1993). *Understanding culture's influence on behavior*. Fort Worth, TX: Harcourt Brace.

Brislin, R., & Yoshida, T. (Eds). (1994). *Improving intercultural interactions*. Thousand Oaks, CA: Sage.

Brislin, R., Cushner, K., Cherrie, C., & Yong, M. (1986). *Intercultural interactions*. Newbury Park, CA: Sage.

Britzman, D. P. (1994). Is there a problem with knowing thyself? Towards a post-structuralist view of teacher identity. In T. Shanahan (Ed.), *Teachers thinking, teachers knowing: Reflections on literacy and language education* (pp. 53–75). Urbana, IL: NCRE.

Brodkey, L. (1987). Postmodern pedagogy for progressive educators. *Journal of Education, 169* (3), 138–143.

Brougham, H. (1828). Speech to the House of Commons. Retrieved November 20, 2008, from http://elt.britcoun.org.pl/elt/e_quote.htm

Brown, J. (2008). Personal communication. July 8.

Bruner, J. S. (1965). *Man: A course of study. Occasional Paper No.3*. Cambridge, MA: Educational Services Incorporated.

Brysk, A. (Ed.) (2002). *Globalization and human rights*. Berkeley: University of California Press.

Buehrer, E. (1990). *New age masquerade*. Brentwood, TN: Wolgemuth & Hyatt.

Burack, J. (2003). The student, the world, and global education. In J. Leming, L. Ellington, & K. Porter-Magee (Eds.) *Where did social studies go wrong?* (pp. 40–69). Washington, DC: Thomas B. Fordham Foundation.

Burbules, N. C., & Torres, C. A. (Eds.) (2002). *Globalization and education*. London: Rutledge.

Burton, S. L., & Greher, G. R. (2007). School-university partnerships: What do we know and why do they matter? *Arts Education Policy Review, 109* (1), 13–

22. Retrieved June 16, 2008, from *ProQuest Education Journals* database. Document ID 1397136611.

Busch, J. W. (1985). Mentoring in graduate schools of education: Mentors' perceptions. *American Educational Research Journal, 22* (2), 257–265.

Butts, R. F. (1969). America's role in international education: A perspective on thirty years. In H. Shane (Ed.), *The United States and international education*, part 1 (pp. 3–45). Chicago: National Society for the Study of Education.

Calder, M. (2000). A concern for justice: Teaching using a global perspective in the classroom. *Theory into Practice, 39* (2), 81–87.

Calder, M., & Smith, R. (1996). Global education: Windows on the world. *Social-Educator,* 14 (2), 23–34.

California International Studies Project (2008). Retrieved April 2, 2008, from www.csmp.ucop.edu.cisp.

Campbell, C. D. (2007). Best practices for student-faculty mentoring programs. In T. D. Allen & L. T. Eby (Eds.), *The Blackwell handbook of mentoring: A multiple perspectives approach* (pp. 325–344). Malden, MA: Blackwell.

Caporaso, J., & Mittelman, J. (1988). The assault on global education. *Political Science and Politics, 21* (1), 36–44.

Carson, R. (1962). *Silent spring.* Boston: Houghton Mifflin.

Carter, C. C. (2002). *Peace education in social studies.* Paper presented at the annual conference of the College and University Faculty Assembly (CUFA) of the National Council for the Social Studies, Phoenix, AZ.

Case, R. (1991). Integrating around themes: An overemphasized tool? Tri-university integration project. Vancouver, Canada: University of British Columbia.

Case, R. (1993). Key elements of a global perspective. *Social Education, 57* (6), 318–325.

Case, R. (1994). *Integration in the global education curriculum.* Paper presented at the conference on Setting Educational Standards as a Basis for Curriculum Development. Ryazan: Russia.

Case, R., & Werner, W. (1997). Building faculty commitment for global education. In M. M. Merryfield, E. Jarchow, & S. Pickert (Eds.), *Preparing teachers to teach global perspectives: A handbook for teacher education* (pp. 189–208). Thousand Oaks, CA: Corwin Press.

Castle, S., Fox, R. K., & Souder, K. (2006). Do professional development schools make a difference? A comparative study of PDS and non-PDS teacher candidates. *Journal of Teacher Education, 57* (1), 65–80.

Chang, D. (2008). Personal communication. May 15.

Chavez, C, R., & O'Donnell, J. (Eds.) (1998). *Speaking the unpleasant.* Albany: State University of New York Press.

Chen, G., & Starosta, W. J. (2000). *Communication and global society.* New York: Peter Lang.

Christensen, L. (1993). Reconstituting Jefferson: Lessons on school reform. In L. Christensen & S. Karp (Eds.), *Rethinking school reform: Views from the classroom* (pp. 266–274). Milwaukee, WI: Rethinking Schools.

Claire, H., & Holden, C. (Eds.). (2007). *The challenge of teaching controversial issues.* London: Trentham Books.

Clark, L. (Ed.). (1997). *Through African eyes*, vol. 2. New York: CITE.

Clement, C., & Outlaw, E. (2002). Student teaching abroad: Learning about teaching, culture, and self. *Kappa Delta Pi Record*, 38 (4), 180-183.

Cochran-Smith, M., & Zeichner, K. M. (2005). *Studying teacher education*: The report of the AERA panel on research and teacher education. Mahwah, NJ: Lawrence Erlbaum. Cochran-Smith, M., Feiman-Nemser, S., McIntyre, D., & Demers, K. (2008). *Handbook of research on teacher education: Enduring questions in changing contexts*. New York: Routledge.Cogan, J. J. (1979). Characteristics of globally minded teachers. *Trends and Issues*. Journal of the Florida Council for the Social Studies, 25 (2 & 3), 25–28.

Cogan, J. J. (1982a). Educating teachers for a global perspective. *World Studies Journal (UK)*, 4 (1), 20–24.

Cogan, J. J. (1982b). *Training teachers for a global age: A critical challenge*. Paper presented at the meeting of the International Higher Education Standing Conference, Oxford University.

Cogan, J. J. (1997). *Multidimensional citizenship: Educational policy for the 21st century*. Executive Summary of the Citizenship Education Policy Study, Saskawa Peace Foundation, Tokyo, Japan.Cogan, J. J., & Derricott, R. (Eds.) (1998, 2000). *Citizenship for the 21st century: An international perspective on education*. London: Kogan Page.

Cogan, J. J., Grossman, D. L., & Liu, M. (2000). Citizenship: The democratic imagination in a global context. *Social Education*, 64 (1), 48–52.

Cole, M., & Scribner, S. (1974). *Culture and thought*. New York: John Wiley.

Collins, P. H. (1990). *Black feminist thought*. New York: Routledge.

Collins, T., Czarra, F., & Smith A., (1998). *Guidelines for global and international studies education: Challenges, cultures, and connections*. New York: American Forum for Global Education.

Cordeiro, P. (2007). A modest proposal for the improvement of scholarship in internationalizing teacher education. *Teacher Education Quarterly*, 34 (1), 151–154.

Council of Chief State School Officers (2006a, November). *Global education policy statement*. Retrieved March 18, 2008, from http://www.csso.org/content/pdfs/Global%20Education%20FINAL%20lowrez.pdf

Council of Chief State School Officers (2006b). Ohio's concept paper for a regional system of science, technology, engineering and mathematics (STEM) high schools. Retrieved July 15, 2008, from http://www.ccsso.org/content/PDFs/System_Reform_Ohio_STEM.doc.

Council on Learning. (1981). *Task force statement on education and the world view*. New Rochelle, NY: Change Magazine Press.

Crew, R. F. (2008). *Schools for a flat world*. Retrieved June 23, 2008, from http://superintendent.dadeschools.net.

Crocco, M., Faithfull, B., & Schwartz, S. (2003). Inquiring minds want to know. Action research at a New York City professional development school. *Journal of Teacher Education*, 54 (1), 19–30.

Crofts, M. (1986). Africa. *Social Education*, 50 (5), 345–350.

Cruz, B. C. (2008). Personal communications. May 13.

Cunningham, G. L. (1986). *Blowing the whistle on global education*. Denver, CO: Region VIII Office, United States Department of Education.

Cushner, K. (1989). Assessing the impact of a culture-general assimilator. *International Journal of Intercultural Relations, 13,* 125–146.

Cushner, K. (1999). *Human diversity in action.* New York: McGraw-Hill.

Cushner, K., & Brennan, S. (2007). *Intercultural student teaching: A bridge to global competence.* Lanham, MD: Rowman & Littlefield.

Cushner, K., & Brislin, R. W. (1996). *Intercultural interactions: A practical guide.* Thousand Oaks, CA: Sage.

Cushner, K., McClelland, A., & Safford, P. (1992). *Human diversity on education: An integrative approach.* New York: McGraw-Hill.

Cushner, K., McClelland, A., & Safford, P. (2000). *Human diversity on education: An integrative approach* (3rd ed.) New York: McGraw-Hill.

Cvetkovich, A., & Kellner, D. (1997). *Articulating the global and the local.* Boulder, CO: Westview Press.

Dahl, R. (2003). *How democratic is the American constitution?* New Haven, CT: Yale University Press.

Darling-Farr, L. (1994). *Global Education as moral education.* Unpublished dissertation, University of British Columbia, Vancouver.

Darling-Hammond, L. (1988). Accountability and teacher professionalism. *American Educator, 12* (4), 8–13, 38–43.

Dasen, P. R. (1992). Cross-cultural psychology and teacher training. In J. Lynch, C. Modgil, & S. Modgil (Eds.), *Cultural diversity and the schools: Prejudice, polemic or progress?* (pp. 191–204). London: Falmer Press.

Davidson, M. N., & Foster-Johnson, L. (2001). Mentoring in the preparation of graduate researchers of color. *Review of Educational Research, 71* (4), 549–574.

Davies, L. (2004). *Education and conflict: Complexity and chaos.* London: Routledge/Falmer Press.

Davydov, V. V. (1981). Printsipy obucheniia v shkole budushchego (Principles of teaching in a school of the future). In I. I. Iliasov & V. Liaudis (Eds.), *Khrestomatiia po vozrastnoi i pedaqoqicheskoi psikholoqii* (Reader in developmental and pedagogical psychology) (pp. 65–99). Moscow: Moscow State University.

Day, C. (1993). The importance of learning biography in supporting teacher development: An empirical study. In C. Day, J. Calderhead, & P. Denicolo (Eds.), *Research on teacher thinking: Understanding professional development* (pp. 221–232). Pittsburg, PA: Falmer Press.

Day, J. (2008). Personal communication. April 14.

De Chardin, T. (1964). *Future of man.* New York: Harper & Row.

De Varona, F. (1987). *Implementation and evaluation of the global leadership training program in the Miami-Dade County Public Schools: 1984–1987.* Paper presented at the American Association of School Administrators Conference: Education and Investment in the Future: New Orleans, LA, February 18–23.

De Varona, F. (1988). *The international dimensions of the Miami-Dade County Public Schools.* Presentation to the Global Awareness Program Advisory Board, Miami: Florida International University, October 28.

De Varona, F. (2008). Personal communication. June 11 and 13.

Deering, T. E., & Stanutz, A. (1995). Preservice field experience as a multicultural component of a teacher education program. *Journal of Teacher Education, 46,* 390–394.

Development Education Association (2004). *Global perspectives and teachers in training*. London: Development Education Association. Retrieved March 14, 2008, from http://www.dea.org.uk/publication-9a85d88eb9fea0bed633d874bdccf9c0.

Dewey, J. (1901). Speech given at the National Education Association meeting. Chicago.

Dewey, J. (1916). *Democracy and education (1966 edition)*. New York: Free Press.

Diawara, M. (1998). *In search of Africa*. Cambridge, MA: Harvard University Press.

Dillard, C. B. (1996, Spring/Summer.) Engaging pedagogy: Writing and reflecting in multicultural teacher education. *Teaching Education, 8* (1), 13–21.

Dneprov. E. (1991). *Mission statement for Russian education: Ten principles of reform*. Speech delivered at the Sochi conference. August, 1991. Sochi, Russia.

Dneprov, E. (1992). *Innovations in Russian education reform*. Speech delivered at Florida International University. Spring, 1992. Miami, Florida.

Dneprov, Е. (2006). Образование и политика Э.Д. Днепров. Chronicle of resistance. In E. Dneprov (Ed.), *Education and politics*, vol. 1 (pp. 174–178). Moscow: Geotech.

Donnelly, J. (2003). *Universal human rights in theory and practice* (2nd ed.). Ithaca, NY: Cornell University Press.

Douglas, C. A. (1997). *Formal mentoring programs in organizations: An annotated bibliography*. Greensboro, NC: Centre for Creative Leadership.

Doyle, J. (2008). Personal communication. May 7 and June 5.

Drum, J. (1986). Project enrichment: A global education program of the Stanley Foundation. In R. E. Freeman (Ed.), *Promising practices in global education: A handbook with case studies* (pp. 66–68). New York: National Council on Foreign Language and International Studies.

Duarte, E. M., & Smith, S. (2000). *Foundational perspectives in multicultural education*. New York: Longman.

Du Bois, W. E. B. (1903/1989). *The souls of black folks*. Chicago: A. C. McClurg.

Du Bois, W. E. B. (1965). The world and Africa: An inquiry into the part that Africa played in world history. New York: International.

Duckworth, R., Levy, W., & Levy, J. (2005). Present and future teachers of the world's children: How internationally-minded are they? *Journal of Research in International Education, 4* (3), 279–311.

Education for a Global Perspective: A Plan for New York State, 1982–2000 (1981). University of the State of New York State Education Department. Retrieved May 22, 2008, from http://www.regents.nysed.gov

Ehrich, L., Hansford, B., & Tennent, L. (2004). Formal mentoring programs in education and other professions: A review of the literature. *Educational Administration Quarterly, 40* (4), 518-540.

Ehrlich, P. (1968). *The population bomb*. New York: Ballantine.

Elkind, D. (1995). School and family in the postmodern world. *Phi Delta Kappan, 77* (1), 8–14.

Ellsworth, E. (1989). Why doesn't this feel empowering? Working through the repressive myths of critical pedagogy. *Harvard Educational Review, 59* (3), 297-232.

English Bill of Rights (1689). Retrieved September 10, 2008, from http://www.constitution.org/eng/eng_bor.htm

Erickson, R. (1986). Regional organizing: Global education in Minnesota. In R. E. Freeman (Ed.), *Promising practices in global education: A handbook with case studies* (pp. 69–76). New York: National Council on Foreign Language and International Studies.

Essex, N. L. (2001). Effective school-college partnerships: A key to educational renewal and instructional improvement. *Education, 121* (4), 732–736. Retrieved June 16, 2008, from *ProQuest Education Journals* database. Document ID 78371797.

Evans, M., & Reynolds, C. (2005). *Educating for global citizenship in a changing world: A teacher's resource handbook.* Toronto and Ottawa: Ontario Institute for Studies in Education of University of Toronto and Canadian International Development Agency.

Fabos, B., & Young, M. D. (1999). Telecommunication in the classroom: Rhetoric versus reality. *Review of Educational Research, 69* (3), 217–259.

Fang, Z., & Ashley, C. (2004). Preservice teachers' interpretations of a field-based reading block. *Journal of Teacher Education, 55* (1), 39–54.

Fine, M. (1991). *Framing dropouts: Notes on the politics of an urban public high school.* Albany: State University of New York Press.

Finn, C. E., Jr. (1988). Among the educationaloids: The social studies debacle. *American Spectator, 21* (1), 14–15.

Finn, C. E., Jr., & Bauer, G. (1986). Globaloney. *American Spectator, 19* (5), 150–152.

Finney, S., & Orr, J. (1995). "I've really learned a lot, but..." Cross-cultural understanding and teacher education in a racist society. *Journal of Teacher Education, 46,* 327–333.

Florensky P. U. (1990). *U Vodorazdelov Mysli. On the watersheds of thought,* vol. 2. Moscow, Russia: Pravda.

Florida Advisory Council on Global Education (1981). *State plan for global education in Florida: Findings and recommendations.* Tallahassee, FL.

Florida International University (2008). Retrieved April 14, 2008, from www.fiu.edu/~globprog/

Ford, T. L., & Dillard, C. B. (1996). Becoming multicultural: A recursive process of self- and social construction. *Theory into Practice, 35 (4),* 232–238.

Foster, M. (1997). *Black teachers on teaching.* New York: New Press.

Foucault, M. (1980). *Power/knowledge: Selected interviews and other writings.* New York: Pantheon.

Franklin, U. (2006a). Stormy weather: Reflections on violence as an environment. In *The Ursula Franklin reader: Pacifism as a map* (pp. 257–262). Toronto: Between the Lines.

Franklin, U. (2006b). What of the citizen? In *The Ursula Franklin reader: Pacifism as a map* (pp. 87–99). Toronto: Between the Lines.

Freeman, R. (1986). The Bay Area global education project. In R. E. Freeman (Ed.), *Promising practices in global education: A handbook with case studies* (pp. 77–84). New York: National Council on Foreign Language and International Studies.Freire, P. (1970). *Pedagogy of the oppressed.* New York: Seabury Press.

Freire, P. (1995). *Pedagogy of hope.* New York: Continuum.

Freire, P. (1998). *Pedagogy of freedom: Ethics, democracy, and civic courage.* Lanham, MD: Rowman & Littlefield.

French Rights of Man and of the Citizen (1789). *Declaration des Droits de l'Homme et du Citoyen*. National Assembly of France, August 26. Retrieved September 8, 2008, from the Declaration of the Rights of Man and of the Citizen Website http://www.constitution.org/fr/fr_drm.htm

Friedman, T. L. (1999). *The Lexus and the olive tree: Understanding globalization*. New York: Farrar, Straus, and Giroux.

Friedman, T. L. (2005). *The world is flat: A brief history of the 21st century*. New York: Farrar, Straus, and Giroux.

Fullan, M. (2000). The three stories of educational reform. *Phi Delta Kappan, 81,* 581–584.

Fuller, R. B. (1970). *Operating manual for spaceship earth*. New York: Pocket Books.

Galtung, J. (1969). Violence, peace, and peace research. *Journal of Peace Research, 3,* 167–192.

Galtung, J. (1996). *Peace by peaceful means: Peace and conflict, development, & civilization*. London: Sage.

Garcia, D. (1985, 1990). Global profile. *Global Awareness Newsletter, 1* (2), 2 & 10 (2) 3.

Gardner, H. (2006). *Five minds for the future*. Cambridge, MA: Harvard Business School Press.

Gates, H. L. (Ed). (1986). *Race, writing and difference*. Chicago: University of Chicago Press.

Gaudelli, W. (2003). *World class: Teaching and learning in global times*. Mahwah, NJ: Lawrence Erlbaum.

Gaudelli, W. (2006). Convergence of technology and diversity: Experiences of two beginning teachers in web-based distance learning for global/multicultural education. *Teacher Education Quarterly, 26* (1), 97–116.

Gaudelli, W., & Heilman, E. (2009). Reconceptualizing geography as democratic global citizenship education. *Teachers College Record, 111* (11).

Gay, G. (2000). *Culturally responsive teaching: Theory, research, and practice*. New York: Teachers College Press.

Germaine, M. H. (1998). *Worldly teachers: Cultural learning and pedagogy*. Westport, CT: Bergin & Garvey.

Gilliom, E. (1993). Mobilizing teacher educators to support global education in pre-service programs. *Theory into Practice, 32* (1), 40–47.

Gilman, S. L. (1985). Black bodies, white bodies: Towards an iconography of female sexuality in late nineteenth-century art, medicine, and literature. *Critical Inquiry, 12* (1), 204–242.

Gilroy, P. (1993). *The black Atlantic: Modernity and double consciousness*. Cambridge, MA: Harvard University Press.

Gioseffi, D. (Ed.). (1993). *On prejudice: A global perspective*. New York: Doubleday.Giroux, H. A. (1997). *Pedagogy and the politics of hope: Theory, culture, and schooling*. Boulder, CO: Westview Press.

Giroux, H. A. (2004). Teachers as transformative intellectuals. In A. S. Canestrari & B. Marlowe (Eds.), *Educational foundations: An anthology of critical readings*. London: Sage.

Gochenour, T. (Ed.). (1993). *Beyond experience: The experiential approach to cross-cultural education*. Yarmouth, ME: Intercultural Press.

Goldstein, E. (2000). *What citizens need to know about world affairs*. Boca Raton, FL: Social Issues Resources.

Gomez, M. L. (1996). Telling stories of our teaching, reflecting on our practices. *Action in Teacher Education, 18* (3), 1–12.

Grant, C. A. (Ed.). (1992). *Research and multicultural education: From the margins to the mainstream*. London: Falmer Press.

Grant, C. A., & Agosto, V. (2008). Teacher capacity and social justice in teacher education. In M. Cochran-Smith, S. Feiman-Nemser, & D. McIntyre (Eds.), *Handbook of research on teacher education: Enduring questions in changing contexts* (pp. 175–200). New York: Routledge.

Greenberg, H. (2008). Personal communication. February 27.

Grellet, S. (1773-1855). Ouoted in G. Benham (Ed.) (1924), *Benham's book of quotations, proverbs, and household words*. London: Ward, Lock & Co.

Grossman, P. (2005). Research on pedagogical approaches in teacher education. In M. Cochran-Smith & K. M. Zeichner (Eds.), *Studying teacher education: The report of the AERA panel on research and teacher education*. Mahwah, NJ: Lawrence Erlbaum.

Gur-Ze'ev, I. (2001). Philosophy of peace education in a postmodern era. *Educational Theory, 51* (3), 315–336.

Gutek, G. (1993). *American education in a global society: Internationalizing teacher education*. New York: Longman.

Gutmann, A. (1993). The challenge of multiculturalism in political ethics. *Philosophy and Public Affairs, 22* (3), 171–206.

Gutmann, A. (2003). *Identity and democracy*. Princeton, NJ: Princeton University Press.

Hall, E. (1959). *The silent language*. Garden City, NY: Doubleday.

Hall, E. (1976). *Beyond culture*. Garden City, NY: Anchor.

Hammond, D., & Jablow, A. (1992). *The Africa that never was: Four centuries of British writing about Africa*. Prospect Heights, IL: Waveland Press.

Hanvey, R. (1976). *An attainable global perspective*. Denver: Center for Teaching International Relations.

Harcourt, W. (1999). *Women@internet: Creating new cultures in cyberspace*. London: Zed Books.

Harding, S. (1998). *Is science multicultural? Postcolonialisms, feminisms and epistemologies*. Bloomington: Indiana University Press.

Heater, D. (1984). *Peace through education*. London: Falmer Press.

Heilman, E. (2005). Towards a eutopic critical pedagogy honoring identity and practice. In I. Gur Ze'v (Ed). *Re-imagining critical pedagogy and critical theory*. New York: Kluwer.

Heilman, E. (2006). Critical, liberal, and poststructural challenges for global education. In A. Segall, E. E. Heilman, & C. H. Cherryholmes (Eds.), *Social studies: The next generation* (pp. 171–208). New York: Peter Lang.

Heilman, E. (2007). (Dis)Locating imaginative and ethical aims of global education. In K. Roth & I. Gur-Ze'ev (Eds.) *Education in the era of globalization* (pp. 83–104). The Netherlands; Amsterdam: Springer.

Heilman, E., & Gaudelli, W. (2007). *We're all global now: A contested typology of global education's terrain*. Paper presented at the College and University Faculty Association of the National Council for Social Studies, November 29, 2007, San Diego, CA.

Henderson, J. G. & Hawthorne, R. D. (2000). *Transformative curriculum leadership*. (2nd ed.), Upper Saddle River, NY: Merrill/Prentice Hall.

Henry, A. (1998). *Taking back control: African Canadian women teachers' lives and practice*. Albany: State University of New York Press.

Henry, N. (Ed.). (1959). *Community education: Principles & practices from worldwide experience*, part 1. Chicago: National Society for the Study of Education.

Hess, D., & Posselt, J. (2002). How high school students experience and learn from the discussion of controversial public issues. *Journal of Curriculum and Supervision, 17* (4), 283–314.

Hett, E. J. (1993). *The development of an instrument to measure global-mindedness*. Dissertation. San Diego, CA: University of San Diego.

Heyl, J., & McCarthy, J. (2003, January 24). *International education and teacher preparation in the U.S.* Paper presented at the conference, Global Challenges and U.S. Higher Education National Needs and Policy Implications, Duke University. Retrieved March 17, 2008, from http://www.jhfc.duke.edu/ducis/lobalchallenges/df/heyl_ aper.pdf

Hicks, D. (2003). Thirty years of global education: A reminder of key principles and precedents. *Educational Review, 55* (3), 265–275.

Hicks, D., & Townley, C. (Eds.). (1982). *Teaching world studies: An introduction to global perspectives in the curriculum*. Harlow, UK: Longman.

Hoffman, D. M. (1996). Culture and self in multicultural education: Reflections on discourse, text, and practice. *American Educational Research Journal, 33* (4), 545–569.

Holden, C., & Hicks, D. (2007). Making global connections: The knowledge, understanding and motivation of trainee teachers. *Teaching & Teacher Education, 23* (1), 13–23.

Huntington, S. P. (1998). *The clash of civilizations and remaking of the world order*. New York: Touchstone Books.

Hursh, H. (2008). Personal communication. March 13.

Huxley T. (1868, 1952). A liberal education. Speech given at the 1868 Working Men's College. In R. B. Inglis, D. A. Stauffer, & C. E. Larsen (Eds.), *Adventures in English literature* (pp. 464–467). Canada: W. J. Gage.

Ibrahim, T. (2005). Global citizenship education: Mainstreaming the curriculum? *Cambridge Journal of Education, 35* (2), 177–194.

International Studies School Association (2008). Retrieved March 10, 2008, from http://www.du.edu/issa/

Istomin, K. (2004). *Domostroi (Foundation of a home)*. Moscow: M. Drofa Drevnerusskaya Literatura (pp. 394–413).

Jackson, V. A., Palepu, A., Szalacha, L., Caswell, C., Carr, P. L., & Inui, T. (2003). Having the right chemistry: A qualitative study of mentoring in academic medicine. *Academic Medicine, 78*, 328–334.

Johnson, W. B. (2002). The intentional mentor: Strategies and guidelines for the practice of mentoring. *Professional Psychology: Research and Practice, 33* (1), 88–96.

Johnson, W. B. (2007). Student-faculty mentorship outcomes. In T. D. Allen & L. T. Eby (Eds.), *The Blackwell handbook of mentoring: A multiple perspective approach* (pp. 189–210). Malden, MA: Blackwell.

Johnson, W. B., & Huwe, J. (2003). *Getting mentored in graduate school*. Washington, DC: American Psychological Association.

Johnson, W. B., & Ridley, C. R. (2004). *The elements of mentoring*. New York: Palgrave Macmillan.

Johnston, M., & Ochoa, A. (1993). Teacher education for global perspectives: A research agenda. *Theory into Practice, 32 (1)*, 64–68.

Kagan, S., & Stewart, V. (2004). International education in the schools: The state of the field. *Phi Delta Kappan*, 86 (3), 229–235.

Kahne, J., & Westheimer, J. (1996). In service of what? The politics of service learning. *Phi Delta Kappan, 77*, 592–598.

Kambutu, J., & Nganga, L. (2008). In these uncertain times: Educators build cultural awareness through planned international experiences. *Teaching and Teacher Education, 24*, 939–995.

Kaplan, R. (2000). *The coming anarchy*. New York: Random House.

Karsten, S., Cogan, J., Grossman, D., Liu, M., & Pitiyanuwat, S. (2002). Citizenship education and the preparation of future teachers: A study. *Asia-Pacific Education Review, 3* (2), 168–183.

Kelly, G. A. (1955). *The psychology of personal constructs*. New York: W. W. Norton.

Kennedy, P. M. (1987). *The rise and fall of the great powers: Economic and military conflict from 1500 to 2000*. New York: Random House.

Kern, R. (2000). *Literacy and language teaching*. Oxford: Oxford University Press.

Kersten, K. (1988). *The radicalization of Minnesota's public school curriculum: The case of Central America*. Minneapolis: Minnesota Association of Scholars.

Khanna, P. (January 27, 2008). Waving goodbye to hegemony. *New York Times Magazine*. Retrieved January 27, 2008, from http://www.nytimes.com/2008/0127/magazine/27worldt.html?r=1&scp=1&sq=Waving+Goodbye+to+Hegemony&st=ny&oref=slogin

Khasan, B. (2007). Personal communications. May 8. Russia: North Caucasus region: Nal'chik.

Kiesler, S. (1997). *Culture of the Internet*. Mahwah, NJ: Lawrence Erlbaum.

King, D., Branson, M., & Condon, L. (1976). Education for a world of change: A working handbook for global perspectives. *Intercom 84/85*. New York: Global Perspectives in Education.

Kirkwood, T. F. (1987). *A content analysis of 45 elementary schools according to the Hanvey conceptual framework*. Unpublished manuscript. Miami: Florida International University.

Kirkwood, T. F. (1989). *Global education at Miami Sunset Senior High School: A case study*. Unpublished manuscript. Miami: Florida International University.

Kirkwood, T. F. (1990). Around the world at Miami High. In K. A. Tye (Ed.), *Global Education: School-based Strategies* (pp. 109–116). Orange County, CA: Independence Press.

Kirkwood, T. F. (1991). Global education as a change agent. In K. A. Tye (Ed.), *Global education: From thought to action* (pp. 142–156). Alexandria, VA. Association for Supervision and Curriculum Development.

Kirkwood, T. F. (1992). *The global perspective in middle schools: Madison and Westview*. Unpublished manuscript. Miami: Florida International University.

Kirkwood T. F. (1995). Teaching from a global perspective: A case study of three high school social studies teachers. Miami, Florida: Florida International University. *Dissertation Abstracts International,* 56 (12). 4851 University microfilms No. ADD 9610888.

Kirkwood, T. F. (1996). Japan studies at W. H. Turner Technical Arts High School Miami, Florida. *Global Connection.* DePere, WI: Association for Supervision and Curriculum Development Global Education Network.

Kirkwood, T. F. (2001a). Our global age requires global education: Clarifying definitional ambiguities. *Social Studies,* 92 (1), 10–16.

Kirkwood, T. F. (2001b, May/June). Building bridges: Miami "ambassadors" visit Russia. *Social Education, 65* (4), 236–239.

Kirkwood, T. F., & Tucker, J. L. (2001). Global education in Russia: Catalyst in the Russian education reform movement. *International Social Studies Forum, 1* (1), 63–75.

Kirkwood-Tucker, T. F. (1998). A tribute to Jan Tucker. In L. Swartz, L. Warner, & D. L. Grossman (Eds.), *Intersections: A professional development project in multi-cultural and global education* (pp. 193–208). Boston: Children's Museum.

Kirkwood-Tucker, T. F. (2002). Teaching about Japan: Global perspectives in teacher decision-making, context, and practice. *Theory and Research in Social Education, 30* (1), 88–115.

Kirkwood-Tucker, T. F. (2003). Global pedagogy in teacher education: Shifting the focus from a curriculum of national citizenship to a curriculum for world-centered citizenship. *World Studies in Education, 4* (2), 91–107. London: James Nicholas.

Kirkwood-Tucker, T. F. (2004). Empowering teachers to create a more peaceful world through global education: Simulating the United Nations. *Theory and Research in Social Education, 32* (1), 56–74.

Kirkwood–Tucker, T. F. (2008). Personal communication. May 18.

Kirkwood-Tucker, T. F., & Goldstein, E. (2007a). *Father of global education: Jim Becker.* Delray Beach, FL: Elliot and Eleanor Goldstein (EGEG) Foundation.

Kirkwood-Tucker, T. F., & Goldstein, E. (2007b). *Pioneers of global education: Charlotte and Lee Anderson.* Delray Beach, FL: Elliot and Eleanor Goldstein (EGEG) Foundation.

Kirkwood-Tucker, T. F., & Morris, J. D. (in review). Will teachers of the twenty-first century embrace the world? The worldmindedness of undergraduate elementary and secondary social studies teacher candidates at five Florida public universities. *Theory and Research in Social Education.*

Kirp, D. L. (1991). Textbooks and tribalism in California. *Public Interest, 104,* 20–36.

Kissock, C. (2002). *An international perspective: Professionalization through globalization* [PDF document]. Retrieved March 20, 2008, from Committee on Global and International Teacher Education (AACTE) Website: http://www.jhfc.duke.edu/ducis/globalchallenges/pdf/kissock.pdf

Kniep, W. (1986). Defining a global education by its content. *Social Education, 50* (6), 437–466.

Kniep, W. (1987). *Next steps in global education: A handbook for curriculum development.* New York: Global Perspectives in Education.

Kniep, W. (1989). Essentials for a global education. *ATA Magazine,* May–June.

Kniep, W. (1994). *Elements of the educational blue-print: Education 2000.* Paper presented at the international conference: Setting Educational Standards as a Basis for Curricula Development. Ryazan, Russia.

Kniep, W. (1996). *The Russian global school initiative.* Paper presented at the Russian Seminar for Global Educators. St. Petersburg, Russia.

Koro-Ljungberg, M., & Hayes, S. (2006). The relational selves of female graduate students during academic mentoring: From dialogue to transformation. *Mentoring & Tutoring, 14* (4), 389–407.

Kozol, J. (1991). *Savage inequalities.* New York: Crown.

Kram, K. E. (1985). *Mentoring at work: Developmental relations in organizational life.* Glenview, IL: Scott and Foresman.

Kramsch, C., & Thorne, S. L. (2002). Foreign language learning as global communicative practice. In D. Block & C. Cameron (Eds.), *Globalization and language teaching* (pp. 83–100). London: Routledge.

Kubow, P. (1995). *Reconceptualizing citizenship education for the 21st century: A study of postbaccalaureate social studies students from Canada, England and the United States.* Unpublished doctoral dissertation, University of Minnesota, Minneapolis.

Kubow, P. (1999). Preparing future secondary teachers for citizenship educators' roles: A possible direction for preservice education in the new century. *Asia-Pacific Journal of Teacher Education and Development, 2* (2), 53–64.

Kuechle, J., O'Brien, B., & Ferguson, P. (1995). A collaborative student teaching program in Australia, New Zealand, and the United States. *Action in Teacher Education, 17,* 36–39.

Kuliutkin, Y. (1995). *Myshleniye i lichnost (Thinking and personality).* St. Petersburg: Christmas, 1995.

Kűng, H. (1991). *Global responsibility: In search of a new world ethic.* London: SCM Press.

Ladd, S. (1985). Interview. *Global Awareness Newsletter, 1:2* (Spring).

Ladson-Billings, G. (1994). *The dreamkeepers: Successful teachers of African American children.* San Francisco: Jossey-Bass.

Lamas, J. I. (2008). Personal communication. May 12.

Lambert, R. (1989). *International studies and the undergraduate.* Washington, DC: American Council on Education.

Lamy, S. L. (1989). Defining global education. In S. L. Lamy (Ed.), Global perspectives in education. *Educational Research Quarterly, 8* (1), 9–20.

Lamy, S. L. (1991). A conflict of images: The controversy over global education in U.S. schools. In K. Tye (Ed.), *Global education: From thought to action* (pp. 49–63). Alexandria, VA: Association of Supervision and Curriculum Development.

League of Nations (2008). Retrieved April 14, 2008, from http://en.wikepedia.org//wiki/Model_United_Nations

Leetsma, R. (1979). Looking ahead: An agenda for action. In J. M. Becker (Ed.), *Schooling for a global age* (pp. 233–243). New York: McGraw-Hill.

Leming, J. L., Ellington, L., &. Porter-Magee, K. (Eds.). (2003). *Where did social studies go wrong?* Washington, DC: Thomas B. Fordham Foundation.

Lentz, E., & Allen, T. D. (2007). Reflections on naturally occurring mentoring relationships. In T. D. Allen & L. T. Eby (Eds.), *The Blackwell handbook of mentoring: A multiple perspectives approach* (pp. 159–162). Malden, MA: Blackwell.

Levinson, D. J., Darrow, C. N., Klein, E. B., Levinson, M. A., & McKee, B. (1978). *The seasons of a man's life*. New York: Alfred A. Knopf.

Lewis, P. (2000). Panel discussant. *Globalization and education*. Board of Trustees Meeting, American Forum for Global Education, December 6.

Liferov, A. (1994). Philosophiyu i praktiku globalnogo obrazovaniya–rossiiskoi shkole. (The philosophy and practice of global education for Russian schools). In *Teoriya i praktika globalnogo obrazovaniya (In theory and practice of global education)* (pp. 59–65, 73–83). Ryazan, Russia: Ryazan State Pedagogical University.

Lister, I. (1987). Global and international approaches in political education. In C. Harber (Ed.), *Political education in Britain* (pp. 47–62). London: Falmer Press.

Lockwood, A. L., Evans, Carr, S., & Eby, L. T. (2007). Reflections on the benefits of mentoring. In T. D. Allen & L. T. Eby (Eds.), *The Blackwell handbook of mentoring: A multiple perspectives approach* (pp. 233–236). Malden, MA: Blackwell.

Long, J. (1997). The dark side of mentoring. *Australian Educational Research, 24*, 115–123.

Lonzetta, M. (1983). The World Affairs Council of Philadelphia: Pre-collegiate education. In R. E. Freeman (Ed.), *Promising practices in global education: A handbook with case studies* (pp. 53–58). New York: National Council on Foreign Language and International Studies.

Lubeck, D. (2008). Personal communication. April 20.

Lysenko, V. (1994). Philosophiyu i praktiku globalnogo obrazovaniya–rossiiskoi shkole (The philosophy and practice of global education for Russian schools). In *Teoriya i praktika globalnogo obrazovaniya. (In Theory and practice of global education).* (pp. 66–72). Ryazan: Ryazan State Pedagogical University.

Macy, J. R. (1983). *Despair and personal power in the nuclear age*. Gabriola, BC: New Society.

Magna Carta (1215/1297). Retrieved September 13, 2008, from UK Statute Law Database Website: http://www.statutelaw.gov.uk/legResults.aspx?LegType=All+ Legislation&title=magna+carta&searchEnacted=0&extentMatchOnly=0&confersPow er=0&blanketAmendment=0&TYPE=QS&NavFrom=0&activeTextDocId=1517519 &PageNumber=1&SortAlpha=0

Mahan, J., & Stachowski, L. (1990). New horizons: Student teaching abroad to enrich understanding of diversity. *Action in Teacher Education, 12* (3), 13–21.

Mahon, J., & Cushner, K. (2002). Overseas student teaching: Affecting personal, professional, and global competencies in an age of globalization. *Journal of Studies in International Education, 6* (1), 44–59.

Mahon, J., & Cushner, K. (2007). The impact of overseas student teaching on personal and professional development. In K. Cushner & S. Brennan (Eds.), *Intercultural student teaching: A bridge to global competence* (pp. 57–87). Lanham, MD: Rowman & Littlefield.

Marshall, H., & Arnot, M. (2008). Globalizing the school curriculum: Gender, EFA, and global citizenship education: RECOUP Working Paper No. 17. *Research Consortium on educational outcomes and poverty.* Retrieved July 16, 2008, from http://recoup.educ.cam.ac.uk/publications/WP17-MA.pdf

Marshall, T. H. (1950). *Citizenship and social class*. Cambridge: Cambridge University Press.

Martin, H., & Schumann, H. (1997). *The global trap: Globalization and the assault on democracy and prosperity.* London: Zed Books.

Massachusetts Geographic Alliance (2008). Retrieved April 22, 2008, from http://www.massgeo.org/

Matiushkin A. M. (1987). Teoreticheskie voprosy problemnogo obucheniia (Theoretical aspects of problem-based education). *Khrestomatiia po psikhologii (Reader in psychology)* (pp. 395–401). Moscow: Prosveshchenie.

Mayer, V. J. (1997). Earth systems education: A case study of a globally oriented science education program. In M. Merryfield, E. Jarchow, & S. Pickert (Eds.), *Preparing teachers to teach global perspectives: A handbook for teacher education* (pp. 25–54). Thousand Oaks, CA: Corwin Press.

McCarthy, C. (1990). Rethinking liberal and radical perspectives on racial inequality in schooling: Making the case for nonsynchrony. In N. M. Hidalgo, C. L. McDowell, & E. V. Siddle (Eds.), *Facing racism in education* (pp. 35–49). Cambridge, MA: Harvard Educational Review.

McCarthy, C. (1995). The problems with origins: Race and the contrapuntal nature of the educational experience. In C. E. Sleeter & P. L. McClaren (Eds.), *Multicultural education, critical pedagogy and the politics of difference* (pp. 245–268). Albany: State University of New York Press.

McCarthy, C. (1998). *The uses of culture: Education and the limits of ethnic affiliation.* New York: Routledge.

McCarthy, C., & Crichlow, W. (Eds.). (1993). *Race identity and representation in education.* New York: Routledge.

McDonnell, K. (2005). *Honey, we lost the kids: Rethinking childhood in the multimedia age.* Toronto: Second Story Press.

McDougal, M., Lasswell, H., & Chen, L. C. (1980). *Human rights and world public order.* New Haven: Yale University Press.

McFadden, J., Merryfield, M., & Barron, K. (1997). *Multicultural and global/ international education: Guidelines for programs in teacher education.* Washington, DC: American Association of Colleges of Teacher Education.

McLaren, P. (1998). Revolutionary pedagogy in post-revolutionary times: Rethinking the political economy of critical education. *Educational Theory, 48* (4), 431–463.

McLaren, P. (Ed.). (2006). *Rage and hope: Interviews with Peter McLaren on war, imperialism & critical pedagogy.* New York: Peter Lang.

McLaughlin, M. W. (1997). Implementation as mutual adaptation: Change in classroom organization. In D. J. Flinders & S. J. Thornton (Eds.), *The curriculum studies reader* (pp. 167–177). New York: Routledge.

McLuhan, M. (1964). *Understanding media: The extensions of man.* New York: McGraw-Hill.

Meadows, D. H., Meadows, D. L., Randers, J., & Behrens, W., III. (1972). *The limits to growth: A report for the Club of Rome's project on the predicament of mankind.* New York: Universe Books.

Mehlinger H. D. (1995). *School reform in the information age.* Center for excellence in education. Bloomington: Indiana University Press.

Meier, D. (1995). *The power of their ideas: Lessons for America from a small school in Harlem.* Boston: Beacon Press.

Mendeleyev, D. (1991). *Granits Posnaniyu predvitet nevosmozhno. (No boundaries to cognition)* (p. 408). Moscow: Sovetskaya Rossiya.

Mercator, H. J. (1636/1986). *Atlas or a geographic description of the world: Facsimile edition in two volumes.* Amsterdam: Theatrum Orbis Terrarium.

Merelman, R. (1990). The role of conflict in children's political learning. In O. Ichilov (Ed.), *Political socialization, citizenship education, and democracy* (pp. 47–65). New York: Teachers College Press.

Merryfield, M. M. (1986). *Teaching about Africa.* ERIC Digest. Bloomington, IN: Social Studies Development Center.

Merryfield, M. M. (Ed.). (1989). *Lessons from Africa.* Bloomington, IN: ERIC and the Social Studies Development Center.

Merryfield, M. M. (1991). Preparing American secondary social studies teachers to teach with a global perspective: A status report. *Journal of Teacher Education, 42* (1), 11–20.

Merryfield, M. M. (1992). Preparing social studies teachers for the twenty-first century: Perspectives on program effectiveness from a study of six exemplary teacher education programs in global education. *Theory and Research in Social Education, 20* (1), 17–46.

Merryfield, M. M. (1993). Reflective practice in teacher education in global perspectives: Strategies for teacher educators. *Theory into Practice, 32* (1), 27–32.

Merryfield, M. M. (1995). Institutionalizing cross-cultural experiences and international expertise in teacher education: The development and potential of a global education PDS network. *Journal of Teacher Education, 46,* 1–9.

Merryfield, M. M. (1996). *Making connections between multicultural and global education: Teacher educators and teacher education programs.* Columbus, OH: Mershon Center.

Merryfield, M. M. (1997). A framework for teacher education in global perspectives. In M. M. Merryfield, E. Jarchow, & S. Pickert (Eds.), *Preparing teachers to teach global perspectives: A handbook for teacher education* (pp. 1–24). Thousand Oaks, CA: Corwin Press.

Merryfield, M. M. (1998). Pedagogy for global perspectives in education: Studies of teachers' thinking and practice. *Theory and Research in Social Education, 26* (3), 342–379.

Merryfield, M. M. (2000a). Using electronic technologies to promote equity and cultural diversity in social studies and global education. *Theory and Research in Social Education, 28,* 502–526.

Merryfield, M. M. (2000b). Why aren't teachers being prepared to teach for diversity, equity, and global interconnectedness? A study of lived experiences in the making of multicultural and global educators. *Teaching and Teaching Education, 16* (4), 429–443.

Merryfield, M. M. (2001). *Learning about Africa through African eyes: When teachers and students challenge European and American constructions of Africa and Africans.* Paper presented at the annual meeting of the American Educational Research Association, April, Seattle.

Merryfield, M. M. (2006). Citizens of the world? Thoughts about cosmopolitanism. In *GlobalTeachNet.* May–June. Retrieved May 18, 2008, from http://www.rpcv.org/GTNMayJun06.pdf

Merryfield, M. M. (2007). The web and teachers' decision-making in global education. *Theory and Research in Social Education, 35* (2), 256–276.

Merryfield, M. M. (2008a). Retrieved April 20, 2008, from www.coe.ohiostate.edu/merryfield/global_resources/default.htm

Merryfield, M. M. (2008b). Personal communication. February 21.

Merryfield, M. M., Jarchow, E., & Pickert, S. (Eds.). (1997). *Preparing teachers to teach global perspectives: A handbook for teacher educators.* Thousand Oaks, CA: Corwin Press.

Metropolitan Miami Report (2005). Miami-Dade County statistical report.

Mertz, N. T. (2004). What's a mentor, anyway? *Educational Administration Quarterly, 40* (4), 541–560.

Metz, M. H. (1978). *Classrooms and corridors.* Berkeley: University of California Press.

Meyer, B., & Geschiere, P. (Eds.). (1999). *Globalization and identity.* Oxford: Blackwell.

Meyerson, D. E. (2003). *Tempered radicals: How everyday leaders inspire change at work.* Boston: Harvard Business School Press.

Miami-Dade County Public Schools (1989). *Dade-County Public Schools system goals.* Miami, FL: Office of the Superintendent of Schools.

Miami-Dade County Public Schools Statistical Highlights for 1984–1985. Office of Public Information. Miami, FL.

Miami-Dade Public Schools Statistical Highlights for 1993–1994. Office of Public Information. Miami, FL.

Miami-Dade Public Schools Statistical Highlights for 2007–2008. Office of Public Information. Miami, FL. http://drs.dadeschools.net/Highlights/Highlights_2007-08.pdf

Michaels, W. B. (1995). *Our America: Nativism, modernism, and pluralism.* Durham, NC: Duke University Press.

Mill, J. S. (1869). *On liberty.* Retrieved September 19, 2007, from http://www.bartleby.com/130/2.html

Model United Nations (2008). League of Nations. Retrieved April 14, 2008, from http://en.wikipedia.org/wiki/Model_United_Nations.

Morris, D. (1977). Global education in elementary schools: Implications for curriculum and instruction. *Social Education, 41* (1), 38–40, 45.

Murray, M., & Owen, M. A. (1991). *Beyond the myth and magic of mentoring: How to facilitate and effective mentoring program.* San Francisco, CA: Jossey-Bass.

Narayan, U. (1988). Working together across difference: Some considerations on emotions and political practice. *Hypatia, 3 (2),* 31–47.

Nash, G. B., Crabtree, C., & Dunn, R. E. (1997). *History on trial: Culture wars and the teaching of the past.* New York: Alfred A. Knopf.

National Commission on Excellence in Education (1983). *A nation at risk.* Washington, DC: Government Printing Office. National Council for the Accreditation of Teacher Education (NCATE) (2008). *Professional standards for the accreditation of teacher preparation institutions.* Washington, DC: National Council for Accreditation of Teacher Education.

National Governors' Association (1989). *America in transition: The international frontier.* Washington, DC: National Governors' Association.

National Task Force on Education and the World View (1981). *Task force statement on education and the world view.* New Rochelle, NY: Council on Learning.Neumann,

A. (1998). On experience, memory, and knowing: A post-holocaust (auto) biography. *Curriculum Inquiry, 28,* 425–442.

Newbold, M. P. (2008). Personal communication. June 16.

Ngugi wa Thiong'o (1986). *Decolonizing the mind.* London: Heinemann.

Ngugi wa Thiong'o (1993). *Moving the centre: The struggle for cultural freedom.* London: James Curry.

Nickel, J. W. (2006). *Making sense of human rights* (2nd ed.). Malden, MA: Blackwell.

Nieto, S. (1992). *Affirming diversity: The sociopolitical context of multicultural education.* New York: Longman.

Noddings, N. (1984). *Caring: A feminist approach to ethics and moral education.* Berkeley: University of California Press.

Noddings, N. (2002). *Starting at home: Caring and social policy.* Berkeley: University of California Press.

Nussbaum, M. (1997). *Cultivating humanity: A classical defense of reform in liberal education.* Cambridge, MA: Harvard University Press.

Nussbaum, M. (2000). *Women and human development.* Cambridge: Cambridge University Press.

Nussbaum, M. (2002). Patriotism and cosmopolitanism. In M. C. Nussbaum & J. Cohen (Eds.), *For love of country: Debating the limits of patriotism* (pp. 2–17). Boston: Beacon Press.

Nye, J. F. (2001). Globalization's democratic deficit. *Foreign Affairs,* 16-24.Ochoa, A. S. (1986). Internationalizing teacher education. In R. E. Freeman (Ed.), *Promising practices in global education: A handbook with case studies* (pp. 46–52). New York: National Council on Foreign Language and International Studies.

Oliva, P. F. (2005). *Developing the curriculum* (6th ed.). Boston, MA: Pearson Education.

Olsen, L. (1997). *Made in America: Immigrant students in our public schools.* New York: New Press.

Omi, M., & Winant, H. (1993). On the theoretical status of the concept of race. In C. McCarthy & W. Crichlow (Eds.), *Race, identity and representation in education* (pp. 3–10). New York: Routledge.

O'Neil, J. M. (1989, January). Global education: Controversy remains, but support growing. *ASCD Curriculum Update.* American Association for Curriculum Development (ASCD): Alexandria, VA.

O'Neil, J. M., & Wrightsman, L. S. (2001). The mentoring relationship in psychology training programs. In S. Walfish & A. K. Hess (Eds.), *Succeeding in graduate school a career guide for psychology students* (pp. 111–128). Mahwah, NJ: Lawrence Erlbaum.

Osler, A., & Starkey, H. (2005). *Changing citizenship: Democracy and inclusion in education.* New York: Open University Press.

Osler, A., & Vincent, K. (2002). *Citizenship and the challenge of global education.* Stoke-on-Trent: Trentham Books.

Osunde, E., Tlou, J., & Brown, N. (1996). Persisting and common stereotypes in U.S. students' knowledge of Africa: A study of preservice social studies teachers. *Social Studies, 87* (3), 119–124.

Paige, R. M. (Ed.). (1993). *Education for the intercultural experience.* Maine: Intercultural Press.

Paige, R. M., & Cogan, J. (2002). Teacher's perceptions of citizen characteristics and environmental concerns in Minnesota, Hong Kong, and Guangdong: A comparative study. *Pacific-Asian Education, 14* (2), 17–35.

Parker, W. C., & Camicia, S. (2007, November). *The new "international education" movement in U.S. schools: Contestation and continuity.* Paper presented at the annual meeting of the College and University Faculty Assembly, National Council for the Social Studies, San Diego, CA.

Parker, W. C., Ninomiya, A., & Cogan, J. J. (1999). Educating world citizens: Toward multinational curriculum development. *American Educational Research Journal, 36* (2), 117–145.

Parry, B. (1987). Problems in current theories of colonial discourse. *Oxford Literary Review, 9* (1 & 2), 27–58.

Partnership for 21st Century Skills (2008). *Our mission.* Retrieved March 21, 2008, from http://www.21stcenturyskills.org.

Pearson, E. (1993). *Global education progress and concerns in the South Area of the Miami-Dade Public Schools.* Speech delivered at the Global Awareness Program Advisory Board meetings, May 2. Miami: Florida International University.

Pence, H., & Macgillivray, I. K. (2008). The impact of an international field experience on preservice teachers. *Teaching and Teacher Education, 24,* 14–25.

Pew Research Center (2003). *Views of a changing world: How global publics view war in Iraq democracy, Islam and governance, and globalization.* Washington, DC: Author.

Pike, G. (2000). Global education and national identity: In pursuit of meaning. *Theory into Practice, 39* (2), 64–73.

Pike, G., & Selby, D. (1995). *Reconnecting from national to global curriculum.* Toronto: International Institute for Global Education, University of Toronto.

Powell, R. R., Zehm, S., & Garcia, J. (1996). *Field experience:* Strategies *for exploring diversity in schools.* Englewood Cliffs, NJ: Prentice Hall.

Powers, M. (2008). Personal communication. June 2.

Pratt, M. L. (1992). *Imperial eyes: Travel writing and transculturation.* London: Routledge.

Pratt, M. L. (1996). Me llamo Rigoberta Menchu: Autoethnography and the recoding of citizenship. In A. Carey-Webb & S. Benz (Eds.), *Teaching and testimony: Rigoberta Menchu and the North American classroom* (pp. 57–72). Albany: State University of New York Press.

Pushkin, A. (1983). *The dead princess and seven knights.* Moscow, Russia: Raduga.

Quezada, R., & Alfaro, C. (2007a). Biliteracy teachers' self reflections of their accounts while student teaching abroad: Speaking from "the other side." *Teacher Education Quarterly, 43* (1), 95–113.

Quezada, R., & Alfaro, C. (2007b). Developing biliteracy teachers: Moving toward cultural and linguistic global competence in teacher education. In K. Cushner & S. Brennan (Eds.), *Intercultural student teaching: A bridge to global competence* (pp. 123–158). Lanham, MD: Rowman & Littlefield.

Quezada, R., & Cordeiro, P. (2007). Guest editors' introduction: Internationalizing schools and colleges of education educating teachers for global awareness. *Teacher Education Quarterly, 34* (1), 3–7.

Rabasa, J. (1993). *Inventing A-M-E-R-I-C-A: Spanish historiography and the formation of ethnocentrism.* Norman: University of Oklahoma Press.

REACH Program (2008). Retrieved August 25, 2008, from www.reachctr.org

Reardon, B. A. (1995). *Educating for human dignity: Learning about rights and responsibilities.* Philadelphia: University of Pennsylvania.

Reischauer, E. O. (1973). *Toward the 21st century: Education for a changing world.* New York: Vintage.

Renn, K., & Lucas, J. (2007). *Internationalizing the student experience: A working group report.* Retrieved September 19, 2007, from http://undergrad.msu.edu/documents/ InternationalizingtheStudentExperienceWorkingGroupReport.pdf

Richardson, R. (1976). *Learning for change in world society.* London: World Studies Project.

Rios, F., Montecinos, C., & van Olphen, M. (2007). Lessons learned from a collaborative self-study in international teacher education: Visiones, preguntas, y desafios. *Teacher Education Quarterly, 34* (1), 57–74.

Roberts, A. (2003). Proposing a broadened view of citizenship: North American's teachers service in rural Costa Rican schools. *Journal of Studies in International Education, 7* (3), 253–276.

Roberts, A. (2004). Analyzing patterns and relationships around a bond of common text: Purposes, dilemmas, and possibilities of a virtual community. *Journal of Research on Technology in Education, 37* (1), 1–27.

Robinson, M. (2002). *Rhetoric to reality: Making human rights work.* Address to London School of Economics, October 2002. Retrieved June 2, 2008, from http://www.Lse.ac.uk/collections/humanrights/articlesandtranscripts/mary_robinson.pdf

Roosevelt, E. (1958). *In your hands.* Retrieved July 14, 2008, from http://www.udhr.org/history/inyour.htm

Roosevelt, F. D. (1941, January 6). *The four freedoms.* Franklin D. Roosevelt's annual address to congress. Franklin D. Roosevelt Presidential Library and Museum. Retrieved July 14, 2008, from http://www.fdrlibrary.marist.edu/od4frees.html

Rosecrance, R. (1986). *The rise of the trading state: Commerce and conquest in the modern world.* New York: Basic Books.

Ross, M. H. (1993). *The culture of conflict.* New Haven, CT: Yale University Press.

Ross, M. H. (2007). *Cultural contestation in ethnic conflict.* Cambridge: Cambridge University Press.

Russell, J. E. A., & Adams, D. M. (1997). The changing nature of mentoring in organizations: An introduction to the special issues on mentoring and organizations. *Journal of Vocational Behavior, 51,* 1–14.

Said, E. W. (1978). *Orientalism.* New York: Random House.

Said, E. W. (1993). *Culture and imperialism.* New York: Alfred A. Knopf.

Said, E. W. (1997). *Covering Islam.* New York: Vintage Press.

Sarason, S. (1982). *The culture of the school and the problem of change* (2nd ed.). Boston: Allyn & Bacon.

Sarason, S. B. (1996). *Revisiting "The culture of the school and the process of change."* New York, NY: Teachers College Press.

Sassen, S. (1996). *Losing control? Sovereignty in an age of globalization.* New York: Columbia University Press.

Sassen, S. (1998). *Globalization and its discontents: Essays on the new mobility of people and money.* New York: Free Press.

Schell, J. (2003). *The unconquerable world: Power, nonviolence, and the will of the people.* New York: Henry Holt.

Schlafly, P. (1986, March 6). What is wrong with global education? *St. Louis Globe-Democrat*, 23.

Schleicher, K. (Ed.). (1993). *Nationalism in education.* New York: Peter Lang.

Schlesinger, A., Jr. (1991). Report of the social studies syllabus review committee: A dissenting opinion. In *New York state social studies review and development committee one nation, many peoples: A declaration of cultural interdependence.* New York: Author.

Schmidt, H. (1997). A universal declaration of human responsibilities. Interaction Council. Retrieved July 1, 2008, from http://www.interactioncouncil.org/udhr/declaration/udhr.pdf

Schneider, A. (2003). *Internationalizing teacher education: What can be done?* Retrieved March 17, 2008, from http://www.internationaledadvice.org/pdfs/What_Can_Be_Done.pdf

Schneider, A. (2006, April). *Preparing internationally-oriented teachers: Some research findings.* Paper presented at the Wisconsin International Outreach Conference. Retrieved March 24, 2008, from http://www.internationaledadvice.org/pdfs/Ann_Schneider_Preparing_Intl_Teachers pdf

Schneider, A. (2007, May). *To leave no teacher behind: Building international competence into the undergraduate training of K-12 teachers.* Retrieved March 26, 2008, from http://www.internationaledadvice.org/pdfs/A.I.Schneider.Complete.Report.pdf

Schubert, W. H., & Ayers, W. C. (Eds.). (1992). *Teacher lore: Learning from our own experience.* New York: Longman.

Schuerholz-Lehr, S. (2007). Teaching for global literacy in higher education: How prepared are the educators? *Journal of Studies in International Education, 11* (2).

Schukar, R. (1986). The center for teaching international relations: A self-supporting university-based program. In R. Freeman (Ed.), *Promising practices in global education: A handbook with case studies.* New York: National Council on Foreign Language and International Studies.

Schukar, R. (1993). Controversy in global education: Lessons for teacher educators. *Teaching into Practice, 32* (1), 52–57.

Scott, J. (1991). The evidence of experience. *Curriculum Inquiry, 17*, 773–797.

Secrest, L., & Flores, L. (1969). Homosexuality in the Philippines and the United States: The handwriting on the wall. *Journal of Social Psychology, 79*, 3–12.

Seelye, H. N. (Ed.). (1996). *Experiential activities for intercultural living.* Yarmouth, ME. Intercultural Press.

Sen, A. K. (1999). *Development as freedom.* New York: Oxford University Press.

Serapion of Vladimir (approx. 1285). *Slovo. (Word).* Retrieved May 13, 2008, from http://www.krotov.info/acts/13/serapion_vl_ru.htm

Shafer, S. (1987). Human rights education in schools. In N. Tarrow (Ed.), *Human rights and education* (pp. 191–206). Oxford: Pergamon Press.

Shane, H. (1969). International education in the elementary and secondary school. In H. Shane (Ed.), *The United States and international education* (pp. 269–298). Chicago: National Society for the Study of Education.

Shea, C. (1993). Diverse, multicultural education. *Buffalo Reporter, 25* (6). Retrieved June 3, 2008, from www.buffalo.edu/reporter/vol25/vol25n6/5b.txt

Simon, K. (2001). *Moral questions in the classroom*. New Haven, CT: Yale University Press.

Sizer, T. R. (1984). *Horace's compromise: The dilemma of the American high school*. Boston: Houghton Mifflin.

Slavin, R. E. (1992). Cooperative learning: Applying contact theory in desegregated schools. In J. Lynch, C. Modgil, & S. Modgil (Eds.), *Cultural diversity and the schools: Prejudice, polemic or progress?* (pp. 333–348). London: Falmer Press.

Sleeter, C. E. (1993). How white teachers construct race. In C. McCarthy & W. Crichlow (Eds.), *Race, identity and representation in education* (pp. 157–171). New York: Routledge.

Sleeter, C. E. (1995). Reflections on my use of multicultural and critical pedagogy when students are white. In C. E. Sleeter & P. L. McClaren (Eds.), *Multicultural education, critical pedagogy and the politics of difference* (pp. 415–438). Albany: State University of New York Press.

Sleeter, C. E. (2008). Preparing white teachers for diverse students. In M. Cochran-Smith, S. Feiman-Nemser, & D. McIntyre (Eds.), *Handbook of research on teacher education: Enduring questions in changing context* (pp. 559–582). New York: Routledge.

Sleeter, C. E., & Grant, C. A. (2003). *Making choices for multicultural education: Five approaches to race, class and gender* (2nd ed.). New York: Merrill.

Sockman, R. W. (1969). The open mind. In W. K. Anderson (Ed.), *Protestantism: A symposium* (p. 209). North Stratford, NH: Ayer Publishing.

Spalding, E., Savage, T., & Garcia, J. (2007). The march of remembrance and hope: Teaching and learning about diversity and social justice through the Holocaust. *Teachers College Record, 109*, 1423–1456.

Sparks, D. (Winter 2003). Interview with Michael Fullan: Change agent. *Journal of Staff Development, 24* (1), 58.

Spellings, M. (2006). *Secretary Spellings delivers remarks at the DePauw discourse*. Retrieved July 15, 2008, from http://www.ed.gov/news/pressreleases/2006/10/10262006.html

Spring, J. (1998). *Education and the rise of the global economy*. Mahwah, NJ: Lawrence Erlbaum.

Stachowski, L., & Chlebo, J. (1998). Foreign educators provide feedback for the improvement of international student teaching experiences. *Action in Teacher Education, 19* (4), 119–130.

Stanley Foundation. Community College (2008). Retrieved March 18, 2008, from http://theglobalcommunitycollege.org/

Stanley Foundation Programs (2008). Retrieved March 18, 2008, from www.vps.stanleyfoundation.org/programs/esp/

State of Florida (2000). *Laws of Florida* (Ch. 2000–2331). Tallahassee, FL: Author.

State Plan for Global Education (1981). Global education for the State of Florida. Global education advisory board. Tallahassee: Florida Department of Education.

Steiner, M. (1996). *Developing the global teacher: Theory and practice in initial teacher education*. England: World Studies Trust.

Stevahn, L., Johnson, D., Johnson, R., & Schultz, R. (2002). Effects of conflict resolution training integrated into high school social studies curriculum. *Journal of Social Psychology, 142* (3), 305–333.

Stori, C. (1994). *Cross-cultural dialogues*. Yarmouth, ME: Intercultural Press.

Study Commission on Global Education (1987). *The United States prepares for its future: Global perspectives in education*. ERIC Document Reproduction ED283758.

Taba, H. (1962). *Curriculum: Theory and practice*. New York: Harcourt Brace.

Tarasov, L. V., & Pushkareva, T. A. (1993). *Nasha planeta Zemlia (Our planet earth)*. Moscow, Russia: Avangard (in Russian).

Tarasov, L. V., & Pushkareva, T. A. (1994). *Chetyre qrani mira (The four facets of the world)*. Moscow, Russia: Avangard (in Russian).

Tarrow, N. (Ed.) (1987). *Human rights and education*. Oxford: Pergamon Press.

Tarrow, N. (1992). Human rights education: Alternative conceptions. In J. Lynch, C. Modgil, & S. Modgil (Eds.), *Cultural diversity in the schools* (pp. 21–50). London: Taylor and Francis Group Press.

Taylor, H. (1970). *The world as teacher*. New York: Doubleday.

Thomas, L. (1974). *The lives of a cell: Notes of a biology watcher*. New York: Viking Press.

Thornton, S. J. (2005). *Teaching social studies that matters: Curriculum for active learning*. New York: Teachers College Press.

Tibbitts, F. (1996). On human dignity: The need for human rights education. *Social Education Archives, 60* (7), 428-43 (n. p.)

Toffler, A. (1970). *Future shock*. New York: Random House.

Torney-Purta, J. (1982a). *Research and evaluation in global education: The state of the art and priorities for the future*. Paper presented at the National Conference on Professional Priorities: Shaping the Future of Global Education. Easton, MD. Reproduced by Global Perspectives in Education. New York.

Torney-Purta, J. (1982b). Socialization and human rights research: Implications for teachers. In M. S. Branson & J. Torney-Purta (Eds.), *International human rights, society, and the schools* (pp. 35–48). Washington, DC: National Council for the Social Studies.

Torney-Purta, J., Lehmann, R, Oswald, N., & Schulz W. (2001). *Citizenship and education in twenty-eight countries: Civic knowledge and engagement at age 14*. Amsterdam: International Association for the Evaluation of Educational Achievement.

Triandis, H. C. (1976). The future of pluralism. *Journal of Social Issues, 32*, 179–208.

Triandis, H. C., & Berry, J. W. (Eds.). (1980). *The handbook of cross-cultural psychology*. Boston: Allyn & Bacon.

Tucker, J. L. (1982a). Developing a global dimension in teacher education: The Florida International University experience. *Theory into Practice, 21* (3), 212–217.

Tucker, J. L. (1982b). International human rights education: The challenge for colleges and universities. In M. S. Branson & J. Torney-Purta (Eds.), *International human rights, society, and the schools* (pp. 71–80). Washington, DC: National Council for the Social Studies.

Tucker, J. L. (1985). *The implementation of global education programs in schools: A progress report*. Speech delivered at the Meeting of North and South Central Area Superintendents, Directors, and Principals. Global Awareness Program. Miami: Florida International University.

Tucker J. L. (1986). Global awareness through global education. In L. E. Freeman (Ed.), *Promising practices in global education: A handbook with case studies*. New York: National Council on Foreign Language and International Studies.

Tucker, J. L. (1988). *Selected annotated bibliography on global education.* Miami: Global Awareness Program, Florida International University. Unpublished Paper.

Tucker, J. L. (1989*). Global inner-city site training (GIST).* Final report. January 3. Miami: Florida International University.

Tucker, J. L. (1990*). Annual report.* Delivered to Global Awareness Program Advisory Board. June. Miami: Florida International University.

Tucker J. L. (1991a). *Education for a global perspective: National leadership in the '90s.* Paper delivered at the Sochi, Russia, First International Conference, September.

Tucker, J. L. (1991b). Global education is essential to secondary school social studies. *NASSP Bulletin, 75* (531), 43–51.

Tucker, J. L. (1994). *Annual report.* Delivered to the Global Awareness Program Advisory Board. June. Miami: Florida International University.

Tucker, J. L. (1996). NCSS and international/global education. In O. L. Davis, Jr. (Ed.), *NCSS in retrospect* (pp. 45–54). Washington, DC: National Council for the Social Studies.

Tucker, J. L., & Cistone, P. (1991). Global perspectives for teachers: An urgent priority. *Journal of Teacher Education, 42* (1), 3–10.

Tye, B. B. (2000). *Hard truths: Uncovering the deep structure of schooling.* New York: Teachers College Press.

Tye, B. B., & Tye, K. A. (1992). *Global education: A study of school change.* Albany: State University of New York Press.

Tye, K. A. (Ed.). (1991). *Global education: From thought to action.* Alexandria, VA: Association for Supervision and Curriculum Development.

Tye, K. A. (1999). *Global education: A worldwide movement.* Orange, CA: Independence Press.

Tye, K. A. (2006). The global ed yellow pages: A directory of global education resources for k-12 teachers. Retrieved August 23, 2008, from http://www.globaledyellowpages.org./

Tye, K. A., & Kniep, W. (1991). Global education around the world. *Educational Leadership, 48* (7), 47–49.

Ukpokodu, N. (1996). Africa in today's social studies curriculum. *Social Studies, 87* (3), 125–132.

Union of Utrecht. 1579. Retrieved September 8, 2008, from *Encyclopædia Britannica* Website http://www.britannica. com/EBchecked/topic/620843/Union-of-Utrecht.

United Nations (1966a). International covenant on civil and political rights. General Assembly resolution 2200A (XXI) of December 16, 1966. Retrieved September 5, 2008, from http://www.unhchr.ch/html/menu3/b/a_ccpr.htm.

United Nations (1966b). International covenant on economic, social and cultural rights, General Assembly Resolution 2200A (XXI) of December 16, 1966. Retrieved September 5, 2008, from http://www.unhchr.ch/html/menu3/b/acescr. htm

United Nations (1972, June). Stockholm declaration of the United Nations conference on the human environment. Retrieved September 8, 2008, from UN Documents Cooperation Circles Website: http://www.un-documents.net/unchedec.htmUnited Nations (1986, December 4). Declaration on the right to development. Retrieved September 8, 2008, from Declaration on the Right to Development Website: http://www.unhchr.ch/html/menu3/b/74.htm

United Nations (1989). Convention on the rights of the child. UN General Assembly resolution 44/25 of 20 November 1989. Retrieved July 1, 2008, from http://portal.unesco.org/education/en/ev.php-URL_ID=8738&URL_DO=DO_ TOPIC&URL_SECTION=201.htmlUnited Nations (1992, June 14). Rio declaration on environment and development. Retrieved September 8, 2008, from United Nations Environmental Programme Website: http://www.unep.org/Documents.Multilingual/Default.asp? Document ID=78&ArticleID=1163.

United Nations Development Program (2002). *Human development report 2002: Deepening democracy in a fragmented world.* New York: Oxford University Press.

United Nations Educational, Scientific, and Cultural Organization (UNESCO) (1974). Recommendation concerning education for international understanding, cooperation and peace and education relating to human rights and fundamental freedoms, November 19, 1974. Retrieved September 5, 2008, from http:// unesdoc. unesco.org/images/0001/000115/011563mb.pdf

United Nations General Assembly (1993). *Vienna declaration and programme of action of the world conference on human rights,* Vienna, June 14–25, 1993. Retrieved July 5, 2008, from http://www.unhchr.ch/huridocda/huridoca.nsf/(Symbol)/A.CONF. 157.23.The United States Bill of Rights (1789, September 25). Retrieved September 8, 2008, from http://www.billofrights.com/HistoryoftheBillofRights.htm

United States Declaration of Independence (1776, July 4). Retrieved September 8, 2008, from U.S. constitution online Website: http://www.usconstitution. net/declar.html

Universal Declaration of Human Rights (1948). Retrieved April 26, 2008, from http://www.un.org/Overview/rights.html

University of Central Florida (2005). Business School. Retrieved April 3, 2005, from www.bus.ucf.edu/ib/content/careers.htm

University of Indiana (2008). Retrieved February 14, 2008, from http://www.indiana.edu/~ssdc/

Urso, I. (1991). Teacher development through global education. In K. Tye (Ed.), *Global education: From thought to action. The 1991 ASCD yearbook* (pp. 100–108). Alexandria, VA: Association for Supervision and Curriculum Development.

Vall, N., & Tennison, J. (1991). International student teaching: Stimulus for developing reflective teachers. *Action in Teacher Education, 13* (4), 31–36.

Van Manen, M. (1990). *Researching lived experiences: Human science for an action sensitive pedagogy.* Albany: State University of New York Press.

Vasak, K. (1977). A 30-year struggle: The sustained efforts to give force of law to the Universal Declaration of Human Rights (pp. 29–32). *UNESCO Courier.*

Vibert, A., & Shields, C. (2003). Approaches to student engagement: Does ideology matter? *McGill Journal of Education, 38* (2), 221–240.

Vygotsky L. S. (1978). *Mind and society: The development of higher psychological processes.* Cambridge, MA: Harvard University Press.

Wade, R. (2007). Sustainable development. In D. Hicks & K. Holden (Eds.), *Teaching the global dimension* (pp. 104–113). London: Routledge.

Walker, M. (2007, Autumn). Globalization 3.0. *Wilson Quarterly,* 2–6.

Wallace, M. (1993). Negative images: Towards a black feminist cultural criticism. In S. During (Ed.), *The cultural studies reader* (pp. 118–131). New York: Routledge.

Ward, B., & Dubos, R. (1972). *Only one earth: The care and maintenance of a small planet.* New York: W. W. Norton.

Ware, P., & Kramsch, C. (2005). Toward an intercultural stance: Teaching German and English through telecollaboration. *Modern Language Journal, 89*, 190–205.

Warren, L. L., & Peel, H. A. (2005). Collaborative model for school reform through rural school/university partnership. *Education, 126* (2), 346–352. Retrieved June 16, 2008, from *ProQuest Education Journals* database. Document ID 982973071.

Warschauer, M. (1999). *Electronic literacies: Language, culture and power in online education.* Mahwah, NJ: Lawrence Erlbaum.

Wellman, C. (1998). *The proliferation of rights.* Boulder, CO: Westview Press.

Werner, W. (1990). Contradictions in global education. In D. Henley & J. Young (Eds.), *Canadian perspectives on critical pedagogy* (pp. 77–93). Occasional Monograph #1. Winnipeg: Critical Pedagogy Network and Social Education Researchers in Canada.

Werner, W. (1997). Teaching for hope. In R. Case & P. Clark (Eds.), *The Canadian anthology of social studies* (pp. 249–253). Burnaby, BC: Faculty of Education, Simon Fraser University.

Werner, W. (2002). Teaching about sectarian violence reported through the media. *Canadian Social Studies, 37* (1), 117–120.

Werner, W., & Case, R. (1997). Themes in global education. In I. Wright & A. Sears (Eds.), *Trends and issues in Canadian social studies education* (pp. 176–194). Vancouver, Canada: Pacific Education Press.

Weston, B. H. (2006). Human rights: Content and concept. In R. P. Claude & B. H. Weston (Eds.), *Human rights in the world community: Issues and actions* (p. 22) (3rd ed.). Philadelphia: University of Pennsylvania Press.

Wheatley, M. J. (2002). *Turning to one another: Simple conversations to restore hope to the future.* San Francisco, CA: Berrett-Koehler.

Wiley, M. (1982). Africa in social studies textbooks. *Social Education, 46* (7), 492–497, 548–552.

Willinsky, J. (1998). *Learning to divide the world: Education at empire's end.* Minneapolis: University of Minnesota Press.

Willinsky, J. (2000). Personal communication. September 13.

Wilson, A. H. (1968). Africa, past and present. *Negro History Bulletin, 31* (6), 6–12.

Wilson, A. H. (1980). The image of Africa in elementary schools. *Social Education, 46* (6), 503–507.

Wilson, A. H. (1982). Cross-cultural experiential learning for teachers. *Theory into Practice, 21* (3), 184–192.

Wilson, A. H. (1983). A case study of two teachers with cross-cultural experience: They know more. *Educational Research Quarterly, 8 (1)*, 78–85.

Wilson, A. H. (1984). Teachers as short-term international sojourners: Opening windows on the world. *Social Studies, 75* (4), 153–157.

Wilson, A. H. (1986). Returned Peace Corps volunteers who teach social studies. *Social Studies, 77* (3), 100–107.

Wilson, A. H. (1993a). Conversation partners: Gaining a global perspective through cross-cultural experiences. *Theory into Practice, 32 (1)*, 21–26.

Wilson, A. H. (1993b). *The meaning of international experience for schools.* Westport, CT: Praeger.

Wilson, A. H. (1995). Teaching about Africa: A review of middle/secondary textbooks and supplemental materials. *Social Studies, 86* (6), 253–259.

Wilson, A. H. (1997). Infusing global perspectives throughout a secondary social studies program. In M. M. Merryfield, E. Jarchow, & S. Pickert (Eds.), *Preparing teachers to teach global perspectives. A handbook for teacher education* (pp. 143–167). Thousand Oaks, CA: Corwin Press.

Wilson, A. H. (1998). Oburoni outside the whale: Reflections on an experience in Ghana. *Theory and Research in Social Education, 26* (3), 410–429.

Wolk, R. A., & Rodman, B. H. (Eds.). (1994). *Classroom crusaders.* San Francisco, CA: Jossey-Bass.

Wood, A. G. (2007). *What do we tell the children? Confusion, conflict and complexity.* Stoke on Kent, UK: Trentham Books.

Yamashita, H. (2006). Global citizenship education and war: The needs of teachers and learners. *Educational Review, 58* (1), 27–39.

Yarrow, P., Lazar, F., Roerden, L. P., & Lantieri, L. (2000). *Don't laugh at me: Teachers guide, grades 6–8.* Retrieved March 27, 2006, from http://www.esrnational.org/

Young, E. (2008). Focus on global education: A report from the 2007 PDK summit. *Phi Delta Kappan, 89* (5), 349–353.

Zeichner, K. M., & Hoeft, K. (1996). Teacher socialization for cultural diversity. In J. Sikula (Ed.), *Handbook of research on teacher education* (pp. 525–547). New York: Macmillan.

Zeichner, K. M., & Melnick, S. L. (February, 1995). *The role of community field experiences in preparing teachers for cultural diversity.* A paper presented at the annual meeting of the American Association of Colleges for Teacher Education, Washington, DC.

Zong, G. (2002). Can computer mediated communication help to prepare global teachers? An analysis of preservice social studies teachers' experience. *Theory and Research in Social Education, 30* (4), 589–616.

Zong, G. (2005). Road less traveled: An Asian woman immigrant faculty's experience practicing global pedagogy in American teacher education. In G. Li & G. Beckett (Eds.), *"Strangers" of the academy: Asian women scholars in higher education* (pp. 251–265). Sterling, VA: Stylus.

Zong, G. (2007). *Improving preservice teachers' conceptual understanding of global education through telecommunication technology.* Paper presented at the annual conference of American Educational Research Conference (AERA), Chicago.

Zong, G. (2008). Personal communication. April 24.

Zong, G., Wilson, A., & Quashigah, Y. (2008). Global education. In L. Levstik & C. Tyson (Eds.), *Handbook of research in social studies education* (pp. 197–216). New York: Routledge.

Pedro R. Bermúdez received his BA, MS, and Specialist Degrees in social studies and global education at Florida International University under the tutelage of Jan L. Tucker. He is a doctoral candidate. After a 20-year career as a high school social studies teacher working mostly with urban students, he currently serves as a curriculum support specialist in the School Improvement Zone of the Miami-Dade County Public School District. His primary commitment is to the implementation of democratic education learning communities that promote social and educational equity in schools. "Pete" Bermúdez is a facilitator of the National School Reform Faculty (NSRF), consults for a variety of organizations including the Early College Program for the National Council of La Raza (NCLR), the Ford Partnership for Advanced Studies (PAS), the Institute for Student Achievement (ISA), and serves as liaison between the National Peace Corps Association and Florida International University. He can be reached at PBermudez@dade schools.net

Kathy Bickmore received her doctorate from Stanford University in 1991. She is an associate professor in the Department of Curriculum, Teaching and Learning at the Ontario Institute for Studies in Education, University of Toronto. She conducts research in education for constructive conflict, equity, citizenship in public school contexts, social justice, and peace-building from an international comparative perspective. Her current research, Safe and Inclusive Schools: A Comparative Analysis of Anti-Violence Policies and Programs, examines intervention and prevention initiatives for handling conflict and violence and opportunities for democratic peace-building in urban Canadian schools. Her international collaborative work includes an antibullying initiative with Japan, a democratic civic education project with Russia, and the Peace Education Council of the International Peace Research Association. Her recent research is published in *Handbook of Research in Social Studies, The Challenge of Teaching Controversial Issues,* and journals such as *Conflict Resolution Quarterly, Theory and Research in Social Education, Curriculum Inquiry, Canadian Journal of Education,* and *Journal of Peace Education.*

John J. Cogan holds a MA (1965) and a PhD in Education (1969) from the Ohio State University. He is Professor Emeritus of Comparative and International Development Education (CIDE) at the University of Minnesota, Minneapolis. His research specializations include educating for citizenship and educational reform in nations in the Asia-Pacific Region. He is an internationally recognized authority on educating for citizenship and has directed three major international studies in this area in the past two decades. He is the co-author of 5 books, 17 book chapters, and more than 100 published juried journal articles. He was a Senior Fulbright Research Scholar at Hiroshima University (Japan), 1982–1983, a Ministry of Education Distinguished Visiting Professor at Nagoya University (Japan), in 1998–1999, and was awarded an Honorary Doctorate of Education degree by Sukhothai Thammathirat Open University (Thailand) for his contributions to the improvement of education throughout the Kingdom over the past two decades. He is the recipient of the Global Engagement Award of the University of Minnesota for nearly four decades of pioneering work to increase the international visibility of the institution both at home and abroad and the Distinguished Global Scholar Award sponsored by the International Assembly of the National Council for the Social Studies.

Bárbara C. Cruz is professor of secondary education at the University of South Florida. She received her MA and EdD degrees from Florida International University under the mentorship of Jan L. Tucker. Her research and teaching interests are in global and diversity issues in education. Dr. Cruz has published a number of young adult biographies of inspirational Hispanics, including *César Chávez: A Voice for Farm Workers* and *Multiethnic Teens and Cultural Identity* for which she received the Carter G. Woodson Book Award. For her nationally recognized research, she has also been honored with the Outstanding Faculty Research Achievement Award and the Faculty Excellence Award. Dr. Cruz is the Director of the Global Schools Project, a collaborative program that prepares teachers and students for an increasingly globalized society.

David L. Grossman is an adjunct senior fellow in the Education Program of the East-West Center and an affiliate graduate faculty member at the University of Hawaii. He received his MA and MAT degrees from Harvard University, and a PhD in international development education from Stanford University. He was Dean of the Faculty of Languages, Arts, and Sciences, and co-head of the Centre for Citizenship Education at the Hong Kong Institute of Education. Prior to that, he was founder and director of the Stanford Program on International and Cross-Cultural Education (SPICE). His research interests include citizenship education, global education, comparative education, and teacher education. His recent publications include three co-edited books: *Social Education in Asia* (with Joe Lo), *Citizenship Curriculum in Asia and the Pacific* (with Wing On Lee and Kerry Kennedy), and *Improving Teacher Education through Action Research* (with Hui Ming Fai).

Elizabeth E. Heilman is an associate professor in the Department of Teacher Education at Michigan State University and has served in leadership roles in social studies and curriculum studies at Purdue and Michigan State University and nationally. Her work is characterized by interdisciplinary scholarship and explores how social and political imaginations are shaped, and how various philosophies, policies, and pedagogies influence the practice of democratic citizenship, especially global citizenship. She is the author or editor of more than 35 book chapters and articles and 5 books including *Reclaiming Education for Democracy* (Routledge); *Harry Potter's World: Multidisciplinary Critical Perspectives* (Routledge/Falmer); and *Social Studies, the Next Generation: Re-searching in the Postmodern World* (Peter Lang).

Toni Fuss Kirkwood-Tucker is an associate professor emeritá in social studies and global education at Florida Atlantic University and now serves as visiting associate professor in the School of Teacher Education, Florida State University. She received her MA and EdD from Florida International University under the tutelage of Jan L. Tucker. Her primary research focuses on teacher education, integration of global perspectives in teacher education and schools, minority and global issues, and global citizenship education. She served as a Fulbright Teacher to China and Fulbright Scholar to Russia and was among the first Western educators to participate in the Russian education reform. She is author of 5 book chapters and 38 juried articles published in *Theory and Research in Social Education, Social Education*, and *World Studies in Education* and *European Education*. She was twice honored as the Florida Global Teacher of the Year and the Agnes Crabtree International Relations Teacher of the Year. She received the Global Apple Award awarded by the American Forum for Global Education. Her email is kirkwoodtf@aol.com

Jacob M. Kolker is professor of education and head of the Department of Linguistics and Intercultural Communication, Ryazan State University, Russia. He serves as Deputy Director of the Ryazan Center for Global Education that offers teacher-training workshops in global education and a vast network for Russian educators. He teaches linguistic methodology and specializes in the theory of translation and practical translation. His innovative ideas are reflected in a number of books. He has translated the full collection of Shakespeare's sonnets into Russian and has become a member of the All-Russia Professional Organization of Writers. He teaches the history of British and American literature from a cross-cultural perspective and served as Visiting Scholar at Indiana University, Florida International University, and Nagoya University. He has been awarded the Professional Medal from the Russian Government for his achievement in education.

Hilary Landorf is an associate professor of social studies and global education at Florida International University. She received her BA from Stanford University, MA from the University of Virginia in English literature, and her PhD in International Education from New York University. She worked as a Peace Corps volunteer in Morocco and has extensive teaching and research experience in a wide variety of schools and universities in the United States and abroad. Her research focus is inclusive of global education. She is known for her work in using the Universal Declaration of Human Rights as a touchstone document for teaching and learning. She has published articles in journals such as *Social Education*, the *Journal of Educational Administration*, and *Teacher Education Quarterly* and has contributed book chapters on globalization and sustainability and service learning. Her latest publication is "Education for Sustainable Human Development: Towards a Definition" forthcoming in *Theory and Research in Education*.

Lena Lenskaya received her doctorate in pedagogy from the Russian Academy of Education in Moscow. She is among the leading Russian scholars in foreign language education, global education, and development education. She has authored more than 120 books, articles, and chapters in books. She has served as Head of International Cooperation and special advisor to the Minister of Education under the Yeltsin government; chaired the curriculum development at the Institute of Educational Innovation; and served as Assistant Director of the British Council. In 2007, she was awarded the Order of the British Empire Award. She was Project Director of the North Caucasus Education Initiative that rehabilitated more than 300 victims of the school siege in Beslan. She presently heads the Education Policy Centre of the Open Society Institute of the Soros Foundation and chairs the Moscow Projects and Development Centre in the School of Socio-Economic Studies.

Merry M. Merryfield is a professor of social studies and global education at the Ohio State University. She began her career as a high school teacher of social studies and Latin in Atlanta and then taught as a Peace Corps volunteer in Sierra Leone. She has carried out research on the role of social studies in the United States and in the national development in Nigeria, Kenya, Malawi, and Botswana. Most recently she worked with Chinese researchers in Hong Kong to examine how its teachers are teaching about the world posttransition. Her interests include cross-cultural experiential learning, teacher decision-making in global education, postcolonial theory, and online pedagogy. You can reach her at merryfield.1@osu.edu.

Irina M. Sheina is an associate professor of philology and is the recently elected Rector of Ryazan State University, Ryazan, Russia. Previously, she served as Head of the Department of English Language and Language Teaching Methodology. She is internationally and nationally recognized scholar in intercultural communication, global education, and linguistics. Among the leading global scholars in Russia, she has trained preservice and in-service teachers in foreign language, American Studies, and intercultural global education. She has presented at numerous international conferences and participated in a number of international projects under the aegis of Open Society Institute, the American Council, and the New Eurasia Foundation. She was a Fulbright Scholar to Florida Atlantic University lecturing in Russian history and culture. Her scholarship is reflected in numerous articles and books published in English and Russian including her most recent book, *A Global Perspective as a Vehicle for Education*, co-authored in Russian and English with A. Liferov, J. Kolker, E. Ustinova, and V. Kriuchkov.

Kenneth A. Tye is a professor emeritus in education at Chapman University. He received his BA degree from San Francisco State, his MA degree from San Diego State, and his EdD from the University of California, Los Angeles. He taught comparative education and curriculum in the School of Education, Chapman University, chaired the Education Department, and served as Assistant Provost for International Programs for the University. Prior to going to Chapman in 1984, he spent 14 years as Program Officer for the Educational Research Center affiliated with University of California in Los Angeles. He was a social studies teacher and a school principal. Ken has traveled extensively and has worked in several countries in Africa, Asia, Europe, the Middle East,

Australia, and New Zealand. He has written extensively, including several books, periodical articles, and chapters in books, many of them about global education. He was the editor of the 1991 ASCD Yearbook *Global Education: From Thought to Action*. He recently developed an Internet website, a directory of approximately 1,000 organizations in North America that provides global education resources for K-12 teachers at www.globaledyellowpages.org

Elena S. Ustinova is an associate professor of education in the Department of Linguistics and Intercultural Communication, Ryazan State University, Russia. She has the distinction of being among the first global scholars in Russian education since the dissolution of the Soviet Union. In addition to her extensive collaborative work in research and writing, she has conducted numerous workshops and seminars in training preservice and inservice teachers in English as a foreign language through global education. She has been invited to American Universities to establish research and faculty exchange partnerships. She served as interpreter during the first international conferences in Sochi and Ryazan working collaboratively with Western educators in the Russian education reform efforts. She teaches linguistic methodology, stylistics, practical translation, and British History from a cross-cultural perspective. Her research is reflected in several books and textbooks.

Guichun Zong is an associate professor of adolescent education and social studies education at Kennesaw State University. She holds a BS degree in Social Studies Education, a MS degree in Comparative Education from Beijing Normal University, and an EdD in Curriculum and Instruction from Florida International University under the direction of Jan L. Tucker. Her research interests include global education, social studies education, and teacher education. Her articles have appeared in journals such as *Social Education* and *Theory and Research in Social Education*. She has contributed a chapter to D. Grossman and J. Lo (Eds.), *Social Education in Asia: Critical Issues and Multiple Perspectives* (Information Age, 2007) and a chapter to L. Levstik & C. Tyson (Eds.), *Handbook of Research in Social Studies Education* (Routledge, 2008).

Author Index

Subject Index

COMPLICATED

A BOOK SERIES OF CURRICULUM STUDIES

This series employs research completed in various disciplines to construct textbooks that will enable public school teachers to reoccupy a vacated public domain—not simply as "consumers" of knowledge, but as active participants in a "complicated conversation" that they themselves will lead. In drawing promiscuously but critically from various academic disciplines and from popular culture, this series will attempt to create a conceptual montage for the teacher who understands that positionality as aspiring to reconstruct a "public" space. *Complicated Conversation* works to resuscitate the progressive project—an educational project in which self-realization and democratization are inevitably intertwined; its task as the new century begins is nothing less than the intellectual formation of a public sphere in education.

The series editor is:

Dr. William F. Pinar
Department of Curriculum Studies
2125 Main Mall
Faculty of Education
University of British Columbia
Vancouver, British Columbia V6T 1Z4
CANADA

To order other books in this series, please contact our Customer Service Department:

(800) 770-LANG (within the U.S.)
(212) 647-7706 (outside the U.S.)
(212) 647-7707 FAX

Or browse online by series:

www.peterlang.com